Understanding Paul and His Letters

VINCENT P. BRANICK

Paulist Press
New York/Mahwah, NJ

The scripture quotations contained herein are translations by the author.

The Old Testament Pseudepigrapha, Volume 2: Expansions of the "Old Testament" and Legends, Wisdom and Philosophical Literature, Prayers, Psalms and Odes [etc]., edited by James H. Charlesworth, et al. New Haven: Yale University Press, 1985. Used by permission. All rights reserved.

Maps: Courtesy of Paulist Press archives
Cover and book design by Lynn Else
Cover photograph courtesy of Michael P. Kerrigan, CSP

Library of Congress Cataloging-in-Publication Data

Branick, Vincent P.
Understanding Paul and his letters / Vincent P. Branick.
p. cm.
Includes bibliographical references.
ISBN 978-0-8091-4581-2 (alk. paper)
1. Bible. N.T. Epistles of Paul—Criticism, interpretation, etc. I. Title.
BS2650.52.B74 2009
227'.066—dc22

2009006898

Published by Paulist Press
997 Macarthur Boulevard
Mahwah, New Jersey 07430

www.paulistpress.com

Printed and bound in the
United States of America

Contents

Appendices

Dedicated to my family
Arlene, Chris, Kevin, and Sean

Preface

For some thirty years here at the University of Dayton and another five years before that at Chaminade College in Honolulu, I tried to give my students something to read as a follow-up to my oral class presentations on Paul. With each revision the manuscript got larger and more complicated. Now in this year commemorating the apostle Paul, I am delighted to share this effort with Pauline students of all ages, in or outside the classroom. I hope I ironed out the inconsistencies that crept into the work by the multiple revisions.

I am particularly delighted to work with Paulist Press in this year of Paul, to have this manuscript on Paul published. Father Lawrence Boadt, CSP, offered much advice that improved this book. Thanks, Larry, and all you hard workers at Paulist Press.

I owe special thanks to my family. My wife, Arlene, proofread the manuscript, catching innumerable mistakes.

January 2008, Dayton, Ohio

Introduction

A colleague of mine had a cordial dislike for Paul. "With all his emphasis on sin and God's anger, where was the good news?" she asked. Where is the gospel picture of God and his love for all? Where is the simple challenge of extending that unconditional love to others? In his own time, Paul saw other Christian missionaries fighting against his teaching. It is not surprising, therefore, to see today both the intense admiration and the intense dislike that religious people continue to have for Paul.

At the end of the nineteenth century, scholars posed the question, "Did Paul corrupt the gospel of Jesus?" This is a good question. Several significant shifts exist between the teaching of Jesus and that of Paul. Jesus focuses on the Father, describing him as the God who loves us unconditionally, who provides food and clothing for the just and the unjust, who manifests his love through the smallest elements of life—the birds outside our windows, the wildflowers in our backyards. Paul, on the other hand, seems to shift the focus from God to Jesus, whose sacrificial death rescues us from God's wrath, whose resurrection is the proof we need salvation. Paul insists on faith in the reality of that resurrection as the necessary condition for attaining salvation. Overall, Jesus' teaching is clear, simple, and basic. Paul's is abstract, abstruse, and complex. Jesus appears as a gentle and unpretentious teacher. At times, Paul emerges as a dogmatic grouch.

Whether or not we agree with this radical criticism of Paul, we are at least warned not to take him for granted. This criticism reminds us that Paul in his own day was very controversial. Hearing this radical criticism of Paul forces us to peel off the calluses of familiarity and think about what he is saying. We will grasp Paul's messages only if we are able somehow to scrape away the dullness of familiarity and reproduce the original freshness of that first Christian generation, if we are able to keep our minds open and listen carefully to what Paul is saying as if it were the first time we were hearing what he is saying.

Our task in this book is to understand Paul as a person of faith, inspired by the Holy Spirit, whose faith as expressed in his writings is a norm for all Christians. Taking Paul's letters as a norm of faith, however, does not mean that we need to find in his writings a statement that reflects everything we as Christians believe. It does not even mean that his beliefs are the same as ours. It means our faith must be in continuity with his faith.

As a matter of fact, it is often a shock to see the gap that exists between Paul's beliefs and those of many Christians today. These gaps occur sometimes because our faith has developed beyond Paul—often from the influence of other New Testament writers. Sometimes these gaps occur because some rich idea of Paul has been forgotten and neglected, sometimes because we have moved in the wrong direction. Thus Paul's ideas can return with their freshness some two thousand years later as a critique of our faith understanding.

I. Understanding Paul in a Historical and Critical Way

Attempting to read Paul with the original freshness of the first Christian generation means reading Paul in the historical context in which he wrote. Such a reading is an attempt to look at the subject matter through his eyes, at the same time critically understanding the perspective of those eyes. It is an attempt to understand what he intended to write as well as how that intention might shape the writing, perhaps even in a way he might not have intended.

Some scholars have recently questioned the value of the search for the intention of the author as a means of understanding the message of a text, particularly of an ancient text.[1] I admit that the task of seeking out the intention of an author is daunting and that the effort to reconstruct psychological motivation might be futile. Nevertheless, the author's intention can function as a kind of North Star that, even if unattainable, can guide our direction. Searching through the text for the intention of the author and for the reality intended by that author thus allows us to see how authors positioned themselves in regard to their intellectual background and culture.

Some texts, of course, do not really lend themselves to a search for authorial intention. When I read some instruction sheet on how to assemble boxed-up furniture, I do not have the slightest interest in the author's intention. When I study some rule book on how to play a new board game, I ignore authorial intention. The Bible, however, is first of all not some instruction manual for assembling the church or some rule book for salvation. The Bible is primarily a collection of stories and communications describing human existence under God. The Bible must be read as mystery speaking to mystery, as person to person. Furthermore, in letters like those of Paul, the person and intentions of the author blare through the text and call for attention.

At the same time, our quest is not just historical. We hope to hear a message addressed to us. We hope to see something that puts us on the spot. If we can see *what* Paul saw, then chances are that this reality will touch our lives. Then *what* Paul said to the ancient Corinthians or Philippians will speak to us. Our study thus involves at once a distancing from the text and an embrace of the text. Our study is at once historical and theological.

We will need enough distance to let Paul speak for himself. We need to bring our faith positions to Paul's letters as questions, rather than as preconceptions of what Paul must be saying. I am not advocating total neutrality or complete distance from the letters of Paul. We cannot do that, and if we could we would probably cease to understand anything of Paul. We probably would not even bother studying Paul. We necessarily bring our own preconceptions to the text. However, we must be willing to test our preconceptions against what Paul actually says. Of course, lurking in our efforts will always be a bundle of presuppositions that we cannot transform into questions, mostly because we may not even be aware of those presuppositions. That is why the study of Paul will continue after us.

As we try to look at the subject matter through Paul's eyes, all the while trying to understand the limits and strengths of Paul's perspective, we never lose our own perspectives, whose limits and strengths we try to recognize. Through this multitude of perspectives, we can begin to walk around the subject matter, as one walks around a large cube, seeing only a few sides at a time. At this point, we begin to see the truth of the matter, the power of the reality to summon us to react one way or another.

II. The Quest for Paul's Faith

Our study will stay close to the historical mode. We will study the person and intentions of Paul, his background and culture, as well as the chronological sequence of his letters and their historical contexts. As we read, we see clearly, however, that Paul intends to share his faith. That faith in its historical forms is the target of our investigation. Thus our study will be theological in its overall thrust.

This theological interest will govern what we focus on and, in some cases, how we see the longer letters should be divided up. This is not the only way to read Paul, but it does seem appropriate for the writings of one whom history called "the theologian." I am not insisting that this approach trump other more literary or sociological approaches, only that it be in continuity with the other approaches so that the reader can move from one to the other without too many bumps in the seams.

We can seek the faith of Paul only if we read Paul with our faith presuppositions as questions. We want to know his concept or image of God, his understanding of Jesus, his grasp of sin and redemption from sin. Those concepts will make sense to us only if we have already struggled with them. Nevertheless, we learn of Paul's faith and in some ways reconstruct Paul's faith by looking at the exact statements Paul makes. We look for the conclusions Paul draws, the associations he makes, the contrasts he describes. We also look for the presuppositions that appear in his statements.

As we develop a sense of Paul's faith, that faith becomes an important context for understanding other statements of Paul. Something of a circular argument appears here. We look at the specifics to grasp the whole, but we need the whole also to grasp the specifics. Yet this is the method we use all the time to grow in knowledge. The circle is really a way of constantly testing our grasp of the whole. When a new statement of Paul fits the conception that we are developing of Paul's faith, we become more confident of our understanding. When a new statement resists incorporation into that conception, we must reevaluate our understanding. The important part is that we let the words of Paul govern our efforts.

Some modern writers object to any such theological method for studying Paul, or scripture in general. Paul, they protest, does not have a well-defined and symmetrical ideology or central idea from which he deduces his positions. In his letters, he is simply reacting to specific problems, gearing his response entirely to the concrete occasion of the letter, making important shifts from one letter to the other.

I understand the objection, but I think it is a caricature of theology. Good theology has left the deductive approach long ago to immerse itself in messy experience. Paul was a good theologian. I too find it hard to identify one central idea or ideology in Paul that enlightens other positions. I do see, however, a cluster of ideas that in their constellation form a type of core. Paul has a position in faith that he rather consistently applies to various church problems and occasions. These problems and occasions in turn also massage his theology as it develops.

Paul's faith is complex. It shares much with other New Testament writers. It arises out of a Jewish apocalyptic worldview. Its many aspects are interrelated and interwoven.

If he were narrating his theology as a story, it would begin with a creaturely revolt that unleashes sin as a cosmic force, not a power rivaling God, but nevertheless a power that is more than human. In many ways, for Paul it is the power of death. God the Father, Yahweh of the Old Testament, the ultimate agent of creation and salvation, is the savior from this sin. He deals with sin on its own level, on the level of death.

Jesus, the Son of God, enters into our sinfulness and is more the recipient of salvation than its agent. He is saved by God from a sinful condition. As part of the sinful condition, Jesus dies. As saved, Jesus is raised from the dead. The risen Jesus is the epitome of saved reality. Still, as part of the ultimate agency of God, Jesus is active as the rescuer and the one who pays the ransom of humanity.

Human beings become beneficiaries of God's salvation by sharing the life of Jesus. In this communion of life, other human beings become part of the death and resurrection of Jesus. In its beginning stage, this communion involves a transformation of the heart, a transformation that should be manifested by a life of love, which, when done with a community, becomes an anticipation of God's kingdom.

The Holy Spirit is a medium by which God's power raising Jesus is communicated to other human beings. Sent by God, this Holy Spirit dwells in our hearts and allows us to experience the saving love of the Father. The community becomes a temple of that Spirit.

The fullness of humanity's salvation will occur only with the general resurrection of all human beings, when the same transformation that occurred in Jesus will occur in us. That general resurrection at the end of time will be the ultimate triumph of God over sin. Such a transformation is in some way a "new creation." Only God can bring this about. To think that we can achieve salvation by our good actions is to trivialize salvation into simply an improvement of behavior.

Such a story involves a texture of distinctive and traditional themes. It is awkward to separate one theme from another. Paul constantly weaves them together. We will try to balance the study by looking at each letter sequentially as a whole then studying each theme by itself.

These themes appear in the early writings and reappear in later letters. I call them trajectories simply because they trace their own paths through the letters. Some of them develop as Paul moves along his writing career and are real trajectories of development. Others are remarkably stable. I will earmark six of them as focal points that seem both to unlock the distinctiveness of Paul and to speak to our faith:

1. The **God** and Father of Jesus and our Father
2. **Christ Jesus**, whom Paul clearly distinguishes from God as God's instrument of justice and salvation
3. **The Spirit of God**, somehow an extension of God's action in the world
4. **Salvation** from sin, considered in a general way
5. The **union of life with Christ**, which gives access to salvation
6. **Eschatology**, the final word of salvation[2]

It is difficult to understand the themes of Paul in such a way that they speak to our faith. Simply repeating Paul's words will not lead to such an understanding. Paul placed his faith in the mystery of God and of God's salvation, a reality that transcends culture, language, and time. When he put that faith into human words, however, that mystery became enfleshed in a particular culture, language, and time. Every generation will see Christ differently, because every generation brings different questions and perspectives. The New Testament canon, with its ancient written documents, measures whether or not the later perspectives are in continuity with those of Paul, with the other biblical writers, and eventually with Jesus. In that continuity, the historical faith of Paul can speak to our faith and enrich it.

The search for the true religious faith of another person requires the recognition that the whole which brings us human beings together for communication involves a divine Person who has already embraced us and looked into our eyes. That divine Person has shared his Spirit with us. Even beyond the historical intention of Paul, our goal will be to read and interpret scripture "according to the same Spirit by whom it was written."[3]

PART I

Background

If we intend somehow to look out of Paul's eyes toward the divine reality he saw, we must learn everything we can about Paul and his mentality. He saw the risen Christ. He grasped something of the salvation God offered humanity through that risen Christ. However, his understanding of those realities took place by a type of integration of his experiences into his mentality. The divine truth became incarnate in a human experience. When Paul wrote about God and his grace, he did so in a language that formed that message and limited that message. Although assisted by the Holy Spirit, Paul was not given a divine perspective of the mystery.

To understand what Paul saw, therefore, we need to have a broad sense of the limits and possibilities of the form and style of writing Paul used to communicate his faith, letter writing. This is a particular literary form or genre, which like every form shapes the truth that it expresses (chapter 1).

The next context for understanding is Paul's life and career, about which we seem to have a great deal of information. A somewhat later writer traditionally known as Luke was quick to see the importance of the story of Paul. What is difficult is ascertaining the historical reliability of that account we find in the Acts of the Apostles. We will start there (chapter 2).

The next step is to try to reconstruct in our heads the education and intellectual background of Paul. Modern historians have gathered a mountain of ancient literary sources that allows us to see both the Greek as well as the Jewish background of Paul, all blended together in what modern scholars call the Hellenistic world. The survey in broad strokes of the cultural history of this Greco-Roman world may help us find echoes in Paul (chapter 3). We will give special attention to Paul's Jewish theological background (chapter 4).

1
A Literary Analysis of Paul's Letters

I. Letter Writing in Early Christianity

Perhaps the most obvious and easily overlooked thing about Paul's letters is simply that he wrote *letters*. The presuppositions involved in Paul's letters as letters, however, are intriguing and must be viewed in the context of the practice of letter writing in early Christianity. Twenty of our twenty-seven "books" of the New Testament are letters. Two others, Acts and Revelations, contain letters. Letter writing in its social character was clearly a very congenial way for the early Christians to express their faith.

Gospel, of course, is the other type of writing or literary form (literary genre) characteristic of early Christianity. Yet writing gospels ceased shortly after the close of the New Testament. A few attempts continued into the second century, but today nobody writes gospels to express their faith.

On the other hand, letter writing continued down through the centuries as a major form of Christian theological discourse. The apostolic fathers like Ignatius and Clement expressed their faith in letters to other groups. Even down to the present time the episcopal and papal encyclicals continue this tradition. Paul's letters stand at the fountainhead of this tradition.

As letters, Paul's writings reflect a crucial stage in early Christianity as its traditions shifted from oral to written form. The reasons for the shift are many: The first generation of witnesses was dying off; the church was spreading beyond the confines of Palestine; the view of an imminent end of the world was shifting to the Lucan perspective of a prolonged future for the Christian community on earth. These and other reasons required writing down the traditions. About a hundred years after Christ, the shift was complete and Christians were collecting their own sacred scriptures to preserve their traditions unchanged for the future.

The shift from oral to written tradition involves a serious trade-off. The oral stage of a tradition enjoys great freedom and creativity. The teller of a story known only by word of mouth does not hesitate to modify that story in order to make it more understandable or to bring out an insight the storyteller has recently attained. Normally, every time we tell a story, we do so differently. Such freedom and liveliness characterized the oral traditions of Christianity.

On the other hand, as a tradition is written down, it becomes fixed in form. Copyists or readers feel a far greater obligation to reproduce the original than do the tellers of a story. The advantages of a fixed, written form are obvious. Written expressions can be pondered at length repeatedly. Written expressions can be shared by many more people, as a text is passed around and comments can be pooled. Written expressions allow for a development of understanding. Religious written expressions allow for a theology. Yet, fixed in its expression, written form loses the vitality, the freedom, and the creativity characteristic of oral tradition. Preservation succeeds development as the main concern of tradition.

Paul's letters, precisely as letters, appear as the first step in that transition from oral to written mode. We will date those letters starting with AD 52 and ending somewhere in the mid-60s. About the mid-60s the sayings and stories of Jesus began to be written down, with Mark's Gospel appearing around AD 70. The remaining New Testament writings will appear in the following decades.

As letters, Paul's writings are basically written conversations. Letters are generally written to speak to someone with whom we cannot converse in person. They are substitutes for a face-to-face conversation. In this intent, letters are quite different from essays. We write essays in order to put our thoughts down in writing. An essay, in a way, is writing for the sake of writing. We may not know exactly who is going to read our essays. Our concern is first of all to articulate our thinking as best we can, to preserve the thought for the future, to fix the word in a permanent form. Our letters, on the other hand, usually have as their purpose communication with particular people in particular situations. Once the communication is made, a letter is often thrown away, having served its purpose. Only when it takes on a new function, such as documentation or souvenir, is a letter saved.

Paul's writings are letters, not essays. They are very close to the oral mode of communication. They respond to questions asked and problems exposed. In this they maintain the dialogical characteristic of oral communication. When Paul includes travel plans in these writings, he in effect is reminding his reader of the way in which these letters are poor substitutes for personal presence. He hopes to explain things better when he arrives in person.

As letters, Paul's communications maintain the liveliness and creativity of the early oral tradition. In his letters, Paul wrestles with grave crises. He does not always have the final remedy, but he is willing to offer stopgap measures. Often his words have the tone of an emergency solution. He probes in directions that are later discarded. By reading these letters, we in effect tune into the most creative period of Christianity's history. We listen to an apostle rejoicing and agonizing with his communities, not having all the solutions, but risking new visions of a dynamic, powerful faith.

To understand Paul's letters means reading them as such and not primarily as essays. However, through a very delicate process of critical interpretation, we can find consistent themes running through Paul's correspondence, themes that allow us to understand his faith and our faith. However, we distort Paul's work if we simply transpose his propositions from his letters into our world.

To muddy the waters a bit, two qualifications are in order. First, there is a great diversity within the writings of Paul. Some, like his writing to Philemon, clearly appear as personal letters. Others, like his writing to the Romans, begin to take on at least some characteristics of an essay.

Following a nomenclature developed in modern biblical scholarship, we will call such a writing an "epistle" as distinct from a letter.[1] A letter, as we have described, is simply written conversation. An epistle, on the other hand, is something of an essay with the form of a letter, that is, with a letter opening and greeting, and with a letter closing.

Paul's Letter to the Romans partially fits this category. Writing to the Romans, Paul appears to be introducing himself and his main teaching. He is interested in a careful expression of his positions. What comes from his pen, therefore, is different from his letters to Galatia or Corinth, where he appears to be writing in haste and deep emotion. Yet also in these letters, Paul frequently breaks into an expository mode of writing, where he tries to explain some mystery of God and salvation whose power and stability extend far beyond the local limits or times of those to whom he is writing.

A second qualification of our understanding of Paul's letters lies in the way Paul always maintains a certain public and even official tone to his writings. Even in his Letter to Philemon, Paul does not write as one private individual to another. Rather, he associates Timothy with himself in the writing, and addresses not only Philemon, but also Philemon's wife Apphia, Archippus, and the whole church that meets in Philemon and Apphia's house (see Phlm 1–2). This naming of others may be a technique of putting pressure on Philemon to do something. In any case, it lifts the letter out of any classification of private correspondence. Similarly, he asks his letters be read by whole communities (see 1 Thess 5:27), he asks that the letters be exchanged and read (Col 4:16), and he frequently identifies himself as an apostle, that is, as an authority in the Christian community.

These two qualifications, nevertheless, leave intact the basic literary form of Paul's writings as that of letter, the first move of Christianity from the oral to the written mode of tradition. They are lively and creative expressions of Christianity in a critical hour of its history, groping for ways of dealing with overpowering forces at play.

II. The Format of Ancient Letters

A cultivated person knows how to use the symbols and stereotypes of his or her day in a free and inconspicuous way. In

Paul's letters we find the stereotype formats, and Paul's modifications give us a special insight into the man and his thinking.

A. Examples of Personal Letters

Two brief letters found on ancient papyri will give us a sense of the Hellenistic style and format of contemporary personal letters:

> Serapion to his brothers Ptolemaeus and Apollonius, greeting (*chairein*).
>
> If you are well,...I myself also am well.
>
> I have made a contract with the daughter of Hesperus and am going to marry her in the month of Mesore. Please send me half a gallon of oil. I have written to you to let you know.
>
> Goodbye. Year 28 [154 BC], Epeiph 21. Come for the day, Apollonius.
>
> [on the back] To Ptolemaeus and Apollonius[2]

> Isias to her brother Hephaestion, greeting (*chairein*).
>
> If you are well and other things are going well, it would be in line with the prayer which I make continually to the gods. I myself and the child and all the household are in good health and remembering you always.
>
> When I got the letter from you through Horus, in which you announce that you are in detention in the Serapeum at Memphis, for your being in good health I straightway thanked the gods, but about your not coming home, when all the others who had been secluded there have come, I am ill pleased, because after having piloted myself and your child through such times and having come to all this owing to the price of corn I thought that now at least, with you at home, I should enjoy some respite, whereas you have not even thought

of coming home nor given any regard to our circumstances, remembering how I was in want of everything while you were still here, not to mention this long lapse of time and these critical days, and you having sent us nothing. As, moreover, Horus who delivered the letter has brought news of your having been released from detention, I am thoroughly ill-pleased. Furthermore, your mother also is annoyed, but for her sake and for mine please return to the city, if nothing more pressing holds you back.

Please take care of your body so that you remain healthy. Goodbye. Year 2 [168 BC], Epeiph 30

[on the back] To Hephaestion[3]

A third letter, showing closer affinity to Paul's format, appears in the opening lines of 2 Maccabees, a work from the late second century BC. Along with many others now embedded in our Bible, this letter gives us a sense of the Jewish Hellenistic letter style and format:

> To the Jewish brethren in Egypt, the Jewish brethren in Jerusalem and those in the region of Juda send greetings (*chairein*) of true peace (*eirênê*).
>
> May God bless you and remember his covenant to Abraham, Isaac, and Jacob, his faithful servants. May he give you all a heart to worship him and to do his will with a great heart and a willing soul. May he open your heart to his law and to the commandments and give you peace and listen to your petitions and be reconciled to you and not forsake you in bad times. And now we are praying for you here.
>
> In the one hundred and sixty-ninth year of the reign of Demetrios, we Jews wrote you of the sufferings and hardships that came upon us in those years after Jason and those with him rose up against the holy land and its kingdom and they set fire to the toll house and spilt

> innocent blood. We beseeched the Lord and we were heard. And we offered sacrifice and fine flour and lit the lamps and set forth the breads. And now [we ask you] so that you might make holy the days of Booths in the month of Chislev.
>
> The year 188 [124 BC] (2 Macc 1:1–10)

In all three we note similarities:

1. The letters begin with the names of the writer and the recipients. In these letters, the name of the writer comes first. Examples exist where the name of the recipient occurs first, as a way of recognizing that the recipient is more important than the writer, as "To King Festus from his loyal subject, Aristobolus."

2. In all three letters we find a word of greeting following the names. In the Hellenistic letters, the writer used the common salutation, *chairein,* which is translated simply "greeting." Literally, it means "rejoice." It meant as much as the "dear" in greetings of our modern business letters. The Jewish letter, on the other hand, contains also the word *eirênê,* translated "peace." "Peace" was the typical greeting of one Jew to another. It evoked the meaning of *shalôm,* which in Hebrew expressed salvation in the whole range of its meanings, starting with having one's debts paid.

3. The Hellenistic letters include frequently a health wish and a rather perfunctory prayer or reference to praying. The Jewish letter, on the other hand, moves into a developed prayer (2 Macc 1:2–6) mentioning many of the essentials of the Jewish faith: God, the patriarchs, worship, the commandments, reconciliation, and divine assistance in time of adversity—a sort of minisynthesis of the Jewish faith.

4. The body of the letter then follows. This body is directly connected to the occasion of the writing this letter. It is therefore difficult to make comparisons.

5. The ending of the Hellenistic letters includes the word *errôsthe,* translated here "goodbye." Such an ending is more common to the Roman period than to the earlier Greek period in this part of the world. The Jewish letter lacks such an ending.

B. Paul's Format

This breakdown of format found in the three sample letters allows us to make some interesting comparisons with Paul's way of writing. We will focus here on the Letter to Philemon because of its simplicity.

1. The Names

Looking at the way Paul in this letter identifies himself and the recipients, we immediately spot important characteristics. First, Paul associates others, in Philemon "Timothy, our brother," with himself in this letter writing. This is typical in his authentic writings, and raises the letter into a more public atmosphere. Paul seems very conscious of the network of relationships that binds him to a community and in many ways engages that community in his actions.

Second, Paul describes himself. In some letters, Paul describes himself as a "slave" or a "prisoner" (Phil 1:1; Phlm 1). In other letters, Paul will have authoritative admonitions for his recipients. In those cases, he will identify himself as "an apostle of Christ" (see 1 Cor 1:1; 2 Cor 1:1; Gal 1:1). Surveying the letters of Paul from the point of view of his self-identification allows us a glimpse at Paul's self-understanding.

2. The Greeting

After naming himself and his recipients, Paul gives his almost invariable greeting, "grace and peace from God our Father and the Lord Jesus Christ." The reference to "peace" reminds us of the Jewish format. The reference to "grace" may be Paul's clever way of adapting the Hellenistic format. The Greek word used by Paul is *charis*. *Charis* is reasonably close to the Hellenistic *chairein*, both words stemming from the same root. *Charis* connotes many things in Greek, including beauty, joy, love. For Paul it is an almost technical term for the idea that overwhelmed him, namely, the unmerited love of God for us. *Charis* as grace describes God's love for us, due to nothing outside of God's love, the basis of our hope.

If in fact Paul is adapting the Hellenistic *chairein* to *charis,* then we can see the genius of this writer. He knows the conventions of his day, but he dominates those conventions, and he does so in a way so quietly that we could easily overlook it.

Furthermore, Paul offers this "grace and peace" not just from himself and Timothy, but "from God our Father and the Lord Jesus Christ." Today we are perhaps used to such language, yet it presupposes in Paul a remarkable self-consciousness—"God and Jesus send their best." Earlier letters do not greet people this way.

The expression "God our Father and the Lord Jesus Christ" is typically Pauline. Paul uses the term *theos,* "God," only for the God he knows from his Jewish faith, the one he calls "the Father." In the letters really written by Paul, he does not use this term for Jesus. Instead, he consistently describes Jesus as *kyrios,* "Lord." This is a practice that consistently extends from the earliest to his last letters (see 1 Thess 1:1).

3. *The Prayer*

The opening prayer in Philemon resembles much more the Jewish letter prayer than the perfunctory references to praying in the Hellenistic letters. Like the Jewish letters, the prayer centers on "God," or as Paul writes here, "my God," whom Paul sees and thanks as the source of all blessing.

The predominance of thanksgiving here, however, reveals something quite distinctive of Paul's epistolary prayers. In general, this note distinguishes the early Christian prayers from contemporary Jewish prayers. Faith in Jesus' resurrection, the experience of the success of the gospel, and other experiences apparently led Paul and the early Christians to an upbeat attitude of joy and confidence.

To this thanksgiving, Paul almost always adds a petition. The combination of thanksgiving and petition also suggests a distinctive mentality. The basic attitude of Paul is positive, one of thanksgiving. This confidence in God's action, however, does not lead to complacence. Paul looks for more. He prays for further development. In Philemon he prays for a perfection of faith in religious knowledge—an interesting way in which knowledge appears as the perfection of Christian living. Combined with thanksgiving, the petition appears as one uttered in confidence, not in desperation. Paul prays for more, but he does so on the basis of what God has already accomplished.

The object of thanksgiving and prayer will differ in the individual letters. In 1 Corinthians, Paul knows that the church lacks a sense of Christian love, but is endowed with an especially charismatic life. It is interesting to see how Paul approaches in thanksgiving this delicate problem (see 1 Cor 1:4–9). Paul's approach in Galatians is quite different (see Gal 1:1–9).

4. *The Body of the Letter*

The body of Paul's letters, where he addresses the particular issues and questions of the churches, is peculiar to each letter and therefore is the hardest to analyze. Some structures do appear. Frequently, for instance, he divides the letters into two major parts, a teaching section and an exhortatory section. In the teaching section (for example, Rom 1:16—11:36 or Gal 1:6—4:31), Paul speaks mostly in the indicative mood. He explains difficult matters to the readers. In the exhortatory section (for example Rom 12:1–15 or Gal 5:1—6:10), Paul switches to the imperative mood.

5. *The Conclusion of the Letter*

As Paul draws to a close in his letters, he adds last-minute recommendations (Phlm 19–22). He includes greetings from companions (Phlm 23–24) and at times greetings to others he knows in the community to whom he is writing (see the long list in Rom 16). Occasionally he mentions a liturgical gesture (2 Cor 13:12), sometimes a stern warning (Gal 6:17), and sometimes something written in his own hand after apparently dictating the letter to a secretary (Gal 6:11 and 1 Cor 16:21). The final words usually form a type of blessing (Phlm 25, and see the elaborate blessing of Rom 16:25–27). This blessing replaces the usual "goodbye" of the Hellenistic letter.

III. Paul's Way of Developing an Idea

As he writes his letters, Paul attempts to develop difficult and complicated ideas and positions. The letters are lively and spontaneous, but they are also thoughtfully composed. This development is not always clear at first reading. In fact, to the modern reader Paul's development sometimes seems haphazard and disorganized. The problem lies primarily in the fact that Paul does not write in paragraphs, as we are accustomed to do. He does not simply present an idea or position and then, with a series of subsequent sentences, explain what he means by that idea before going on to the next. Rather, like most writers of ancient times, his development consists of positive and negative associations. Paul links an image or idea to another, or contrasts it with another.

Understanding Paul's underlying theology, therefore, means paying attention to the way he makes these connections and contrasts. Sometimes in a sentence the words or statements are simply placed in apposition to each other, basically repeating the same idea. Sometimes the words are connected by carefully chosen prepositions and conjunctions, where a causal relationship or a spatial relationship might be intended. A careful look at the very sentence structure in detail is thus the first step in understanding Paul.

A second step is to see how Paul uses the literary structures of his day to connect sentences or phrases. One of the most common ways of accomplishing this association is by way of parallel statements, repeating the same idea in different words or from another angle. For example, Paul writes to the Corinthians,

> I urge you brothers...
> that all of you agree in what you say,
> that there be no divisions among you,
> but that you be united in the same mind and in the same purpose. (1 Cor 1:10)

The first and the third repetition are both positive statements. This is known as "synonymous parallelism." The second repetition, however, is a restatement of the same idea by denying the opposite. This is known as "antithetical parallelism." By recognizing these parallel statements, we can see one parallel concept that he associated with "agreeing" and one he distinguished from it. Thus we can better understand what he is urging his readers to do. Rewriting the texts of Paul in this form of structural verse often helps us see the flow of Paul's thought.

This parallelism can link up two separate statements in such a way that their internal parts can be interrelated and thus better understood. Here the association of ideas takes the form of a more elaborate weave.

One form of this weaving involves simply alternating two or more ideas in the same order creating an A-B-A′-B′ pattern. The parallel alternation can be short and simple:

A. "We are fools on Christ's account,
  B. but you are wise in Christ;
A′. we are weak,
  B′. but you are strong." (1 Cor 4:10)

Or the parallelism can be subtle and extended. Thus Paul writes,

A. "Our ancestors were all under the cloud and all passed through the sea,
  B. and all of them were baptized into Moses in the cloud and in the sea.
A′. All ate the same spiritual food, and all drank the same spiritual drink
  B′. for they drank from a spiritual rock that followed them, and the rock was the Christ." (1 Cor 10:1–4)

A-A′ describes stories in the Bible, the passage through the Red Sea and God's care in the desert.

B-B′ gives a Pauline interpretation going beyond the story and relating the biblical narration to Christian realities. He is saying the same thing twice but with different nuances. The key to understanding this rhetoric is to identify the corresponding parts of Paul's exposition and then make comparisons between them. If the idea is important, Paul will say it several times.

In addition to this alternating parallelism, ancient writers had a second method of weaving ideas together using a kind of bookends construction. Paul, for instance, sometimes interrupts the parallel by going on to something else, then later returning to the first idea, thus relating ideas by weaving the thoughts around each other.

This bookends composition, or "inclusion," results in a type of A-B-A′ pattern. The pattern not only provides an interesting parallelism, but indicates a unit of related thoughts. Note how Paul starts and closes the opening prayer in 1 Corinthians by repeating the name "Christ Jesus...Jesus Christ" (1 Cor 1:4–9).

At times this bookends composition gives us a clue to major sections of some of the more lengthy letters. A major section of 1 Corinthians begins with Paul's concern about meat offered to idols (1 Cor 8:1–13) and ends with the same topic (1 Cor 10:23–33). A composition teacher today would have criticized Paul for breaking up the unified material. In his own day, Paul's composition teacher would have given him a high mark for his subtle signal of a major division in this letter.

This structure might likewise explain an aspect of 2 Corinthians that has puzzled modern readers. Paul begins this letter at 1:8 by a narration of his recent experiences. At 2:13, however, the account is broken off and resumed again at 7:4–16. Between these bookends Paul explains the theology of his "ministry of the new covenant," of "death and life in his ministry," and of his "ministry of reconciliation." While some explain this structure as the work of a later editor, Paul may very well himself have wanted to integrate his theology with his concrete experience.

Finally, sometimes, a series of concentric bookends inside each other link up several thoughts in a form of inverse symmetry. This type of construction results in a pattern like A-B-C-B′-A′. Today, scholars call that elaborate inversion a "chiasm" after the form of the Greek letter *chi*, which looks like a big X. Note, for instance, the development in the very wording in 1 Corinthians 9:15–18:

A. I have not used any of these rights...(15)
B. an obligation has been imposed on me...(16a)
C. and woe is me if I do not preach it...(16b)
B'. I have been entrusted with a stewardship...(17)
A'. I offer the gospel free of charge so as not to make full use of my right in the gospel. (18)

Similarly in the reprise of Paul's "travel log" in 2 Corinthians 7, we find a subtle chiastic structure in the basic ideas:

A. Paul's joy and encouragement in regard to the Corinthians (7:4)
B. Paul's meeting with Titus in Macedonia (7:5–7)
C. Paul's harsh letter (7:8–13a)
B'. Titus's joy with the Corinthians (7:13b–15)
A'. Paul's joy and confidence in regard to the Corinthians (7:16)

The chiasms may have any number of elements, but often the central element of a chiasm (C) is the focal point meant to color the entire structure. This is the statement that the writer has in mind from the start, around which he associates other ideas as a development of the central element. Likewise, the outside inclusion (A-A') gives a framework to the development and provides a special light for reading the whole development.

As we read the letters of Paul, then, we need to recognize these literary structures of Paul's letters and then identify the ideas or images that Paul apparently wants to associate. We will find that these associations are fairly consistent in Paul. Our restatement of Paul's theology then becomes an effort to rethink the nature of the associations he insists on.

IV. Conclusions

This study of Paul's use of the Jewish-Hellenistic letter form paints a picture of a well-educated writer. He knows the conventions of letter writing. His writings are much smoother than the stilted Hellenistic examples we saw.

More important, he can adapt those conventions both to reinforce his intentions in the letter and also to express his faith. Few of us would ever think to adapt the simple conventions of beginning a letter as we do, "Dear so-and-so," into an expression of our faith. Paul does it masterfully. His style is an indication of how all pervasive his faith was in his life. He cannot even write a personal letter without showing his amazement for the gifts of God in Christ Jesus.

2

The Life of Paul—The Use of Acts

I. Testing the Waters: A Comparison of Acts 9—15 and Galatians 1—2

A. The Texts

The two principal sources for reconstructing the life of Paul are his own letters and the account of Paul by Luke in the Acts of the Apostles. Since Acts gives us a much more complete picture of Paul than the snippets gleaned from the letters, many have begun with the Acts account and then simply fit or squeezed in the details from the letters. We must, however, be careful. The purposes and literary forms of ancient writers of historical narratives differ greatly from those of modern history writers.

Fortunately, Paul gives something of his own life in the autobiographical sections of his letters, particularly in Galatians 1—2. With that information from Paul we can test the parallel account in Acts 9—15. Both sources describe the events in Paul's life from his "conversion" to the meeting in Jerusalem and the immediate aftermath of that meeting. The two accounts seem to break down in the following way:

Gal 1—2	*Acts 9—15*
Paul the persecutor (1:13–14)	Paul the persecutor (9:1–2)
The calling (1:15–16)	The conversion (9:3–7)
revelation of the Son	encounter with Jesus
Arabia (1:17)	Damascus (9:8–22)
and return to Damascus	cure: preaching and escape
[three years]	
Jerusalem (1:18–20)	Jerusalem (9:23–30)
sees Cephas and James only	after some time with Barnabas

	introduced to apostles,
	escape to Caesarea and Tarsus
Syria and Cilicia (1:21)	From Tarsus to Antioch (11:25–26)
	one year
(not known to Judea)	Jerusalem (11:29–30; 12:25)
	with Barnabas
	brings collection, return to Antioch
[14 years] (2:1)	First missionary journey (13:1—14:22)
Jerusalem (2:1–10)	Jerusalem (15:1–29)
re: the liberty of Gentiles	re: the liberty of Gentiles
with Barnabas and Titus	with Barnabas
meets Cephas, James, and John	meets Peter, James, apostles, and presbyters
agreement:	agreement:
remember the Poor	Gentiles to abstain from blood,
Paul to Gentiles	blood meats, food offered to idols, and illicit sex
Antioch (2:11–14)	Antioch (15:30–34)
dispute with Peter and Barnabas	dispute with Barnabas
departure for 2nd journey	

B. Analysis of the Differences

1. Paul, the Persecutor

In a comparison of the two texts, we are struck with both the similarities of the main lines of Paul's life and the discrepancies in the details. Both accounts begin by describing Paul as a persecutor of the church. The authority Paul supposedly had from the high priest in Jerusalem to arrest Christians in Damascus, as recounted by Acts, seems a bit improbable. The high priest, as presiding officer of the Jerusalem Sanhedrin, had authority over the internal affairs of the Jewish community in Judea. It is difficult to see how he could have had extradition rights in Damascus. Yet we know little of the times and their actual lines of authority.[1]

2. The Call

The differences in the descriptions of the conversion of Paul are due mostly to the literary form in which they are told. Luke's account follows very much the typical apocalyptic description of the inaugural vision of the seer.[2] The light, the collapse to the ground [no horse], the divine words, and the mission all seem to fit into the stereotype of an apocalyptic experience. On the other hand, Paul's brief description (Gal 1:15–16) parallels the description of Jeremiah and his prophetic call (Jer 1:4–19; see also Isa 49:1). To describe his experience, Paul picks another stereotype, the call of a prophet, and by so doing tells us about his understanding of the experience.

For Paul this experience was less a "conversion," a leaving of one religion for another, than a "calling," a vocation like that of the prophets to the fullness of his faith. The experience involved a major change or turning point in his life. In that sense it was a "conversion." However, the turning point was much like that of Jeremiah or the prophets whose lives became consumed by an insight into God's plan. Paul never leaves his Jewish faith. Rather, he sees the "Christian" reality within that faith.

3. Immediately after the Call

When we look at the third step, the discrepancy becomes more difficult. Paul insists that he "immediately, without seeking human advisers," went off to Arabia (Gal 1:16–17). Luke clearly describes Paul getting in contact with Ananias, apparently a leader of the Christian community in Damascus. In fact, in the dialogue between Jesus and Paul in Acts 9:6, Luke insists on the active role of Ananias giving Paul his instructions. It would take difficult mental gymnastics to reconcile these two accounts.

Paul clearly is stressing that he has his commission directly from God and Christ, as did the first apostles, and hence his authority is no less than theirs. (See Paul's insistence in 1 Cor 9:1 and the way he associates his experience of the risen Lord with that of the Twelve in 1 Cor 15:5–8.) Luke's purpose in this account seems likewise to uphold the authority of Paul. Luke in effect associates Paul with Jewish Christianity as soon as possible.

Soon afterwards, according to Luke, Paul is introduced to the pillars of Jerusalem, who accept him. Both Paul and Luke agree in the basic idea, but approach this idea with contradictory stories.

4. A Trip to Jerusalem

The first trip to Jerusalem as told by both accounts differs only in minor details. Paul then summarizes the next fourteen years or so as a stay in the province of Syria and Cilicia, the territory around the northeastern corner of the Mediterranean. This is the period in which Acts describes Paul's first missionary journey from Antioch in Syria into the area which today is southern Turkey, not far from the ancient province of Syria and Cilicia (Acts 13:4—14:25).

One particular difficulty with this account in Acts lies in the visit to Jerusalem (11:29–30), an account that is confusing due to variants in the manuscripts at 12:25, and one that may well have been garbled in the tradition. In any case, it is difficult to reconcile this trip to relieve the famine in Jerusalem with the account of Paul in Galatians. Many years later, however, Paul did make a trip to Jerusalem to come to the material assistance of the "holy ones" there. He describes his intentions to make that trip in several letters as it develops (1 Cor 16:1–4; 2 Cor 8—9; Rom 15:25–29). Luke may have had wind of this trip without knowing when it occurred.

5. The "Council" of Jerusalem

The principal difficulty with the Lucan account of Acts 11:29–30 lies in the fact that the trip in Gal 2:1–10 seems almost certainly the trip recounted by Luke in Acts 15:1–29. Many important details are the same. The liberty of the Gentile Christians is discussed and secured. Paul meets with the leaders of the Jerusalem church, specifically Cephas (Peter) and James. Barnabas is Paul's companion. Paul, however, identifies this trip as his *second.* He describes the encounter as a private meeting with the leaders of Jerusalem. Luke describes it as a great council of the church. Later in Acts 21:25, Luke betrays the real possibility that the description of the Jerusalem council in Acts 15 may very well have been a conflation of two separate meetings, one with Paul and another without him.

Most striking, however, is the discrepancy dealing with the agreement reached regarding the obligations of the Gentile Christians. According to Paul, the only stipulation was "to be mindful of the poor." According to Acts, three stipulations are insisted on: (1) to abstain from food offered to idols, (2) to abstain from blood and meat not drained of blood (strangled), and (3) to abstain from "illicit sex," *porneia,* a word that could refer to anything from simple fornication to incestuous marriages.

Paul's account of the stipulation, "to be mindful of the poor," probably refers to an agreement to remember the church of Jerusalem. Later, Jewish Christians were known as "the poor" or the *Ebionites*. The theme of "the poor of Yahweh" was one stemming from the prophets denoting the remnant of Israel that remained faithful to God despite dispossession. This theme fits very well what we know about the consciousness of the first Jewish Christians as a faithful remnant. Hence, the stipulation to be mindful of the poor was probably referring to an agreement to remember the priority of the Jerusalem church, the priority of that stock, to which Paul would later refer when he describes Gentile Christians as wild branches grafted onto the stock of Israel.

Luke's stipulations are puzzling in many respects. Taken together, they represent the things most abhorrent to a Jew; hence, an agreement on these matters would in fact be an agreement regarding the respect of Gentiles for Jews in the church. Yet this solemn stipulation regarding the avoidance of blood and meat from strangled animals becomes one of the most quickly forgotten regulations in Christianity. We never hear of it again. Nowhere in Paul's letters is it ever mentioned.

The provision of abstaining from food offered to idols is especially puzzling. This provision likewise is never mentioned again. This is all the more significant with Paul involved, because he later would deal directly with this question when writing to the Corinthians (see 1 Cor 10:23–30). The silence about any Jerusalem agreement is deafening.

Luke, on the other hand, could possibly be thinking on a theological plane at this point. The law forbidding blood stems from the story of Noah (Gen 9:4). In that story, God makes a covenant promising never again to destroy the Earth by water. In turn, Noah must respect life and express that respect by refraining from blood. This covenant is the last covenant in the Old Testament that God makes with humanity as a whole. After this covenant, God will deal with only more and more restricted portions of the human race. For Luke, this universal aspect of the Noahic covenant would have great significance. Developing the story of the Jerusalem agreement, Luke may be simply insisting on its significance as a covenant embracing all humanity, not just Jews.

"Remember the poor" may be an agreement about the unity of Jewish and Gentile communities within the church. Abstaining from blood and blood meats may be a reference to the Noahic covenant with all humanity, Jews and Gentiles. In broad strokes, Luke and Paul agree. In the historical details, they differ.

6. The Fight at Antioch

Finally, we compare the scene in Antioch describing Paul in a serious argument with a leader of the Jerusalem church. In Galatians 2:11–14, Paul is arguing with Peter. Here two important leaders are in dispute about a fundamental matter, the unity of Jews and Gentiles in the church. The crisis must have been severe for the early Christian community.

Luke may very well be giving us a version of the same event in Acts 15:30–39. The argument is with Barnabas, a leader of the Jerusalem church, who is mentioned in the Galatians account (2:13). The event occurs in Antioch. The dispute happens sometime after the agreement about church unity. However, in Acts, the issue is a family problem. It is not a fundamental issue about Christianity. Barnabas wants to bring along his cousin; Paul does not. Luke appears to want to allude to the event, while in effect trivializing the argument.

C. Conclusions

Through this test case, then, comparing Galatians 1—2 with Acts 9—15, we have some evidence for evaluating the reliability of Acts as a source of information for the career of Paul. It would seem clear from the discrepancies that Luke did not know the epistles of Paul. He certainly did not read Galatians, with Paul's account of his early years, and probably never knew Paul at all.[3] In the light of this distance between Luke and Paul, the similarities between the two accounts become all the more significant. The two accounts agree in the main lines.

At times, however, the details of the two accounts are clearly incompatible. If Paul is speaking of his own life, writing at least twenty years earlier than Luke, then it would seem only reasonable to accept the Pauline version of the accounts. In Paul we have it, as it were, from the proverbial horse's mouth.

We see Luke as one who fills in the gaps with his own theologically motivated details. We see Acts as much like the gospels, where theology often replaces historical accuracy (newspaper reporting) as the guide to the narration. We thus have a basis for using Acts for drawing the broad strokes of the rest of Paul's life. We have no reason for rejecting Acts as totally unreliable. Nevertheless, we are warned to see the details in Acts about Paul as far more Lucan than Pauline, as far more representing the Lucan understanding of Paul in the history of salvation than giving us the actual words and deeds of Paul. Wherever possible we need to evaluate the Lucan accounts by comparing them to Paul's references to his own life.

II. Luke's Story of Paul

A. Pre-Christian Paul

We can find some details about the early life of Paul from the descriptions in Acts, especially in the latter part of this book where the Lucan Paul defends himself by allusions to his youth. We can compare these allusions with Paul's own statements in his letters about himself.

About his birth and early background, Acts speaks of Paul as "a Jew from Tarsus in Cilicia" (21:39, also 22:3). Paul himself does not mention Tarsus, but does insist on being an Israelite of the tribe of Benjamin (Rom 11:1; Phil 3:5). Both Acts and Paul specify Paul's Jewish background as that of the Pharisaic tradition (Acts 23:6, 26:5; Phil 3:5). Both Acts and Paul are clear about his persecution of the early Christians (Acts 9:2, 22:1–5, 26:9; Gal 1:13; Phil 3:6; 1 Cor 15:9).

Acts describes Paul as having studied in Jerusalem, "at the feet of Gamaliel," where he was educated in the law (Acts 22:3). Gamaliel was the second generation (actually, grandson) of teachers in the School of Hillel, the school of liberal interpretation, often contrasted with that of Shammai, the school of strict interpretation. This description of Paul's studies is surprising after what we know about Paul's harsh persecution of the Christians. Paul himself speaks about "my excess of zeal to live out all the traditions of my ancestors" (Gal 1:14). A more important difficulty in accepting Luke's description of Paul studying in Jerusalem is Paul's total silence about this. Paul faced several challenges to his Jewish orthodoxy, which he vehemently defended, especially by referring to his Pharisaic background. He never mentioned, however, studying in any prestigious school of Jerusalem. On the other hand, Luke typically locates important events in Jerusalem. He sees this holy city as the place of salvation from which salvation radiates to the world. The Lucan picture of Paul studying in Jerusalem, therefore, may well be based on theology rather than historical knowledge.

Concerning the broad strokes of Paul's education and family background in general, we can detect an important agreement. Luke clearly insists on Paul's intense education, and toward the end of the Acts, Luke describes Paul, the "citizen" of Tarsus and Rome, hobnobbing with governors and kings (Acts 24—25). The description suggests a Roman aristocrat. While speaking of beatings that would argue against the elevated social status Luke gives him (see 2 Cor 11:24–29), the very quality of his letters, along with the occasional allusion to poets and philosophers, reveals the education he must have received in his youth. Furthermore, a good education of the children was one of the most significant signs of a rich family. Paul may not have been of the almost senatorial rank suggested by Acts, but he probably came from a well-to-do family when he left all to become an itinerant preacher.

B. PAUL'S TRAVELS

Luke dedicates all of the second half of Acts to Paul and organizes the missionary work of Paul into three major trips. Each journey ends with a trip to Jerusalem. The final one leads to his imprisonment in the Middle East and his eventual voyage as a prisoner to Rome.

1. The First Journey (Acts 13:1—14:28)

The first journey begins in Antioch (modern-day Antakya). After Jerusalem, Antioch was the most important Christian city at the time of Paul and apparently the seedbed of a Hellenized Jewish Christianity. Later, a somewhat Hellenistic but very Jewish scribe will write the Gospel of Matthew from here. The commissioning of Paul and his companion, Barnabas, is important. No one less that the Holy Spirit designates the two for a work to which the same Holy Spirit has called them (Acts 13:2). The intervention of the Spirit occurs during a community liturgy, one apparently involving the exercise of Christian prophecy. The two then receive a "laying on of hands" by the prophets and teachers of the Antioch community. The work of Paul is thus carefully inserted into the life and functioning of the church.

The journey first takes Paul and Barnabas, along with Barnabas's cousin, John Mark, to the island of Cyprus. They travel to the cities of Salamis and Paphos, the homeland of Barnabas. From here on, Paul (called Saul here for the last time) appears more and more as the leader of the expedition. The missionaries preach the word first in Jewish synagogues and then to more receptive Gentiles, a pattern repeated throughout Acts.

The missionary group then sails to Pamphylia, on the southern coast of modern-day Turkey. Their first stop is Perga, where John Mark leaves them. This move by John Mark becomes the subject matter for the later argument in Antioch between Paul and Barnabas. The two then continue on to Antioch in Pisidia, to Iconium (modern-day Konya), then to Lystra and Derbe, before returning to Antioch in Syria. Luke summarizes the message of Paul in the speeches at Antioch in Pisidia (13:16–41) and Lystra (14:15–17). Paul's words to the Jews are filled with allusions to

Fig. #1: Paul's first missionary journey—Acts 13:4—14:28

the Old Testament. On the other hand, his words to the Gentiles speak of the God of nature. Luke focuses, however, far more on the person of Paul than on his theology. We hear very little of the intricate theology Paul expresses in his letters. The pattern throughout the trip is that of (a) some success among the Jews, (b) greater success among the Gentiles, and then (c) severe opposition from the unconvinced Jews, who force the missionary group to move on. When after this trip Paul and Barnabas return to Jerusalem, the scene is then set for the "council" that discusses the freedom of the Gentiles.

In his Letter to the Galatians, Paul gives us little information to help us test this account from Acts. As we saw, Paul speaks only of some fourteen years spent in the region of Syria and Cilicia during this time (Gal 1:21—2:1). Nothing precludes an intense missionary activity and travels, although Luke places Paul's travels somewhat more to the west. The picture of one grand circuit through the land appears as a Lucan effort to systematize, and the absence in Paul of any mention of Cyprus makes the Lucan descriptions of Paul there a bit suspect.

Paul's indications of durations are important as he speaks of this time period. He speaks of three years elapsing between his call and his first trip to Jerusalem (Gal 1:18) and of fourteen years elapsing until his second trip to Jerusalem to discuss the freedom of Gentiles (Gal 1:18—2:1). Adding the two durations as successive periods involving seventeen full years poses some problems down the road as we try to correlate Paul and Luke. However, some ambiguity in Paul's account allows for flexibility. According to the ancient ways of counting, where a part counted as a whole, three years could mean anything from one year with a few days on either end to three full years; fourteen years, from slightly more than twelve to the full fourteen. Moreover, Paul's descriptions in Galatians, "after three years" and "after fourteen years," could be read either as successive intervals or as concurrent intervals (that is, "three years after my call...fourteen years after [my call]). The interval between his call and the meeting in Jerusalem could thus stretch from thirteen years to seventeen years. As we will see, the "Council of Jerusalem" as described by Luke should probably be dated to around AD 49. According to Paul's figures taken in their minimal extension, his call would then be dated no later than AD 35 or 36.

2. The Second Journey (Acts 15:40—18:22)

After the return of Paul and Barnabas to Jerusalem and the ensuing decisions regarding Gentile membership in the church, Paul sets out again on a missionary journey, with the important "commendation" by the brethren. After their "sharp argument," however, Barnabas and Paul split. Paul's new companion is Silas, whose name had the Latinized form of Silvanus (see 1 Thess 1:1). In Acts, Silas had already functioned as a special representative of the Jerusalem church (15:22).

The journey retraces some of the steps from the first journey along with a special trip to the Galatian territory. Timothy, who will become a lifelong companion of Paul, is recruited at Lystra. Characteristic of this journey, however, is the impulse by "the Spirit of Jesus" (16:7) as well as by visions in the night (16:9) to travel westward into Europe.

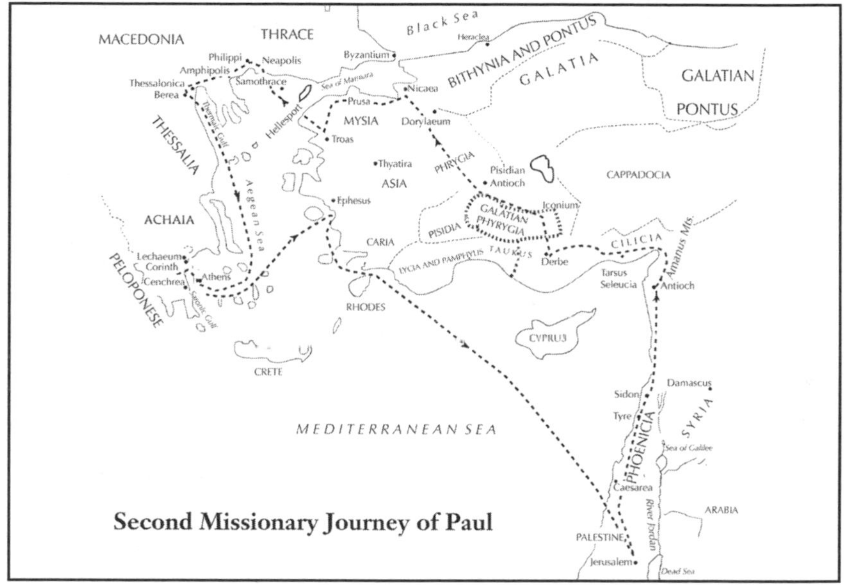

Fig. #2: Paul's second missionary journey—Acts 15:39—18:22

Once in Europe, the three travel to Philippi, Thessalonica, and Beroea, all in the Roman province of Macedonia. From there they travel to Athens and Corinth in the province of Achaia. Except in Athens, Paul establishes Christian communities. The pattern of success and persecution, seen in the first journey, occurs again for the most part during this second journey.

Luke portrays Paul as appearing before Gallio in Corinth (18:12–17). If accurate, this scene provides us with the unique peg to hook the relative chronology onto our modern calendar. Historians point to AD 51–52 as the time of Gallio's proconsulship in Corinth. We therefore date Paul's stay in Corinth to the year AD 52. Allowing for the approximate amount of time necessary for Paul to have journeyed this far, we can generally assign the "Council of Jerusalem" to the year AD 49. The second journey appears, therefore, to cover the years AD 50–53.

As we will see in the study of the letter, 1 Thessalonians can easily be situated at this moment of the second journey. The itinerary hinted at by Paul (1 Thess 2:2, 17) as well as the mention of

Paul's companions (1 Thess 1:1, identifying Silvanus with Silas) accord well with the description of Paul in Acts 18. We date this letter therefore from the year AD 52, making it the oldest extant writing in Christianity.

3. The Third Journey (Acts 18:23—21:14)

The third journey begins abruptly at 18:23: "After spending some time there he set out again." Nothing is said about a community mandate. As depicted by Luke, this period in Paul's life is characterized by a two- or three-year stay in Ephesus (19:1–40). First Corinthians was written from Ephesus (1 Cor 16:8) and mostly likely was written at this time. Part of 2 Corinthians appears also to have been written at this time and place.

Luke then briefly mentions a trip through Macedonia and "Greece" (Achaia) (20:1–3a). The bulk of 2 Corinthians was written from Macedonia (2 Cor 7:5). Other details of the letter suggest this period of Paul's life. The stay in Greece at this time also

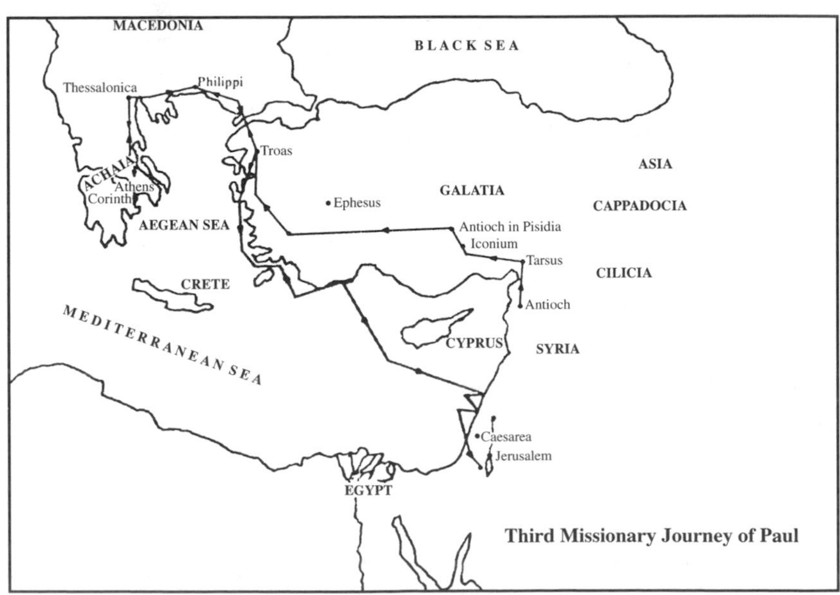

Fig. #3: Paul's third missionary journey—Acts 18:23—21:16

appears to be the setting for Paul's Letter to the Romans (Rom 16:1) and probably that to the Galatians.

Plots against Paul's life lead to a journey back to the Middle East (20:3b—21:14). Again using only estimated times required for traveling along with the duration of his stay in Ephesus, we can estimate the time of this third journey to be around AD 54–58.

The concluding part of Acts brings Paul back to Jerusalem, where he receives a curious reception by James, "the brother of the Lord," now the leader of the church of Jerusalem. After a riot in the Temple provoked by his presence, Paul is arrested and imprisoned in Caesarea for two years. Appealing to his Roman citizenship, Paul asks for a trial before Caesar and is granted this request. The trip to Rome, which includes a shipwreck at Malta, takes about a year. In Rome, as Acts concludes, Paul is held in a kind of house arrest for two years. The years AD 58–63 are for Paul years of imprisonment, first in Caesarea and then in Rome.

These concluding chapters on the imprisonment of Paul and his trip to Rome pose special problems for their historicity. Paul's hobnobbing with kings and governors and his treatment as a person of almost senatorial class are hard to correlate with Paul's own descriptions of labors and beatings. This Lucan description may be part of a Lucan intention to portray the applicability of Christian faith for the upper crust of the Roman Empire after Luke's insistence in his Gospel on the poor.

Acts abruptly ends with Paul's house arrest in Rome. Paul may have been released according to a probable Roman legal provision to release the accused if an accuser does not appear within two years to make accusation.[4] As described by Luke, this Roman imprisonment certainly does not suggest "death row." Nevertheless, we might wonder why nothing is mentioned at all about Paul's death. Writing in the 80s, Luke must have known about this tragic end, which for us would have been a fitting end of the story.

An explanation for this abrupt end, however, may appear in the programmatic command of Jesus in Acts 1:8: "You will receive power when the Holy Spirit comes down on you; then you are to be my witnesses in Jerusalem, throughout Judea and Samaria, yes, even to the ends of the earth." The first half of Acts, centered on Peter and the Twelve, concentrates on the witnessing in Jerusalem,

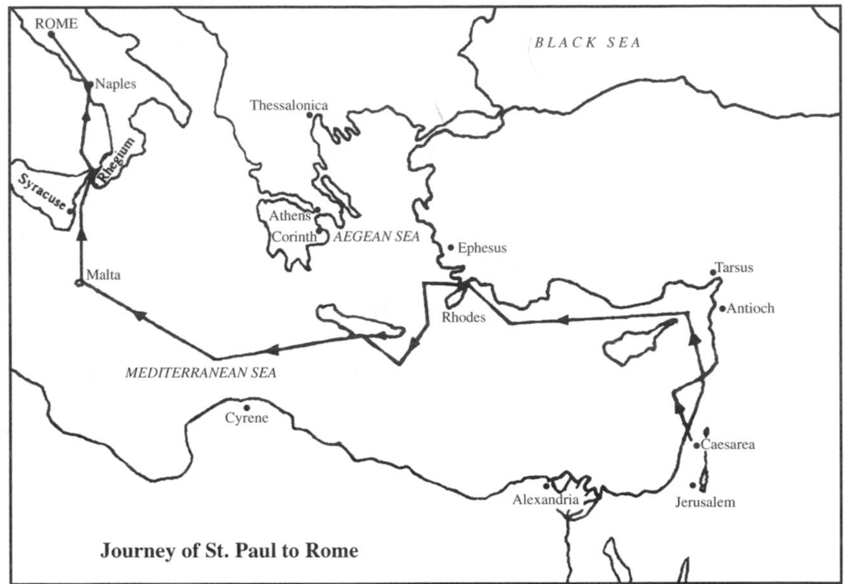

Fig # 4: Paul's prison journey to Rome—Acts 27:1—28:16

Judea, and Samaria. The second half, centered on Paul, concentrates on the witnessing "to the ends of the earth." Paul's arrival at Rome was his arrival at the hub of the known world. From Rome lines of communication connected the whole empire. Very probably, Luke saw the fulfillment of Jesus' command with Paul's witnessing in Rome. Although Luke tells the story by focusing on persons and their activities, the real subject of the story is "the word" and the acts of preaching and witnessing to that word. The story for Luke really is achieved with Paul preaching in Rome (28:31).

Paul's letters to Philemon, to the Philippians, and to the Colossians are all difficult to date and situate geographically. However, they were all written from prison (Phlm 1; Phil 1:13; Col 4:3) and appear to reflect the later mature thought of Paul. Tradition situates these letters in this Roman imprisonment during the years AD 61–63. Given the somewhat suspect historicity of the final chapters of Acts, however, I will suggest another imprisonment a few years later.

Later tradition places the death of Paul in Rome, beheaded under Nero in AD 67. The earliest detailed account of this death is from the Acts of Paul 11:3–5, an early Christian writing generally dated from the second century AD. We have a fuller account from Jerome writing in the fourth century.[5] This tradition can also be traced back to the 90s, when 2 Timothy—a letter, as we will see, written by a later disciple of Paul—describes Paul's death row in Rome (2 Tim 1:16–18). Also in the 90s, Clement of Rome wrote of Paul's death and associates his death with those who died under Nero.[6] The discrepancy between Paul's presumed release in AD 63 and death in AD 67 led to the idea of a second imprisonment in Rome after a final few years of ministry. The fourth-century historian, Eusebius, described such a final preaching and second Roman imprisonment, but qualifies such information "as reported."[7]

III. Conclusion

The absence of any letter writing is quite striking in Acts' extended account of Paul. Paul later would quickly become most famous for his writings. Luke seems to know nothing about them. As we have seen, however, it is not difficult to situate a large number of Paul's letters in the itineraries provided by Acts.

Rather than presenting Paul as an influential writer, Luke presents him as a man of imposing presence and a powerful speaker (see especially Acts 14:11–18). Paul, on the contrary, accepts the criticism, "his bodily appearance is weak and his speech of no account" (2 Cor 10:10), and often speaks of his physical infirmity (Gal 4:13–14). In his own mind and as his letters confirm, Paul is rather a man with a powerful pen.

The material from Acts supplemented with some later traditions thus forms something of a framework in which to integrate the fragmentary information Paul himself gives us about his life and work. From the earlier comparison between Galatians 1—2 and Acts 9—15 we saw the difficulty of using Acts uncritically as a basis for understanding the life of Paul. We also saw a general agreement between Acts and Galatians regarding the major points and events in Paul's career, an agreement all the more remarkable given our conclusion that Luke neither knew Paul nor read his letters. Despite the problems posed by Acts 23—28, we are justified in using the earlier chapters of Acts as a tentative frame of reference for Paul, provided we do so critically and with a great deal of suspicion regarding the details of Acts' description of Paul, the speeches, the amount of time spent in places, and the exact companions. Our procedure must be first to cull from Paul's own writings where he is and what he is doing. With these details we will try to correlate Paul's letter writing with Acts, always ready for significant discrepancies.

3
Paul's Intellectual and Religious Background: Hellenism and Judaism

Paul was a thinker of his time, yet he was faced with the newness of the gospel, the newness of Christ. His effort to understand this new reality and to explain it to others required finding the images and concepts of his day that could express his faith-filled understanding. As it turns out, Paul was an exceptionally capable person to do just that. The Acts of the Apostles portrays Paul quite willing to speak in terms understandable to his Greek audience for missionary purposes (Acts 17:22–31).

Acts places his birth in Tarsus in Cilicia (Acts 21:39; 22:3). Paul himself says of his birth only that he was of the race of Israel and the tribe of Benjamin (Rom 11:1; Phil 3:5). If we can accept Tarsus as the place of Paul's birth, we have a city that helps explain Paul's extraordinary cultural background. Tarsus was located at a strategic spot on the caravan route from the western end of the Roman Empire to the eastern end. Travelers by land from the west would generally travel along the Anatolian plateau, the central section of present-day Turkey, then cross the Taurus Mountains to the plains of Cilicia, whence they could move easily eastward to Mesopotamia. Because of its strategic position, Tarsus was an important intellectual center. The currents of East and West mingled in its market place, the *agora*. We can picture in such a place young Paul, as he was known to the Greek-speaking neighbors, or Saul, as he was known to his fellow Jews, growing up a young man of two worlds, Hellenistic and Jewish.

For the sake of clarity, we will divide the elements of Paul's background somewhat artificially into these two aspects, examining first the Hellenistic, then the Jewish, including a brief glance back to Hellenic culture, especially as expressed in the thought of Plato. Our sketch is simplified and aims at grasping the major lines of Hellenistic philosophies as they would have impacted on Paul.

I. Paul's Hellenistic Background

A. Hellenic Roots

Hellenism at the time of Paul was an amalgam of cultures stemming from the world empire of Alexander the Great who, died in 323 BC. It was rooted in the classic Greek culture of the fifth and fourth centuries BC, a culture we can designate as Hellenic in distinction from the later Hellenistic culture. Alexander dreamt of a world culture modeled after Greece. What resulted was a rough synthesis of West and East, the rational view of the Greeks and the mythical thrust of the Middle East.

The classic Hellenic culture had many currents, some very spiritual, some very materialistic. Lumping the currents of this culture together is a simplification. Yet we can trace certain common major lines.

The dominant line of this culture was the emphasis on reason. This emphasis is the drive to give a "rational explanation" lying behind things. Other cultures had spoken of cosmic origins in terms of stories of gods. The Greeks around this time began to speak of cosmic origins in terms of principles or constitutive elements (*archai*). For some philosophers, the principles were elements like fire, water, air, and earth. For others, they were atoms. It was the beginning of the scientific spirit.

These principles were named by abstractions drawn from experience. They themselves were not experienced by the senses, but they could be thought of. They could be known by the mind. Moreover, the concrete realities experienced by the senses are distinguished by time ("now" not "then") and place ("here" not "there"). However, the principles we think of are stable through time and universal through place. I can see and touch a rock here in front of me that is more or less circular, and it will remain circular until I crack it in half. However, the circle as a geometric shape will not change. It remains a circle if thought of in Athens, as well as if thought of in Jerusalem. Reason and thought are engaged in a search for stability and universality.

The attempt to communicate this thought leads to the literary form of abstract "exposition." Expository writing or speaking attempts to lead us to the understanding of a reality in terms of stable principles grasped on some level of abstraction. Narration on the other hand leads us to see the concrete individual precisely in its temporal flow and local existence. The oldest cultures have left us narrative literature or stories, especially of their origins and critical moments. From these cultures we also have "gnomic" literature, a type of moral instruction in the form of proverbs or sayings, as well as legal texts. Only with the classic Greeks, as far as I can see, do we perceive the development of expository writing as an attempt to explain the way things are in terms of principles intended to be grasped by any reader at any time or any place.[1] Large sections of Paul's letters consist of similar types of expositions of his faith.

Plato, who died in 347 BC, by no means represents the full spectrum of Greek philosophy, but his understanding marked Greek thought in an unparalleled way. Following the lead of his teacher, Socrates, Plato took the rational method into the realm of human behavior and society. Whereas pre-Socratics asked the question of the rational basis for the cosmos, Socrates and Plato asked about the rational basis, the principles, or "ideals" of life, developing the ideal or principle of "justice." Justice made a human society a good society. However, the justice we experience on earth is always partial, always more or less, always temporary. Socrates and Plato sought to understand the *principle* of justice behind these partial and temporary forms.

This principle of justice would be the presupposition of all discourse about justice. If not experienced as a reality in this world, it is experienced as an ideal to be sought after. It is also experienced as independent power, a power that summons and commands us, not depending on any particular society or person—else it would cease to be an ultimate standard.

Plato saw this experience as evidence that the universe must, in fact, be of a dual nature. On the one hand, there exists this material world, where we experience justice and the other ideals lived out in partial form or at times totally absent. On the other hand, there must exist another separate world, where with our mind's eye we see the reality of absolute justice and the other ideals, not in partial form but in absolute and eternal form. In a famous allegory, Plato pictured this dual universe like a world divided between a cave world of shadows and a "real" world illumined by the sun. In the cave, people mistake shadows for reality. In effect, people cannot understand reality unless they climb out of the cave and experience a superior world, illumined by a great sun. From the experience of sunlight, a wise person can recognize the shadows as shadows.[2]

For Plato this cosmic dualism must be matched by an anthropological dualism. The question arises how Plato (or how *we*) can make this analysis. If we were totally immersed in the cave, we would be incapable of recognizing the cave as such. Yet it is clear we are part of this world, immersed in transitory concrete reality with its partial reflections of ideals. However, our quest for the ideal, our sense of fulfillment or joy at understanding the ideals, means we belong also to that world of ideals.

Hence, Plato concluded that the human person was really two realities bundled together, a body with its senses immersed in this world and a mind with its vision of ideals. Plato insisted on the independence and superiority of the mind over the body. Following this logic, Plato reasoned to the immortality (and preexistence) of the human mind. In this logic, death is not the end of the person but the liberation of the mind, the movement of the mind to the realm of ideals, the spiritual world of perfection.[3] For Plato and for the Hellenism that followed in his tradition, the resurrection of the human body had no place. Only the mind was important.

Platonic thought and the classic Greek thought deeply influenced by Plato are thus characterized by two parallel dualisms: a cosmic dualism and an anthropological dualism. Echoes of these dualisms clearly appear in the later Hellenistic movements that become the matrix of Paul's thought. Paul will resist the Platonic depreciation of the body (1 Cor 6:15–20). He will, however, eventually accept the view of a soul living separate from the body (Phil 1:23). This background is thus important for Paul's eschatological trajectory.

One word of caution is necessary for any attempt to understand classical Greek thought and culture. This culture was dominated by a search for an understanding of the ordered world, the cosmos. Even as it studied human life, this classical thought focused on the makeup and place of human beings in the cosmos, not on the internal experience of being human with all our human limits This was a rather extroverted interest. How do the gods, the elements, and things all fit together? It did not reflect on the way our internal and past experience molds and limits our experience of the cosmos.

Today, our culture is far more interested in subjectivity, with its goals of autonomy and individual expression, as well as the limits to our understanding reality and attaining our goals. Thus, the modern reader encounters serious difficulties grasping the classical mind.

B. Stoicism

As Hellenism under the banner of Alexander the Great encountered and assimilated the Eastern mind, an amalgam arose that modern scholars call "Hellenistic culture." Perhaps the most important Hellenistic philosophy forming Paul's intellectual context is Stoicism.

Following its Platonic heritage, Stoic philosophy represented the cool, rational approach of the West, with a sprinkling of the mystic and imaginative. This philosophical movement caught fire in the Roman world. It was called Stoicism from the *stoa* or covered walkways where the original Stoic philosophers first propounded their ideas. For the purposes of comparing with Paul, we can focus on (1) the Stoic emphasis on reason over passion, (2) the Stoic use of the body image for a society, and (3) the Stoic diatribe.

1. The basic interest of Stoicism was reason. Like our word reason, the Greek equivalent, *logos,* connoted both the mental process of thinking as well as the basic meaning behind or the

reason for an event or thing. The word *logos* also meant simply "word." The Stoics marveled at the regularity of nature and saw behind it all a universal *logos*, something like a world reason or soul that gave meaning to the whole universe, which began to resemble a living body.[4] As Seneca writes, "All this which you see, which is comprised of the divine and the human is one. We are members [*membra*] of a great body [*corpus*]."[5]

The Stoics also spoke often of a cosmic "spirit" [*pneuma*] that held together the universe much like the human spirit holds the human being together. This cosmic spirit was something like a substance in itself, along with the traditional fire, water, air, and earth, something like the "quintessence" of Aristotle. In fact, this spirit permeated and gave a kind of life to all forms.[6] The human mind was seen as a portion of this cosmic spirit inserted into the human body.[7]

The good life, according to the Stoics, communed with this cosmic *logos*. It was one in tune with the supreme reason of nature. Such a communion was possible through each individual's reason, that power in the human person which was part of the cosmic reason and which allowed people to function on the same order as that of the whole universe.

If reason was the key to salvation, then the obstacles to reason clearly were the basic evils of life. According to the Stoics, the things that prevent us from reasoned activity are our emotions and bodily senses. We cannot think straight when we are angry or in pain. Even intense pleasure can prevent us from cool reason. Hence, the Stoics developed the ideal of *a-patheia*, a lack of passion or emotion or at least a state of mind that resists any influence by these forces. This is not the "apathy" signified by our English cognate. Rather, Stoic *a-patheia* meant intense energy, one directed and lived entirely on the level of the mind. This for the Stoic mental energy led to the great ideal of *eleuthereia*, freedom.[8] Writing to the Galatians, Paul speaks frequently of the "freedom" we have from Christ (Gal 2:4; 5:1, 13).

2. Another image in Paul, one important for understanding the church, is "body" (*sôma*). Paul probably got the idea from the Stoics of his culture, where the term rang much like our expression "student body." The philosopher Chrysippus (280–207 BC),

one of the founders of Stoicism, specifically uses this image to describe an assembly or *ekklêsia*: "Here then we have a single body [*sôma*] composed of diverse bodies, like an assembly [*ekklêsia*] or an army or a chorus."[9] Much later, Seneca uses this terminology to distinguish a political body and the parts or members that compose it.[10]

The great concern of the Stoics using this body figure was to explain the ethics of dealing with others. Plutarch wrote of the need for "citizens, as parts of one body [*hosper henos mere sômatos*], to feel and sympathize with one another."[11] As Seneca writes, "'To harm one's country is wrong. Therefore, likewise, it is wrong to harm a fellow-citizen, since he is a part of the country....What if the hands should desire to harm the feet, or the eyes the hand?"[12] Urging Nero to be merciful toward the citizens of Rome, Seneca describes the city as Nero's "body." "You are the soul [*animus*] of society [*res publica*], which is your body [*corpus*]."[13]

About a century earlier, the Greek historian Dionysius of Halicarnassus recounted the speech by Menenius Agrippa to a plebeian group in revolt against the senate of Rome. The text contains interesting parallels to Paul's Letter to the Corinthians urging them to overcome factionalism and accept a sense of interdependence in society. In the speech, Agrippa starts by asserting, "A society [*polis*] resembles in some measure a human body [*sôma*]... and no one of the parts either has the same function or performs the same services." He then describes an absurd situation where the parts vaunt their importance and rebel against the stomach:

> Should the feet say that the whole body rests on them; the hands, that they work the crafts, secure provisions, fight wars and contribute many other useful things toward the common good; the shoulders, that they bear all the burdens; the mouth, that it speaks; the head, that it sees and hears and possesses the other sense by which the thing is preserved; and then they say to the stomach, "And you, fine thing, which of these things do you do? Of what use are you to us?"...If, I say, they are of such opinion and none of the parts should any longer perform its own work, could the body possibly

> exist for long and not rather be destroyed within a few days by the worst of all deaths, starvation?

For Agrippa and Dionysius the lesson is clear regarding a society:

> Now consider the same thing for a society. For this also is composed of many peoples not at all resembling one another, every one of which contributes some particular service to the common good [*to koinon chreios*], just as the members do to the body.

In the story, Agrippa then urges the plebeians not to revolt against the senate, which also contributes in its own way to the good of the whole body. To cause one member like the senate to perish would lead to destruction of the whole.[14] (For fuller texts of these ancient writers, see Appendix 1.)

Writing to the Corinthians, Paul will employ this image to describe the cohesion of the church in Christ and the mutual dependence of the "members" (1 Cor 12:12–26).

3. Another aspect of Stoicism that had a strong influence on Paul is a style of writing. The Stoics developed a way of teaching that they called the "diatribe." Again, this word should not be confused with "a prolonged, bitter argument," which our English word *diatribe* has come to mean. Rather, for the Stoics a diatribe described a literary form, a way of explaining their lofty message to those uninitiated into the technical aspects of Stoicism. The diatribe was a speech involving examples, lists of virtues and vices, rhetorical questions, imaginary dialogues, and other pedagogical devices. Epictetus was a master of the diatribe. He writes about controlling passions:

> Passion is only produced by a disappointment of one's desires and an incurring of one's aversions. It is this which introduces perturbations, tumults, misfortunes, and calamities; this is the spring of sorrow, lamentations, and envy; this renders us envious and emulous, and incapable of hearing reason....Shall I tell you what you have shown yourself? A mean, dis-

> contented, passionate, cowardly person, complaining of everything, accusing everybody, perpetually restless, good for nothing.[15]

Very characteristic of the Stoic diatribes was the imaginary partner who objected to the matter at hand. This interlocutor was not the real audience, but rather a literary device to allow the speaker to answer objections and further develop his thought. As Epictetus writes about the power of arguing and of persuasive reasoning, he creates a dialogue with some partner:

> In general any such power is dangerous for weak and uninstructed persons, as being apt to render them arrogant and elated.... What, then? Was not Plato a philosopher? Yes, and was not Hippocrates a physician? Yet you see how he expresses himself.... If Plato was handsome and stalwart, must I set myself to becoming handsome and stalwart?... What then? Do I reject these special faculties? By no means! Neither do I reject the faculty of sight. But if you ask me what the good of man is, I can only tell you that it is a kind of power of choice.[16]

Similarly, writing about freedom:

> For he is free to whom all happens agreeably to his desire, and whom no one can unduly restrain. What, then, is freedom mere license? By no means, for madness and freedom are incompatible.[17]

Other dramatic devices of the diatribe included personifications, even identifications, of the speaker with characters or things described in the discourse. The purpose of all these rhetorical devices was to aid a neophyte to understand the complex idea being explained.

All these elements of Stoicism are particularly important for the study of Paul, whose letters show hints of Stoic ideals: freedom, conscience, virtue, as well as distrust of "the flesh." His letters, with their lists of virtues and vices, their rhetorical questions, and imaginary interlocutors, likewise reflect the manner of the Stoic diatribe.

C. Mystery Cults

Another influence, at one time thought to be major in Paul but now considered questionable, is that stemming from the "mystery cults." These religions centered around secret dramas often portrayed on stage, through which salvation was offered to those initiated into these dramas. These cults centered around stories about life and death. Stories included descriptions of gods, like Attis, Osiris, or Dionysus, who died and rose from the dead. Watching the drama unfold on stage, the participant identified with the story and thus began to deal with the perplexing problem of death.

One such cult developed around the story of Isis and Osiris.[18] This was the story of a hero, Osiris, killed by his enemies and hacked to pieces. His enemies then tossed his parts into the Nile, which carried them in its flow down to Hades. At this point of the story, the audience responded with lamentation and dirge, allowing the horror of death to sweep over it. The story then continued with Isis, Osiris's loving wife, finding her way down to Hades, where she dutifully collected Osiris's body parts. Once Osiris pulls himself together, as it were, he returns to life to become the lord of Hades. The audience now rejoiced with great exultation.

A similar mystery cult celebrated the story of Persephone. This cult, with its center at Eleusis, today a suburb of Athens, portrayed the drama of Persephone, a beautiful, radiant girl.[19] Wherever she went on earth her radiance provoked the birds to sing, the flowers to bloom, the sun to shine. All of nature responded to her beauty and vitality. Pluto, the god of the underworld, however, becomes jealous of earth and kidnaps Persephone. At this loss, the flowers die, the birds disappear, and the cold blast of stormy weather replaces sunshine. To the rescue comes Persephone's mother, Ceres, who complains to Zeus, the chief god. Zeus then works out a compromise. Persephone will remain with Pluto six months of the year and return to earth the other six months. The audience responds appropriately, as it had been doing throughout the drama.

Throughout these stories, the theme was similar, the cycle of life and death. By participating in the mythical representation of this cycle, the members of the cult would purge their fears of death and experience the exuberance of life. Participating in the mystery cult constituted a sort of peak experience, giving them courage to face drab reality. To heighten the experience of the drama, members solemnly vowed never to disclose the contents of the drama to outsiders, hence, the name *mystery* cult.

Although the cults seemed to gather people together, these religions were quite individualistic. They were concerned about the unity of life between the devout individual and the god of the drama. The devotee would be concerned about how he or she as an individual could be united in a type of mystic isolation with the beloved god and thus rise above the sadness and suffering of earthly life. Nothing is ever said in these writings about the formation of a group or assembly, who together shared the death and resurrection of the god. This individualism contrasts with Paul's insistence on community.

The resemblance, nevertheless, between the mystery-cult dramas and the ancient Christian rituals is quite striking, especially when the Christian rituals are portrayed as providing entrance into the greater drama of Christ's life and death. Because the sources for our knowledge of the mystery cults are later than Paul, we must be careful about drawing conclusions. Nevertheless, it seems fairly certain that the mystery cults were part of the social milieu in which Paul preached. They could be important in the investigation of the Pauline trajectory of union of life with Christ, especially as Paul connect this union with the ritual dramas of baptism (Rom 5:3–4) and the Lord's Supper (1 Cor 10:16).

D. Gnosticism

Somewhat akin to the mystery cults is a religion and philosophy that flourished in the centuries immediately following the period of the New Testament called Gnosticism.[20] Although it existed as a systematic religion only after the New Testament,

Gnosticism appears to have its beginnings as a general movement in times preceding and coinciding with those of the New Testament.

We can probably best understand Gnosticism if we recall its basic story or myth. A typical Gnostic story is the short "Hymn of the Pearl," which we find in the *Acts of Thomas*, a Christian Gnostic document from the third century AD.[21] This short hymn is about a heavenly prince who descends to the evil earth in search of a pearl. For a while, he clothes himself in filthy human clothing. At one point, he becomes drunk and must be awakened by a special message from his heavenly father, a message that reminds the prince of who he really is. Eventually he seizes the pearl from a sea monster and returns to heaven. (See Appendix 2 for the text of the story.)

This story involves roughly seven major points, usually found in the many varieties of ancient Gnosticism:

1. God, the source of all goodness, dwells in a realm totally apart from this universe. This divine realm is one of pure spirits. God never had and never would have anything to do with the universe that human beings inhabit.
2. On the other hand, this universe in which we live is essentially evil. The evil lies in its material nature, which is directly opposed to spirit. All of reality falls into one of two categories: matter or spirit, evil or good, darkness or light. Thus, Gnosticism adheres to a radical dualism.
3. The human person finds itself caught between the two realms of spirit and matter. In its interior life, the human person is spirit, a spark of the divine spirit. However, the human body consists of evil matter. The body of the human person is thus a form of evil prison, in which the real spiritual person is entrapped. Such an entrapment occurred because of a fall or sin.
4. Redemption, therefore, consists of escaping from this evil body and returning to the spiritual realm of God. Redemption is in effect a spatial movement, a journey back to where we belong.
5. This return to God begins with knowledge. In Greek the word for this knowledge is *gnosis*, as in the English

words, prognosis or diagnosis, hence the name Gnosticism. This saving knowledge is above all knowledge of self, knowledge that one is truly a spark of the divine, that one is really an alien on earth.

6. This knowledge comes by way of revelation, a special message from God, sent to rescue human beings from their entrapment. In many forms of Gnosticism, this revelation comes by way of a revealer, a messenger of light who descends into the realm of darkness to bestow the saving message.
7. Because this material world with its history is inherently evil, what occurs on earth cannot contribute to human salvation. For the Gnostic, salvation cannot occur in or through history. What counts now for salvation is primarily one's thinking, one's interior life. Hence, according to the Gnostic view, this saving knowledge can come in the form of a myth, an imaginary story unrelated to historical events.

When Paul describes the radical antithesis between "spirit" and "flesh" (see especially Rom 8:6–8), we can ask about the possible influence of Gnosticism on Paul. Jesus and the evangelists never spoke of "flesh" in such negative terms. Where did Paul get this idea? Why is Paul recasting the traditional biblical idea of sin in almost metaphysical categories? A possible Gnostic background could be important for understanding Paul's trajectory of salvation.

Likewise, the picture of Jesus as living with God before becoming human, of Jesus' "degrading" himself to the earthly level (see especially Phil 2:6–8) can again lead us to ask about the influence of Gnostic imagery. In neither Matthew, Mark, nor Luke do we have this picture of Christ descending from heaven. When Paul and John introduce this idea into Christian preaching, are they simply accommodating their message to Gnostic listeners, or are they developing something implicitly present from the beginning? The question is important for tracing Paul's trajectory of the identity of Christ Jesus.

II. Paul's Jewish Background

Although Hellenism had a profound impact on Paul, by far the most dominant background influence on his writing was his Jewish heritage. Paul was a very good Jew. He describes himself as a circumcised Hebrew of the tribe of Benjamin, whose life and thought was governed by the Pharisaic interpretation of the law (Phil 3:5–6). In effect, Paul looks like a well-educated rabbi who became a Christian. He never gave up a sense of mission to the Jews, for whom he was quite willing to "become like one under the Law" (1 Cor 9:20). He reinterpreted all religious matters in the light of Christ but never felt he was less a Jew for that. It is no exaggeration to say that Paul's theology is incomprehensible without an understanding of his Jewish background.

A persuasive argument today asserts that whatever Hellenism we find in Paul, or the New Testament in general, had already been assimilated by some form of the Judaism of the Greco-Roman world contemporary with Paul. Philo, a Jewish author in Alexandria at this time, bent over backwards to show the basic compatibility of Platonic philosophy with his Jewish faith. Even in the most insulated Jewish circles in Israel, we find Hellenistic influence, for instance, in the stark dualism of light and darkness at Qumran. The Hellenism in Paul may in fact be a function of his Jewish faith.

Judaism at the time of Paul involved a variety of movements or traditions, a mosaic in which Christian Jews could easily fit. The relatively homogeneous rabbinic Judaism that we think of today is a reduction of the pluriform Judaism at the time of Paul. Until the destruction of the Temple and much of Jerusalem by the Romans in AD 70, this religious tradition included such contrasting movements as that of the Sadducees and the Zealots, the Pharisees and Diaspora Judaism, the schools of wisdom and the movements of apocalypticism. The destruction of the Temple by the Romans in AD 70 and the second military disaster at the hands of the Romans in AD 135 basically wiped out the Sadducees and Zealots and colored Jewish apocalypticism in shame and ridicule.

The Sadducee group was concerned mostly about Temple worship. They appear to be a type of priest party, with a view that limited scripture to the Torah, or the first five books of the Bible. Because of that restriction they refused to accept any authoritative teaching about the resurrection of the dead or the existence of angels, elements found only in later parts of the Bible. Paul seems little influenced by Sadducee theology, apart from the occasional attempt to see the death of Jesus as a Temple sacrifice (see Rom 3:25; 5:8–9; perhaps 1 Cor 5:7). Like the Pharisees we read about in the gospels, Paul may have harbored a hostility toward the Sadducees.

A. The Pharisees and the Bible

On the other hand, the Pharisee group had a major influence on Paul, as Paul himself admits (Phil 3:5; see Act 23:6; 26:5). Pharisee children grew up with an intense devotion to the Law and the Prophets, as well as the other Writings[22] and the oral traditions collected by the Pharisees as the Jewish scriptures.[23]

The Pharisee was the lawyer or rabbi and therefore the authority on scripture. The institution of the synagogue, where scripture was read, prayed, and studied, was the platform for the Pharisee. Although some questions arise today about the existence of Pharisees outside Palestine at the time of Paul, Paul's own testimony suggests a Diaspora presence. It could well be, therefore, that even outside Judea and Galilee the Pharisee was a leader in the synagogue. Frequently it was he who would give the scriptural exposition or homily after the readings from the Torah and Prophets.

The Pharisees became known especially for their separatism. They were not the only exclusivist sect in Judaism at the time of the New Testament. The Essenes at Qumran took the matter of the exclusion of outsiders to even greater lengths. However, the Pharisees practiced this separatism in the midst of city life and thus by shear dramatic effect became known for their focus on boundary building, where the boundaries give identity to the group, and where group leaders reinforce that identity by pointing out the dangers of being outside the boundaries and the advantages of being inside.[24]

The gospels depict the Pharisees as hypocrites. We must, however, be careful to remember the theological bias or perspective of these writings. Jewish memories of the Pharisees are much more positive. The goal of the Pharisee was to do all things in perfect conformity to the will of God. This goal means seeing all things somehow regulated by that will, which for the Pharisee was expressed above all in the Torah. To this end the Pharisaic tradition developed an elaborate code of behavior, the *halaka*, which formed an ideal to live up to, regulating every detail of life, and forming a type of hedge around the Torah itself (see Mark 7:3).

Perhaps the most important influence of this Pharisaic background on Paul was his general concern for scripture. Paul brought to his experience of Christ his deep faith that God was present and revealing himself in the history of Israel and in its foundational documents. This God of the Jewish scriptures is the same God who is the Father of Jesus Christ. Paul was convinced of a general continuity between the Old Testament and the New. He expressed this continuity not so much like the Gospel of Matthew, with the image of "fulfillment" (for example, Matt 1:22; 5:17), but rather with a special method of drawing on Old Testament prophet themes (as we will see).

It is hard to trace the development of the idea of looking at the stories and writings about the foundation and development of Israel in order to find God. The earliest indication seems to be a reference to "the book of the law" and its authority in the story of Josiah (2 Kgs 22:8–13). The expression is used in Deuteronomy for the scroll associated with the covenant at Horeb or Sinai (Deut 29:30; 31:26). This story of finding the "book of the law" in the Temple and the effect that it had on King Josiah may well describe an historical event, although this story is written much later. Before Josiah, the authoritative expression for measuring conformity to the covenant and statutes of God was rather the preaching of the prophets (2 Kgs 17:13–18). Moreover, whether the authority was the word of the prophet or the word of the book, the issue of obedience concerned far more the public policy of the king than the position of theological authorities or the personal faith of the people.

During the Exile in Babylon (598–538 BC), the Jews developed the synagogue, gatherings of Jewish people in a community of faith, where the emphasis lay entirely on the word—narrations, exhortations, prayers, and legal texts, many of which were probably written down and edited into collections. A hundred years or so after the Exile we hear about "the book of the law of Moses" also called "the book of the law of God," an earlier and much shorter form of the Torah, as the basis for the reconstruction of Israel (Neh 8). A reading of this book described in chapter eight of Nehemiah apparently took place at the beginning of the fourth century BC.

It was during this period of reconstruction that the Old Testament as we know it took form. The various strands of the Torah came together. Shortly afterward, the writings preserved by the followers of the literary prophets were collected along with a narrative stretching from the stories of Joshua to the Babylonian Exile. This became the second major part, "the Prophets," of the Hebrew Bible. From then on, efforts continued to include other traditional and not so traditional literature into this "Bible," such as the Psalms, the Proverbs, the story of Job, the midrashim like Ruth, Esther, Judith, even the stories of Ezra, Nehemiah, and the Maccabees. These came to be known as "the Writings." The later Pharisees had a sense of "the more the merrier," while dour Sadducees put their foot down on anything beyond the Torah.

Although God does not appear in any of the later books as speaking, the whole collection of the biblical books eventually was seen as the word of God. The description of God dictating much of the books of Exodus, Leviticus, and Numbers to Moses on Sinai was taken as a factual report. The literary prophets continually referred to the source of their messages as the word of the Lord, and Ezekiel introduced the Spirit, or "inspiration," as the basis of his message (Ezek 2:2; 3:12, 24; and so on). In the end, the whole collection, "the Law and the Prophets and the Writings," was seen as divinely inspired and the source of all wisdom.

When we study the Judaism that moves toward the time of Paul, we see clearly the authority that the Bible had for Jews in general, not just as guiding public policy. In the second century BC, ben Sira identifies the Torah with wisdom herself (Sir 24:23), as coming forth from the mouth of God before creation (24:3–6) and finding a dwelling in Israel (24:7–9; see Baruch 4:1). Fourth Maccabees refers to the law as the source of Jewish culture and wisdom (1:17). It is hard to find such rave reviews for the Prophets and the Writings, but we found copies of and commentaries on the prophets at Qumran, testifying to the way that Isaiah and Habakkuk, Hosea, Micah, and Nahum were treasured in that community.[25] We also know of the prominent place of the Psalms in the ancient synagogue service along with the special role of the Song of Songs, Ruth, Lamentations, Ecclesiastes, and Esther (the *Meggilloth*).

Paul's background as a Pharisee appears especially in his methods of developing scripture texts. Like the rabbis of his day, Paul used allegories and typology to understand scripture, as for instance in his comparison of Adam and Jesus (Rom 5:12ff.), in the lessons he draws from the Sinai experience (1 Cor 10), or his allusions to Jewish legends (1 Cor 11:8). Another typical exegetical method of the rabbis was Paul's way of stringing up texts from different parts of the Jewish scriptures.[26] He probably heard this approach many times as he listened to homilies in the synagogue, and we see it in 1 Corinthians 1—2 or Galatians 3. Like the Pharisees, Paul drew on stories from the Torah (1 Cor 10:1–13; 2 Cor 3). Unlike the Pharisees, Paul gravitated more toward the Prophets in his search for continuity between the covenants.

B. The Diaspora and the Greek Bible

The Acts of the Apostles describes Paul as born in Tarsus in Cilicia, what today is southeastern Turkey (Acts 22:3). Such an origin would make Paul part of "Diaspora" Judaism. The name "Diaspora" is a Greek term describing the scattering of seed. The term depicts a scattering that began with the Babylonian Exile of the sixth century BC and continued through the subsequent centuries on a more voluntary basis with Jewish communities eventually scattered around the Greco-Roman world. Here Jews were constantly challenged with the issues of accommodating to a "pagan" environment while maintaining faithfulness to the Jewish religious traditions.

It is in this environment that Jewish teachers adopted the often abstract perspectives of their Greek counterparts while holding their focus on their own ancient traditions. The author of the Wisdom of Solomon, writing in the middle of the first century

BC, describes Solomon as speculating on the origins of the universe, on immortality, and on divine wisdom as the all-pervading effusion of the divinity. Philo of Alexandria interpreted many of the biblical figures to show how the ideas found in Platonic philosophy were already taught by the Bible.

This Judaism, for the most part, had no temple in which to offer sacrifices. Instead, Jews gathered in a synagogue to read, study, and pray the scriptures. The Greek word *synagogos* means a "gathering." Eventually it means the group that gathered, and finally the place where they gathered. The word has basically the same meaning as the Greek word, *ekklesia,* which we translate as "church," which went through the same shift of meanings.

Some time around the early second century BC, Jewish scholars of the Diaspora translated the Hebrew scriptures into Greek. At the same time, they wrote Greek texts and added them to scripture. The collection we know best is called the "Septuagint," indicated by the abbreviation LXX.[27] This Greek translation became the Bible for Paul and for the earliest generation of Christians.

Besides including several books not found in our present Hebrew Bible, which is based on the Massoritic School of the Middle Ages, the text of the Septuagint sometimes differs significantly in wording and chapter order from the corresponding Hebrew text. Some of those differences can be attributed to poor translation or even deliberate changes. However, since the discovery of several Hebrew manuscripts dating from the first century BC at Qumran, known as "the Dead Sea Scrolls," the general opinion of this Greek Bible has changed. The Hebrew manuscripts at Qumran are often closer to the Septuagint than to the Massoritic texts. We now suspect that the Septuagint reflects other Hebrew text traditions that existed at the time of Paul and the New Testament and have since been lost.

The Greek Bible also contains such works as the Wisdom of Solomon and the Book of Sirach, which may have had a significant influence on Paul and other writers. These and other books are found in the modern Catholic and Orthodox Bibles as part of canonical literature. They are not part of the Hebrew Bible. In modern Protestant Bibles they are often included as "the Apocrypha."

C. Apocalyptic and Noncanonical Judaism

From roughly 200 BC to AD 200 a special body of Jewish literature arose that has a special importance for understanding early Christian faith. These are the writings that for the most part never made it into either the Hebrew or the Greek canon of scripture. Many of them were actively spurned and even banned by Jewish leaders after the second Roman war of AD 135.

An exception to this disrepute was the Book of Daniel, most likely because authorities saw it as written during the Babylonian captivity of the sixth century BC, as it purports to be. Internal literary evidence dates this book from around 190 BC, during the terrible persecutions of Antiochus IV, whom we read about in the books of Maccabees. It appears to be written to give good Jews, bewildered and suffering from a hostile government and culture, the courage to endure the hard times. Its focus lies in God's control of all events in history. Its message is an assurance of God's victory over all forces of evil.

The *Book of Enoch* appears to have been started at this time and gradually developed over the next two hundred years. The books of *4 Ezra, 2 Baruch,* along with the *Testament of Moses,* appear to have been written a century or two later. When we recognized the common literary form of these works and saw how Daniel fit this form, we began to understand the common literary devices and themes used by the authors to convey their message of hope. The devices and themes include the following:

1. Attributing the writing to a much earlier writer whose writings are then kept secret until the end time (see Dan 12:4–9)
2. Portraying evil as energized on a cosmic scale (Dan 10:20ff.)
3. Seeing political history as a part of God's great preordained plan of salvation (Dan 11)
4. Seeing material creation, especially the human body, as part of God's plan of salvation and drawn up into the conflict of good and evil (Dan 7; 12:2)
5. Expressing absolute confidence that the forces of good

under the power God will prevail at the end, and that this end will come soon, relative to the discovery and first reading of the book (Dan 7:9–18; 12:2–13)

6. Referring this insight into God's plan to a revelation from God (Dan 7:1; 8:1; 9:20–22; 10:1)

The literary form became known as "apocalyptic" from the Greek word *apokalypsis*, which means "revelation."

These and other Jewish writings today known as the "pseudepigrapha" flourished during this period of discouragement and suffering caused by the religious persecutions. The Jewish writers developed a way of expressing hope in a hopeless situation. They portrayed the mysterious plan of God as allowing evil, even on a cosmic scale, for a limited time, an evil time which eventually ended in God's absolute triumph over evil. They portrayed this triumph as part of a great climax of history in some end time, in some new epoch to come.

After inspiring two disastrous revolts against Roman rule, AD 67 and AD 135, this literature was basically banned by Jewish authorities who encouraged instead the collection of rabbinic interpretations of the law, moving the culture of Judaism from apocalyptic speculation to detailed observance of ethical norms. Around the third century, the *Mishnah* developed; in or about the sixth century, the *Babylonian Talmud*. Although late in their codification, these writings often testify to much earlier understandings and practices.

Similarly and roughly at this time, biblical stories were retold with imaginative elaborations. Perhaps the best-known collection of these stories is the multivolume *Midrash Rabbah*. The elaborations, however, can also be found in the Aramaic translations of the Bible, the *Targumim*. Although scholars disagree on the classification, books like that of Ruth, Judith, Jonah, and Esther are early midrashim that made it into at least one of the biblical canons, along with late wisdom writings like the Book of Wisdom (The Wisdom of Solomon) and Sirach (Ecclesiasticus). Other retellings like *Jubilees*, *The Martyrdom and Ascension of Isaiah*, and *Joseph and Aseneth*, today are relegated to the pseudepigrapha, for which, however, there is no official canon.[28]

In the last century, documents of the Essenes were discovered, first in a storeroom (Giniza) of an ancient Jewish synagogue in Cairo, then in several caves near the Dead Sea, above the ruins of a community at Qumran. Some of these writings like the *War Scroll* share the characteristics of apocalyptic literature, others like the *Genesis Apocryphon* look like midrashim, still others are commentaries on scripture and descriptions of the community.

In all this ancient Jewish literature, themes vary widely. They include speculation about angels and the cosmos, about the resurrection, the age to come, and the messiah-king. Despite their differences, the groups behind these writings all drew inspiration from the scriptures of Judaism, whose canon was beginning to close. (Appendix 3 contains short descriptions of the many Jewish sources used in this study.)

When we look at Paul and the other New Testament authors, we see that the texts of the Old Testament, especially those of the literary prophets, were fundamental for expressing their faith. However, often the Old Testament texts came into the Christian writings filtered by these later Jewish writings. A study of Judaism at the time of Paul therefore requires a bifocal vision, at once looking to the Old Testament texts and the later Jewish writings.

III. Conclusions

The intellectual and faith world of Paul was no spiritual and cultural vacuum. It was teaming with questions and ideas about meaning and life. It had inherited the love of logic and precision characteristic of Plato and the Greeks, yet it also contained the sense of mystery and imagery we associate with the Oriental mind, where intensity and commitment might be more important than precision. It was in the cities of Paul's world where this intellectual and spiritual ferment could be felt most. Urban intellectuals discussed the issues of life and death, society and justice.

Paul can thus be seen as the chosen instrument to take the agrarian message of Jesus—with its lilies of the field and its lost sheep—to the forums and agoras of the empire, where social functions and dysfunctions glared. Paul appears to be able to speak the language of his world. A comparison between the parables and proverbs of Jesus and the teachings of Paul illustrates the influence of Hellenism in Paul. Paul felt the need to explain things. He developed concepts, images that by their abstractness contain an involved but stable insight into reality. Like a good Hellenist, Paul tried to resolve the perplexing complexity of life into simpler principles, often in opposite pairs: life and death, flesh and spirit, freedom and slavery.

Paul translated Jesus—as indeed we translate Paul. Our concern here is to understand his faith. That faith will remain inseparable from the culture in which it is incarnated. Yet the mysterious reality that he touched by his faith transcends Hellenistic culture and any culture and therefore in principle can be translated and incarnated universally.

4
Paul's Theological Background in Judaism

We must now scan the content of the Jewish faith at the time of Paul for two reasons. First, this will allow us to sketch the heuristic outline of what to look for in Paul, one that is faithful to historical criticism.[1] The six focal positions that I see characterizing Paul's theology—and used in this scan—obviously are formulated within the context of my faith. However, I want to use these focal positions as open-ended questions without simply trying to find confirmation of my faith as I now understand it. The positions as they appear in Jewish faith give a wider scope and direction to these questions, giving us a more subtle sense of what to look for. In this way we can obtain preliminary understandings of those focal points as they may well have been understood by Paul.

The second reason for scanning this Jewish faith is to sift through the soil from which Paul grew his major theological positions. Where we see correspondences, we may be touching some direct influence on Paul or we may have parallel testimony of a tradition of which Paul was also a part. Where we see differences, we may have a foil from which we can identify special and perhaps unique elements of Paul's faith. Our guiding goal is to look at the Jewish texts the way Paul himself looked at them. We are searching for the faith positions that would be of major interest to Paul.

I. God the Father

In Hebrew, the noun for "God" is *ʾel* or *ʾelohim;* in Greek, *theos*. The proper or personal name in Hebrew of Israel's God is *Yhwh,* probably pronounced "Yahweh." At the time of Paul, this name was generally read aloud as *ʾAdonay*, which means, "the Lord" (literally "my Lords"). Avoiding the pronunciation of "Yahweh" was an act of reverence. Our earliest Hebrew manuscripts of the Old Testament that contain vowel markings generally place the vowels of *ʾAdonay*, a-o-a, under the consonants of *Yhwh*.[2] Another common substitute for *Yhwh* was simply *ha-Shem*, which means "the Name." Paul will in effect choose these names very carefully to describe and distinguish God, the Father, and Jesus, the Lord.

Paul's theology is clearly theocentric, in accord with his Jewish faith. Four aspects of this faith appear repeatedly in the expositions of his theology: (a) God as creator and covenant maker, (b) God as loving Father, (c) God as one who manifests anger at human sinfulness, and (d) God as the God of justice. All four of these aspects are clearly rooted in Paul's Jewish faith.

A. Covenant Lord and Creator

At the foundational level of the Jewish faith this God is the God of the Sinai (or Horeb) Covenant. This is the God who chose Israel as his people, promised to bless and protect them, and demanded loyalty and obedience to his words (Exod 19—20).

Also fundamental to this faith is the conviction that there is only one God. "Hear, O Israel! Yahweh is our God, Yahweh alone" (Deut 6:4). In its earlier form, this faith was a type of monolatrism. Israel was to worship only Yahweh, whether or not other gods existed for other nations. "I, Yahweh, am *your* God.... *You* shall not have other gods besides me" (Exod 20:2–3, my emphases). If Chemosh was the god of Moab and Milcom the god of Ammon, Yahweh was the God of Israel.

During the Babylonian Exile of the sixth century BC, however, prophets expressed this faith as strict monotheism. There *is* no other God besides Yahweh, even if other nations think they are worshiping other gods. "I am God, there is no other; I am God, there is none like me" (Isa 46:9). Although some modern scholars have challenged the monotheism of the Judaism at the time of Paul in the light of Jewish interest in heavenly and divine mediators (see below),[3] the evidence strongly argues the solid monotheism of "mainline Judaism" at that time,[4] if that expression may be used for a very complex and diverse religious tradition. For all his desire to express the divinity of Jesus, as we will see, Paul never deviates from this basic monotheistic faith (1 Cor 8:5–8).

Closely connected with the development of this strictly monotheistic faith was a faith in God as the creator of the universe (Gen 1:1–4; Isa 42:5; 45:5–7). This faith was not simply ontological speculation on the origins of the universe but rather motivation for confidence in God to save from the hopelessness of exile (Isa 40:26–28). It was also background for understanding how all peoples and governments of the world fall under his dominion and care (Isa 45:1–4). God remained the God of Israel through a special covenant but now could be seen to be the God of all peoples through creation.

B. Fatherly Kindness

The prophets did much to sketch the primary traits of God's personality, who is pictured predominately as masculine. Three of those traits will dominate the Pauline sketch of God: love, anger, and justice (or righteousness).

The form of divine love that dominates the Old Testament is that of a covenantal "kindness and mercy" (*chesed*). The divine self-identification to Moses on Sinai proclaims this type of love:

> Yahweh, Yahweh, a merciful and gracious God, slow to anger and rich in kindness and fidelity, continuing his kindness for a thousand generations, and forgiving wickedness and crime and sin. (Exod 34:6–7)

The eighth-century prophet Hosea canonized the images of God as loving husband (2:21–25) and as parent (11:1–4) of Israel. The images of the tender mother or father are particularly moving in their attempt to describe the love of God:

> When Israel was a child I loved him, out of Egypt I called my son.... It was I who taught Ephraim to walk and took them up on my arms;...I drew them with

> human cords, with bands of love; I was to them like one who raises a child to his cheeks. (Hos 11:1–4)

Those texts of the Old Testament that stemmed from the monarchy period seem to avoid calling God "Father" (*ʾAb*), although contemporary names like "Abijah" or "Absalom" seem to reflect an ancient tradition of doing so. Nevertheless, we see that the early prophets like Hosea described God dealing with Israel as his children (11:1–4; see also Isa 1:2). In the context of the covenant, Israel was God's son (Exod 4:22–23; Hos 11:1–4) as was in particular the king (1 Sam 7:14–15; Ps 2:7).

When we turn to postexilic texts, however, Old Testament writers feel more comfortable referring to God as "our Father" (Isa 63:16; 64:7) or "a Father" for Israel (Mal 1:6). In the centuries before Paul or Jesus, the wisdom writers like ben Sirach address God as "Father and Lord" (Sir 23:1, and see 23:4; 51:10; Wis 14:3). Addressing God as "Father" in prayer seems fairly common in Judaism at the time of Paul.[5]

A fifth-century prophet, whose preachings were added to the Book of Isaiah, reinforced the image of God as a loving spouse (Isa 62:4–5) and suggested the image of "mother" along with the traditional image of "father" as a way of expressing the heartfelt love of God for his people:

> As a mother comforts her son so I will comfort you; in Jerusalem you shall find your comfort.
> (Isa 66:13; see Isa 42:14; 49:15)

C. The Anger of God

This divine love of God for Israel, however, was a dangerous love, as the divine self-identification to Moses continues:

> Yet he does not remit all punishment, but visits the iniquity of parents upon children and children's children, up the third and fourth generation. (Exod 34:7)

In fact, the trait of God most written about in the prophets is divine anger, especially against Israel (Amos 2:6–16). Descriptions of this anger and of divine destruction usually follow long lists of the people's sins and are proclaimed like the sentence of a judge in trial ("therefore...woe..." Hos 12–13; Isa 5). The prophets of the Old Testament are clear. God deals with sin. He does not simply walk away from it. Like the loving parent of a rebellious child, God is not indifferent. He punishes.

That punishment is destructive. It is often death. Stories abound in the Torah, or Pentateuch, of God killing or ordering the death of sinners (Lev 10:1–3; Num 16). God threatens even to exterminate the whole people because of their sin (Exod 32:10).

Sin, then, is a serious matter. The combination of divine holiness and human sinfulness is death for the sinner. Isaiah understood very well the destructive presence of God (Isa 6:1–6). Although so personally moved by the love of God for his people, Hosea is also among the first to describe God as the destroyer of his people:

> Therefore, I will be like a lion to them; like a panther I will stalk them by the road, I will attack them like a bear robbed of her cubs and will tear out their hearts, I will devour them there like a lion, a wild beast of the field tearing them apart. (Hos 13:7-8)

D. Divine Justice

Jewish faith held together the divine traits of life-giving love and deadly anger by a third personality trait, divine justice or righteousness (Jer 9:24; Zeph 3:5; Zech 8:8). If God brings calamity on his people it is because of the wickedness of the people and the justice of God (Dan 13—14).

The Hebrew word behind these English translations is *zedek*, or its feminine form *zedekah*. The word is difficult to translate. The Greek translators of the Old Testament used the word *dikaiosynê*, which then enters into Paul's religious vocabulary. The basic idea is "being right" or "making things right," hence the common translations "righteousness" or "justice."[6]

This righteousness or justice often appears in the Bible in images of God as judge. In the prophetic tradition, God arises as judge against his people and against the nations to punish their sins (Isa 3:13–15; Hos 4:1; 5:1; Mic 6:1–5; Zeph 3:8; see Ps 50:4–7; Ps 75:8–9) where God is both witness, accuser, and judge in a forensic scenario. Yet God is not capricious or arbitrary. Unlike the kings and judges of the earth, God is not mean and evil. As a just judge God upholds what is right. He protects and restores what is right especially for those who are deprived of their rights. "Yahweh is just in his deeds, he brings justice to the oppressed" (Ps 103:6). "I, Yahweh, bring about kindness, justice, and uprightness on the earth, for with these things I am pleased, says Yahweh" (Jer 9:23).

In later apocalyptic literature, the day of divine judgment is an ambiguous event, punishing evil nations, but restoring Israel (Joel 4:1–2), eventually punishing evil individuals and rewarding the good (Dan 12:1–3). Usually in this literature, God himself is the final judge (*1 Enoch* 47:3; 90:15–27; *4 Ezra* 7:33–44).

The justice of God is thus closely connected with the salvation of God (Isa 45:21). God is good and can be trusted. Israel's prayers are often appeals to Yahweh's justice for deliverance from troubles (Ps 31:2) and from wicked enemies (Ps 5:9; 143:1). Yahweh's just judgments are saving judgments (Ps 36:6–7). Paul will tie into the divine trait of justice to develop his theology of salvation.

The justice of God is also closely connected to the covenant. God is just in the fulfillment of his promises (Neh 9:8). God grants justice to those who fulfill his will (Ps 7:9–10) and brings justice and kindness to those who fulfill his covenant (Ps 103:6–18; see 116:5–6). The reconstruction of Israel after the Exile and the reestablishment of the covenant is an act of God's justice. "I will bring them back to dwell in Jerusalem. They shall be my people, and I will be their God in faithfulness and justice" (Zech 8:8).

The justice and covenant of God lead directly to the obligation of his people to "hear" or "obey" (*shamaʿ*). This obligation constitutes the people's part in the covenant with God, "If you listen (*ʿim shamoʿa*) to my voice and observe my covenant..." (Exod 19:3–6). From the earliest Jewish writings to those closer to Paul, the covenant was inseparable from the law of God. We see this link in the poetic parallelism of the texts. Hosea describes the impending punishment of Israel, "Since they have violated my covenant, and sinned against my law" (Hos 8:1; see 6:7; Deut 4:12–13). Ben Sira writes, "An everlasting covenant he has made with them, his commandments he has revealed to them" (Sir 17:10; see 24:22; 28:7). In effect, God demands that his people reflect his divine righteousness or justice to one another, especially to the poor and weak. This demand for justice on earth is more important than any requirements for cult (Isa 1:10–16; Hos 6:6; Amos 5:21–25).

II. The Divine Mediator with God

Jesus is not described in the Old Testament.[7] It would seem impossible to find in the writings and culture that orbited around belief in one God any description of a divine person other than Yahweh, Israel's God and Father. Paul, however, was convinced that the reality of Christ was present in the times of the Old Testament in a hidden manner (1 Cor 10:4; Rom 16:25–26; Col 1:26) and the reality of Christ had divine traits (Phil 2:6–11; Col 2:9). He did not have to develop his understanding of this figure, as we have said, in a vacuum. We can in fact find in the Old Testament and in later Jewish writings figures who functioned as representatives of God, instruments of God's salvation, at times even reflecting divine attributes, images that Paul may have used to develop his Christology.[8]

We need to look carefully at four of these figures: (a) the poetic personifications of aspects of God, especially the figure of Wisdom; (b) descriptions of a "superangel," like Michael, who takes on divine features; (c) descriptions of heavenly human beings, like the heavenly "Son of man"; and (d) the figure of the "Messiah," especially in Hellenistic Judaism.

A. Divine Wisdom

From the actual vocabulary that Paul uses to describe Jesus, it is clear that an important background for Paul's Christology is the figure of divine wisdom found in the later wisdom traditions of the Old Testament.

The earliest forms of Israel's wisdom appear in the central section of the Book of Proverbs, chapters 10–29. These are sayings, remarkably secular in their tone, culled from experience dealing with a happiness or success in life. It was probably the counselors and sages (perhaps the scribes) of Israel's kingly courts that developed these sayings. Eventually the collection included books like Job, Ecclesiastes, many psalms, and, in the Greek scriptures, the Wisdom of Solomon and the Book of Sirach.

As we get closer to the New Testament times, these wisdom traditions take an important twist. The sages of Israel began speculating about God's wisdom. If the king was supposed to have wise counselors, God must have the greatest of counselors, Wisdom herself. And so the wise men of Israel began to speak about Wisdom as a person in the divine realm distinct from God.

Proverbs 8 is a good example of this way of speaking about Wisdom. Here we see the feminine figure first of all making an appeal to human beings, offering happiness and salvation. At verse 22 we see her properly divine role. She is with God at creation. She preexists all that God created. She was with him at the beginning. She then instructs human beings:

> Does not Wisdom call out? Understanding lifts up her voice.
> At the top of the heights on the way she takes her stand....
> Yahweh created me from the beginning of his way, before his works of old
> From eternity [*'olam*] I was poured forth from before the earth
> When there were no depths, I was brought forth
> When there were no springs carrying water,
> Before He made the earth and the fields or the first dust of the world....

Then I was with him as his craftsman and I was a delight to him every day
Rejoicing before him at all times
Rejoicing at the world of the earth, I was a delight to the sons of man
And now, children, listen to me
Happy is the one who keeps my ways.... (Prov 8:1–32)

The authors of this description are using the literary device of personification. They are speaking about an attribute of God as though it were a person apart from God. Yet the description is bold, especially in the suggestion of a feminine consort for God. Israel remembered the struggle against the goddess Astarte, wife of Ba'al. And in this later period, when the nation was still struggling against polytheism, such descriptions of female consorts with God were daring. The poetic personification created an image of a reality with divine traits who is yet clearly distinct from God himself.

The figure of Wisdom as a heavenly person appears also in *1 Enoch*. There she is described as descending from heaven and returning again:

Wisdom could not find a place in which she could dwell;
but a place was found (for her) in the heavens.
Then Wisdom went out to dwell with the children of the people,
but she found no dwelling place.
(So) Wisdom returned to her place
and settled permanently among the angels. (42:1–2)

Similarly, a poem inserted into the Book of Job celebrates wisdom, stressing its inaccessibility and its presence at the time of creation:

Where will wisdom be found? And where is the place of understanding? Mortals do not know the way to it, and it is not found in the land of the living.... God understands the way to it, and he knows its place. For he

> looks to the ends of the earth, and sees everything under the heavens. When he gave to the wind its weight, and apportioned out the waters by measure; when he made a decree for the rain, and a way for the thunderbolt; then he saw it and declared it; he established it, and searched it out. (Job 28:12–27)

Written around the middle of the first century BC and included in the Greek Bible but not the Hebrew Bible, the Wisdom of Solomon (also entitled simply the Book of Wisdom) describes divine Wisdom as a feminine person distinct from God, who is instrumental in bringing people close to God (7:27). Besides giving Wisdom a long list of attributes that belong properly to God (7:22–23), this author develops the view of Wisdom as an "image" of God (7:25–26). In this way the author can speak of Wisdom as properly divine without implying that there is a second God:

> For Wisdom, the maker of all, taught me.
> For in her is a spirit that is intelligent, holy, only
> begotten, multiform, subtle, active, clear, unsullied,
> certain, not baneful, loving the good, keen,
> unhampered, beneficent, philanthropic, firm, secure,
> tranquil, all-powerful, all-seeing, and pervading
> all spirits, who are intelligent, pure, and subtle.
> For Wisdom is mobile beyond all motion,
> and she penetrates and pervades all things by her
> purity.
> For she is a breath of the might of God
> and a pure effusion of the glory of the Almighty;
> therefore nothing impure enters into her.
> For she is the radiance of eternal light,
> the spotless mirror of the power of God,
> the image of his goodness.
> And she, who is one, can do all things,
> and renews everything while herself remaining.
> And passing into holy souls of every generation
> she produces friends of God and prophets.
> (Wis 7:22–27)

Perhaps the aspect of this imagery that saves it for monotheism is this description of divine Wisdom as a kind of radiance or mirror image of God. Nowhere in these texts is divine Wisdom described as a second divinity other than Yahweh. Instead it is a type of extension or reflection. The idea will be key for the high Christologies of the New Testament.

The personification of Wisdom seems related to the personification of the word of God. In exile, Deutero-Isaiah[9] writes, "Just as the rain and snow come down from heaven...so will be my word that goes out from my mouth. It will not return to me empty, but will do my will, achieving the end for which I sent it" (Isa 55:10–11; see Wis 18:14–18). Philo, a Hellenistic Jew more or less contemporary with Paul, calls this Word, in Greek, *Logos*, a "second God."[10] For Philo, he functions as "the administrator and steward of the world."[11] In another text, Philo describes this Word or *Logos* as a superangel, who even possesses the name of God. In the end, this Word represents Israel:

> God's firstborn, the Word [*Logos*], who holds seniority among the angels, an archangel as it were. And he has many names, for he is called the Beginning, and the Name of God, and his Word, and the Human Being [*anthropos*] according to his Image and the One who Sees, that is to say, Israel.[12]

B. The Great Angel

After the Babylonian Exile, angels began to figure prominently in Judaism. They appear with distinct personalities and names, functioning as agents of God, participating in God's activity on earth, yet not blocking God's immediacy on earth. For instance, in the Book of Tobit, the angel Raphael is the instrument of God's healing power. He introduces himself, "I am Raphael one of the seven angels who enter and serve before the Glory of the Lord" (Tob 3:17). Later he describes himself as presenting the prayers of Tobit and Sarah to God (Tob 12:12), although Tobit and Sarah in fact pray directly to God.

Centuries earlier, Jewish piety pictured one angel in particular who stands in God's place with divine characteristics, sometimes almost indistinguishable from God. In Genesis, for instance, "the angel of Yahweh" (*mal'ak Yahweh*) appears to Hagar and encourages her (Gen 16:7–12). The narrator then continues, "She called Yahweh who spoke to her, 'You are the God of Vision'" (Gen 16:13). Again, "the angel of Yahweh" appears to Abraham to prevent him from sacrificing Isaac (Gen 22:11–14). That same angel then speaks as God, "I swear by myself, declares Yahweh, that because you acted as you did...I will bless you abundantly" (Gen 22:15).

A special great angel clearly distinguished from Yahweh functions in Exodus to accompany the Israelites (Exod 23:20–23). God commands obedience to this angel because "[m]y name resides in him" (Exod 23:21; see also 14:19–20). Similarly, an armed angel appears to Joshua at Jericho, describing himself as "chief commander (Hebrew: *sar*; Greek: *archistratêgos*) of Yahweh's army" (Josh 5:13–15). Perhaps also describing a great angel standing in the place of God, Ezekiel describes "the likeness of the glory of Yahweh" as "a likeness of the appearance of a man...from his waist up like gleaming amber, from his waist down surrounded by fire, all surrounded by splendor" (Ezek 1:26–28; see 8:2–4).

Many other Old Testament texts describe angels and a superangel, but the texts mentioned are the ones that later Judaism often reflected on as they developed an elaborate angelology. The vision of the glorious angel in Daniel 10:2–9 resembles the glorious figure in Ezekiel. This angel, who might be Gabriel (Dan 8:15–26; 9:21), however, needs the help of Michael, "one of the chief commanders" (*sar;* 10:13). Michael is later described as "the great commander" (*sar)* who will arise in the end time (12:1).

As we move to the noncanonical Jewish literature roughly contemporary with Paul, Michael as a "chief commander" (*archistratêgos*) acts as an agent of God with Abraham and visits him at Mamre, to assist him with dying.[13] Another Jewish writer of the same time, the author of the *Apocalypse of Abraham*, also described an angel by the name of Iaoel, who visits Abraham to strengthen him.[14] This is an angel in whom God's name dwells, an allusion to the accompanying angel in Exodus 23:20–21. He therefore has control over the "living creatures" who surround God's throne and over "leviathan" (10:8–17). The description of this angel with white hair and rainbow colors reminds us of the visions in Daniel 7:9 and Ezekiel 1:26–28.

At Qumran, the Essenes saw the end time as the time when God will "raise up the kingdom of Michael in the midst of the gods, and the realm of Israel in the midst of all flesh."[15] Scholars have also found references to Michael at Qumran also under the name of Melchizedek, who will protect the elect from "the hand of Belial" and "restore them and proclaim liberty to them, relieving them of [of the burden] of all iniquities."[16]

Perhaps the most elaborate description of Michael[17] is found in an ancient Jewish romance called *Joseph and Aseneth,* written sometime between 100 BC and AD 150, a narrative midrash elaborating on the brief biblical mention of the marriage of Joseph and Aseneth, the daughter of Potiphera (Gen 41:45). According to the later Jewish story, "a man from heaven" appears assisting Aseneth's conversion from idolatry to Judaism. This heavenly figure is "the chief of the house of the Lord and commander [*archistratêgos*] of the whole host of the Most High" (14:8). He appears in great light. His face is like lightning; his eyes, like sunshine; hair, like a fire; hands and feet, like iron shining forth from a fire with sparks (14:3–9). He does not give his name because it is an ineffable name, but he repeats that he is before all others because he is "chief of the house of the Most High" (15:12). After he leaves in a chariot of fire (17:8), Aseneth says, "I did not know that [a] god came to me" (17:9).

C. The Heavenly Son of Man

Another Jewish writing begun probably around 200 BC and progressively written over the next two centuries is *1 Enoch*. In one of the last sections to be added, chapters 37–71, the heavenly figure, combining angelic and human characteristics, appears with the names of "Son of man" and the "Elect One." He is described with divine power and glory.

Most likely, the writer of this section is drawing on the portrayal of "one like a son of man" in Daniel:

> I saw one like a son of man coming with the clouds of heaven. And he came to the Ancient One and was presented before him. To him was given dominion and glory and kingship, so that all peoples, nations, and languages should serve him. His dominion is an everlasting dominion that shall not pass away, and his kingship is one that shall never be destroyed. (Dan 7:13-14)

In Daniel the figure is eventually identified with the people of Israel (Dan 7:27). Yet as described, this one looks more like an angel. Perhaps the image of the guardian angel of Israel is, in the author's mind, an image that is distinct yet reflects the group protected (see Dan 10:13–21).

In the later *1 Enoch*, this Son of man functions as a helper, healer, and revealer of wisdom:

> He will become a staff for the righteous ones in order that they may lean on him and not fall. He is the light of the Gentiles and he will become the hope of those who are sick in their hearts. All those who dwell upon the earth shall fall and worship before him; they shall glorify, bless, and sing the name of the Lord of the Spirits.... And he has revealed the wisdom of the Lord of the Spirits to the righteous and the holy ones. (*1 Enoch* 48:4–7)

Although he is carefully distinguished from God, the Son of man sits on God's throne of glory (51:3; 61:8; 62:6) and will never pass away from the face of the earth (69:27). In one of those "seatings" the Elect One appears like an eschatological judge:

> On that day, my Elect One shall sit on the seat of glory
> and make a selection of their deeds,
> their resting places will be without number,
> their souls shall be firm within them when they see my
> Elect One.
> those who have appealed to my glorious name. (45:3;
> see 55:4; 61:8)

First Enoch then continues to describe the Son of man as a victorious warrior, punishing powerful evildoers presumably at the end times:

> This Son of man whom you have seen is the One who would remove the kings and the mighty ones from their comfortable seats and the strong ones from their thrones. He shall loosen the reins of the strong and crush the teeth of the sinners. He shall depose the kings from their thrones and kingdoms. For they do not extol and glorify him, and neither do they obey him, the source of their kingship. The faces of the strong will be slapped and be filled with shame and gloom. Their dwelling places and their beds will be worms. They shall have no hope to rise from their beds, for they do not extol the name of the Lord of the Spirits. (*1 Enoch* 46:4–6; see 62:2)

It is difficult to know if the author of *1 Enoch* intended to develop the figure of "the Messiah" by the image of the "Son of man/Elect One." The figure in *1 Enoch* is associated with the Messiah in two texts. In one "the kings of the earth and the mighty landowners" are punished in the days of the Son of man because "they have denied the Lord of the Spirits and his Messiah" (48:1–10). In the second, Enoch has a vision of "the secret things of heaven and future things," including a series of mountains of metal. An angel interpreter explains, "All these things which you have seen happen by the authority of His Messiah so that he may give orders and be praised upon the earth" (52:4). This vision occurs after the Elect One sits on God's throne and proclaims the secrets of wisdom (51:1–5). Furthermore, the Son of man functions much like the eschatological Messiah. He bashes kings of the earth (46:4–5) and rules over everything (62:6). In the name of God he judges even angels (55:4; 61:8) and men (45:3). Although angelic in authority, he is described as "the One who was born of human beings" (46:2).[18]

On the other hand, if the author of this section of *Enoch* intended a distinction between "the Son of man" and the

Messiah, then we have a second figure to examine as possible Jewish background for Paul's description of Jesus. This figure preexists creation, hidden in times past:

> At that hour, that Son of man was given a name, in the presence of the Lord of Spirits, the Before-Time; even before the creation of the sun and the moon, before the creation of the stars, he was given a name in the presence of the Lord of Spirits...he was concealed in the presence of [the Lord of the Spirits] prior to the creation of the world, and for eternity. (*1 Enoch* 48:2–6)

> For the Son of man was concealed from the beginning, and the Most High One preserved him in the presence of his power; then he revealed him to the holy and the elect ones. (62:7)

D. The Messiah

Since Paul applies the name "Christ" to Jesus, it is important to look directly at the figure of the messiah or christ.[19] In Judaism at the time of Paul, the "messiah" clearly had a technical meaning as a representative or messenger of God as part of the drama of the end times.

The image is rooted in the theology of the Davidic kings, several of whom are described as being anointed at the beginning of their reign: Saul (see 1 Sam 10:1), David, (1 Sam 6:13), Absalom (2 Sam 19:11), and Solomon (see 1 Kgs 1:39). Others at critical times in the monarchy enjoy this description (2 Kgs 9:6; 11:12; 23:30). More important, the designation especially in hymnic texts of "the anointed one" became a stock title for kings in general (1 Sam 2:10; 2 Sam 22:51; Ps 2:2; 18:51; 20:7; 28:8; 84:10; 89:39, 52; 132:10, 17; Lam 4:20; Hab 3:13). Hence the messiah was a king.[20]

In several Old Testament texts the "anointed" king is also designated as a "son of God" (2 Sam 7:14; Ps 2:7; 89:27–28; 110:3). In the Old Testament, the title "Son of God" had a broad meaning,[21] but it is never used to indicate a divinity equal to God. The Book of Job describes "sons of God" in God's heavenly throne room as God's counselors (Job 1:6; 2:1; see Ps 29:1) and at the moment of creation (38:7). The stress in such use of the term is usually to insist on the subordination to God of such divinelike beings (see Ps 29:1; 89:7). A "son of God" therefore could describe a godly person (Wis 2:18). To insist on Israel as a whole as God's beloved, Hosea relates the words of God, "When Israel was a child I loved him, out of Egypt I called my son" (11:1; see Exod 4:22; Jer 31:9). Using the title "son of God" for the king seems to be an adaptation of ancient Near Eastern court hyperbole. The expression was meant to describe the king's association with God. The Hebrew usage said nothing about the king being divine.

The idealized memories of David, along with the prophecy of Nathan with its promise of unending duration and divine sonship for the Davidic monarchy, cast a glow over that dynasty (2 Sam 7:13–16; also in Ps 89:2–5, 27–29). Disappointment with the successors of David led not to a revision of expectations but to a projection into the future, even when the monarchy was destroyed. The righteous shoot of David would govern wisely, bringing salvation and security to Israel (Jer 23:5–6). A new Davidic prince would shepherd his people in a function that parallels God as shepherd (Ezek 34:23–24; see Ezek 37:22–28).

As we move to the Judaism closer to the time of Paul, the Messiah appears more frequently with the power of God, ushering in the eschatological days or the period preliminary to the eschatological days. Eventually, as apocalyptic speculation colored more and more Jewish theology, this representative of God took on angelic qualities and became more dominant in the transformation of earth and Israel's role. The portrayal of this messianic instrument of God, however, is anything but consistent.[22]

In Psalm 17 of the *Psalms of Solomon,* a collection of hymns from the first century BC, "the Lord Messiah" is a king of the Davidic dynasty, a victorious warrior who subjugates alien nations, leads Israel, and purges Jerusalem (17:21–32). Psalm 18 of the same collection speaks of "those days" when the Messiah will reign:

> May God cleanse Israel for the day of mercy in blessing,
> for the appointed day when his Messiah will reign.

Blessed are those born in those days,
to see the good things of the Lord
which he will do for the coming generations;
(which will be) under the rod of discipline of the Lord
Messiah. (18:5–7)

Composed around AD 100, *4 Ezra* describes the eschatological consequences that will happen when the Messiah is revealed:

> For my son the Messiah shall be revealed with those who are with him, and those who remain shall rejoice four hundred years. And after these years my son the Messiah shall die, and all who draw human breath. And the world shall be turned back to primeval silence for seven days. (7:28–30)

This description is one of the few texts that speak of the death of the Messiah. It is also important for the clear delineation between the time of the Messiah, four hundred years, and the end of the world, which includes the resurrection of the dead and the final judgment along with eternal reward of the good and eternal punishment of those who have not served God (7:32–44).

In a second text of *4 Ezra*, the Messiah arises "from the posterity of David," although his appearance is a revelation by God of the one "whom the Most High has kept until the end of days" (12:32). He is the one who will judge all peoples, including the Roman Empire, symbolized by an eagle, which he will destroy because of its wickedness (12:32).

Roughly contemporary with *4 Ezra, 2 Baruch* also speaks of an eschatological revelation of the Messiah, or Anointed One. This occurs after a succession of oppressive kingdoms:

> And it will happen when the time of its [the fourth evil kingdom] fulfillment is approaching in which it will fall, that at that time the dominion of my Anointed One, which is like the fountain and the vine, will be revealed. And when it has revealed itself, it will uproot the multitude of its host. (*2 Baruch* 39:7)

The scene continues until the last living ruler is bound and his army destroyed:

> And they will carry him on Mount Zion, and my Anointed One will convict him of all his wicked deeds and will assemble and set before him all the works of his hosts.…And his dominion will last forever until the world of corruption has ended and until the times which have been mentioned before have been fulfilled.
> (40:1–3)

Later in *2 Baruch*, the Messiah, or Anointed One, appears again as eschatological judge of all the nations, separating those who have oppressed Israel from those who have not:

> After the signs have come of which I have spoken to you before, when the nations are moved and the time of my Anointed One comes, he will call all nations, and some of them he will spare, and others he will kill.
> (72:2; see 70:9–10)

As portrayed in these later Jewish writings, the Messiah is no ordinary king or human being. Rather, he operates with the power of God and ushers in an eschatological period of God's justice.

III. The Spirit of God

Paul's view of the Spirit of God has its direct roots in the Old Testament and Judaism. This is a Jewish image with many facets. The Hebrew word for "spirit," *ruach*, means also "wind" or "breath." It is an image of life and invisible power, power that is either gentle or destructive. The image of God's spirit is basically that of God's breath, which in its divine dimensions could be either a life-giving breath (Gen 2:7; 6:3; Ezek 37:5, 9–10) or a hurricane-force wind (Exod 15:8; Job 1:19).

Sometimes the spirit of God appears as an inanimate liquid that is "poured out" like water. "I will pour out water upon the thirsty ground...I will pour out my spirit upon your offspring and my blessing upon your descendants" (Isa 44:3; see Ezek 39:29; Joel 3:1–2 [2:28–29]). At other times the spirit "comes upon" or "rests on" people (Num 11:25–26; 2 Kgs:2:18; Isa 11:2). The description of the spirit "hovering over" the primeval waters (Gen 1:2) intrigued later Judaism. The *Babylonian Talmud* makes the connection between this action and the image of a dove. "And the spirit of God was hovering upon the face of the waters, i.e., as a dove which hovers over her young, but does not touch them" (*Babylonian Talmud, Hagigah* 15a).

In general, various forms of agency are ascribed to the spirit of God, although nowhere in the Old Testament or in Judaism is the spirit of God given the vivid personification that was attributed to the Wisdom of God.[23] The spirit of God remains an image of the power of the transcendent God, extended into the world for the working out of his will. For this reason, it is best not to capitalize the English translation "spirit" for the Old Testament and the later Jewish writings.[24]

A. Spirit and Power

Ruach is a term for wind. It is, therefore, not surprising to see the portrayal of the divine spirit as conveying power, especially a type of temporary but extraordinary power in the leaders of the people. The oldest stories of the Bible describe the ancient judges as receiving their military power from the spirit of God (Judg 3:10; 6:34; 11:29; 15:14). King David stands out by the way "the spirit of Yahweh came mightily" on him from the day of his anointing (1 Sam 16:13).

Isaiah links the extraordinary governing ability of the promised sprout from Jesse with the spirit of God (Isa 11:1–9). This link is echoed in the servant of God described by Deutero-Isaiah (Isa 42:1–4). In these descriptions the fruit of the spirit is less some transient or chaotic power than an enduring conduit connecting earth with the justice and peace of God. Through this spirit of wisdom, knowledge, and understanding, Immanuel judges the poor with justice and transforms nature into a peaceful paradise. Through this spirit, the Servant with his gentle manner establishes justice on the whole earth (42:1–4).

Later Jewish writings link this governing power of the spirit with messianic and eschatological figures, apparently reflecting Isaiah 11. The *Psalms of Solomon* describe the Davidic Messiah: "God made him powerful in the holy spirit" (17:37). The Elect One or Son of man in *1 Enoch* is also empowered by the spirit: "The Lord of spirits sat down [or seated him] on the throne of his glory; and the spirit of righteousness was poured out upon him [the Elect One]" (62:2).

B. Spirit and Life

Ruach is also a term for breath. Breath gives life (See Gen 2:7: *nishmat chaiim*). It is not surprising then to see the portrayal of the spirit of God as giving life to human beings. Job expresses this view as he protests that he will speak the truth "so long as I have life in me and the *ruach* of God in my nostrils" (Job 27:3). Elihu echoes the same sentiment: "The spirit (*ruach*) of God made me, the breath (*nishmat*) of the Almighty keeps me alive" (Job 33:4).

Perhaps the most dramatic portrayal of the spirit as life-giving occurs when Ezekiel has a vision of the restoration of the people. The message consists of hope for new life for the nation. However, the vehicle for this message is an allegory presuming the role of the divine spirit in the gift of life. The scene is a plain covered with dead, dry bones. God commands:

> Prophesy over these bones, and say to them: Dry bones, hear the word of the Lord Yahweh! Thus says the Lord Yahweh to these bones: See! I will bring spirit into you, and you will live.... Say to the spirit: Thus says the Lord Yahweh: from the four winds come, O spirit, and breathe into these slain and they will live. I prophesied as he ordered me, and the spirit came to them; they came alive and stood upright, a vast army....O my people! I will put my spirit in you that you may live, and I will settle you upon your land; thus you shall

> know that I am Yahweh. I have said it, and I will do it, says Yahweh. (Ezek 37:4–14)

This famous image stresses the communitarian role of the spirit. The spirit gives life to the vast nation of Israel. In fact, even in the portrayals of special power to particular individuals, the power was given for the good of the people.

C. The Spirit and Prophecy

The classic literary prophets did not make any connection between prophecy and the spirit of God. The eighth-century BC prophets attributed their message rather to "the word of Yahweh" (Hos 1:1; Micah 1:1; Isa 1:10) or to the description, "Thus says Yahweh" (Amos 1:3, 6, 9, 11, 13; Isa 7:7; 8:11).

Nevertheless, the roots of the connection are old. The depiction of prophetic mania or ecstasy was clearly attributed to the spirit of God (1 Sam 10:6–10; 19:20–23). The story of the seventy assistants to Moses prophesying is also probably a story of mantic prophecy (Num 11:16–25). Interesting in this story is the way the spirit bestowed by God on the elders is described as "the spirit that was on Moses" (11:25).

A bridge connecting the spirit of God to the preaching style of prophecy lies in the story of Elisha succeeding Elijah. Both of these prophets function to mediate the will of God in an intelligent way to the leaders of Israel. In one final request before the transfer of roles, Elisha asks Elijah for "a double portion of your spirit" (2 Kgs 2:9), apparently an allusion to the privilege of the firstborn's inheritance (Deut 21:17). In a story that bears the earmarks of the ancient Elohist (E), the "pagan prophet" Balaam gives his message through the spirit of God—against his will and that of his employer (Num 24:2–9). The last words of David appear as a message of the spirit of God speaking through the king (2 Sam 23:1–7).

Ezekiel, however, makes an emphatic link between his prophetic mediation of God's word and the spirit of God entering the prophet (Ezek 2:2; 3:24), moving him (3:12, 14), and speaking with the prophet (3:24). Here the spirit is now a divine force that enlightens, a force that gives insight into the plan of God (see 11:5).

Trito-Isaiah connects the word of God in the mouth of the prophet with the spirit of God upon the prophet: "My spirit which is upon you and my words that I have put into your mouth shall never leave your mouth" (Isa 59:21). This prophet is probably describing his calling when he says, "The spirit of the Lord Yahweh is upon me, because Yahweh has anointed me; He has sent me to bring good news to the lowly, to heal the brokenhearted..." (Isa 61:1).

Joel reinforces the image of the divine spirit of prophecy, the outpouring of which then becomes one of the major signs of the end times: "Then afterwards, I [God] will pour out my spirit on all flesh. Your sons and your daughters will prophesy. Your old men will dream dreams. Your youth will see visions" (Joel 3:1 [2:28]). Joel is distinctive in his insistence on the widespread endowment of the spirit and the ensuing prophecy.

As we get closer to Paul's time, Jewish writings speak often of the divine spirit in prophecy. In this historical period, the Aramaic translations of the Torah, the Targumim often substitute the expression "spirit of prophecy," (*ruach nebu'ah*) where the original Hebrew text would have used simply "the spirit" or the "the spirit of God."[25] The Essenes at Qumran speak of all that "the prophets have revealed through His holy spirit" (1 *QS* 8:16).

Connected to this prophetic role of the spirit is the more general picture of the spirit enlightening or instructing human beings in things religious.[26] The Essenes at Qumran frequently wrote about a special revealed knowledge or enlightenment attributed to a "spirit of truth" who opposes a "spirit of lies" (1 *QS* 3:18–19). The "ways in the world" for the enlightenment of the heart include the following "counsels of the spirit":

> A spirit of humility, patience, abundant charity, unending goodness, understanding and intelligence; [a spirit of] mighty wisdom which trusts in all the deeds of God and leans on his great loving kindness; a spirit of discernment in every purpose, of zeal for just laws, of holy intent with steadfastness of heart, of great charity

> towards all the sons of truth, of admirable purity which detests all unclean idols, of humble conduct sprung from an understanding of all things, and of faithful concealment of the mysteries of truth. These are the counsels of the spirit to the sons of truth in this world.
> (1 *QS* 4:2-6)

Moral uprightness and enlightenment are not distinguished. The language seems to allude to Isaiah 11:2, where the string of "a spirit of" is attributed to the spirit of Yahweh.

Similarly, the leader at Qumran praises God and attributes his knowledge of God to the spirit of God:

> I, the Master, know you, O my God, by your spirit which you have given to me, and by your holy spirit I have faithfully hearkened to your marvelous counsel.
> (1 *QH* 12:11; see 13:18-19)

D. The Spirit and Covenant

In Ezekiel the divine spirit is an important element of the new or restored covenant. As we saw, his vision of the dry bones and the life-giving spirit ended with the promises of resettlement in the land and knowledge of Yahweh (Ezek 37:1–4). These are covenantal promises. Five times Ezekiel mentions here the coming of the spirit that regenerates life and restores the covenant. Like Jeremiah, Ezekiel insists on internal renewal and reform as constituting any restored covenant. For Ezekiel this internal renewal was nothing less than a "new heart and a new spirit" (Ezek 18:31). Ezekiel then proclaims that this new spirit is nothing less than God's spirit:

> I will give you a new heart and place a new spirit within you, taking from your bodies your hearts of stone and giving you a heart of flesh. I will put my spirit within you and make you live my statutes, careful to observe my decrees. You shall live in the land I gave your

> fathers; you shall be my people and I will be your God.
> (36:26–28; see 11:17–20)

Describing the spirit of God on the prophet, Trito-Isaiah includes a promise of the eternal presence of the word of God. This, according to Trito-Isaiah, constitutes the covenant that God has made with his people:

> This is the covenant with them which I myself have made, says Yahweh: My spirit which is upon you [singular] and my words that I have put into your mouth shall never leave your mouth, nor the mouths of your children nor the mouths of your children's children from now on and forever, says Yahweh. (Isa 59:21)

If we look on the divine covenant as epoch making, then the new epoch is defined by the spirit of God. Joel took this spirit-epoch image as the heart of his eschatology. Here we see the confluence of the final period in God's history, the gift of prophecy, and the gift of the spirit:

> Then afterwards, I will pour out my spirit on all flesh. Your sons and your daughters will prophesy. Your old men will dream dreams. Your youth will see visions. Also over your servants and maids in those days I will pour out my spirit. I will give forth signs in the heavens and on earth: blood, fire, columns of smoke. The sun will be darkened to black, and the moon to blood, before the coming of the day of Yahweh, the great and terrible day. And all who call on the name of Yahweh will be saved, because on Mount Zion and in Jerusalem there will be escape, as Yahweh has said, and in the survivors whom Yahweh shall call. (Joel 3:1–5 [2:28–32])

From this prophecy of Joel on, the spirit of God will be understood as the eschatological gift and the sign of the end times.[27]

E. The Cosmic Spirit of Creation

Old Testament writings attributed toward the end of the Exile (Deutero-Isaiah) and those during the Persian period (Job, Judith, many psalms, the priestly editing of the Torah) show a new interest in creation. At the same time the spirit of God takes on a world-creating power. God is portrayed as forming the world by his spirit. In Job that spirit is clearly connected with the breath of God as he talks:

> By his power he stirs up the sea,
> and by his understanding he crushes Rahab;
> With his spirit [*rucho*] he makes the waters fair.
> (Job 26:12–13)
> The spirit [*ruach*] of God made me,
> the breath [*nishmat*] of the Almighty gives me life.
> (Job 33:4)

Similarly:

> By the word of Yahweh the heavens were made;
> by the spirit [*ruach*] of his mouth all their hosts.
> (Ps 33:6)

Other texts suggest greater distinction between God and his creative spirit:

> When you send forth your spirit [*ruchaka*] they are created
> and the face of the earth is made new.
> (Ps 104:30; see Jdt 16:14)

It is at this time that the image appears of the *ruach ʾelohim* hovering or sweeping over the abysmal waters at creation (Gen 1:2). On one level, the expression suggests a hurricane-force wind adding to the chaos. On another level, as the spirit of God hovering over chaos, this *ruach* suggests the beginnings of a divine intervention that will lead to the creation of the ordered cosmos.[28]

Later Jewish writings do not lose the sense of the creative spirit. As he discusses the generations of those who have died and the number yet to come, the author of *2 Baruch* quotes God: "No creature will live again unless the number that has been appointed is completed. For my spirit creates the living, and the realm of death receives the dead" (23:5). In the Wisdom of Solomon, the cosmic spirit appears with characteristics of the spirit in Stoicism: "The spirit of the Lord fills the world, is all-embracing, and knows what man says" (Wis 1:7).

F. The Spirit and the Good Person

In sharp contrast to Paul, the Judaism just prior to Paul does not seem to make any strong link between the individual person and the spirit of God, especially in terms of a personal endowment making that person a good person or rewarding that person. This is the period when the prevalent view held that prophecy and the holy spirit were absent from Israel because of Israel's sinfulness, the destruction of the Temple, or just bad timing.[29]

Only in Ezekiel can we find a connection between the spirit of God and interior renewal, eventually of the individual Israelite. Ezekiel predicts a renewal of the covenant on the basis of "a new heart" and "a new spirit within you." "I will put my spirit within you and make you live by my statutes, careful to observe my decrees" (Ezek 36:26–27). In Ezekiel the stress is on Israel as a whole and its covenant with God. Yet the promise implies some sort of law-abiding attitude, some special bond of intimacy with God on the part of individuals on the basis of the gift of the Spirit.

Even in much later Judaism, we can find only isolated descriptions of the spirit received by a good, law-abiding person. A second-century AD Jewish writing, the *Mekilta*, states: "Whosoever takes upon himself one precept in faith is worthy that the holy spirit should rest upon him."[30] In the third century, the Mishnah included a text describing a long linkage of holy actions and conditions with a mention of the holy spirit in a climactic position: "The Torah leads to watchfulness, watchfulness to strictness...sin fearing to holiness, holiness to the holy spirit, and this last to the resurrection of the dead."[31] Written probably in the fifth century AD, the *Midrash Rabbah on Leviticus* cites a fourth-century rabbi: "He who learns [the law] in order to live it is worthy [to receive] the holy spirit."[32]

IV. Salvation

When Paul attempted to understand the basic good thing God did through Jesus for humanity, he writes repeatedly of "salvation," using also related words like "redemption" and "rescue." This is vocabulary directly drawn from Paul's Jewish heritage. In that heritage, however, the notion of salvation ranged over a wide span of meanings, with divergent understandings of who is saved, from what are people saved, and how God accomplishes his salvation.

The God of Israel was a saving God. Israel's faith was rooted in the story of God's rescue of the Hebrews from the slavery of Egypt (Exod 1—15). If this story became the primordial story for Israel, then the basic image of Yahweh was that of a God who saves, delivers, or rescues (*yashaʿ, gaʾal, padah*) from constraints and confinements (Ps 3:8; 68:19–20). Yahweh is the God or rock of salvation (Ps 79:9; 85:4; 95:1). A large part of the psalter, the psalms of thanksgiving or deliverance, combine a description of distress along with an action of God rescuing either individuals (Ps 30; 32; 34; 40; 41; and so on) or the nation (Ps 65; 66; 67; 68; and so on) from that distress.

A. Personal and National Salvation

In these stories and songs, salvation for an individual is usually rescue from sickness and death or from wicked and powerful enemies. For the people, salvation is rescue from a powerful foreign enemy.

Later prophets called this national rescue an act of God's "justice" (*zedek*; Isa 42:6; 46:13; 62:1–2). "God, our savior" is the God who works "mighty deeds of justice" (Ps 65:6). In the mouth of the psalmist, the individual needing salvation also prayed for God's "justice" (Ps 4:1; 35:24–28). When God "justifies" (*hizdiq*), he rescues from oppression (Ps 82:3), punishing evildoers and rewarding the good (2 Chr 6:23) or simply proving the good person to be right (Isa 50:8–9). This verb is also used to describe a cleansing or rescue of evil people from iniquities, although this rescue is not described as an act of God. The suffering servant of Deutero-Isaiah "will justify many and he will bear their iniquities" (Isa 53:11; see Dan 12:3).

In general, salvation is maintenance of an earthly life and the possession of land, a share in the inheritance of a people. The Torah is essentially the "law" of a social reality, describing how one behaved in a society with others and how one related to God as Father of the people. Sin and punishment revolved around cutting oneself off from the "inheritance" of Israel or Israel as a whole losing its "inheritance."

If the final punishment for sin was an early death (Exod 32:25–29), salvation from sin was a recovery from a deadly situation, like that in the story of the bronze serpent (Num 21:4–9). As the people came into contact with hostile peoples, the drama of sin and salvation took on a military form. The Book of Judges develops the repeated pattern of sin, oppression from foreign enemies, repentance from sin, and salvation in the form of military conquest:

> Because the Israelites did what was evil in the eyes of Yahweh by forgetting Yahweh their God, serving the Baals and Asherahs, the anger of the Lord Yahweh flared up against them and surrendered them into the power of Cushan-rishathaim, king of Aram Naharaim, whom they served for eight years. But when the Israelites cried out to Yahweh, he raised up for them a savior [*moshiaʿ*], Othniel, son of Caleb's younger brother Kenaz, who saved them [*yoshiʿem*]. (Judg 3:7–9)

The pattern of sin, divine anger, prayer, and salvation is repeated over and over again as the history of Israel passes through the stories of Saul and David, and then those of the kingdoms of Judah and Israel. In fact the basic structure of Joshua, Judges, 1 and 2 Samuel, and 1 and 2 Kings seems to be the result of a specific school of theology, whose basic teachings are formulated in the Book of Deuteronomy. This pattern is ultimately the explanation of the destruction of the two kingdoms. The northern kingdom of Israel is destroyed in 722 BC by the Assyrians. The historian explains, "This came about because the Israelites sinned against Yahweh, their God, who had brought them up from the land of Egypt" (2 Kgs 17:7; see 17:7–20). The southern kingdom of Judah is destroyed in 587 BC by the Babylonians. Again the historian explains, "This befell Judah because Yahweh had stated that he would surely put them out of his sight for the sins Manasseh had committed in all that he did; and especially because of the innocent blood he shed, with which he filled Jerusalem, Yahweh would not forgive" (2 Kgs 24:3–4; see 24:19–20). This "Deuteronomistic history" is thus the story of God's continued punishment and salvation that is played out in the political and military turmoil of this earth.

This theology sets up the major conundrum for the Old Testament: As saving and delivering, God is also the one from whose anger one is saved and delivered! As punishing sin, God is also the cause of the deadly situation. Why then does God save from God?

In one sense, the problem is monotheism. It is the one and the same God who saves and who destroys his people. If there were two gods, one good and one evil, theology would be much simpler. In another sense, the problem arises with the fusion of the Exodus tradition and the covenant tradition.[33] God not only rescues a people from Egyptian slavery, he establishes an intimacy of life with these people and sets up high obligations, which from the beginning Israel fails to honor (Exod 32). At the very least, this makes God look very questionable, especially from the perspective of the Egyptian outsider, as Moses is quick to explain to God:

> "Why, Yahweh, should your wrath blaze up against your own people, whom you brought out of the land of Egypt with such great power and with so strong a hand? Why should the Egyptians say, 'With evil intent he brought them out, that he might kill them in the mountains and exterminate them from the face of the earth'?"
> (Exod 32:11–12)

The "wrath" of God against his sinful people is a theme that dominates the writings of the prophets (Isa 5:25–26; 9:12—10:4; Jer 4:8, 26; Ezek 5:13). Later apocalyptic writers would speak of an eschatological or "coming wrath" that involved the entire universe (Zeph 1:2–18; *1 Enoch* 18:14–16; 84:4). This was the "day of Yahweh" that Amos warned against (Amos 5:18).

In the Jewish faith only God can save from the wrath of God. No magical practices would help. Hence, for the prophets only the people's "turning" from sin would lead to God "turning" from his wrath (Jer 4:4; 35:7; Mal 3:7). In the later Priestly (P) strand of the Torah, religious procedure also functioned to avert divine anger: "The Levites shall encamp around the meeting Tent of Testimony so that there may be no wrath against the community of the sons of Israel" (Num 1:53). Later Jewish writings spoke of prayer (*1 Enoch* 84:5), the life of a good person like Noah (Sir 44:17), or intercessory prayer from the blameless person (Wis 18:21), especially people like Elijah (Sir 48:10; see Mal 3:23–24), as effective ways of diverting the wrath of God.

In the early stories of Israel, the drama of sin and salvation plays itself out on earth. In these stories there are no images of a "heaven" of ultimate salvation or a "hell" of ultimate condemnation. From roughly the sixth century BC, obscure hints of something like human immortality or life after death emerge in texts like Isaiah 53:8–10, where the suffering servant is granted life as a compensation after his suffering and death. Job trusts that his redeemer lives and afterwards he will see God (Job 19:25–27; see Ps 16).

As national solidarity crumbled under foreign oppression and concern grew for the individual who would die for God, some writers became more confident in individual recompense and retribution after death (2 Macc 7:9–29; Dan 12:2). Apocalyptic theology emphasized more and more "the world to come," and hope for salvation, as the Essenes at Qumran expressed it, became above all a longing for an "eternal joy in life without end" (*1 QS* 4:7–8).

B. Salvation from Sin

In the seventh century it became clear to the prophets of Israel from the constant pattern of sin, punishment, and the need for salvation that the situation had become hopeless. Israel was "hard-hearted." The covenantal relationship with God constituted a disaster, as the destruction of the two kingdoms demonstrated. Any real divine "salvation" would require a change within the human heart. Only in that way could the covenant be restored.

At this time, Jeremiah continuously repudiates hope for political and military success. Along with its neighboring kingdoms, Israel must submit to the yoke of Babylon (Jer 27) and accept exile. Instead, Jeremiah promises a renewal of God's covenantal love (Jer 31:1–6), especially in the form of a divine intervention in the human heart. The result will be Israel's fidelity to the law in the form of a "new covenant":

> The days are coming, says Yahweh, when I will make a new covenant with the house of Israel and the house of Judah. It will not be like the covenant I made with their fathers the day I took them by the hand to lead them forth from the land of Egypt; for they broke my covenant and I had to show myself their master, says Yahweh. But this is the covenant which I will make with the house of Israel after those days, says Yahweh. I will place my law within them and write it upon their hearts; I will be their God, and they will be my people. No longer will they have need to teach their friends and kinsmen how to know Yahweh. All, from least to greatest will know me, says Yahweh, for I will forgive their evildoing and remember their sin no more.
>
> (Jer 31:31–34)

Ezekiel promises similar salvation consisting in internal renewal:

> I will take you away from among the nations, gather you from all the foreign lands, and bring you back to your own land. I will sprinkle clean water upon you to cleanse you from all your impurities, and from all your idols I will cleanse you. I will give you a new heart and place a new spirit within you, taking from your bodies your stony hearts and giving you hearts of flesh. I will

> put my spirit within you and make you live by my statutes, careful to observe my decrees. You will live in the land I gave your fathers. You will be my people, and I will be your God. (Ezek 36:26; see 11:20; 18:31)

The Old Testament rarely speaks explicitly of God saving or rescuing from sin (Ps 130:8). However, a lasting rescue of Israel by God meant God dealing with sin. Deutero-Isaiah reminds the exiles of "Yahweh…your savior" (*moshiʿeka*) who will "wipe out your offences…remember no more your sins" (Isa 43:3, 25). Jeremiah speaks of Yahweh promising to heal Israel from its "faithlessness." In doing such, Yahweh is "the salvation of Israel [*tshuʿat Yisraʾel*]" (Jer 3:22–23).

Psalm 51 brings many of these aspects of salvation together. This lamentation begins by a prayer to "blot out my offense, wash me from all my guilt, and cleanse me from my sin" (51:3–4). Like Ezekiel, the psalmist prays, "Fashion a pure heart for me, O God; create in me a steadfast spirit" (51:12). God is addressed as "the God of my salvation" [*ʾelohe tshuʿati*] who saves from "blood (guilt)" (51:16). Lines added probably around the time of Nehemiah ask God to "rebuild the walls of Jerusalem" as part of this plea for removal of sin and renewal of inner spirit (51:20).

C. Salvation through Blood

If suffering and death are a consequence of sin, suffering and death are also then a saving remedy for sin. The idea will be central in Paul, who insists, "Christ died for us…we are justified by his blood" (Rom 5:8–9). Paul could draw from four aspects of his Jewish background to establish some connection between salvation and blood. One came from the Temple sacrifices, particularly the rite of atonement (*kipurim*); the second, from the story of the covenant ritual, where the connection with salvation is not explicit, but the context is the divine rescue from Egypt; the third, from the Passover story; the fourth, from the prophetic tradition.

1. The Temple liturgy included many sacrifices for sins involving the death of animals. One ritual for sin, however, stands out by its prominence among the feasts and by the way it survived

the destruction of the Temple, the great Day of Atonement, later called *Yom Kipur*, celebrated on the tenth day of Tishri, in close connection with New Year's day and the Feast of Succoth.[34] The feast is described in detail in Leviticus 16 and later in the *Mishnah* tractate, *Yoma* (also Lev 23:26–32; Num 29:7–11). According to these texts, the days consisted of fasting and prayer culminating in the Temple sacrifice of a bull, the blood of which the high priest sprinkled on the *kapporeth*, the golden plate on top of the ark of the covenant, in Greek the *hylasterion*, (Exod 25:17–22) and then on the ark itself. After the ark disappeared at the destruction of the first Temple, a substitute stone, the *shotiyah*, was used.[35] The high priest then sprinkled the blood of a goat on the altar of incense, while another goat (the "scapegoat") was led into the wilderness and killed. This ritual was intended to cleanse or atone for any sins against God.

In the Temple sacrifices involving animals, the blood was central. The sprinkling of blood on the altar was reserved for the priest. Leviticus is explicit: "The life of the flesh is in the blood, and I have given it to you upon the altar to make an atonement for your souls, for it is the blood that makes an atonement for the soul" (Lev 17:11). Centuries later, the *Babylonian Talmud* expresses the principle, "No atonement but through blood."[36]

While the sacrificial system was not central to the spirituality of the Pharisees, who stressed far more the importance of personal repentance for dealing with sin (see Sir 34:18–19), the celebration of the Day of Atonement survived the destruction of the Temple in the spiritualized rabbinic Judaism that ensued. While no animals were killed or blood sprinkled, the Torah texts and their descriptions of these bloody rituals were central to the rabbinic celebration of this feast. Paul makes a clear connection between the death of Jesus and the Day of Atonement when he refers to Jesus as the one "whom God set forth as a *hylasterion* through faith in his blood" (Rom 3:24).

2. "The blood of the covenant" is the defining expression of the second source for Paul's sense of salvation through blood and death. Exodus 24 describes the ratification of the Sinai covenant with the people chanting, "We will observe all the commands that Yahweh has decreed" (Exod 24:3). Moses then writes down the

commands, builds an altar, and sacrifices bulls as "communion sacrifices," and then splashes the blood of the slain animals on the people:

> Half of the blood Moses took up and put into basins, the other half he cast on the altar.... Then Moses took the blood and cast it towards the people. He said, "This is the blood of the Covenant that Yahweh has made with you, concerning all these commands." (24:6–8)

The texts make no connection between this blood and sin. Furthermore, we find no particular cultic commemoration of this bloody ratification of the covenant.[37] We know of no Jewish repeated ceremony in which the splashing of blood on the people took place.

However, the expression Paul used to describe the cup at the Last Supper of Jesus recalls this covenantal significance of blood: "This cup is the new covenant in my blood. Whenever you drink it, do this as a memorial of me" (1 Cor 11:25). The connection with the Exodus account is even stronger in the Marcan description of the cup: "He took the cup...and said to them, 'This is my blood, the blood of the covenant, which is to be poured out for many" (Mark 14:23).

3. The third Jewish basis for Paul's link between salvation and blood was the story of the Passover lamb, where the blood of the roasted lamb smeared on the Hebrew's doorposts and lintels saved the family from God's "destructive blow" (Exod 12:13). The ritualized Passover celebration became a major feast in the Jewish annual cycle (Exod 12:1–27; Deut 16:1–8; *Mishnah, Pesahim*). At the time of Paul, Passover, a pilgrim feast, was celebrated in Jerusalem in connection with the Temple. The celebration involved two parts. The first involved the ritual or sacrificial killing of the lambs by priests and the sprinkling of the animal's blood on the altar. The second involved a domestic meal where the lamb's roasted meat was eaten along with wine and herbs. The meal involved a "memorial" session, with an account of the Exodus from Egypt along with subsequent deliverances of the nation. In the Diaspora at the time of Paul, the feast may have been cele-

brated entirely at home, with a blood ceremony on the doors of the house (Exod 12:21–23). In later rabbinic tradition, all blood rituals cease, and the "memorial" takes on greater prominence (see *Mishnah, Pesahim* 10, 5).

4. The Jewish basis for linking salvation and blood is implied also in the portrayal of the suffering servant of Deutero-Isaiah (52:13—15:22), who appears to have suffered and died for the health and salvation of the people (Isa 53:8–9). This figure is important also for the background of collective solidarity with a messiah figure (see below), but here our focus is on the connection between salvation, on the one hand, and blood and death, on the other. It is the suffering and presumed death of the servant that brings health—not his success or power.

The connection seems to grow first of all from the connection between sin and punishment, especially punishment by death, a ubiquitous theme in the Old Testament. However, on a more subtle level, we can find in the prophetic tradition a theme that links sin and suffering. In this theme the suffering is first of all that of God. The prophets frequently describe the "pathos" of God as he confronts the sin of his people. Hosea portrays the anguish of God who loves unfaithful Israel as a parent loves an infant son: "My heart is overwhelmed, my pity is stirred" (Hos 11:8). In Micah, God reproaches his people, "O my people, what have I done to you; how have I wearied you? Answer me!" (Mic 6:3).

In this prophetic tradition, the life of the prophet is often drawn up into the suffering of God as a vivid revelation of this suffering. The suffering of the prophet often begins as he is drawn into his mission. The clearest example is Hosea, who lives with an adulterous wife as a revelation of God living with adulterous Israel. Likewise, Isaiah is called only to fail (Isa 6:10–13). Jeremiah is not only called to fail as well, but to suffer deeply from that failure (Jer 20:7–18). The link between the prophet's suffering and God's pain appears in the association of the two ideas at the concluding oracle to Baruch:

> The word which the prophet Jeremiah spoke to Baruch.... Thus says Yahweh, God of Israel, concerning you Baruch, "Because you [the prophet Jeremiah] said,

> 'Alas! Yahweh adds grief to my pain; I am weary from groaning, and find no rest,' say this to him, thus says Yahweh, 'What I have built, I am tearing down; what I have planted, I am uprooting, even the whole land.'"
> (Jer 45:2–4)

The pain of the prophet is explained by the pain of God. Anticipating this decision of God, the call of Jeremiah is precisely "to root up and to tear down, to destroy and to demolish, to build and to plant" (1:10).

The suffering and death of the "servant" in Deutero-Isaiah is nothing new in the prophetic tradition. What is new is the positive issue of that suffering. "Upon him was the chastisement that makes us whole, by his stripes, we are healed" (Isa 53:5). Salvation comes through suffering, perhaps because it reveals the suffering of God.

This fourth servant song in Deutero-Isaiah may have been a sixth-century reflection on the suffering of Jeremiah. Early on, an application of the servant was made to understand the suffering of Israel as a nation (Isa 49:3). Centuries later, the fourth song became a wellspring for writers of the New Testament to understand the sufferings of Jesus (see especially Acts 8:26–35; also Matt 8:17; Luke 22:37; 1 Pet 2:22–25). It does not, however, seem to be cited again in the Old Testament or later Jewish writings.

D. The Scope of Salvation

To the degree that salvation was seen primarily as a rescue of the nation from their enemies, divine salvation appears to be limited to the nation of Israel. This exclusive view of divine salvation will dominate the Old Testament and Judaism. We see this view particularly in concerns for postexilic reconstruction (Ezek 44:4–9; Ezra 9). This view gains sharp intensity in Pharisaic circles as we move into Judaism at the time of the New Testament (*4 Ezra* 5:23–27).

However, a universalist view runs less prominently below the surface. The international and even "cosmic" dimension of God's salvation appears in the psalms of Yahweh's kingship (Ps

47; 93; 95—99). Psalm 96 invites the audience to "announce his [God's] salvation day after day," which is to "tell God's glory among the nations, God's marvelous deeds among all peoples" (96:2–3). This invitation is made to all the "families of nations" (96:7) and all the elements of nature (96:11–12). The psalmist refers to God's creation of the heavens (96:5) and promises that God "will come to govern the earth with justice and the peoples with fairness" (96:13). In their use of Canaanite imagery, these psalms appear to be rather ancient.

The ancient Elohist strand (E) in the Pentateuch also shows a remarkable openness to other nations. While the Yahwist (J) hints at universalism by stories of the human race before Abraham, the Elohist focuses more on individual non-Israelites contemporary with the patriarchs and Moses. In the story of the birth of Moses (Exod 1:15—2:10), the Elohist shows how the genocidal policy of the pharaoh was frustrated by those who appear to be Egyptian midwives of the Hebrews, disobeying the king of Egypt because they were "God [Elohim] fearing" (Exod 1:17, 21). The theme of the "God-fearing" non-Israelite runs throughout the Elohist strand from Abimelech, who acknowledges Elohim as *ʾAdonai* ("my Lord"; Gen 20:4) and obeys God's instructions not to touch Sarah, to Jethro, Moses' Midianite father-in-law, who offers holocaust and sacrifices to Elohim and then shares a sacred meal with Moses, Aaron, and the elders of Israel (Exod 18:12).

Similarly, later prophetic writers will envision future salvation as a renewal of the whole natural order (Isa 9:2–7) or will find hope in future salvation by recalling God's power in creation (Isa 51:9–16). There is clearly a sense that Yahweh is the God of the entire universe and therefore the God of all peoples. Thus Isaiah and Micah together describe nations streaming to the Temple (Isa 2:1–4; Micah 4:1–4). Trito-Isaiah is even more emphatic about including foreigners and others traditionally excluded from Israelite religion (Isa 56:3–7; 66:18–21): "My house will be called a house of prayer for all peoples" (Isa 56:7). The canonical books of Jonah and Ruth seem to protest loudly against exclusion of the Gentiles (see also Tob 13:11).

V. Salvation through Union with a Mediator Figure

We will find no formulation in the Old Testament of Paul's view of life "in Christ" and solidarity in Christ's death and resurrection. We can, however, look for the building blocks of Paul's view of this intense sharing in the life and death of the Messiah, perhaps the most characteristic aspect of Paul's theology.

One of those building blocks was the sense of solidarity of the community under God. Modern readers are often shocked by stories of God punishing the whole people for the sins of one, like the story of David's sinful census (2 Sam 24). This solidarity is often explained today with the concept of "corporate personality." The nation of Israel seemed to function as one person, and sometimes one person in Israel seemed to sum up the whole nation, as seen in the way in which the patriarchs gave their names to the tribes.

In some cases this solidarity worked for the good of the people. The ancient Yahwist (J) and Elohist (E) stories of Moses effectively interceding on Sinai on behalf of Israel in the story of the golden calf (Exod 32:11–14, 30–35; see also Num 14:13–19; Deut 9:26–29) portrays a solidarity by which the actions and prayers of good individuals bring forgiveness for the whole group. Within one of the prayers, Moses asks God to remember "Abraham, Isaac and Jacob, your servants" and God's own promise of offspring (Exod 32:13). God's memory and his fidelity to his promises become the basis of solidarity through the succession of generations. In another prayer, Moses offers his own life to God either as a substitution for Israel or as a way of insisting on his solidarity with the sinful people: "If you would, forgive their sin, but if not, then blot me out from the book that you have written" (32:32). This scene may have developed under the influence of the eighth-century prophets, where we find also the prophetic role as intercessor representing the sinful people and pleading for forgiveness (Amos 7:1–6).

The story of Adam and Eve with their fall and punishment (Gen 2—3) implies a solidarity of all humanity with this couple.

The stress in this story on the sufferings of childbirth (3:16), the drudgery and frustration of work (3:17–18), and even the inevitability of death (3:19) would be read by the faithful as a reflection of their sufferings and suggestion of a source common to humanity. As told in Genesis 2—3, however, the stress lies more on external circumstances rather than on an internally shared life. Humanity is affected by Adam and Eve's sin because they are banished from the garden and isolated from the tree of life (Gen 3:23–24).

While later Jewish writings returned to the image of solidarity with Adam in sin (Sir 49:16), the Hebrew and the Greek Old Testament outside the opening chapters of Genesis are remarkably silent about Adam.[38] Later Jewish writings especially saw the loss of immortality as due to the sin of Adam.[39] Philo uses the story of Adam to illustrate his adaptation of Platonic dualism. Philo sees the man of Genesis 1 and the Adam of Genesis 2 as two different persons, one heavenly and one earthly,[40] an understanding that Paul seemed to know about (see 1 Cor 15:45–49).

With his teaching concerning personal responsibility (Ezek 18), Ezekiel throws a major monkey wrench into this sense of solidarity of all humanity or at least of Israel. For Ezekiel, only the wicked person is to be punished (18:18, 24) and the good parent cannot save his wicked child (18:10–13). The historical context for this teaching was the Babylonian Captivity (587–538 BC) with its loss of all the structures of national solidarity, Temple, king, the land. Ezekiel begins a long priestly and rabbinic tradition of personal ethics, stressing the need of each person to observe the law.

Later rabbinic reflection developed the idea of personal merit (*zakuth*), as a type of spiritual currency produced by good deeds that could grow and be stored in a kind of heavenly treasury.[41] Rabbinic reflection continued to speculate on the way this merit could be transferred from one person to another, so that, for instance, the good actions of Moses and Aaron could help their contemporaries during the Exodus[42] or the good deeds of patriarchs like Abraham worked for the good of later generations.[43] There is here, however, less an issue of solidarity than one of the spiritual exchange through the currency of merit, as the treasury of one person could be exchanged for the good of another.

The experience of martyrdom, especially at the time of the Maccabees, reinforced the idea of the suffering of good people for the sake of the law bringing benefits to the people. Shortly before the end of the second-century BC a Jewish writer tells the story of the death of the seven brothers under the persecution of Antiochus IV. The account of their suffering comes to a climax with the prayer of the seventh brother about to be tortured to death:

> I offer up my body and my life for our ancestral laws, imploring God to show mercy soon to our nation.... Through me and my brothers, may there be an end to the wrath of the Almighty that has justly fallen on our whole nation. (2 Macc 7:37–38)

Sometime in the middle of the first century AD, a Jewish writer again reflects on the deaths of these and other martyrs of the time and develops a theology of atonement:

> The tyrant was punished and our fatherland purified since they became as it were a ransom [*antipsychon*] for the sins of the nation. Divine providence rescued Israel through the blood of those pious persons, and through the propitiation [*to hilasterion*] of their death.
> (4 Macc 17:21–22; see also Eleazar's prayer in 6:28–29)

Again the image of the ransom suggests an exchange of goods rather than a solidarity as the medium for the nation being rescued by the suffering and death of a good person.

On the other hand, the fourth servant song found in Deutero-Isaiah (Isa 52:13—53:12) describes the atonement of one person for others where solidarity with the servant seems to be stressed more than any exchange of merits as the basis for the atoning suffering. This sixth-century text written within the Babylonian Captivity may well be a reflection on the suffering of the prophet Jeremiah some fifty years earlier, whom Deutero-

Isaiah sees as not only vindicated but also responsible for the healing of the nation:

> He bore our infirmities and he endured our sufferings....
> He was pierced for our sins; he was crushed for our
> iniquities.
> The punishment on him made us whole, his bruises
> healed us....
> Yahweh visited on him the guilt which is all ours....
> My just servant will justify many; he will bare their guilt.
> (Isa 53:4–6, 11)

Paul twice cites lines from this passage (Rom 10:16; 15:21). Neither citation, however, deals with the vicarious nature of the servant's suffering. It is difficult therefore to know how much Paul had this suffering servant in mind when he developed his theology of sharing in the death and resurrection of Christ.

VI. Eschatology and Apocalyptic Hope

First announced as a day of punishment (Amos 5:18–20; Isa 2:9–17; Zeph 1:14–16), "the day of Yahweh" in postexilic writing became a saving intervention of God like no other past intervention (Isa 61:2; Joel 3:4; Mal 3:1–2, 23–24). The day brings destruction to the godless but salvation to the good people. It is therefore above all a day of distinction between the good and the bad. From his earliest writing (1 Thess 5:2) to his much later (Phil 1:10), Paul never loses focus on that day.

The theme of that day connects with many other aspects of Old Testament theology. The great psalms that celebrated the kingship of Yahweh introduced the image of a coming of Yahweh to govern or rule the earth (Ps 96:13; 98:9). By combining the themes of creation, future coming, and judgment with universalism, they further prepared for the later development of apocalyptic salvation. The promises of salvation made by the prophets likewise nudged the people away from the past toward the future. As prophecy was preserved in writing and the written promises led to disappointments in the present, the heart of Israel moved more toward a vision of the future. Eventually, apocalyptic writers envisioned the ultimate future of God's salvation.

Paul tied almost every aspect of his theology into that eschatological and apocalyptic vision, although he made very significant changes. He dabbled in explicit apocalyptic descriptions in his earliest letters, especially in 1 Thessalonians. Eventually, he stopped describing the end of the world. Nevertheless, the apocalyptic view with its many facets continued to color his understanding and descriptions of God and salvation.

A. The Conflict of Good and Evil

Using the imagery of the day of Yahweh and the coming kingship of God, apocalyptic writers attempted in effect to deal with the problem of evil in the world. Jewish apocalyptic writers depicted in gruesome terms a growing conflict of good and evil. As Daniel declares, "It shall be a time unsurpassed in distress since nations began until that time" (Dan 12:1).

These forces of good and evil were pictured as raging in a magnitude of struggle that enveloped the whole universe. This was not a struggle between good and bad people—much less between the good and bad elements of the human heart. Rather, this was a struggle involving the stars, the moon, the harvest, the earth and its quaking. As described in the *Testament of Moses,*

> And the earth will tremble, even to its ends shall it be
> shaken.
> And the high mountains will be made low.
> Yea, they shall be shaken, as enclosed valleys will they fall.
> The sun will not give light.
> And in darkness the horns of the moon will flee.
> Yes, they will be broken in pieces.
> It will be turned wholly into blood.
> Yea, even the circle of the stars will be thrown into disarray.
> And the sea all the way to the abyss will retire,
> to the sources of waters which fail.
> Yea, the rivers will vanish away. (10:4–6; see *4 Ezra* 9:2–4)

The source of this evil, however, remains a human or creaturely rebellion, not some metaphysical structure of reality or divine dualism. The figure of Adam becomes central in this consideration: "For a grain of evil seed was sown in Adam's heart from the beginning, and how much ungodliness it has produced until now and will produce until the time of threshing comes!" (*4 Ezra* 4:30).

On a deeper level, the conflict of good and evil involves opposing cosmic powers. The angel revealing the mysteries to Daniel had to contend with "the prince of the kingdom of Persia" and is rescued by "Michael, one of the leading princes" (Dan 10:13). We see in this picture the traces of Hellenistic dualism. However, the Jewish writers refused to root evil in any absolute principle or evil god. Instead, they maintained a picture of God as above this conflict, as allowing this conflict, and ultimately resolving this conflict.

B. Cosmic Salvation from God

In the apocalyptic vision, salvation shifts from national redemption to cosmic transformation. Trito-Isaiah spoke of God creating "a new heavens and a new earth" (Isa 65:17; 66:22). Like the Isaiah of the eighth century, this prophet too sees a coming return to paradise where "the wolf and the lamb feed together" (Isa 65:25; see 11:6–9). Only God can bring this about. That, of course, is the main point. The new kingdom of God comes about by God's action alone. A heavenly Jerusalem comes down from heaven or a new creation comes into existence, something totally beyond the powers of human beings.

Later speculation will describe this transformation in terms of two worlds or ages, "this world" and "the world to come" (*ha-ʿolam ha-zeh* and *ha-ʿolam ha-baʾ*). In *4 Ezra* the angel interpreter states, "Listen to me, Ezra, and I will instruct you, and will admonish you yet again. For this reason the Most High has made not one world but two" (7:50). "This world" is the sick world: "Creation [is] aging and passing the strength of youth" (5:55). Hope of salvation lies not in this world but in the one coming.

This sick world must be destroyed or in some way perish so as to make room for the "world to come." The evil universe or eon is overcome by being destroyed. This view of cosmic destruction leads back again to the theme of salvation through blood and death, only this time on a cosmic scale. At times this destruction is pictured as total, leading to a radical discontinuity between "this world" and "the world to come" (See 6:7–20; 7:30; *Testament of Moses* 10:4–6).

Life in the world to come is a life without death. This is a world where the good and the wise, after sleeping in the dust of the earth, will awake and "will shine as brightly as the vault of heaven, and those who have instructed many in virtue as bright as the stars for all eternity" (Dan 12:3). In *2 Baruch* God himself tells the visionary about the future of the righteous:

> And I will tell about their blessedness and shall not be silent about their glory which is kept for them. For surely as you endured much labor in the short time in which you live in this passing world, so you will receive great light in that world which has no end. (48:49–50).

For most Jewish apocalyptic writers at this time, such a "new life" meant the resurrection of the body:

> For the earth will surely give back the dead at that time; it receives them now in order to keep them, not changing anything in their form. But as it has received them so it will give them back. And as I have delivered them to it so it will raise them. For then it will be necessary to show those who live that the dead are living again, and that those who went away have come back.
> (*2 Baruch* 50:2–3; see 2 Macc 7:9; 12:43–44; 14:46)

Second Baruch continues the scene after the final judgment, stressing this time how people are changed:

> Time will no longer make them older. For they will live in the heights of that world, and they will be like the angels

> and be equal to the stars. And they will be changed into any shape which they wished, from beauty to loveliness and from light to the splendor of glory. (51:9–10)

On the other hand, some Jewish writings more influenced by Platonic philosophy spoke of this final glory in terms that suggest the immortality of the soul as the essential part of the human. About a hundred years earlier, a Jewish writer, attempting a bold integration of Greek philosophy and Mosaic faith, wrote:

> The souls of the just are in the hands of God
> and no suffering shall touch them.
> In the view of the foolish they seem to be dead;
> And their passing away was thought to be an affliction
> And their going forth from us, complete destruction
> But they are in peace....
> Their hope is full of immortality.
> (Wis 3:1–4; see also 4 Macc 9:22)

Probably written about the same time as Paul, *4 Ezra* writes of an intermediate stage of "those who have kept the ways of the Most High, when they are separated from their mortal bodies." The writer describes the joy and rest of these bodiless persons:

> They shall see with great joy the glory of him who receives them.... They have now escaped what is moral and shall inherit what is to come; and besides they see the straits and toil from which they have been delivered, and the spacious liberty which they are to receive and enjoy in immortality. (7:91–96)

In a section of the book also probably written around the first century AD, *1 Enoch* describes the resting place and the dwelling of the righteous with the holy angels from where "they interceded and petitioned and prayed on behalf of the children of the people" (39:4; see also 71:1–17). The *ʿolam ha-baʾ* becomes at once the future world and a present heavenly world.

C. Eschatological Exclusion from Salvation

If the success story of salvation is magnified by the eternity of the world to come, the horror of failure is magnified into eternal damnation. In the cosmic proportion of the conflict of good and evil, there was no room for intermediates. Either you functioned as a child of God, the principal agent behind the forces of good, or as an agent of Satan, the chief power behind all evil.

With a distinct focus now on individuals rather than on peoples and nations, Daniel seems to provide the earliest description of individual exclusion from salvation and eternal condemnation as he describes the resurrection of both the good and the bad: "Of those who lie sleeping in the dust of the earth many will awake, some to everlasting life, some to shame and everlasting disgrace" (Dan 12:2).

As the hope of national glory fades under foreign oppression and as Ezekiel's theme of individual responsibility takes hold (see Ezek 18), the final judgment of individuals becomes the key to salvation and damnation, which now have eternal dimensions (see *4 Ezra* 7:70–99; *2 Baruch* 30). *Fourth Ezra* describes the fate of the wicked as "the pit of torment" and the "furnace of Hell" (*4 Ezra* 7:36). *First Enoch* describes the "chains of Satan" being prepared for the kings and potentates of this earth" (*1 Enoch* 53:4–5) as well as "the armies of Azaz'el" (54:4–5).

Fourth Ezra is particularly pessimistic about the number of the saved: "And now I see that the world to come will bring delight to few, but torments to many" (7:47; see 9:14–22). In a parable of the sower, similar to that of Jesus (see Mark 4:1–9), the angel explains to Ezra:

> For just as the farmer sows many seeds upon the ground and plants a multitude of seedlings, and yet not all that have been sown will come up in due season, and not all that were planted will take root, so all those who have been sown in the world will not be saved. (8:41)

The old issue of exclusivism dealt with Israelite society, with its insistence excluding Gentiles from Israel. Now, however, the issue of exclusivity deals with eternal salvation. It would seem only right that nothing of this evil world should enter the world to come. Hell becomes a convenient place to relegate the evil things and persons of this world. Divine anger now issues in eternal damnation, not just an early death.

Jewish apocalyptic is absorbed by early Christianity with a major shift. Jesus becomes the figure through whom God rescues people from the realm of evil and transfers them to that of goodness. The return of Jesus becomes the main event of the end times.

PART II

The Letters of Paul

We will study the letters of Paul in their apparent chronological order, starting with 1 Thessalonians, then 1 Corinthians, 2 Corinthians, Galatians, and Romans, letters that are relatively easy to correlate with the second and third missionary journeys of Paul as described in Acts. We will then treat Philippians, Philemon, and Colossians as late letters written outside the time frame described in Acts. As we study each of these letters, we will examine the evidence for this chronological placement.

Colossians poses a special problem because many reasons exist to see this letter as belonging in the next part of our study, that about letters written in the name of Paul after his death. In my opinion, Colossians could go either way. From the point of view of style and vocabulary, Colossians belies the work of another hand. However, the theological trajectories continue in this letter with striking consistency. We will treat it as one of the last letters written by Paul, most likely penned by another person but under Paul's supervision.

Our study of each letter will be in three steps. First, we will look at the background for the letter, where we try to reconstruct the historical situation and the reasons for the letter writing. Second, we will do a sequential scan of the letter. This requires establishing some sort of outline or structural order of the letter so that we can recognize the compositional steps of Paul. The thoughts that will be picked up and further developed in the thematic study will be marked by a key word in bold print. Third, we will pull together Paul's statements according to the six theological themes that we will follow throughout the Pauline writings. As we progress in the study, we will refer to the background material and to his earlier letters to follow any theological development of these themes in Paul's mind.

The English translations of Paul's text follow the Greek as closely as possible, even when this closeness leads to an awkward English expression. Every translation involves some interpretation of the meaning of the text, often ironing out ambiguities and confusing statements. Unfortunately, the sense that is ironed out might be important for understanding Paul's theology as a whole. Where the thought is dense and complex, I will try to make the relationships of ideas clearer by structuring the lines of Paul in a type of verse format.

5

First Thessalonians

From 146 BC on, Thessalonica was the capital of the Roman province of Macedonia. Some 170 years earlier, Cassandrus founded the city under Alexander the Great around 316 BC. In 42 BC it became a "free city" with its own local government. At the time of the New Testament, Thessalonica was a cosmopolitan city with a large Jewish colony and many pagan cults.

I. Background for the Letter

A. The Founding and Development of the Church

The first half of Paul's First Letter to the Thessalonians contains a number of details about the founding and development of the church there. Paul had arrived from persecutions at Philippi and had run into difficulties at Thessalonica (2:2). Yet he praises the recipients of this letter for having received the good news with great conviction (1:5–6). As Paul says, "As soon as you heard the message… you accepted it for what it really is, God's message" (2:13).

This part of the letter gives us also some details about the development of the church after its founding. Paul alludes to continued difficulties suffered by the Thessalonians (1:6; 3:3). Despite these difficulties, however, the church in Thessalonica prospered. According to Paul, this church had even become a source of evangelization not only in its own province of Macedonia, but also in neighboring Achaia (1:7–8). A bit of hyperbole rings in the words of Paul: "The news of your faith in God has spread everywhere" (1:8). Nevertheless, from these details we can construct a picture of a basically healthy, although battered church. Some very early and interesting aspects of church life and structure appear throughout this letter, but especially in the final words of Paul.

B. The Circumstances for Writing

Paul describes the circumstances leading up to his writing to the Thessalonians:

1. A short time after leaving the Thessalonians, he tried several times to return. Paul describes a sense of great urgency in his need to return. Apparently, bad news had reached him about the church there. In a typically apocalyptic perspective, he attributes his inability to return to Satan (2:17–18).
2. Because he was unable to return, Paul, now in Athens, sent Timothy back to Thessalonica (3:1–2).
3. Timothy eventually returned to Paul with the good news "of your faith and your love, telling us that you always remember us with pleasure and want to see us quite as much as we want to see you" (3:6). From the nature of the Letter to the Thessalonians, we can surmise that Timothy brought back a number of questions for Paul to answer. These questions appear behind the remarks of Paul that begin with "and concerning" (*peri de tôn/tês*, 4:19, 13; 5:1).

C. Correlations with Acts

If we look in the Acts of the Apostles for a description that would correspond to the circumstances Paul gives for writing this letter, we must find the following events:

- Paul has founded the church in Thessalonica.
- He had arrived there from Philippi.
- He has recently left there and traveled to Athens.
- His companions are Timothy and Silvanus.
- He is presently still close enough to Thessalonica for Timothy to make a return trip.

Acts 17—18 explicitly mentions events that correspond for the most part with these circumstances. For Luke, Paul is on his "second missionary journey." A few details here in Acts show some discrepancies, best attributable to Luke's free handling of the story:

- According to Luke, Paul's stay in Thessalonica is only "three Sabbaths" (Acts 17:2). This time is hardly long enough to allow for the intense bonds of friendship Paul has developed with the community or for the development of that community presupposed in Paul's letter.
- Timothy's presence with Paul in Athens after his departure from Thessalonica contradicts the description in Acts 17:15 and 18:5 of Timothy and Silas (presumably the same person as Silvanus) remaining in Macedonia and rejoining Paul only in Corinth.

Thus we have a reasonable basis for coordinating the writing of 1 Thessalonians with the Lucan picture of Paul's stay in Achaia on his second journey.

This coordination with Acts leads to an important conclusion regarding the date of this letter. Although he briefly mentions Athens (1 Thess 3:1), Paul is probably writing from Corinth, the next extended stay after his brief stopover in Athens. If this is correct, we can date this letter to approximately AD 52, the time of the proconsulship of Gallio, mentioned in Acts 18:12–17.

D. Integrity of the Letter

This first letter of Paul brings up the question of whether or not later editors changed the text in any way. This is the question of "integrity." Many years may have passed between Paul's writing of this letter and the subsequent copying of the letter for distribution. We have no indication that the copyists had anything like a modern curator's concern for preserving documents for the future.

Paul's letters in fact contain many "lumps." These are sections that somewhat abruptly change the topic and are loosely connected to the surrounding text. Of course, by the very nature of letters as we have seen, such lumps are to be expected. However, when a statement within the lump seems to run counter to what Paul has said in other authentic sections, when the lump seems to reflect the concerns of a later time of the church, or when its wording is unusual for Paul, we can legitimately suspect a later addition to the letter by a copyist or editor. Such additions are called "interpolations."

Questioning the integrity of a letter in the light of a suspected interpolation is not questioning the value of the section. It is not questioning the inspiration of the passage or even of its right to hold its place in the canon. It is, rather, a question of understanding the consistency of Paul's mind. If Paul did not write a passage, the passage may reflect a very early interpretation of Paul, but it does not reflect Paul's thought. If our efforts are to understand the consistency of Paul's mind in distinction from the many other currents of the New Testament, it is essential to identify interpolations and set them apart.

For some time, scholars have questioned the integrity of the prayer found in 1 Thessalonians 2:13–16. In no other letter does Paul interrupt his "newsy" section with a prayer. This prayer repeats many of the thoughts of the opening prayer, especially the thoughts found in 1:2–7. In fact, the description here of the Jews as those "who killed the Lord Jesus and the prophets" reflects a Matthean tone (See Matt 5:12; 23:29). Calling the Jews "opposed to everyone" reflects an animosity not found anywhere else in Paul. When Paul explicitly reflects on the lack of belief of the Jewish people, as he does in the later text of Romans 9—11, he speaks in terms of his personal sorrow (Rom 9:2–3) and of the need to respect these people (Rom 9:4). We know of no persecution between the Jewish follows of Jesus and the non-Christian Jews in the early 50s, the time of the writing this letter. The "lynching" of Stephen (Acts 7:54–60) occurred in the mid 30s. The attack by the Herodian king, Agrippa I, on the leadership of the church occurred around AD 40.

After the Roman war broke out in the late 60s, intense animosity developed between Christians and Jews. As extended into the 80s and 90s, this animosity forms the backdrop for the anti-Jewish texts of the gospels. In fact, the reference to the "anger of God having come on them in a final way [*eis telos*]" reflects a Christian interpretation of the Roman war, an interpretation evidenced in the 80s (Matt 23:37–39; see 2 Chron 36:15–16).

All these observations suggest that 1 Thessalonians 2:13–16 was not written by Paul, but by an editor-copyist two or three decades later. While these verses are an important reflection on Christian suffering and a vital insight into the early Christian experience of separating from Judaism, they do not seem to reflect Paul's thought.

II. The Sequential Study of the Letter

A. The Overall Structure of the Letter

The letter as a whole falls clearly into two major sections: chapters 2—3, where Paul describes the recent events dealing with himself and the community, and chapters 4—5, where Paul answers the Thessalonians' questions. These sections are preceded by the opening greeting and thanksgiving (1:1–10) and followed by the conclusion of the letter (5:23–28). The following outline of the letter shows the further breakdown into specific topics:

I. Opening and thanksgiving (1:1–10)
II. Paul and the community (2—3)
  A. The foundation of the community (2:1–12)
    [Insertion? An anti-Jewish prayer (2:13–16)]
  B. After Paul's departure (2:17—3:10)
  C. Prayer (3:11–13)
III. Instructions (4—5)
  A. Moral duties regarding sex and love (4:1–12)
  B. Eschatology (4:13—5:11)
    1. About those who have already died (4:13–18)
    2. About the timing of the end (5:1–11)
  C. Various directives (5:12–22)
IV. Conclusion: blessing, greetings, prayer (5:23–28)

Such an outline helps us view the letter as a whole as well as divide the letter into significant units for concentrated reading. Trying to read carefully and digest entire letters of Paul at a time often results in theological indigestion. From this outline we can orient our search for the principle ideas or themes of Paul as he explains them to the Thessalonians.

B. The Opening Greeting and Prayer (1:1)

The opening of the letter with its mention of "God the Father" and "the Lord Jesus Christ" is significant for the **God trajectory** and the **Jesus Christ trajectory**. We will examine these expressions below. Also significant here is the way Paul describes the church as both "in God" and "in Christ" (1:1). This is the beginning of the fifth trajectory or major theme we need to follow, the theme of **union of life with Christ** to which all are called, a union which lets the drama of salvation begin in Christ and flow into all who share his life.

C. The Opening Prayer and Christian Suffering (1:2–10)

In a letter prayer, Paul reflects on the experience of the Thessalonians as well as on his own experiences. Throughout his writings, Paul frequently mentions the sufferings that he and other followers of the gospel must undergo. He uses mostly the term *thlipsis* to describe this suffering (1:6; 3:3, 7). In 5:3 he refers to the *ôdis* or labor pains of a pregnant woman. The terms are interesting. In apocalyptic literature, these terms frequently describe the great "tribulation" programmed by God to precede the end of the world (see Isa 26:17; *4 Ezra* 4:40; see also Jer 4:51). The New Testament refers to this type of suffering as a necessary yet hopeful condition of being a follower of Jesus (John 16:21). Paul here is introducing the **eschatology trajectory** that he will develop later in this letter.

Here he does not say a great deal about this suffering or about its meaning. He simply points out that it is "our common lot" (3:3), that he foresaw this suffering as inevitable (3:4), and that this particular suffering can coexist with joy (1:6).

This coexistence of suffering and joy is the work of "the Holy Spirit," mentioned a few lines earlier in connection with the "power" and "conviction" that allow the gospel to be more than "mere words" (1:5). Mention of the Holy Spirit here in connection with inner transformation inaugurates the third trajectory that we need to follow through Paul's writings, the **Spirit trajectory**.

The prayer climaxes with a description of the Thessalonians as having converted "to serve the living and true God and to await his Son from heaven, whom he raised from the dead, who delivers us from the coming wrath" (1:9–10). The line that rings like an early formula combines the **trajectories** regarding **God, Christ, salvation**, and **eschatology**.

D. Personal Memories and News (2:1—3:12)

As Paul gives us important glimpses into the founding of the church at Thessalonica and into the events leading up to the writing of this letter, he also refers to the affection and care that he feels for the Thessalonians. He writes of an intense bond of friendship between this founder of the community and the members as he switches between the imagery of "a mother feeding and looking after her own children" (2:7) and that of "a father [caring for] his children" (2:11). This bond of affection will appear again in Paul's relationships with his other churches and reflects an important dimension that Paul sees in the nature of being a founder and pastor of a church. He is far more than a business manager or group leader.

As he began the letter with a prayer, so he ends this section with a prayer (3:11–13). His petitions include himself and his travels. "May God himself, our Father, and our Lord Jesus direct our way to you." He also prays for the Thessalonians: "May the Lord make you increase and abound in love for one another and for all." These are the two crucial elements of the mission, which Paul now places in God's hand. He ends with an eschatological perspective that includes the presence of God, the coming of our Lord Jesus, and the need for strong hearts and irreproachable holiness. The coming of Jesus "with all his holy ones" is probably a reference to the holy angels who appear frequently in apocalyptic writings (Matt 24:31; Mark 13:27). Holy men and women are probably not intended here since, as Paul will explain, those who have died on earth will have to rise from the dead first before they become part of Jesus' entourage.

E. Sexual Morality and Love (4:1–12)

In his letters to Macedonia and Achaia, Paul frequently has to deal with the issue of sexual morality. Sacred prostitution was common in the Greek cults of this time. "Greek love" was the current euphemism for homosexual love.

Writing here to the Thessalonians, Paul treats the theme briefly as he begins his instructions in chapter four. His approach is interesting. His argument is not a Stoic appeal to discipline. Even less does he approach sex from a Gnostic despising of the body. By means of antithetical parallelism, he simply contrasts sexual immorality (*porneia*) with growth in holiness: "It is God's will that you grow in holiness: that you abstain from sexual immorality" (4:3). He is in effect saying that the body and its sexual functions have an important significance in a person's holiness, that a believer has a particular obligation regarding his or her body, not because sex is bad, but because of that person's call to intimacy with God.[1]

Concluding these instructions on sexual morality, Paul alludes to "brotherly [or sisterly] love" (*philadelphia*, 4:9), only to exclude it from further discussion. Apparently, Timothy related to Paul a question on this topic from the Thessalonians. What Paul does say without further development, however, is intriguing: "You have been taught by God (*theodidaktoi*) how to love (*agapan*) one another" (4:9). Paul does not elaborate on what he has in mind by this divine instruction.

F. Eschatology (4:13—5:11)

After dealing with the moral duties of the Thessalonians, Paul picks up the topic that dominates this letter, that of the coming or *parousia* ("presence") of the Lord Jesus (4:13—5:11). With this reflection, Paul returns to his **eschatology trajectory** for a major development. Concerning this coming of Jesus, Paul deals with two issues, that of the deceased members of the community and that of the timing of this end.

1. Those Who Have Already Died

Paul's general instruction in 4:13–18 consists in assuring the Thessalonians that their dead will not miss out on the last day, that one of the first events of that day will be their rising from the dead (4:16). This is an eschatological view directed intensely to the future.

Verses 14 and 15 indicate two bases for this conviction and hope. Verse 14 refers to the resurrection of Jesus. Paul here writes in an elliptical manner, in effect leaving out a thought. He does not mean, as his words here literally indicate, that the belief of the Christians is the basis or cause of the resurrection, but rather that one belief should lead us to another: "For if we believe that Jesus died and rose, then [we should also believe that] God will bring forth with him from the dead those also who have fallen asleep in Jesus."

It appears that Paul here is referring to a faith formula or creedal statement circulating in the church. The expression, "Jesus died and rose," is not typically Pauline. Paul otherwise refers to Jesus being raised by the Father. For Paul, the resurrection of Jesus is not his proof of divine power—as it is for John. For Paul, rather, the resurrection is the manifestation of the Father's power to save. This theocentric perspective appears clear in the second half of the verse. It is God who will "bring forth" those who have died through Jesus.[2] It is interesting, however, to catch a glimpse of the faith formulas prior to Paul's understanding—formulas that Paul occasionally integrates into his letters.

Verse 15 then provides a second basis for the faith in the resurrection of the Christians: "This we say to you in a word of the Lord." This expression could have a few meanings. It could indicate a word passed down from Jesus. Paul will use the expression at other times for teachings that form part of the traditions regarding Jesus' own instructions, some of which have close parallels with instructions we now find in the gospels (see 1 Cor 7:10). The term is also frequent among the Old Testament prophets for a prophetic utterance, that is, one made in the name of God himself (see Isa 1:24; 28:13–14; Jer 1:2–4; Ezek 1:3; and so on). If this is the meaning that Paul has in mind, then the basis here for Paul's instruction is some utterance of a Christian prophet (see 1 Thess 5:19; 1 Cor 14:1–5) or perhaps an insight of Paul himself functioning as prophet.

After identifying the bases of the instruction, Paul then provides a miniapocalypse. He describes the second coming of Jesus:

> The Lord himself will come down from heaven
> with a summoning call,
> with a voice of an archangel,
> and with a trumpet of God;
> and those who have died in Christ will rise first.
> Then we, the living, the survivors, will be caught up with them
> in the clouds to meet the Lord in the air.
> Thenceforth we shall be with the Lord unceasingly.
> (4:16–17)

When we compare this description with a text of Exodus we notice many common details. The text is that of the Sinai theophany, where Yahweh is described as coming down to earth to give his law and form a covenant with his people:

> On the morning of the third day there was thunder and lightning, and a heavy cloud over the mountain, and a very loud trumpet blast.... And Moses led the people out of the camp to meet God, and they stationed themselves at the foot of the mountain. Mount Sinai was wrapped in smoke, for the Lord [YHWH] came down upon it in fire.... The trumpet blast went on louder and louder while Moses was speaking and God was answering him with thunder. (Exod l9:16–19)

The two accounts, that by Paul and that in Exodus, both refer to "clouds," "a trumpet," "the Lord coming down," and the people "going to meet" the Lord. Many of these details occur repeatedly in other apocalyptic literature. We see the trumpet in Revelation 1:10 and 4:1 as well as in Joel 2:1. The clouds appear with the eschatological "son of man" in Daniel 7:13–14. The archangel Michael is associated with the end times in Daniel 12:1–3. Michael is also described by the Essenes as an agent of God at the end times, protecting Israel during the great war against the forces of evil (*1 QM*17:6–8).[3]

Apocalyptic writers, including Paul, made efforts to use the same stage props in their descriptions of the end of the world, and these props are rooted in the ancient descriptions of the Sinai event, a description that Jewish people knew very well, although Paul's account here stands out from other Jewish apocalyptic description by the concentration of Sinai details. The details seem to constitute literary stereotypes. In the minds of the Jews, especially in the minds of the apocalyptic writers, this is the way the Lord is supposed to look. The dependence of Paul's description on stereotypes argues that Paul did not have factual information about the events at the Lord's coming. Rather, he was simply describing it in ways that would make sense to those who shared his apocalyptic mentality.

In the Exodus text, "the Lord" is Yahweh, the God of Israel. As a rule, when Paul is citing or alluding to an Old Testament text, he maintains the theological sense of "the Lord." Otherwise, "the Lord" has a christological meaning. However, in 1 Thessalonians Paul is clear that the *parousia* of the Lord is a description of the coming of Jesus. Earlier he prays that the Thessalonians are holy and irreproachable, "at the *parousia* of our Lord Jesus" (3:13). He makes the same prayer at the end of the letter referring to the "*parousia* of our Lord Jesus Christ" (5:23). "The Lord" who is coming (4:15) is Jesus. This subtle substitution of Jesus in the place of Yahweh alerts us to Paul's **Christology trajectory**.

2. The Timing of the End

In the description of the Second Coming, Paul seems to presuppose that it will occur soon. He seems to presuppose his own survival to that day: "We the living, the survivors, will be caught up..." (4:17). When, however, he deals with the question of the exact timing, Paul backs off: "As regards specific times and moments, brothers, we do not need to write you" (5:1).

Both in his presumption that the end is coming quickly and in his unwillingness to speculate about the exact time, Paul is conforming to a typical Christian tradition. We see this tradition in Mark's portrayal of Jesus' words, "I assure you, this generation will not pass away until all these things take place.... As to the exact day or hour, no one knows it, neither the angels in heaven nor even the Son, but only the Father" (Mark 13:32, 34).

Paul reminds his readers about the importance now of being "children of the light" rather than "of the darkness" (5:5), describing how this future unforeseeable event already qualifies the present. Paul concludes this eschatological discussion by declaring that now we are oriented not "toward wrath but toward salvation through our Lord Jesus Christ, who died for us" (5:9–10). This is a major theme for Paul, and we will try to follow it in the **salvation trajectory**, specifically including the theme of death and destruction as the vehicle of salvation.

G. The Conclusion of the Letter (5:12–28)

As Paul comes to a conclusion with this letter, he briefly alludes to several interesting points:

1. He refers to "those among you whose task it is to preside over you in the Lord" (5:12), giving here a brief glimpse of an emerging authority within the local community.
2. He refers also to the gifts of the Spirit. "Do not stifle the Spirit. Do not despise prophecies. Test everything; retain what is good" (5:19–21). Here Paul is insisting on some cooperation with this Spirit, adding an important element to the **Spirit trajectory**.
3. The conclusion includes a reminder of the "coming of our Lord Jesus Christ" where Paul mentions a view in Stoic philosophy of the human person as divided into "spirit, soul, and body" (5:23).

Paul ends with references to liturgical gestures, "the holy kiss" (5:26; see also 2 Cor 13:12) and the community reading of the letter (5:27).

III. The Thematic Summary of the Letter

Here our task is to summarize that theological content around the six trajectories, drawing together details from various parts of the letter, linking them where possible to prior theological positions.

A. God, the Father

In this letter, Paul does not present a developed view of God in any one section, yet we can find specific theological presuppositions behind the views that he does develop. To understand the **God trajectory** in this letter, therefore, we need to gather many scattered statements and presuppositions.

As we saw in the study of this letter greeting, Paul very quickly names God "the Father" (1:1), picking up especially on the postexilic image of God. He also refers to him as "our Father" (1:3; 3:11, 13). In Paul's authentic letters, only this Father is called "God" (*theos*), a title that becomes in effect the proper name of the divine Father. This God is "the living and true God" (1:9) toward whom one has faith, toward whom one turns in a conversion away from idols (1:8–9).

This God is present with his people and becomes a standard of human behavior. Paul stands "in the presence of God" (3:9), and prays for the Thessalonians to be strengthened in holiness "in the presence of God" (3:13). Unlike the gods of other religions, the God of Paul does not require some cultic action to make contact. No mediator is necessary to relay Paul's prayers to God. This God appears to be always present. Thus Paul can say he prays "unceasingly" (1:2) and can urge his readers to pray "unceasingly" (5:17).

Paul's own work with the Thessalonians as an apostle is particularly oriented to the presence of God. Paul remembers the Thessalonians before God (1:3). He gives uninterrupted thanks to

God for the Thessalonians (1:2; 3:9). In God Paul finds audacity to speak the gospel (2:2), which is in fact "the gospel of God" (2:2, 8–9). God tests Paul's heart, approves him to speak the gospel (2:4), and can witness to Paul's sincerity (2:5, 10). In contrast to any attempt to please and be approved by other human beings, Paul is trying to please and gain the approval of God (2:4). Likewise, Paul sees also Timothy his partner as a "co-worker of God" (3:2).

The intimate relationship of God to the Thessalonians is dramatized by the unexplained description of the church as "taught by God" (*theodidaktoi*) in the matter of fraternal love (4:9). The Thessalonians are likewise "beloved of God" (1:4). God wills "the holiness of the Thessalonians, that is, abstaining from immorality" (4:3). He calls them to holiness (4:7) and calls them "into his kingdom and glory" (2:12). In turn, the Thessalonians have "faith toward God" (1:8). They are to act in a way that is "worthy of God" (2:12) and "pleasing to God" (4:1). Like Paul, they are also to give thanks in all things. This is God's will "in Christ" (5:18).

At the same time, this is a dangerous God, the God whose "coming wrath" requires rescue (1:10). God, however, did not set us up for this wrath but rather for salvation (5:9). Paul echoes here the prophets' image of God who demands fidelity to his covenant. The prophets described the "wrath" of God against his sinful people as the serious consequences of national sin (Isa 5:25–26; 9:12–10:4; Jer 4:8, 26; Ezek 5:13). The "coming wrath" gave this theme an apocalyptic spin (Zeph 2:2; see Amos 5:18). For Paul as for the prophets, sin remains a serious matter. God does not walk away from sin but punishes in anger, like the demanding father of a rebellious child. Yet for Paul as for the Old Testament, the justice and judgment of God that lie behind his anger come from a justice that delivers (Ps 31:2; Isa 45:21) and a saving judgment (Ps 36:6–7). The final word of God is not wrath but salvation.

B. Jesus Christ

The **Jesus trajectory** likewise requires the gathering of scattered statements throughout the letter. First, we see Paul's insistence on calling Jesus "Lord" (*Kyrios*). In his Christian conversations Paul heard the formula, "Jesus is Lord." Throughout this letter Paul refers to "the Lord Jesus Christ" (1:1, 3; 2:19; 5:9; 5:23; 5:28) or simply, "the Lord Jesus" (2:19; 3:11; 4:1, 2). In the rest of his letters, this title will be Paul's favorite for Jesus.

Paul clearly distinguishes Jesus from God. For Paul, Jesus is not "God" since Jesus is not the Father. There cannot, of course, be two Gods. Yet Paul intimately associates him with God, and he can do this particularly by the title "Lord," the name that in Paul's faith functioned as almost a second or substitute name for God. This title for Jesus often occurs in the paired expression, "God the Father and the Lord Jesus" (1:1; 3:11; see also 1:3; 3:12; 5:18). Perhaps most significant in this letter is the way the title "Lord" is used for Jesus as he functions like God coming from heaven on "the day of the Lord" (5:1). Jesus embodies "the Lord," precisely as a name that normally points to Yahweh. From this earliest letter, Paul seems to be struggling to affirm some form of divinity for Jesus. Furthermore, this "lordship" is not something Jesus will have only at his coming. Jesus is now the Lord in whom the church exists (1:1), in whom the Thessalonians can now stand (3:8), and who as Lord can direct Paul's travels (3:11).

On the other hand, Paul is not clear whether Jesus in the eschatological scene is to be distinguished from the "archangel" mentioned in the text. The descent of the Lord from heaven is described with three details of sound, "with a summoning call" (*en kaleusmati*), "with a voice of an archangel" (*en phônê archaggelou*), "and with a trumpet of God" (*en salpiggi theou*) (4:16). Do the first two sounds describe some kind of ambient setting or do they describe the sounds of Jesus as he descends?

At the beginning of the letter, Paul names Jesus as God's "Son," whom we are to await from heaven, whom God raised from the dead, and who will save us from the coming wrath (1:10). This Pauline reference to the eschatological Son of God could possibly tie into the late Jewish expectation of an eschatological messiah,[4] except for the way Paul in general seems unconcerned about Jesus as Messiah. Paul's frequent use of "Christ" for Jesus seems more like a second name than the designation of a role. This eschatological "Son," a title given without explanation, appears to be already an accepted designation of Jesus.

Writing some six years later, Paul describes the revelation in which he encountered the risen Christ. "It pleased God to reveal his Son to me" (Gal 1:15–16). The event described in Galatians took place some eighteen years before writing 1 Thessalonians. Although the zigzag chronology makes it difficult to reconstruct the christological development in Paul's mind, it is important to note that Paul used the title "his Son" to describe his revealed understanding of Jesus. Paul saw this understanding coming from a direct intervention of God rather than as a development of his past religious education.

C. The Holy Spirit of God

Four times in this letter Paul refers to "the Holy Spirit" or "the Spirit" that is from God.[5] The first refers to the first reception of Paul's gospel. In contrast to receiving the gospel "in word alone," the Thessalonians received it "in power [*dynamis*] and in the Holy Spirit and with much conviction [*plêrophoria*]" (1:5). This is the first of many times in later letters that Paul will associate the Spirit of God with "power." The contrast with "word alone" suggests an inner transformation and thus the association with "conviction." Paul will later insist on the interiority of the Spirit's working.

In the next verse of this opening prayer, Paul again refers to the initial reception of his preaching and mentions "the joy of the Holy Spirit" that coexisted with the "great suffering" in which the word was received (1:6). For Paul, joy and love will become the earmark of the Spirit.

In the third brief reference, this "Holy Spirit" is given to the Thessalonians by God and is a reason for not resisting Paul's teaching (4:8).

The fourth mention of "the Spirit" deals with a continuing operation within the community. In a final admonition, Paul writes about not "stifling" the Spirit or "quenching" prophecies, while "testing" everything (5:19–21). The association with prophecies suggests the Spirit is seen here as the spirit of prophecy, as

Paul understood it from his Jewish background (see Ezek 2:2; 3:12, 14, 24; Isa 59:21; 61:1; Joel 3:1 [2:28]).[6]

The implications of the admonitions here are worth noting. The action of the Spirit appears as something that needs cultivation, something that could otherwise be stifled. At the same time, Paul sees the need for "testing" even what might be the work of the divine Spirit. We do not see the mindless compulsions of the Hellenistic rites sometimes associated with "spirit."

Paul's implied connection between the Spirit and the community is typically Jewish. In the Old Testament and Jewish writings, the special powers of the spirit were usually for the good of the people, not just for the individual endowed with the Spirit. Here, however, Paul is somewhat distinctive with his hint at an individual or personal relationship to the Spirit on the basis of some personal decision, namely, accepting the gospel. We find only isolated descriptions in Judaism centuries after Paul of a reception of the Spirit of God precisely because of one's personal goodness.[7]

D. Salvation

Paul describes salvation in the opening of this letter as Jesus "rescuing [*rhyomenos*] us from the coming wrath" (1:10) and as God "calling you into his kingdom and glory" (2:12). Toward the end of the letter, Paul describes something like salvation at the resurrection of the dead as an eternal conscious and communitarian existence in personal communion with Jesus. "We will be with the Lord [*syn kyriô*] forever" (4:17). "Together [*hama*] we will live with him [*syn autô*]" (5:10). Especially in this letter, salvation cannot be separated from eschatology and Christology.

1. *Agency in Salvation*

The description of Jesus rescuing us from "the coming wrath" is one of the few statements in Paul where Jesus is the principal agent of salvation, specifically saving us from God's wrath. In Jewish faith, the repentance of the people (Jer 4:4; 35:7), the prayers of great people (Sir 44:17; Wis 18:21; see also

1 Enoch 84:5), even the functioning of priests and Levites could divert the divine wrath (Num 1:53).

Without further explanation here, Paul attributes this rescue to Jesus, raised by God from the dead and awaited by the Thessalonians from heaven as the Son of God (1 Thess 1:10). In this description, agency for salvation is thus in some way shared by Jesus and the Father. Jesus rescues—but does so as raised by the Father from the dead. As agent of Jesus' resurrection, God will also raise those who have died, through and with Jesus (4:14).

Using a type of inclusion for the whole letter, Paul returns to the theme of divine anger in a more developed statement toward the end of his letter:

> God did not set us up [*etheto*] for wrath but to gain salvation through our Lord Jesus Christ, who died for us awake or asleep that we together might live with him.
> (5:9–10)

The statement corrects any sense of God being appeased. Here God is the active agent for our salvation from divine wrath. Jesus is the means through whom this divine salvation takes place.

For the first time, Paul describes the means as Jesus who died "for us" (*hyper hêmôn*), giving that death an atoning significance. Salvation comes out of death, out of some form of destruction. The thought echoes a broad tradition in the Old Testament of salvation through blood, whether it be the traditions connected with the Temple liturgy (Lev 17:11), those of the covenant ceremony (Exod 24:6–8), or those of Passover (Exod 12:1–27). For Paul, however, this death is not the death of the sinner or animal substitute, but the death of "our Lord Jesus Christ" through whom God sets us up for salvation.

2. *Scope of Salvation*

Who then is saved? Does Paul follow the current pessimistic view that only a few are saved (Matt 7:13–14; Luke 13:23–24; *4 Ezra* 7:45–91) or does Paul intend a more optimistic view? Paul does distinguish people now alive who are in a bad situation. He contrasts the holy behavior of his readers to "the Gentiles with lustful passions, who do not know God" (4:5). He contrasts the "children of the light" to those "of the darkness" (5:5).

However, he includes no such distinguishing at the end time. In the miniapocalypse Paul gives here, there is no judgment scene dividing the good from the bad, a scene that dominates many apocalyptic accounts (see Dan 12:1–3; *4 Ezra* 7:36; 8:41; Matt 25:31–46). Describing those involved in "meeting the Lord in the clouds," Paul mentions simply "we, who are alive, who are left" (4:17) along with the resurrected "dead in Christ" (4:16), probably also described as "those who have fallen asleep through Christ" (4:14). Paul is not clear about who these "dead in Christ" are. He does not seem to be limiting the group to martyrs. In fact, throughout the description here, he gives no hint of excluding anyone.

E. Union of Life with Christ

The theme of union of life with Christ is not developed in this letter, but there are hints of that idea. First of all, Paul promises future salvation as life "with" Jesus forever (4:17; 5:10). Furthermore, Paul's description of the resurrection, with its references to "the dead in Christ" (4:16) and "those who have fallen asleep through Christ" (4:14), is an important allusion to a life and a death somehow marked by a connection with Christ.

Scattered throughout the letter are other uses of the "in Christ" or "in the Lord" phrase. At the beginning of the letter, Paul greeted the church "in God the Father and the Lord Jesus Christ" (1:1). His readers are to stand firm "in the Lord" (3:8) as he beseeched them "in the Lord Jesus" (4:1). He mentions some who preside over you "in the Lord" (5:12) and refers to the will of God for you "in Christ Jesus" (5:18).

The word *en* in Greek could be very general as is its Hebrew counterpart, *b*^{e}, as in the expression, "In the beginning" (Gen 1:1). Yet as we will see throughout Paul's writings, something more is at stake here. Paul sees all blessings as flowing through some connection we have to Christ, as though we were "plugged into" Jesus. From 1 Thessalonians, we can only infer that the association with Christ expressed by the phrase "in Christ" is a relatively permanent condition remaining in death. It involves both

Paul and his readers as a church and as individuals with specific church activities.

F. ESCHATOLOGY

The theme of eschatology dominates this letter. It is mentioned in both the opening prayer for the whole letter (1:10) and in the concluding prayer of the first half (3:13). It is explicitly then developed in a major section of the letter (4:13—5:11).

In the opening prayer, Paul brings up eschatology after mentioning the sufferings of the Thessalonian church. The second mention at the end of the first half of the letter is also connected with the need for God to "strengthen your hearts" (3:13). The major development in chapters 4 and 5 occurs in the context of grief over the dead.

The problem of suffering was a serious one for the early Christians. After all, Jesus had died to save us from the death and misery incumbent on humanity because of sin, and he had risen or been raised from the dead. Yet suffering and death, wars and famine, sin and evil continue to be part of humanity's existence. Where is this salvation? Is our continued suffering and sickness the indication of our lack of true faith in Jesus and his resurrection?

The Jewish apocalyptic traditions of this time dealt with sin and suffering in terms of God's plan for history, a plan that provided for "evil times," especially in the times just preceding his ultimate victory (Dan 12:1; *Testament of Moses* 10: 4–6; *4 Ezra* 9:2–4). Christian apocalyptic currents held to the victory already accomplished in Christ but had to say, in effect, that the victory was not yet complete, that something was left undone in the redemption of Christ, that Christ would come again to complete the work. In the meantime, Christians were to endure patiently the distress of the times, never doubting either the redemptive power of God or the validity of their faith in Christ. Such suffering should be filled with hope, and thus joy.

In chapter 4, Paul appears to be thinking specifically of Exodus 19, or he may be unreflectively using the apocalyptic stereotypes that in turn depended on the Exodus text. Paul may thus be suggesting a covenantal significance to the *parousia* of Jesus.

In chapter 5, where he shifts to the issue of timing, Paul refers to the end as "the day of the Lord" (5:2) or simply "the day" (5:4). By associating this day with blessings, he is tying into the postexilic prophetic theme of a future definitive saving intervention of God, which also has dire consequences for evildoers (Isa 61:2; Joel 3:4; Mal 3:1–2; 23–24).

At the same time, Paul does not see the end time as totally future. He refers to the believers in Thessalonica as already "sons of light." They are already qualified by the end times.[8] In some way, the end times are anticipated to the present, into the life of the believer. This sense of a "realized eschatology" will become more pronounced in later writings, but it appears already in the earliest. At this point, Paul simply sets up two thoughts, vectors as it were, trying to move the reader in two different directions and in effect steering that reader in a third.

Paul expresses the purpose of this complicated description and hence the intended meaning of the whole instruction in verse 18: "Console one another with this message." This is a message given to convey hope and encouragement, not to satisfy intellectual curiosity about the end of the world. The important idea that pervades this apocalyptic description is the message of hope, the message that Christians will "be with the Lord unceasingly."

Paul is silent about life immediately after death in some spiritual world parallel to this world. The more common Jewish apocalyptic theology had developed the imaginative scenarios of one world succeeding another in a flow of time into the eschaton, at which time the dead rise bodily.[9] Platonic philosophy and some Jewish currents influenced by this philosophy had a view of parallel worlds, one earthly and the other heavenly, to which spiritual souls move at death.[10] If Paul here is trying to console his readers about their beloved dead, he could very aptly have referred to the souls of the dead going "to a better place," as we generally speak at Christian funerals. The silence of Paul about immortal souls and life in heaven immediately after death is therefore significant. Paul appears at this point to be thinking only in the more prevalent Jewish categories of resurrection at the end of time.

IV. The Message of the Letter

Opening this letter, Paul writes about the readers "receiving the word in great affliction" but "with joy from the Holy Spirit (1:6). A few lines later he praises the readers for the way they "turned to God" (1:9) "to await his Son from heaven, whom he raised from the dead" (1:10). The lines belong together as they form an interesting trinitarian description of Christian life. The Holy Spirit can bring the experience of joy even in great affliction. This is possible because the readers are awaiting the future coming of Jesus. Jesus is in control of their future. This is the Jesus whom God raised from the dead. Deliverance from affliction is assured. In this divine perspective of history, the joy that the Spirit brings is the joy of hope.

A good part of the rest of the letter describes this eschatological hope (4:13—5:11). Paul presents this description with its cosmic details to soothe the readers' affliction of grief. He does not intend his account of the apocalyptic trumpet, clouds, and movement into the air ("the rapture") to absorb the readers' attention as if the details could give information and control over the future.

As we read 1 Thessalonians from our perspective, we hear Paul tell the readers to focus their lives on the end times, the coming of Christ as Lord, which gives meaning to death, an otherwise hopeless core of life. We move beyond our lifetime to a broader perspective. The readers are not to deny death and its ugliness but are to look at a divine power far greater than death. They are not to simply distract themselves from the lines of rot that run through human existence, but rather to see a glorious and public union with Christ that brings hope and joy even in the midst of suffering. This attitude becomes all the more urgent to the degree "we the living" will be part of the final drama (4:17).

At the same time, Paul urges the readers against an unhealthy fixation on the end times, one that would distract them from present responsibilities. He does this in two ways. First, he excludes any calculation of the timing of the end. The end comes like "a thief in the night." Believers must be prepared right now. Present energy must not be wasted on such calculations. God and his absolute future remain mystery. Second, he describes those waiting for the end as already sons and daughters of the light. Believers are already qualified by the end times. If there is a joy and fullness associated with the return of Jesus, then that joy and fullness should be in their lives now and thus radiated to those around them now.

Christian morality is a morality of hope. It is also a morality of holiness, and this holiness is not just that of a future age where the presence of God transforms all things. It is also an anticipation of that eschatological holiness, one that begins now.

6

First Corinthians

Formerly known as Ephyra, ancient Corinth lay on the narrow isthmus connecting the Peloponnesus with the mainland of Greece. Settlements extended back to Neolithic times. The Dorian Greeks occupied the site from the beginning of the first millennium BC. In 146 BC, however, the Roman consul L. Mummius captured, burned, and razed the city, killing all its men and selling into slavery all its women and children.

After about a hundred years of desolation, the city appeared again as a Roman colony, Colonia Laus Julia Corinthiensis. In 29 BC the city became the capital of the senatorial province of Achaia and the residence of a proconsul. Because of its two harbors, Cenchreae on the east and Lechaeum on the west, the city prospered.

At the time of Paul, the city reportedly had a population of about 600,000, two-thirds of whom were slaves. The city was infamous for its immorality. "Korinthizing" was a popular euphemism for fornication. Typifying the sexual tone of the city was the temple to Aphrodite (Venus), the goddess of erotic love, situated on the Acrocorinth, a citadel on a towering peak above and behind the city. Reports tell of one thousand sacred prostitutes active day and night for the devotees of this cult—all fervent men.

Recently discovered among the ruins, a block of white marble contains the partial inscription of a building's name, "The Synagogue of the Hebrews," testifying to the presence of a Jewish colony in Corinth at the time of Paul. Corinth may have attracted many Jews expelled from Rome by the emperor Claudius in AD 49.

I. Background for the Letter

A. The Founding and Development of the Church

Unlike his Letter to the Thessalonians, Paul's First Letter to the Corinthians does not give us a great deal of information about the founding of the church. We can, however, glean some details from the letter.

Paul had come to Corinth "in weakness and fear and with much trepidation" (2:3). He insists that his message was focused on the crucifixion (2:2).

As the church in Corinth developed, it found itself exceptionally endowed with the gifts of the Spirit. This is a matter of special thanksgiving in the opening prayer of the letter (1:5) as well as the extended topic of instruction within the letter (chapters 12–14). It appears as a particularly "charismatic" church.

He can address this church as rather low on the social ladder, "not many well-born" (1:26). Given the general population of the city, we can surmise a large proportion of slaves in this church, whom Paul explicitly addresses in this letter (7:21). At the same time, we see evidence of many wealthy people within the community, those whose dining rooms could host "the Lord's Supper." Later writing to the Romans from Cenchreae, Paul sends greetings from "Erastus, the city treasurer" (Rom 16:24). All this seems to indicate a rather mixed group.

The household of Stephanas appears to be the first converted to Christianity in Achaia and as a result held some form of preeminence in the church of Corinth (16:15–16). This household was personally baptized by Paul, an exception to his usual practice (1:16).

Paul mentions Apollos as a person who had been influential in the development of the Corinthian church, and yet whose work had led unwittingly to factions developing within the community (1:12; 16:12). In Acts we also hear of Apollos at Corinth as an eloquent and learned Jew who was connected with the movement of John the Baptist and had become a follower of Jesus (Acts 18:24–28).

Acts 18 provides us with further details about the founding of the church. There we find mention of Aquila and Priscilla (known by Paul as Prisca), Jews expelled from Rome under Claudius, living in Corinth, who hosted Paul for a time. Paul, on the other hand, now writing *to* the Corinthians, mentions Aquila and Prisca as with him and sending their greetings back to the Corinthian community (1 Cor 16:19).

B. The Circumstances for Writing

Paul is in Ephesus (1 Cor 16:8), but is hoping to come to Corinth in the near future. He plans to wait in Ephesus until after the Jewish feast of Pentecost and then to winter in Corinth (4:19; 16:5–6). As he says, Paul already wrote to the Corinthians about not associating with immoral people (5:9). We no longer have this earlier letter as such. He also sent Timothy to the Corinthians so recently that Paul is not sure if Timothy has arrived or not (4:17; 16:10). Timothy is to report back to Paul.

In the meantime, either before or after Timothy's departure, Paul receives apparently two different delegations from Corinth. In the opening of the letter, Paul speaks of "Chloe's people" reporting serious difficulties within the church of Corinth (1:11). The second delegation appears at the end of the letter, where Paul simply mentions his pleasure of receiving Stephanas, Fortunatus, and Achaicus (16:17). These three men may have relayed a series of questions to Paul, to which he responds with the expression, "And now concerning…" (7:1; 8:1; 12:1; 16:1).

In fact, this letter to the Corinthians appears to deal with two types of issues—serious problems within the community and questions that the Corinthians addressed to Paul. The letter is thus highly situational. Paul is addressing the concrete concerns of a particular community, sometimes writing down stopgap measures until he can be personally present.

If we search the Acts of the Apostles, we find the events in chapter 19 a likely situation for the writing of 1 Corinthians. Paul is in Ephesus on this "third missionary journey" about to leave for Greece. There we hear of Paul sending Timothy along with Erastus to Macedonia (Acts 19:22).

C. The Integrity of the Letter

Like 1 Thessalonians, 1 Corinthians contains a brief passage that looks un-Pauline. This is the infamous command for women to be silent in the church (14:33b–35). The text has puzzled readers because of Paul's earlier instructions about women prophesying in church, a ministry that could hardly be exercised without speaking in church (1 Cor 11:3–16).

These verses in fact interrupt an instruction regarding the decorum and orderliness of prophecy (14:29–33a). With its reference to "the word of God," 14:36 looks like a continuation of these instructions for local prophets, as do the next three verses. The section on women, 14:33b–35, could be removed without disturbing the flow of thought.

Furthermore, the reference to the law as a norm of conduct (14:34) does not sound like Paul. The law has not been a topic in this letter. Moreover, writing a few years later to the Galatians and to the Romans, Paul will make an enormous effort to stop believers from measuring their conduct by the law (see Gal 5:18; Rom 7:1–6).

Some early manuscripts of 1 Corinthians do not have this instruction in this place, but rather place it after verse 40. This textual variation reinforces the impression that the verses were added after Paul during the subsequent recopying of Paul's letters.

D. Paul's Incorporation of Previously Written Material

On the other hand, other "lumps" in 1 Corinthians are very consistent with the thought and writing of Paul as expressed in this letter, and sometimes a later allusion in the letter to the lumpy section shows that this section was there from the beginning. We might suspect the typical meanderings of a letter, but the lumpy sections sometimes contain intensely thought-out and carefully composed theology (for example, 1 Cor 1:18–2:16; 1 Cor 13).

A simple hypothesis consists in seeing these other lumpy sections as written previously by Paul but for another audience and another issue and now incorporated into the letter that Paul is writing. Paul did not have any "cut-and-paste" buttons on his papyrus, of course, but he did have an excellent memory, from which he could bring forth verbatim poems and homilies he had previously composed or studied.

Several sections of 1 Corinthians in fact make better sense if read as composed by Paul but independent of Paul's immediate need to respond to the Corinthian situation:

1. The section from 1:18 to 2:16, along with 3:18–23, is loosely connected to the letter context and follows the general composition pattern of a rabbinic homily.
2. First Corinthians 10:1–13, not at all connected to the preceding material and very loosely to the following, appears likewise to be a rabbinic type of homily.
3. First Corinthians 13, Paul's poetic praise of love, is only loosely connected to the letter and has a very different rhythm than the surrounding prose context.

If we understand these passages as written by Paul—but apart from his writing of the letter—then the challenge to understand these passages requires us to approach them in two ways. First, we need to see the theology that they contain in themselves, which might far exceed their application to the Corinthian context. They are like little letters in themselves. Second, we need to then see how Paul applied these passages to the Corinthians. Typically, when he addresses a moral or practical issue, Paul does more than simply tell people what to do. He looks for a theological root to the moral problem and moves to the theological level. In the precomposed passage we need to find the theological perspective that Paul wants to apply to the practical issue.

Understanding these passages as written independently of the letter also warns us not to use these passages to reconstruct the historical situation of the church to which he is writing. Much has been written about the "Gnostic" terminology of 1 Corinthians 1:18–2:16 in an attempt to describe the particular Gnosticism at Corinth. If Paul actually composed 1 Corinthians 1:18—2:16 earlier for another group, such use of the text to reconstruct the history of the Corinthian church is a mistake.

II. The Sequential Study of the Letter

After the opening greeting and thanksgiving (1:19), Paul plunges into the problem of disunity within the Corinthian church reported to Paul by Chloe's people. He treats this topic, as we will see, within the broader context of the Holy Spirit and the Spirit's role in the life of the believer (1:10—4:21). Next, Paul treats three problems, probably also reported by Chloe's people, that of a case of incest, that of using pagan courts, and that of fornication (5:1—6:2). In the rest of the letter, for the most part, Paul then picks up a series of questions, perhaps addressed to Paul by Stephanas, Fortunatus, and Achaicus. These questions deal with marriage and virginity, food offered to the idols, conduct at Christian worship, the spiritual gifts, and the resurrection of the dead (7:1—15:58). After some concluding remarks (16:1—18), Paul closes with his usual greetings and blessings (16:19–24).

The following outline indicates the various problems and questions Paul tries to deal with in this letter:

I. Opening: Address and thanksgiving (1:1–9)
II. Concerning disunity in the Corinthian church (1:10—4:21)
 —Homily on true wisdom and the Spirit (1:18—2:16; 3:18–23)
III. Three major problems (5—6)
 A. Incest in Corinth (5:1–13)
 B. Use of pagan courts (6:1–11)
 C. Illicit sex (6:12–20)
IV. Response to questions and reported problems (7—15)
 A. Marriage and virginity (7)
 B. Food offered to idols and other matters (8—10)
  1. Eating food offered to idols (8)
   a. Paul's rights and life as an apostle (9)
   b. Homily on immorality and grumbling (10:1–13)
   c. Warning against idolatry (10:14–22)
  1′. Eating food offered to idols (10:23—11:1)
 C. Conduct at public worship (11)
  1. Men and women at worship (11:2–16)

2. The Lord's Supper (11:17–34)
D. The spiritual gifts (12—14)
—Hymn about love (13)
[Insertion? Women to be silent in church (14:33b–35)]
E. The resurrection of the dead (15)
V. Conclusion (16)

A. The Opening Greeting and Prayer (1:1–11)

Paul identifies himself by name and by his role as "apostle of Christ Jesus," a practice he will now use rather consistently in his letter openings. He is calling on his authority, probably thinking already of what he is going to have to write. Sosthenes, now Paul's companion, might possibly be the Jewish opponent of Paul in Corinth, the synagogue official who was beaten up by the Romans in Acts 18:17. If so, much has happened since Paul first visited the city.

Paul identifies his readers as "the church of God which is in Corinth," a much more pregnant expression than the simple "church of the Thessalonians" that he used earlier (1 Thess 1:1). *Ha-qahal,* ("the assembly") sometimes translated in the Old Testament Greek as *hê ekklêsia*[1] ("the church"), is often a reference to Israel as a whole gathered before God (Deut 9:10; 18:16). *Qahal Yahweh,* "the church of Yahweh," meant the same (Deut 23:2–4; cf. Judg 20:2). In this letter, Paul uses the term "church of God" for the group that he persecuted (1 Cor 15:9), namely the Jewish-Christian community. The expression "which is in Corinth" suggests a way in which the church is at once larger than the Corinthian community and yet is present in that community. In fact, Paul seems to be making a deliberate effort to widen the ecclesial scope to "all those who call on the name of our Lord Jesus Christ in every place" (1:2).

The actual greeting here, "Grace and peace from God our Father and from the Lord Jesus Christ" (1:3), from now on will become the fixed formula in Paul's letters. As we saw in 1 Thessalonians, the designations here of God and Jesus are important for the **God trajectory** and the **Christology trajectory**. Speaking for God and Jesus, Paul also says much about his sense of his own role.

Paul is faced with a delicate problem. The Corinthians have a good thing going with their bountiful gifts of the Spirit. Yet these same gifts have led to serious problems within the community, including a type of "spiritual clericalism," where one group felt itself superior to another because of its gifts. The result is a divided and bickering church. Paul has to move the Corinthians to a more Christian use of the gifts without stifling the Spirit in the community.

Paul therefore starts in his introductory letter prayer with sincere thanks to God for the Corinthians' gifts (1:4–7). He omits, however, thanking God for their faith and love, as he had for the Thessalonians (1 Thess 1:3), a thanksgiving that will become rather standard in his later letters. Instead, Paul singles out the Corinthians' "speech and knowledge" (*logos kai gnôsis*, 1:5). From the discussions in chapters 12 and l4, these gifts appear as forms of inspired discourse and insight about Christian mysteries. They are special spiritual gifts (*charismata*, 1:7).

The prayer ends with a reference to "the day of our Lord Jesus Christ" (1:8), an eschatological theme he brings from 1 Thessalonians, where he referred simply to "the day of the Lord" (1 Thess 5:2). Here Paul sees this day as "the revelation [*apokalypsis*] of our Lord Jesus Christ" (1:7). The expressions are important for following Paul's **eschatology trajectory**. Jesus is on center stage here, yet it is God who strengthens us for that day and who in his faithfulness "calls us into a sharing [*koinônia*] with his Son Jesus Christ our Lord" (1:9). Thus Paul introduces his **union with Christ trajectory** and develops that of **Christ**.

B. Disunity in the Corinthian Church (1:12—4:21)

Immediately after this opening thanksgiving, Paul accuses the community of a divisive and quarreling attitude (1:10–16). Factions are mentioned. Paul then jumps to his ministry of preaching under the shadow of Christ's cross. He is now ready to treat the issues at depth.

This extended treatment begins with 1:18 and runs through the end of chapter 2. Surprisingly, Paul in this section never mentions the problems of disunity or partisan spirit. Rather, he speaks about the authentic wisdom of Christian life and the essential role of the Spirit in that wisdom.

This section is punctuated by repeated use of the Old Testament in the manner of a rabbinic homily, selecting texts from diverse parts of scripture strung together by key words. This section is carefully worked out. The part from 1:16 to 2:5 is essentially negative, the judgment of worldly wisdom. The part from 2:6 to 2:16 is essentially positive, the spiritual wisdom possible for the believer. If we add 3:18–23 to this composition, we end up on the topic of true wisdom along with a "double-whammy" citation possibly characteristic of rabbinic homilies.

The section is also rather loosely connected with the rest of the letter, so that we can suppose this section was composed at another time, probably for another audience, perhaps a scriptural homily that Paul composed on the topic of wisdom and the Spirit in the life of the believer. What Paul does here is reapply these thoughts to the difficult situation of the Corinthians.

We have to understand this section first on the level of the original composition, where the thoughts far exceed the issues of community spirit, and then on the level of Paul's reapplication of this composition to the problems of Corinth.

1. The Spirit in the Life of the Believer in General

Throughout the first part of this homily (1:18–24), Paul holds up the cross of Jesus as a sign of the uselessness of worldly wisdom. For those "being destroyed" (1:18), for those without the Spirit, the cross is a stumbling block and an absurdity. On the other hand, for those "who are called" (1:24), for "us who are being saved" (1:18), the cross is "the power of God and the wisdom of God" (1:24). Paul's contrast with those "who are being saved" certainly appears to exclude from salvation those "being destroyed" in this development of his **salvation trajectory**.

In 2:10–12, a revealing role of the Spirit appears. "God has revealed this wisdom to us through the Spirit" (2:10), an important aspect added here to Paul's **trajectory of the Spirit of God**. This thought is not new. From the time of Ezekiel, Jews recognized the role of the Spirit of God in prophecy. Even the Hellenistic cults at the time of Paul often dealt with a kind of spirit-induced mania, from which revelations could be drawn.

In the next verses (2:13–16), Paul deals with the transformation that the Spirit brings about in those who receive him. Here Paul divides human beings into "the spiritual" (*pneumatikoi*) and "the natural"[2] (*psychikoi*). The labels Paul uses derive from Hellenistic religious language. Paul's intention is to insist on a permanence in the action of the Spirit in the life of the believer, not simply a transitory help for extraordinary tasks (see Acts 2:4; 4:8; 7:55). The Spirit transforms the very being of the human person.

In the preceding verses (2:6–9), Paul provides a contrast with the "spiritual person." He describes "the leaders of this age," the respected and powerful rulers who could not even grasp the meaning of Jesus. The lack of the Spirit in the lives of these "leaders" and the resulting ignorance of God's "wisdom in mystery" is dramatized in their act of crucifying Jesus, whom Paul here calls "the Lord of glory" (2:8).

For Paul, therefore, the contents of this "wisdom in mystery" revealed through the Holy Spirit is not some esoteric secret given to only a few. It is, rather, the basic message of salvation rooted in the cross. It is in effect nothing less than the gospel itself. This is the "gift" of God that is known by those who have the Spirit from God. This message remains incomprehensible without the interior revelation of the Spirit.

2. The Spirit in the Corinthian Community and Paul's Apostolic Ministry

Applying the homily on wisdom and the Spirit to the situation in Corinth (3:1–4), Paul attacks a moral problem by moving to a theological level. The real issue is not just moral weakness, a refusal to be harmonious and loving as a community. The real issue is a blatant contradiction in the life of the Corinthians.

The homily grouped people simply into two groups, those who have received the Spirit and those who have not, "those who are being saved [*hoi sôdzomenoi*]" and "those being destroyed [*hoi apollymenoi*]" (1:18), those for whom the crucifixion of Jesus is God's wisdom and power and those for whom it is a stumbling block. This is the same division as that distinguishing the "the spiritual" (*pneumatikoi*) and "the natural" (*psychikoi)* (2:14–15).

After having made this point in the homily, Paul then turns to the Corinthian church and says in effect that he cannot speak to them as people endowed with the Spirit. To suture the homily into his letter to the Corinthians, however, he has to shift the meaning of the classification "spiritual" and "nonspiritual." Here in contrast to the "spiritual" and "mature," he will have to speak about "fleshy people...infants [*nêpioi*] in Christ" (3:1). Nevertheless, their jealousies, quarrels, and partisan spirit are in such contradiction to the work of God's spirit that Paul cannot speak to the Corinthians as spiritual people. Despite their charismatic gifts, the behavior of the Corinthians puts them dangerously close to "those being destroyed," those for whom the crucifixion of Christ is meaningless. He ends up calling them *sarkikoi* (3:3), which roughly means "hell-bent on the flesh"—hardly complimentary for a church proud of its spiritual gifts.

As he applies his theology of the cross and of the Spirit to Corinth, Paul makes a reflection on the role of God's ministers, leaders like Paul and Apollos (3:5), whom some Corinthians are using as division banners. Here Paul uses the image of architecture, where Christ is the foundation and various materials of different worth are used to build, materials that will be tested by fire (3:13).

In the middle of this reflection Paul makes an enigmatic statement, "If someone's work is burned up, that one will suffer loss [*zêmiôthêsetai*]. The person, however, will be saved [*sôthêsetai*], but only through fire" (3:15). Paul does not explain. The presupposition here is imperfection in the ministry. The point seems to be an eschatological purification by God. The interesting pattern behind the brief statement, however, joins the **salvation trajectory** with some form of destruction. A few verses later, Paul refers to the time when "the Lord comes" in a revealing role, when "he will manifest the thoughts of hearts, and then each person will receive praise from God" (4:5). Nothing is said about punishment.

In the remaining verses of this section of the letter (chapter 4), Paul deals with himself and his companions as "servants of Christ" (4:1). He insists on his foolish and weak role in the plan of God (4:10). Like Christ, he suffers and has become like the world's rubbish, but he does so with blessing and gentleness. This is the pattern of ministry that makes sense only through the Spirit. This is the pattern of **salvation** that God in his "foolishness" and "weakness" has chosen for the redemption of the world.

C. Sexual Morality and Lawsuits (5—6)

In several places in this letter Paul deals with issues of sex and marriage. In chapter five he accuses the community of laxity or indifference regarding a case of incest. There he demands an expulsion of the culprit, "getting rid of the offender" (5:2). Paul adds an enigmatic statement, "Hand the culprit over to Satan for the destruction [*olethron*] of the flesh, in order that the spirit may be saved [*sôthê*] on the day of the Lord" (5:5). Comparing the expulsion of the culprit to the act of cleansing the house for the Passover feast, Paul adds another enigmatic statement, "Christ, our Passover lamb, has been sacrificed" (5:7). Again the **salvation trajectory** appears connected with the images of some form of destruction.

In chapter 6 he deals with sexual immorality in general (*porneia*). Somewhat reminiscent of the Stoic diatribe, Paul here starts by responding to rather sophisticated objections: one from liberty and one from biology. The first objection comes in the form of a slogan that rings somewhat Pauline: "Everything is lawful for me." Paul answers briefly, accepting the slogan but qualifying it, "not everything is good for me," and warning against another form of slavery.

The second objection compares sex with other biological functions, implying that the exercise of sex should be as morally unencumbered as other functions, such as eating. When we are hungry, we eat. "Food is for the stomach and the stomach is for food" (6:13). "When we are sexually aroused, why not have sex?"

Paul's response here is to reject the analogy. "The body, however, is not for immorality, but for the Lord, and the Lord is for the body" (6:13). Some functions of the body, like eating, are trivial. They have no significance beyond this passing age. Sex is different. It unites the whole person with another. It engages the whole "body" or *sôma* of the person. "Body," unlike "flesh" (*sarx*), has eternal significance. The "body" is a dimension of our existence common to both our present reality and also our postresurrection reality, as Paul will insist in chapter 15.

As he did for the Thessalonians (1 Thess 5:3–8), Paul links sexual morality to the call to holiness. He sums up his argument for the Corinthians:

> Do you not know that your bodies are members of Christ?…Do you not know that your body is a temple of the Holy Spirit, who is within—the Spirit you have received from God? You are not your own. You have been purchased, and at a price. So glorify God in your body. (6:15–20)

Here Paul is connecting sexual morality with the **union with Christ** trajectory, the **Spirit trajectory**, and the **salvation trajectory**.

Between the two responses to sexual immorality, Paul responds also to another objectionable practice, lawsuits before unbelievers (6:1–8). The response is eschatological, "Do you not know that we will judge angels?" (6:3), and an appeal to Christian wisdom, "Is there none among you wise enough to be able to judge in a matter among your brothers?" (6:5). This litigious practice appears to Paul as a way of cheating and being unjust to one's brothers and sisters.

At this point, Paul speaks explicitly of exclusion from salvation. The list of ten vices reminds us of the style of Stoic diatribes and is meant by Paul to explain the meaning of "the unjust":

> Do you not know that the unjust will not inherit the
> kingdom of God?
> Do not deceive yourselves.

> Neither fornicators, nor idolaters, nor adulterers, nor the effeminate, nor male homosexuals, nor thieves, nor the greedy, nor drunkards, nor slanderers, nor robbers will inherit the kingdom of God. (6:9–10)

As describing ultimate salvation, "inheriting the kingdom" is an expression more typical of Jewish Christianity (see Matt 25:34).[3] Exclusion from salvation on the basis of personal actions and vices is also a major theme in Jewish Christianity (Matt 4:7–10; 5:22; 7:21, 26–27; 25:31–46). Confronted with the discouraging lack of morality in his Corinthian church, Paul falls back on this Jewish background, expressing again an exclusionary note in his **salvation trajectory**.

D. Marriage and Virginity (7)

In chapter 7 Paul deals with the related issues of marriage and virginity. Paul starts by responding to an ascetic position advocating total abstinence from sex, even in marriage: "It is good for a man not to touch a woman" (7:1). This is the position of Paul's imaginary conversation partner. Paul responds, "Yes, but...." He, too, does not seem to have a high opinion of conjugal sex, but he insists that any such abstinence must be by mutual agreement (7:5) and according to the "gift" (*charisma*) that might differ for each person (7:7). His general teaching is to place virginity above marriage and simply accept marriage as permissible.

This general attitude regarding marriage must be seen in the context of Paul's **eschatological trajectory**. "In the present time of stress...I tell you brothers, the time is short.... The world as we know it is passing away" (7:26, 29, 31). In the light of the nearness of the end, Paul counsels radical detachment from the activities of this world (7:29–31).

The context is very similar to that of Jeremiah, ordered by God not to marry as a sign of the impending destruction of Jerusalem by the Babylonians:

> The word of Yahweh came to me: do not marry any woman; you shall not have sons or daughters in this

> place. For thus says Yahweh concerning the sons and daughters who will be born in this place, the mothers who will give them birth, the fathers who will beget them in this land: of deadly disease they shall die. Unlamented and unburied they will lie like dung on the ground. By the sword and by famine they will be consumed. Their corpses will become food for the birds of the sky and the beasts of the earth. (Jer 16:1–4)

Celibacy here is a witness against the future of the world, a witness that the end is near. Marriage and having a family is an investment in an earthly future, but the end of this age is coming quickly. Celibacy, of which Paul himself is an example (7:8), is therefore an apocalyptic testimony to God's plans, as above and beyond human plans.

Later in the chapter, Paul again apparently addresses rigorists who seem to be advocating divorce in all marriage where only one spouse is a Christian (7:12–16). Paul allows such a divorce where peace is impossible in the marriage (7:15). For Paul, however, such divorces are neither needed nor desirable where the unbeliever is willing to live with the Christian spouse (7:12–13).

The justification for this position is perhaps more interesting than the actual moral directive. Paul states that the unbelieving spouse is "made holy" (*hêgiastai*) through or in (*en*) the believing spouse. "For the unbelieving husband is made holy through his wife, and the unbelieving wife is made holy through the brother. Otherwise your children would be unclean, whereas in fact they are holy" (7:14). To the degree holiness and salvation are connected, Paul is adding a remarkable openness to nonbelievers in his **salvation trajectory**.

At the same time, this sanctification through or in one's spouse is not automatic or some form of magic. Paul allows the believer to divorce his or her nonbelieving spouse if the nonbelieving spouse refuses to live with the other (7:15). Here Paul expresses flexibility with the otherwise unconditional command of Jesus about no divorce (Mark 10:11–12). Paul explains, "How do you know…if you will save [*sôseis*] your husband…if you will save [*sôseis*] your wife" (7:16). The believing spouse does not have to assume the total responsibility for the holiness or salvation of the other, a responsibility that remains personal for each individual and remains shrouded in the mystery of God.

E. Offerings to the Idols (8—10)

After dealing with marriage and virginity, Paul picks up another question from the Corinthians ("And now concerning..." 8:1). What are believers to do about the meats that are part of the pagan religious ceremonies and then offered for public consumption? Some in the community have a liberal view. The pagan gods are nothing, therefore there is nothing special about the meats offered to them. Others have a much more scrupulous view. Participating in anything connected with idols is equivalent to giving up your faith. Paul deals with this issue at the beginning of chapter 8, before breaking off in digressions.

Paul's initial response to the issue of the meat is basically to agree with the liberals, "the knowledgeable" people, in contrast with "the weak" members of the community (8:1–13). These "knowledgeable" people are probably the wealthy people for whom eating meat was a common thing. In the midst of this agreement, Paul adds what appears to be a short hymn that becomes an important part of Paul's **Christology trajectory**:

> There is one God, the Father from whom all things come
> and for whom we exist,
> And one Lord Jesus Christ, through whom all things exist
> and through him we exist. (8:6)

God the Father has the traditional role as source or creator of all things and the ultimate end point or purpose of the universe. However, Christ appears also in a cosmic role. He is a type of instrument through which God creates all things and all peoples. Paul's point is to agree that the pagan gods are nothing. Certainly, they in no way compete with Christ, through whom all things exist.

Having made this point, Paul then puts the issue of eating the meat in a larger, more important context, possible scandal to others. Such misinterpreted but offensive action is equivalent to causing a weak person "to be destroyed [*apollytai*]" (8:11) and "sinning against Christ" (8:12), thus describing the weak person's extraordinary **union with Christ**. For the benefit of others, forego your freedom to eat, Paul urges his educated readers.

Paul then interrupts his thought to deal with at least three different topics. He begins with a reflection on his own role as an apostle (chapter 9), which he roots in having seen the risen Lord (9:1). Here he speaks about his rights or authority (*exousia*), mostly to say that he does not want to use them.

Instead, Paul sees his effectiveness precisely in the loss of rights. In almost poetic structure, he starts a pattern that he will use repeatedly in later letters to describe the way Christ saves through loss. The pattern involves a present participle describing a positive condition, an aorist active verb describing a contrasting condition, and a purpose clause (*hina*) describing the intended befits. Here Paul speaks about himself:

> Being a free person [present participle] in regards to all,
> I made myself a slave [aorist] to all
> so that [*hina*] I might gain [*kerdêsô*] a good number [*tous pleionas*].
> I made myself a Jew to Jews
> so that I might gain the Jews.
> [I put myself] under to law to those under the law
> so that I might gain those under the law.
> [I put myself] outside the law to those outside the law…
> so that I might gain those outside the law.
> I made myself weak to those who are weak
> so that I might gain those who are weak.
> I made myself all things to all
> so that by all means I might save [*sôsô*] some [*tinas*].
> (9:19–22)

Paul ends this topic comparing his strenuous efforts to that of an athlete, lest he be found disqualified (*adokimos*, 9:27).

The second topic of the digression is a homiletic-style story of Israel in the desert with a description of Christ's presence in the desert as the "spiritual rock that followed them"[4] and present in the situation of the Israelites "testing Christ" (10:1–13). It is connected very loosely to the following section in the letter by the reference to "spiritual food" and "spiritual drink" (10:3–4). However, the main thoughts of immorality and grumbling have nothing directly to do with the problems that Paul is addressing in this part of the letter. I suggest that this section is also a previously composed rabbinic style homily on scripture passages.

This story is meant to flow ("therefore") somehow into the third topic, which is a reflection on the Lord's Supper with its insistence on "communion" (*koinônia*) with Christ (10:14–22). These intervening digressions from the issue of meat offered to the idols afford brief hints at Paul's **salvation**, **Christology**, and **union with Christ trajectories**.

Coming back to the topic of meat offered to idols after the digressions, Paul repeats the principle that it is all right to "eat anything sold in the market" (10:25). However, the conscience of others like Paul should be a guide to decision. The point is not to seek one's own benefit but that of all, "that they may be saved [*sôthôsin*]" (10:33). The contrast between "being destroyed" and "being saved" touches the **salvation trajectory**. However, the contrast here is developed outside of an eschatological context, suggesting that earlier descriptions of "being destroyed" and "being saved" (1:18) might also be less than eschatological.

F. Conduct at Public Worship (11)

Chapter 11 deals with two issues that arose at the public or communal worship of the Corinthians. On the first issue, proper dress at church (11:1–15), Paul starts by praising his readers. On the second, proper celebration of the Lord's Supper (11:16–34), Paul starts by refusing to praise the group.

Paul's concern with dress at communal worship centers on gender. He wants women to look like women and men to look like men. He gives instructions for both. The distinguishing mark seems to have been the veil on the head. Paul did not like the unisex look. The real issue here might have been homosexuality at Corinth, an accepted practice among the Greeks.

Here Paul makes an oblique but important reference to women who prophesy in church (11:5). This speaking and teaching function was one of the most important in Paul's communities. He will deal with Christian prophecy at length in the next section.

Paul's concern with the Corinthians' celebration of the Lord's Supper centers on divisions in the community during the celebration. References to some going hungry (11:21) or coming in late (11:33) sounds like descriptions of poor people arriving at "the church of God," which would always have to be the villa of some rich person, a villa with a dining room large enough to accommodate at times the whole church of Corinth (see Rom 16:23). The meal appears to be an evening dinner (*deipnon*). Only rich members of the community could handle the logistics. In a culture where wealth and poverty separated people by social chasms, huge efforts were needed if the community was to function as "one body" partaking of the "one loaf" (1 Cor 10:17).

Paul wraps his scolding admonitions around a gospel tradition. This is the brief account of the Last Supper of Jesus with his disciples, which focuses on the words and actions of Jesus on the bread beginning the meal and the wine ending the meal. We have this account also in Matthew 26:26–29, Mark 14:22–25, and Luke 22:14–20. All four renditions are somewhat different. Paul's wording, by far the earliest, is closest to Luke's rendition. Both Paul and Luke have Jesus describe the bread as "my body which is [given] for you" (1 Cor 11:24; Luke 22:19). The expression recalls Paul's description in 1 Thessalonians of Jesus' death as "for us" (1 Thess 5:10) and suggests again the atoning or substitutionary character of Jesus' death. Both have Jesus describe the wine as the cup of "the New Covenant in my blood" (1 Cor 11:25; Luke 22:20). The description evokes the "blood of the covenant" that Moses splashed on the altar and on the people (Exod 24:6–8). From his Jewish-Christian predecessors, Paul is drawing a key element in his **salvation trajectory**. Both Paul and Luke add the explicit designation of Jesus' actions as ritual to be repeated: "Do this in remembrance [*anamnêsis*] of me" (1 Cor 11:24, 25; Luke 22:19).

G. The Spiritual Gifts (12—14)

In chapter 12 Paul begins an extended discussion of the diverse functions within the church, which he calls *charismata*, spiritual gifts. In this section of the letter, the stress is on the role of the Spirit, mentioned nine times in connection with the gifts. The gifts are called "manifestations" of the Spirit (12:7). They are given "through the Spirit" (12:8), "according to the same Spirit (12:8), "in the same Spirit" (12:9). "One and the same Spirit is at work in all of these gifts as he wishes" (12:11). The section is thus important for Paul's **Spirit trajectory**.

In this development Paul stresses that these spiritual gifts or "manifestations of the Spirit" are given "to each individual" (12:7). He had said earlier in connection with the gift of celibacy, "Each person has a particular gift from God" (7:7). Paul makes no distinction between a gifted "clergy" and a passive "laity."

Chapter 12 probably continues the discussion on the same church assembly begun in chapter 11, where he spoke of the Lord's Supper. This chapter spotlights the exercise of the gifts of the Spirit. Again Paul insists on the harmony and unity inherent in the gifts of the Spirit. There are many gifts, but they are all rooted in the same Spirit, the same Lord, and the same God, a parallelism that constitutes the first of several "trinitarian" expressions of Paul. There are many gifts, but all are aimed at the same goal, the edification of the church of Christ (12:4–11). Diversity and unity work together when the Spirit is present.

As he had done in his instructions on the Lord's Supper (10:17; 11:29), Paul draws on the image of "body," an image he must have heard from his Stoic acquaintances. Here he uses it to explain the possibilities of diversity and unity within the church at Corinth and the mutual dependence of its "members" (*melê*) in what he calls "the body of Christ" (12:27). The theme is that of a vital union between the believer and the person of Christ that produces a community among believers. This reflection is an important development of the **union with Christ trajectory**.

When Paul lists the diverse functions of the church again in 12:27–31, he specifically lists them as functions of body parts or members. The list varies each time Paul gives it, indicating that he is not attempting a systematic or complete list of roles in the church.

Here Paul shows some concern for priorities, describing "apostles," "prophets," and "teachers" as first, second, and third in the church, a set of church roles that Paul probably inherited from Jewish Christianity (see Acts 2:42; 13:1). Just prior to this list, however, Paul made a strong appeal against insisting on any hierarchy of honor. There Paul insists that the trappings of honor *(timê)* should gravitate toward the "less presentable" (*atimotera*) parts of the body (12:23–24).

The point here is an interesting contrast with the later view that offices like that of bishop are "noble" (*kalos*) (1 Tim 3:1). The voluntary associations or clubs at the time were deeply interested in hierarchies of honor and nobility. People who gave money to clubs or provided meeting places wanted to be treated as a cut above the others. Titles, special seats, and special robes in clubs constituted the only way hoity-toity persons not born into political power could experience such honors.

Except for the brief mention of rank as regards apostles, prophets, and teachers, Paul avoids any discussion of "who's more important." Instead he focuses on mutual dependence. The "head" needs the "foot" (1 Cor 12:21). Furthermore, all the roles and functions must be directed to some "benefit" of the body of Christ, which is the church (12:7).

Into this context, Paul inserts an ode to love (*agapê*, chapter 13). The ode has nothing to say about church unity. It reads like carefully worked-out poetry, composed at a time far more meditative and tranquil than that presupposed by this letter. Except for the brief mention of "prophecy" as a form of esoteric "knowledge" (contrast 14:3) and the mention of "faith" as a power to work miracles (13:2), the ode has virtually no direct connection to the discussion about diverse functions in the church. However, in Paul's mind this ode to love goes to the very root of the issue. As giving the ability to forget about the question of who is more important and noble, love is the gift that surpasses all the others, even the power to work the most spectacular of miracles.

As used in this letter, this ode presents a high moral ideal. However, as standing by itself, this text rings with subtle **soterio-**

logical tones. Paul associates love with the coming of "the perfect"[5] (*to teleion*) as contrasted with "the partial" (*to ek merous*) (13:10) or "the things of an infant" (*ta tou nêpiou*) (13:14). With its focus on opposite stages, its description of replacement, and especially with its description of the final-stage "coming," Paul seems to be suggesting something like the "two-age" theory of Jewish apocalyptic[6]—even as he uses concepts of human development. As a reality that comes, "the perfect" thus suggests an epoch that replaces a previous one. Morality is seen as life arising from the transforming epoch, rather than the term of human effort and development.

In its present context, the ode is an affirmation that the first gift of the Spirit is love. Without that love every other spiritual gift looks suspect. Thus, love is the key to a healthy church, where functions and positions are seen as acts of service not grounds for priority and honor (see also Mark 9:34–35; 10:43–44).

H. The Resurrection of the Body (15)

At the beginning of chapter 15, Paul shifts topics to the resurrection of the body after death. Apparently, the Corinthians questioned Paul on this teaching. Influenced by a Platonic depreciation of the body (see Acts 17:32), the Greek Corinthians could have serious difficulties with this teaching.

As in 1 Thessalonians (4:14), Paul starts, not with a philosophical refutation of dualistic presuppositions, but rather with the event of Christ's resurrection. This event alone for Paul is the basis of any hope in a resurrection for individual Christians. Whereas in 1 Thessalonians he says simply, "If we believe that Jesus died and rose…" (4:14), writing to the Corinthians here, Paul cites a statement of a faith tradition, already codified into a short creed, "I handed on to you first of all what I myself received…" (15:3-7). The traditional statement refers to the death, resurrection, and appearances of Jesus after his death, by far the earliest testimony of Christian faith to the resurrection of Jesus. Paul here speaks of the descriptions as a tradition already around AD 52 when he presumably "handed it on" to the Corinthians. Paul adds to this statement his own experience of the risen Christ (15:8). From this faith in the risen Christ, Paul reasons to the resurrection of Christians (15:12–19).

Paul goes beyond his teaching in 1 Thessalonians and deals with the questions of the why and the how of such a resurrection. He first deals with the significance of bodily resurrection. It is in effect nothing less than the ultimate triumph of God over sin and death (15:20–28). This section may be the most important contribution of this letter to Paul's **salvation trajectory**.

The description of this final triumph likewise picks up the thread of the **Christology trajectory**. Recreating the eschatological scene here as he had done in 1 Thessalonians, Paul describes the role of Jesus in a warlike scenario. Jesus is a person of divine-like power yet the one who clearly stands under God, the one through whom the saving work of God operates. The reflections on Christ blend into the **God trajectory**.

Paul then picks up the question of *how* there can be a resurrection (15:35–57). Although he scoffs at the desire to have a clear answer (15:36), Paul tries to explain. By a series of synonymous antitheses, he insists on a radical transformation of the risen body:

> What is sown is subject to decay; what is raised is incorruptible.
> It is sown ignoble; it is raised glorious.
> It is sown in weakness; it is raised in strength.
> A natural [*psychikon*] body is sown; a spiritual [*pneumatikon*] body is raised. (15:42–44)

The terms *natural* and *spiritual* are the same words Paul used in chapters 1 and 2 to describe the people incapable and capable of receiving the wisdom of the Spirit, those being destroyed and those being saved. The other adjectives in this description of the two forms of body appear in synonymous parallelism explicating what is meant by "natural" and "spiritual." The reflections on the role of Christ and God in the resurrection thus include a contribution to the **Spirit trajectory**.

With his description of the resurrection as the transformation from "natural" to "spiritual," Paul is trying to say two things.

First of all, he insists on a continuity between ourselves as mortal and ourselves as raised. What is sown is what is raised. This continuity is located in our "body" (*sôma*). At the same time, however, Paul insists on a discontinuity between the manner of our existence before death and after the resurrection. The resurrection is not simply the return to our earthly way of living. It is not simply the resuscitation of a corpse. The shift is from a "natural" mode to a "spiritual" mode. This discontinuity is located especially in our "flesh" (*sarx*). "Flesh" is left behind. "Flesh" does not inherit the kingdom—"body" does.

Paul's use of the term *pneumatikon*, "spiritual," to explain the risen body suggests a presence or action of the divine *pneuma*. The Greek adjectives ending in *-ikos* were used often to express the material out of which something was made, like the adjective *kerameikos*, from the Greek word *keramos* for a potter's clay. The Spirit, with its qualities of power, glory, and incorruptibility, begins to appear here as the very structure of salvation.

As if to explain the transformation of the risen body from "natural" to "spiritual," Paul ties into a Jewish interpretation of the creation of Adam that we find in Genesis 1—2, where the interpreters struggled with the double account of this creation in Genesis 1:27 and Genesis 2:7. Philo described the Genesis accounts as the creation of two Adams, one ideal and heavenly (Gen 1) and the other earthly (Gen 2) according to the Platonic view of parallel universes.[7] Paul apparently likes the interpretation but incorporates it into his Christian faith, where Jesus becomes the heavenly man and Adam the earthly man, hence the need to reverse the order of their appearance (1 Cor 15:45–48). He describes Adam as "natural" (*pychikos*) and "earthly" (*choikos*), while he describes Jesus as "spiritual" (*pneumatikos*) and "heavenly" (*ex ouranou*). From what Paul says about our future "bearing the image of the heavenly one" (15:49), it is clear that for us rising with a spiritual body is becoming like the heavenly risen Christ. This description of Jesus contributes to the **Christology trajectory**, although the exact meaning of a "heavenly" Jesus remains obscure.

On the other hand, if we connect Paul's multiple descriptions of this transformation of the resurrection with the "mystery" of universal change he describes a few verses later, we can see a vital link for understanding Paul's **salvation trajectory**. He introduces the new thought solemnly with what looks like a universal exclusion from salvation. "This I declare, brothers. Flesh [*sarx*] and blood cannot inherit the kingdom of God; any more then corruption could inherit incorruption" (15:50). He then goes on to insist, "We will all be changed," either through death and resurrection or through some other transformation (1 Cor 15:51). This is the "mystery" he declares. In effect, the resurrection of the body and the ensuing transformation become the essential conditions for "inheriting the kingdom of God."

The instructions on the resurrection end with another miniapocalypse, similar to that in 1 Thessalonians. We hear again of the now familiar trumpet. Other details, however, fade behind the message of hope: "Thanks be to God who has given us the victory through our Lord Jesus Christ" (15:57).

I. Conclusion (16)

Paul concludes the letter with a collection of isolated points. He gives his first instruction regarding the collection of money for the Jerusalem church, "the holy ones" (16:1). He adds the travel plans for himself as well as for Timothy and Apollos, indicating his own intentions to visit Corinth in the near future (16:5–12). He adds isolated instructions and greetings. The Aramaic prayer, *Maran atha*,[8] "Our Lord, come!" (16:21) reminds us of the eschatological tone of the letter and the deeply eschatological culture of the Jewish-Christian community that Paul here extends to the Greeks. He then ends with a blessing, "The grace of the Lord Jesus be with you. My love to all of you in Christ Jesus" (16:23–24).

Paul may have been a bit discouraged at the news of the difficulties at Corinth. His occasional gruff tone in this letter shows moments of irritation. Yet he is confident. "You know," he writes to the Corinthians, "that your toil is not in vain when it is done in the Lord" (15:58).

III. The Thematic Summary of the Letter

Our job here again is to summarize Paul's position in 1 Corinthians regarding the main themes we are following, if necessary gathering separated and isolated statements. We can also now compare Paul's position with his earlier writing, in this case, 1 Thessalonians.

A. God, the Father

By citing the Old Testament here in 1 Corinthians in his reference to God (for example, 1:20; 2:9), Paul is even clearer that his God is Yahweh of the Old Testament, who for Paul is "God the Father" (1 Cor 1:3; 8:6). This identification is not an issue in this letter, and Paul seems to see it as a normal presupposition of his thought. It will continue more or less as an unreflected premise in his later letters.

With even more emphasis than in 1 Thessalonians, Paul stresses God as active in Paul's apostolic role. Paul is an apostle "by the will of God" (1:1; also 4:9) and by "the grace of God given me" (3:10; 15:10). As in 1 Thessalonians, Paul describes himself and his associates as "co-workers of God." Here in 1 Corinthians he develops the image with details from construction and farming (3:4–11).

The church that Paul works to build up is "the church of God" (1:2; 10:32; 11:22; 15:9). Members of the church are graced by God (1:4) and called by God (1:9). They receive the Spirit from God (2:12; 6:19), who is also the source and "activator" of all spiritual gifts (7:7; 12:6). It is God who "constructs" the body that is the church (12:24) and "places" each of the members in that body (12:18, 23) by a special call (7:17, 24). Therefore in the church, God should be loved (2:9; 8:3), praised and thanked (14:18; 15:57), as everything should be done for the glory of God (10:31).

As in 1 Thessalonians, Paul sees the resurrection of Jesus—and our resurrection—as the action of God (1 Cor 6:14; see 15:4). Similar to the short description of the end of the world in 1 Thessalonians, Paul in this letter attempts one last apocalyptic scenario, this time detailing the way the risen Christ brings all things under the authority of God. Jesus himself is included in this ultimate eschatological subjection to God. "Christ hands over the kingdom to his God and Father.... Then the Son himself will be subjected to the one subjecting all things to him, in order that God be all in all" (15:24–28). God is clearly the supreme being and "head of Christ" (11:3; see 3:23), as he is the supreme purpose and end of all humanity, "for whom we exist" (8:6).

At this point in 1 Corinthians, Paul begins a related trajectory placing the eschatological saving role of God in the context of creation. Drawing on a Jewish heritage that developed from the Exile (Isa 40:18–20; 41:6–7), Paul insists that the gods of the nations mean nothing, because the true God created everything (Gen 1:1–31; Isa 42:5; 45:5–7). Hence, all things are "from God" (1 Cor 8:6; 11:12).

For Paul this God, however, remains a great mystery. Only the Spirit of God knows the depths of God (2:10). There is no way to "figure out" God or the ways of God. The actions of God clash with the standards of wisdom and strength of "this world." In this world, God's ways thus look "weak" and "foolish" (1:18–29). The result, as we will see, is a divine salvation through suffering, through crucifixion. To accept God, therefore, is to leap into a frightening mystery, supported simply by the belief that God is "faithful" (1:9). He is faithful by not letting us suffer beyond our strength (10:13). His wisdom is from eternity (2:7).

B. Christ Jesus

1. Jesus Crucified, Risen, and Coming

The foolishness and weakness of God appears above all in Jesus Christ crucified (1:18–25). The dying crucified Christ is in fact "the wisdom and power of God" (1:24). As crucified, Jesus is "the Lord of glory" and the sign that the wisdom of this age is not God's wisdom (2:8).

This letter includes also a great insistence on the resurrection of Christ and on the appearances of this risen Christ. Christ died, was raised by God the Father (6:14), was seen by various groups in the first Jewish-Christian community, and then by Paul

(15:3–8), an appearance that Paul understands to be on the same order as that to the apostles, thus making him an apostle (9:1).

This is the same Jesus Christ who will appear at the end of time in a warlike scenario active in the destruction and subjection of all evil powers and the subjection of all creation to himself (1 Cor 15:25–27). Like the figure of the Messiah in noncanonical Jewish writings, Jesus appears as an agent of God at the end times destroying evil powers and kingdoms.[9] As the eschatological warrior, Jesus here resembles Michael the archangel in the Dead Sea Scrolls.[10]

However, bracketing this portrayal of an all-powerful Christ is Paul's insistence on the subordination of Jesus to God the Father. "He hands over the kingdom to his God and Father.... Then the Son himself will be subjected to the one subjecting all things to him, in order that God be all in all" (15:24, 28). For Paul, Jesus is the one through whom God becomes "all in all," through whom the saving work of God operates. He does not displace the Father as the Most High.

2. Jesus, the Son

Jesus, the loyal vassal who "hands over the kingdom to his God and Father" (15:24), Paul names simply as "the Son" (15:28). In Paul's earlier description of God, Jesus was named as "his Son" (1:9). Referring here to Jesus for the first time simply as "the Son," Paul suggests the designation had become a title with its Johannine ring rather than the very general sense of "belonging to" or "characterized by" as it does in the Hebrew construct state, *ben-*, "son of...." The expression in its absolute form, "the Son" draws attention to a special quality of filiation that defines the person. The title seems to have its roots in early gospel tradition (see Mark 13:32; Matt 11:27 [Q]). I know of no parallel in Old Testament or Jewish literature where the divine mediator is known simply as "the Son."

3. Jesus and Creation

In this letter Jesus is also the medium of creation, "through whom all things exist" (8:6), a cosmic aspect of the christological trajectory that will be picked up and developed by Colossians. Does this cosmic "through whom" function imply preexistence? Is Jesus somehow with God at creation? As Paul plays with Philo's imagery of the heavenly and earthly man, Paul does say that Jesus is "from heaven" and "heavenly" (15:48–49). Yet Paul insists here on Jesus as after Adam, who was first (15:45–46). And the "heavenly" nature of Jesus seems here to be connected to his resurrection, who then is "a life-giving spirit" (15:45).

4. *Jesus as Wisdom*

Also interesting—yet tantalizingly vague—is the identification of the crucified Jesus as "the power of God and the wisdom of God" (1:24). In later currents of Jewish faith, the wisdom of God is personified as a distinct person alongside of God at creation (Prov 8) endowed with divine qualities (Wis 7:22–27). In fact, the pairing of divine "power" (*dynamis*) and "wisdom" (*sophia*) appears already in Job (12:13), where wisdom's inaccessibility and its presence at creation is also celebrated (Job 28:12–27). All this suggests that Paul is willing to play with the possibility that Jesus, who was crucified in time as a vulnerable human being and who will return at the end of time as the powerful Lord, was also with God in the way divine wisdom was with God from the beginning of time.

For Paul, Christ existed before his birth in some "spiritual" way. In the desert of the Exodus he was with the Israelites as "the spiritual rock" that provided water (10:4). This presence in the desert is definite enough for Paul that he can conclude that the moral sinfulness of the Israelites was a way the Israelites tested Christ (10:9).

5. *Jesus as Lord*

In 1 Thessalonians, Paul began a kind of parallelism associating Jesus with God, especially by attributing the title "Lord" (*kyrios*) to Jesus in contexts applicable to God (1 Thess 1:1; 4:16–17). The parallelism between God and Jesus is developed in 1 Corinthians. Paul wishes grace and peace to the Corinthians specifically from "God our Father and the Lord Jesus Christ"

(1:3). Paul is an apostle "by the will of God" (1:1; 4:9) and by "the grace of God given me" (3:10; 15:10), but he is an apostle "of Christ Jesus" (1:1), who sent Paul to preach (1:17). Paul insists he is "not outside God's law" because he is "within the law of Christ" (9:21). All things are "from God" but all things are "through Christ" (8:6). Inviting the Spirit into the parallelism, Paul also insists that there are many different gifts but "the same Spirit...the same Lord...the same God" (12:4-6).

Paul calls Jesus dying on the cross "the Lord of glory" (2:8). In all the New Testament or contemporary Jewish literature, the title shows up again only in James, where it refers to Jesus Christ, the object of a faith that should exclude discrimination against the poor (Jas 2:1). In the Old Testament the closest parallels refer to God as "the king of glory" (Ps 24:7–10) or "the God of glory" (Ps 29:3).

All these diverse descriptions of Jesus leave us with no clear and distinct christological identification. Rather, they form a spread of diverse vectors all contributing to some final but unexpressed direction.

C. The Spirit of God

In 1 Thessalonians, Paul briefly mentioned "the Holy Spirit" only three times, as part of the power and conviction of faith (1 Thess 1:5), as being joy in sufferings (1:6), and as the Spirit of prophecy (5:19–21). On the other hand, 1 Corinthians contains three extended discussions and two briefer mentions containing important details for an understanding of "the Spirit of God."

1. The Spirit and Wisdom

The first extended discussion consists of the rabbinic homily on understanding the crucifixion through the Spirit of God (1:18—2:16). Here Paul speaks of God revealing through the Spirit by allowing us to receive his Spirit, who alone understands the "depths of God" (2:10–12).

By associating the Spirit with religious knowledge, Paul is tying into his Jewish roots. These roots include the link between

Spirit and prophecy (2 Kgs 2:9; Num 24:2–9; 2 Sam 23:1–7; Ezek 2:2; 3:12, 14, 24; Isa 59:21; Joel 3:1 [2:28]). For the sectarians at Qumran at the time of Paul, the Spirit of God was likewise the source of knowledge of God himself and of his counsels.[11]

Paul's comparison of the "Spirit of God" (*to pneuma tou theou*) with the "spirit of a human being" (*to pneuma tou anthrôpou*) is interesting (2:10). This comparison is part of Paul's explanation of the revelation through the Spirit (2:10b–12). As he continues, the Spirit of God "scrutinizes" "the "depths of God [*ta bathê tou theou*]," as the spirit of the human being "knows" "the...of the human being [*ta tou anthrôpou*]. As common in Greek, Paul leaves out a word in this expression, but on the basis of the parallel expression and the grammatical agreements with the definite article, *ta*, we can read "*the depths* of the human being" here. Verse 12 then explains that human beings "have received the Spirit which is from God" [*to pneuma to ek tou theou*] so that we might know "the gifts of God" [*ta hypo tou theou charisthenta*].

The thought of Paul can be diagramed in the following way:

agent of knowledge		*object of knowledge*
The Spirit of God	⟶	the depths of God
The human spirit	⟶	the [depths] of the human being
We with the Spirit from God	⟶	the gifts of God

For Paul, this human spirit is a special element of the person along with a person's soul and body (see 1 Cor 14:14–16; 16:18), here described as a principle of intimate self-awareness. The parallels that Paul sets up here suggest a view of "the Spirit of God" like that of the human spirit, God's inner sense of self, his inner consciousness, his immediate presence of self to self. "The Spirit *from* God" suggests an externalization and sharing in that inner awareness. The object of such a sharing is not the depths of God but the gifts of God, again an expression that suggests something of an externalization and sharing.

Through the reception of the divine Spirit, human beings can share in a type of knowledge proper to God and his Spirit. In effect, the divine gifts can be known by human beings by a sharing in God's own self-awareness. For Paul, this Spirit communicates simply by being "received" (2:12), as if the very presence of the Spirit gives insight into the gifts of God. This is not the Lucan concept of the divine Spirit as a spiritual force in the community alongside human beings speaking into the ears of church leaders and instructing them from the outside (Acts 13:2; 15:28; 16:7). Rather, for Paul the Spirit of God reveals the depth of God to us by simple presence, just as our self-consciousness "communicates" our identity to us by direct presence.

In the context of the homily, the object of knowledge at issue is Christ crucified. By its presence in the believer, the Spirit can interpret this death and suffering as God's saving wisdom and power. Whereas in 1 Thessalonians, Paul spoke of the Spirit allowing the believer to experience joy in moments of general suffering (1 Thess 1:6), here Paul speaks of the Spirit as giving insight into the real meaning of Christ's suffering and death.

For Paul, this insight is so very important that any claim to being spiritual by a community where the crucifixion of Christ is not an operative principle, where bickering and divisions dominate over self-sacrifice, is a bogus claim (1 Cor 3:1–4). This insight into Christ's suffering and death is true wisdom, hidden from ages past now revealed through God's spirit (2:7–10).

2. The Gifts of the Spirit

The second extended discussion deals explicitly with the spiritual gifts (1 Cor 12—14). Paul roots the unity of the gifts in the "same Spirit," the "same Lord," and the "same God" (12:4–6). The parallelism of this expression suggests seeing the Spirit as a person in the same divine realm as God and Jesus (see 2 Cor 13:13).

At this point, Paul seems closer to the Lucan or more traditional view of the Spirit as giving extraordinary and unpredictable powers to individuals for the good of the community. On the other hand, he contrasts these gifts of the Spirit with the mindless impulses of pagan idolatry (12:2) and then insists that acceptance of Jesus as Lord is an essential work of the Spirit (12:3). Paul is stressing the unity of these actions of the Spirit.

In the next part of this discussion, however, Paul points out the mutual care and concern that should ensue from the distribution of these gifts. He uses the Stoic image of the social body where all the parts are in need of each other as members or parts (12:14–26). He concludes, "If one part suffers, all the parts suffer; if one part is honored, all the parts share its joy" (12:26). Paul starts this description of the body and its mutually dependent functions with the role of the Spirit in the individual's incorporation into the body. "For in one Spirit you were all baptized into one body, whether Jew or Greek, slave or free, all were imbued with the one Spirit" (12:13).

The stress on mutual care and concern leads Paul easily to think of "the more excellent way," the way of love (chapter 13). Presupposed here, perhaps, is the role of the Spirit at work in love as the spiritual gift that forms the foundation of every other gift of the Spirit. Paul will be more explicit about this role in future letters.

3. The Spirit and the Resurrection

The third discussion is that of the resurrection (15:35–49). Here the Spirit as such is not mentioned except in the description of Christ, "the last Adam," who became "a life-giving Spirit" (15:45–46). However, Paul describes the risen body as "spiritual" (*pneumatikos*), the same term Paul used in chapter 2 for the person who has received the Spirit so as to know the gifts of God. He contrasts that quality of the risen body with the quality of the dead body as "natural" (*psychikos*), the same term Paul used in chapter 2 for the person who is incapable of knowing the gifts of God because, presumably, that person has not received the Spirit. This terminology strongly suggests an action of the Spirit in the resurrection that parallels or continues the action of the Spirit in life. Further, this terminology suggests that the wisdom of the Spirit described in chapter 2 is an anticipation of the eschatological resurrection. In later writings, Paul will make explicit the role of the Spirit in the resurrection of the dead (see Rom 8:11).

The description of Christ as life-giving Spirit (*pneuma*) is a play on the Greek description of Adam as a "living *psychê*" (1 Cor

15:45, citing Gen 2:7). That allows Paul to describe Christ and Adam respectively as *pneumatikos* and *psychikos* (1 Cor 15:45). Paul is not so much identifying the Spirit of God with Christ as connecting the Spirit's work of making humans *pneumatikos* with Christ, who is "the firstfruits" of the resurrection (15:23).

4. *The Spirit Dwelling in You*

Besides these developed discussions, Paul makes several isolated statements about the Spirit that are important for understanding his "pneumatology." Twice Paul refers to the Spirit "in you" (*en hymin*) as in a temple. The first refers to the dwelling (*oikeô*) of the Spirit in the community of the Corinthians, making the community the temple of God (3:16). The second refers to the individual bodies of the Corinthians in whom the Spirit lives also as in a temple (6:19). Since the preposition *en* can be translated either as "among" or "within," the two references to the Spirit appear more closely aligned than in the English, where the first reference probably should be translated "among you." Nevertheless, the issue here is that of a relatively permanent presence of the Spirit with humans.

The temple image suggests the interiority of that presence. Paul suggests the aspect of interiority also where he describes the act of "receiving" the Spirit and by his comparison of the Spirit from God with the human spirit (2:10–12). Here Paul's debt to Ezekiel appears. Paul knew the text of Ezekiel where God promises to reestablish the covenant by giving his people a new heart and a new spirit: "I will put my spirit within you" (Ezek 36:27; see 11:19; 2 Cor 3:3). No other prophet in the entire Old Testament connects the Spirit of God to the interior of the human being with such an emphasis. This stress on the interior role of the Spirit will be developed in later letters (see Rom 8:9, 11; Gal 4:6).

5. *The Spiritual Rock*

Finally, the reference to Christ present with the Hebrews at the time of the Exodus as the "spiritual [*pneumatikos*] rock" (10:4) suggests a role of the Spirit in the unity between "ages past" and "now" (Rom 16:26–26), between the "old covenant" and the "new" (2 Cor 3:6, 14). Nothing is explained here, except to say that this presence of Christ is "spiritual," and therefore possibly attributable to the Spirit, whom Paul knew in his Jewish background as the Spirit of prophecy.

D. Salvation

1. *Salvation as Resurrection*

For the most part, Paul in 1 Corinthians as in 1 Thessalonians presents salvation as eschatological. Salvation consists in the resurrection of the dead and the life that ensues. "The last enemy to be destroyed is death," Paul asserts. With this final triumph, all of created reality will become subject to Christ, who will in turn subject himself to the Father, "so that God may be all in all" (15:28). As in Thessalonians, Paul is thinking in an apocalyptic mode. Redemption is not just "saving souls," or getting spiritual substances into a spiritual heaven. Rather, it is a transformation of all created reality. It is the subjection of all "powers" to God, through Christ.

Moving beyond 1 Thessalonians, Paul in 1 Corinthians adds a clearer picture of the action of God raising the dead as a radical transformation modeled after the resurrection of Christ. What happened to Christ on "the third day" after his death is the model of salvation itself. As the first of a series representing the whole, Christ is "the firstfruits" of this salvation as resurrection (15:23). Hence if there is no resurrection, "your faith is worthless; you are still in your sins" (15:17). The resurrection of Christ is not just an epilogue to the gospel, showing that Jesus was right all along, along the lines of the Fourth Gospel. For Paul the resurrection of Christ is the gospel. The salvation of the world begins in the act of God raising Jesus. The full realization of that salvation occurs in the general resurrection of the dead.

In two of the precomposed sections that Paul probably inserted into this letter, a nuance of realized resurrection appears. The homily on wisdom (1:18—2:16) describes the believer as "perfect" (*teleios*) and "spiritual" (*pneumatikos*) because that believer has received the Spirit from God. Thus the life of the believer should be characterized by true wisdom, revealed by the Spirit. The ode to love (chapter 13) describes the believer as having put away "the things of an infant" "when the perfect comes" (13:10). Thus the life of the believer should be characterized by love, the more excellent gift of the Spirit. The fundamental saving gift of God here appears as a kind of perfection or maturity that seems to anticipate the full transformation of the resurrection.

2. The Scope of Salvation

Paul begins the letter with what appears to be very selective salvation. The opening chapter categorizes people into "those being destroyed [*hoi apollymenoi*]" and "those being saved [*hoi sôdzomenoi*]" (1:18). He reinforces the issue of selective salvation by the specification that God "was pleased to save those who believe [*hoi pisteuontes*] through the foolishness of the proclamation" (1:21).

This view fits quite well into the Jewish apocalyptic context of the two eons, where often the first evil eon and what belongs to this evil age must be destroyed to make room for the "age to come."[12] For Paul this present world, or at least "the form of this world is passing away" (*parageô*) (1 Cor 7:31). Furthermore, Paul is clear, "The rulers of this age are being abolished" (*katargeô*) (2:6). In this theology, destruction and salvation are paired, although the destruction envisioned here is not the same as punitive condemnation in hell. The pairing of death and resurrection, even that of Christ, is part of this theology.

Significantly, Paul never mentions hell or eternal damnation in this context. Nevertheless, as defining the "outsiders," the situation of those "being destroyed" places them smack in the middle of this age that must pass away. Three other times in this letter Paul uses the verb *apollymi* (to destroy) to refer to harming or scandalizing a weak brother (8:11), to dying as a punishment (10:9–10), and once to dying in some definitive way in contrast to "falling asleep in Christ" (15:18).

For whatever its full meaning, this picture of selective salvation functions also to give identity to the believing group he is addressing. The development of social boundaries for the purpose of group identification usually involves showing the advantage of being an insider and the disadvantages of being an outsider. The two contrasting situations described by Paul in this opening chapter, "those being saved" and "those being destroyed," characterize people now, not after death or after some judgment. Paul is speaking of concrete people of his own time, including "the rulers of this age" and all those for whom the cross is foolishness in contrast to "those who are called." Paul is dividing people of his day into the "in-group" and the "outsiders." In effect, we see here one of the developments of social boundaries, necessary to transform a movement into a society.[13] Yet in other contexts, Paul foresees the presence of "outsiders" (*apistoi*) in the Christian assembly (14:23) and in Christian marriage (7:12–14).

An even more somber presentation of an apparently limited scope of salvation returns with Paul's list of people, characterized by vices such as fornicators, idolaters, thieves, and so on, who "will not inherit the kingdom of God" (6:9–10). This statement is a development of his pronouncement, "The unjust will not inherit the kingdom of God" (6:8). This somberness also appears in the restrained language regarding those whom he hopes "to gain" or "to save" (9:19–22). While his efforts are aimed at all (*pantes*), his hopes are limited to "a large part" (*oi pleiones*) or "some" (*tines*). We seem to hear echoes of a pessimistic sense of salvation found in contemporary Judaism where only a few are saved (see Matt 7:13–14; Luke 13:23–24; *4 Ezra* 7:45-91).

The letter genre of 1 Corinthians as moral exhortation may also help us understand better Paul's apparent pessimism here. He is writing to admonish the community. He is drawing their failures into view—hence, the role of warning and threat in the style of the prophets. Paul likens the efforts of the community as well as his own efforts to those of a competitive runner (9:24–26). This is not a time for overconfidence. Everyone—including himself—should worry about being "disqualified" (9:27). Writing both on restricted inheritance of the kingdom (6:8–10) as well as on his own less than enthusiastic sense of apostolic success (9:19–22), Paul's focus is on human activity and effort, "so that I might gain…so that I might save some."

At the end of the letter, Paul seems at first to intensify radically the limits of inheritance of the kingdom. "Flesh and blood cannot inherit the kingdom of God" (15:50). "Flesh and blood" is a way of talking about human beings in general (see Gal 1:16; Matt 16:17). What Paul, however, is affirming here in chapter 15 is not a general exclusion of all from salvation, but the need for the transforming power of God (see Mark 10:27 and parallels). He goes on to insist, "We will all be changed," either through death and resurrection or through some other transformation (1 Cor 15:51).

The result appears to be an affirmation not of universal exclusion but of universal salvation. This is the "mystery" he insists on. In effect, the resurrection of the body and the ensuing transformation become the essential conditions for "inheriting the kingdom of God." Paul basically excludes all humanity until it is subject to the transforming power of God. According to Paul's position on this point, even Jesus before the resurrection would have been excluded! The key element in salvation is not human actions and decisions but the grace of God that transforms the "natural" into the "spiritual," a grace that brings life out of death, a grace modeled on the resurrection of Jesus.

Although the limited nature of Paul's discussion prevents us from drawing clear conclusions, the discussion of mixed marriages in chapter 7 includes important soteriological presuppositions. Paul explains that one should not necessarily separate from an unbelieving spouse, because that nonbelieving (*apistos*) spouse is "made holy" (*hêgiastai*) through the spouse. Paul alludes to the holiness of children as a foregone conclusion. The allusion is based on this view of solidarity in holiness apart from personal decision (7:14). The holiness of the believing spouse is in effect contagious and can spread to an unbeliever simply by the close association of marriage. No conversion, act of faith, or personal decision is envisioned here. The nonbelieving spouse and the children are represented in some way by the believing spouse.

In this text about mixed marriage, Paul speaks of being holy (*hagios*), not of being saved. He contrasts this holiness with being "unclean," which is more an issue of ritual propriety than of salvation (7:14). Yet for Paul in this letter, holiness is something to which "the church of God" is called, and it is something that occurs "in Christ" (1:2). Paul places "being made holy" in parallel with "being washed" and "being justified" (6:11). The "contagion" of holiness in the family of at least one believing spouse seems to be quite relevant to salvation, which here appears the result more of divine gift than of any human performance.

All these diverse positions and images of Paul leave us in a dialectic formed by Paul's apparent pessimism and optimism regarding salvation. Paul is not offering us a choice of one position or the other. In effect, he is urging us to hold on to both, where one thought corrects the other as we move in a direction described by neither.

3. The Active Role of Jesus

Besides seeing Jesus as the model of salvation, the "first-fruits" of a series to come, Paul in 1 Corinthians begins also to articulate an active role of Jesus in our salvation, mostly with a focus on Jesus' death. This articulation is typically expressed through isolated one-liners about this role, suggesting that Paul is simply jogging the memory of traditional material or material he himself explained at length earlier.

In 1 Thessalonians, Paul had mentioned without explanation the atoning character of Jesus' death (1 Thess 5:9–10). In 1 Corinthians he repeats the idea as part of a tradition passed on to the Corinthians, namely, "that Christ died for our sins in accordance with the scriptures" (15:3). The tradition that Paul cites connects the death with "our sins" and emphasizes the plan of God in this death, "in accordance with the scriptures."

The Jewish background of this tradition appears clearest in the "suffering servant" of Deutero-Isaiah, who "was pierced for our offenses, crushed for our sins" (Isa 53:5). The portrayal of the martyrs' death as atoning for the people in the books of Maccabees suggests a relatively wide acceptance of this view (2 Macc 7:37–38; 4 Macc 17:21–22).

Paul evokes the atoning character of Jesus' death when he cites the Lord's Supper tradition where the bread is Jesus' "body which is for you" (11:24; see Luke 22:19). This same tradition connects the wine with the covenant and the blood ceremony (Exod 24:8): "This cup is the new covenant in my blood" (1 Cor 11:25; Luke 22:20).[14]

The blood recalled in this tradition, however, has the meaning more of a religious sacrifice than of an atoning death.

Earlier in the letter Paul writes, "Christ, our Passover lamb, was sacrificed [*etythê*]" (5:7). The context deals with expelling the incestuous man as one cleanses the house of leaven (5:1–8). Paul's remark, however, refers to the killing of the lamb the day before the Passover feast, which at the time of Paul was a pilgrim feast, one involving a ritual killing by priests in Jerusalem. The image here suggests salvation through blood, as the blood of the first Passover lamb on the doorposts and lintel saved the Jewish family from God's destruction (Exod 12:1–27), a gesture that was ritualized at the time of Paul by the sprinkling of lamb's blood on the altar.[15] This line in 1 Corinthians is Paul's earliest description of the execution of Jesus as a ritual sacrifice willed by God.

Switching the imagery, Paul twice states, "You were purchased [*êgorasthête*], and at a price" (6:19; 7:23). The two contexts of this repeated statement deal with, first, the sacredness of the human body as a motive to avoid sexual immorality (6:12–20) and, secondly, with slavery, freedom, and the importance of not becoming enslaved to other human beings (7:21–24). Although Jesus is not mentioned, the aorist form of the verb, "you were purchased," like the verb "he was sacrificed" (5:7), suggests the death of Christ as the definite past event that effects the purchase. The religious tradition seems to be drawing on the Jewish reflection of how one person's good acts can benefit others, earning a kind of spiritual currency that could be spent for another.[16]

4. *Salvation through Loss*

In a number of other places in 1 Corinthians, Paul connects "being destroyed" and "being saved," not just as a contrast (1:18) but where destruction becomes a means of salvation, like the death of Jesus. Paul makes the enigmatic statement about the incestuous man, "Hand the culprit over to Satan for the destruction [*olethron*] of the flesh, in order that the spirit may be saved [*sôthê*] on the day of the Lord" (5:5). He describes the imperfect minister whose work is burned but who himself "will be saved [*sôthêsetai*] as though through fire" (3:15).

Seeing himself and his associates as "co-workers" of God, Paul recognizes the same pattern of salvation through loss in his own work. He came in weakness and fear so that "your faith might rest on the power of God" (1:3–5). He insists on being a fool and becoming weak like the scum of the earth on Christ's account, while the Corinthians "are wise in Christ…strong…held in honor" (4:10). Below the sarcasm in Paul's tone here, we see the familiar pattern, which he repeats later without the admonishing tone: "Being free in all respects I made myself a slave to all so as to gain a large part.… I made myself all things to all so that by all means I might save some" (9:19–22). Paul's success depends far less on his academic brilliance than on his weakness and loss. If God's power enters the world looking like weakness and foolishness, Paul becomes God's co-worker by being drawn like the prophets into God's pathos.

E. Union of Life with Christ

1. Sharing in Christ

Opening the letter, Paul thanks the God by whom "you were called to a sharing [*koinônia*] with Christ" (1:9). Later in the letter, Paul will speak of the blessing cup of the Lord's Supper as "a sharing [*koinônia*] in the blood of Christ" and the bread that is broken as "a sharing in the body of Christ" (10:16). The word could mean an association or fellowship when directed to persons and a type of participation when directed to things or actions. These texts are the first of many times Paul will use the term.[17] In 1 Corinthians the sharing or association is consistently related to Christ.

2. In Christ

As in 1 Thessalonians, Paul peppers his Letter to the Corinthians with the phrases "in Christ" or "in the Lord." Three times "in Christ" refers to an action of God for the Corinthians, as in the thanksgiving for the grace of God bestowed on them "in Christ" (1:4) or the promise "in Christ we will be brought to life" (15:22; see 1:30). Seven times "in Christ" or "in the Lord" refers to a relationship connecting Paul with the community, as in the way Paul becomes their father "in Christ" (4:15) or the way Paul sees his work and the seal of his apostolate as "you in the Lord" (9:1; see 4:17; 15:31; 16:19, 24). Six times the phrases simply qualify the Corinthians or other human beings, as in the description of the Corinthians as "infants in Christ" (3:1) or "wise in Christ" (4:10; see 7:39; 11:11; 15:18, 19, 58).

Again, the indeterminate nature of the phrases makes it difficult to understand what Paul intends to say. However, the description of graces of God bestowed in Christ and especially the description of being brought to life in Christ by God both suggest Christ as the medium through which God acts on behalf of other people. Such a medium would bring Paul and his community together and would in general qualify people in their Christian status. Being "in Christ" would mean being in the medium by which we can receive God's saving activity. The resurrection of Christ can therefore be seen as "the firstfruits" of the resurrection, the first of a series, the representation of the whole, because Christians are raised from the dead by an action of God in Christ (15:23).

3. *The Body of Christ*

In 1 Corinthians, Paul makes a great effort to connect this life in union with Christ to something that happens through the church. Paul uses the Stoic image of "the body"[18] to describe the church and then identifies that body as "the body of Christ." By naming this church body "the body of Christ" (12:27) into which Christians are incorporated, however, Paul moves the metaphor beyond the Stoic usage. For Paul "the body" as a whole is much bigger than the sum of its members and exists prior to its members, into which they are incorporated. The whole is nothing less than Christ himself.

Paul's point here not only underlines the mutual dependencies within the church but also accentuates the intense union of the church as a whole with Christ and the intense union of the individual believer as a gifted "member" of Christ (see also 6:15). Christians do not simply together form a body; they are incorporated into a body that already is Christ. They are "baptized into one body" (12:13).

Thus, divisions within the church are equivalent to attempts to divide Christ (1:13). Sinning against a weak member of the church is equivalent to sinning against Christ (8:12). The imagery and message here are very close to the Matthean view of Christ present in the suffering of "the least of my brethren" (Matt 25:35–45).

Paul states, "If one member of the body suffers, all suffer. If one member is honored, all share its joy" (1 Cor 12:26). The primary sense here in Paul's mind is the need to show concern for others in the body. Honor must not be seen as the property of any one member.

In the light of the Paul's view about union with Christ, another deeper meaning surfaces that reflects Paul's view of salvation and the role of all members of the body in that salvation. The suggestion that lurks below the surface is the way in which all members of the body suffer because Christ suffered, the way in which all members of the body work at the salvation of the world, because Christ suffered and died for our sins.

F. Eschatology

Connecting again to the prophetic theme of "the day of the Lord," Paul brings his opening prayer to a close by turning his gaze toward the "the day of our Lord Jesus Christ" (1:8), described as a day of "the revelation of our Lord Jesus Christ" (1:7). Paul connects the spiritual gifts of the Corinthians with their waiting for that revelation, thus giving an eschatological color to those gifts.

In effect, this prayer prepares for the end of the letter, where Paul dedicates an entire chapter to describing that "day of the Lord" with its general resurrection and the ultimate triumph of God over all enemies (chapter 15). During his stay at Corinth about five years earlier, Paul had written to the Thessalonians about resurrection (1 Thess 4:13–18). There he simply insisted on its certainty as an event that will allow the dead to participate in the return of Jesus. Writing now to the Corinthians, he repeats the point that our faith in the general resurrection is based on our faith in the resurrection of Jesus (1 Cor 15:3–7). The resurrection of Jesus must be seen as the "firstfruits" of this general resurrection (15:23). Therefore, the resurrection of Jesus must be seen as the beginning of the end of the world. The end has already begun in a small but representative portion of the universe, namely, the human body of Jesus.

So likewise the spiritual transformation of the body from "natural" to "spiritual" at the end (15:42–44) is also anticipated in the present in the transformation of the community of "those called" from "natural" to "spiritual" people (2:14–15). The eschatological spirit of Joel 3 is already present in the church, as Luke clearly saw (Acts 2:16–21). Paul sees this spirit in the Spirit received by the believer and especially in the spiritual gifts of God to the church.

Paul, however, envisioned much more to come. We are to wait "until the Lord comes" (4:5). We are to remember and proclaim the death of Jesus at the Lord's Supper "until he comes" (11:26). At that coming, Jesus "will bring to light what is hidden in darkness and will manifest the motives of our hearts, and then everyone will receive praise from God" (4:5). Following Jewish eschatology, Paul sees this moment as the time when "the holy ones will judge the world" (6:2), and "we will judge angels" (6:3; see Wis 3:8; Sir 4:15; Matt 19:28). The only mention of God as the future judge deals with "outsiders" (5:13).

Paul's practical teaching regarding marriage and virginity in chapter 7 is dominated by the thought of an impending kingdom. "Time is running out" (7:29). The present time is a time of distress (7:26), for "the world in its present form is passing away" (7:31). Paul presents this eschatological urgency as a motive for "using the world as if not using it" (7:30). Thus, he advises staying in one's social status (7:14–28). This advice presupposes an end coming in the lifetime of his readers, a position similar to that which we see in 1 Thessalonians where Paul presumed "we the living" will be caught up in the clouds to meet the Lord (1 Thess 4:17). Paul's recommendation of his own celibate state for the same eschatological reason (1 Cor 7:32) reminds us of Jeremiah, whose celibate state was a sign that the world as he knew it was coming to an end (Jer 16:1–4).

In this letter, perhaps more than all his other letters combined, Paul uses "kingdom of God" language to describe this future eschatology. This is a kingdom that comes "in power" not just "in words" (4:20). This is a kingdom that is to be "inherited" (6:9–10) but by such a select group of heirs that no one would qualify were it not for God's power to transform "flesh and blood" into the "spiritual body" (15:50). This is the kingdom that Christ at the end "hands over to God" (15:24).

IV. The Message of the Letter

First Corinthians speaks to readers who are worried about the church and about Christian life in a vicious world. The letter proclaims basic principles of constancy and reform: reminders of the mysterious wisdom and power of God, which appear in this world as foolishness and weakness, reminders of the Spirit who alone will attune believers to God's ways, reminders of the need for moral discipline, but above all reminders of the love that allows diverse functions in the church to serve the edification of the whole.

At this point Paul is not discouraged by the failures of the Corinthians. The church of Corinth is the construction site of God, and Paul is just a worker at that site. He is working with many others whose contributions are of various worth, some like gold, some like straw. Unlike Matthew, Paul does not see their failings as the work of "the enemy" (Matt 13:28). Like Matthew, he does see the need for an eschatological fire, but for Paul that eschatological fire purifies and saves.

Ultimately, the fire of death and burial opens the way for God to raise up new life characterized by the Spirit. The topic of the resurrection of the dead may have arisen in this letter because of some doctrinal dispute. But faith in the resurrection is also his faith in the ultimate success of the Corinthian community. This success will be the work of God, transforming a corruptible body, a lowly body, a weak body into one that is incorruptible, glorious, and powerful—a truly spiritual body. Salvation will come through loss and destruction. The Spirit who allows joy to coexist with suffering can bring life out of death.

7

Second Corinthians

I. Background for the Letter

A. Events Leading Up to the Letter

The "newsy" sections of 2 Corinthians provide many surprises. In 1 Corinthians we left Paul in Ephesus ready to come to the Corinthians. Not a great deal of time has passed. The collection of funds that Paul announced in 1 Corinthians 16:1–4 is now nearing completion, as we can see in 2 Corinthians 8—9. However, Paul is now in Macedonia defending several recent actions he took in what appears to have been a serious breakdown of relationships between the apostle and his community. The events seem to be as follows:

1. Timothy apparently returned from Corinth with bad news. In 1 Corinthians, we read of Timothy's mission to Corinth and his expected return to Paul in Ephesus (1 Cor 4:17; 16:10–11). Now Timothy is with Paul (2 Cor 1:1).
2. Paul then made a special trip to Corinth. This visit "in painful circumstances" (2:1) does not look like the first trip of Paul to Corinth, when he founded the church. Rather, this trip was one on which he received some serious offense, for which some individual was responsible (2:5–8). This trip would explain how Paul can write about coming to Corinth "a third time" (12:14; 13:1).
3. This painful trip does not seem to have been successful because Paul then mentions two actions he had to take. The first is a mission to the Corinthians of Titus and an

unnamed "brother" (12:18). Paul was quite concerned about Titus's mission and became more and more worried as Titus was away (2:12–13; 7:5–7).

4. The second action of Paul was a letter that he wrote "in tears" to this church (2:4), a letter that eventually led the Corinthians to sorrow and repentance (7:8–9). This letter does not sound like 1 Corinthians. Hence, we now have evidence for speaking of at least four letters of Paul to the Corinthians: the "earlier letter" mentioned in 1 Corinthians (1 Cor 5:9), 1 Corinthians, "the letter in tears," and 2 Corinthians.
5. Paul then meets Titus in Macedonia and receives a reassuring report about the Corinthians (2 Cor 7:7–8). It is in response to this report that Paul writes 2 Corinthians—or at least a good part of what we call 2 Corinthians.

Acts 20:1–3 is the only place in the Lucan account where we can find a possible correspondence. There Paul is on his third journey. He leaves Ephesus and travels through Macedonia to Greece, where he spends three months before returning to the Middle East. No other details are given.

B. The Integrity and Editing of the Letter

As it appears today, 2 Corinthians breaks down into three easily defined sections: chapters 1–7, where Paul reflects on his reconciliation with the community; chapters 8–9, where Paul asks for help completing a collection of money intended for the Jerusalem church; and chapters 10–13, where Paul argues at times with sardonic bitterness about his authority.

Chapters 8 and 9, where Paul describes the collection he is coming to get and bring to Jerusalem, may have been composed separately. Both together as they now stand may not have been part of this letter of reconciliation. The question is almost impossible to resolve and makes little difference for our understanding. Seeing them as originally part of the whole letter does not pose any great problems.

On the other hand, chapters 10–13 seem incredibly out of place after an appeal for money. They seem to contradict the reconciliation described in the earlier part of the letter (contrast 7:16 with 10:9–10). They could in fact be at least part of the lost "letter in tears." If this is so, then we must think of an editor after Paul, probably from Corinth, joining "the letter in tears" to "the letter of reconciliation." As the letters of Paul were being exchanged between the churches, such editing would preserve the precious but embarrassing letter of bitter admonition, placing it in the more positive context of Paul's reconciliatory letter. This hypothesis allows the whole letter to make better sense.

Another, much smaller section of 2 Corinthians likewise fits poorly in its context, suggesting also the work of a later redactor. This is the section from 6:14 to 7:1. The material in 6:14—7:1 interrupts the flow of thought from 6:13 to 7:2 and corresponds in content to the very first letter Paul wrote to the Corinthians, as described in 1 Corinthians 5:9. It deals with not associating with immoral people. We could have at least a fragment of that very first letter now embedded here in 2 Corinthians. We will treat it as such. No clear reason appears, though, why any editor would have placed it here.

Interesting also is the way in which 1:8—2:17, describing recent events, flows directly into 7:5–16, also describing recent events. Perhaps an editor is responsible for this split. However, no real difficulty exists in seeing Paul organizing the letter in this way. As written by Paul, the two sections on recent events form a neat inclusion for the doctrinal section of the letter. The mention of consolation and affliction in 7:4 could easily lead Paul back to the topic of recent events, just as he introduced those recent events in the first place by references to afflictions and consolation (1:3–7). This verse thus becomes a hinge.

II. The Sequential Study of the Letter

The overall outline of 2 Corinthians as we now have it seems as follows:

I. Introduction: Greeting and prayer (1:1–14)
II. Part One: The letter of reconciliation (1—9)
  A. Paul and the Corinthians
    1. Recent events (1:15—2:13)
    2. Paul's theology
      a. Prayer (2:14–17)
      b. The ministry of the new covenant (3:1—4:6)
      c. Life and death in Paul's ministry (4:7—5:10)
      d. The ministry of reconciliation (5:11—7:4)
        [Insertion: Fragment of the early letter? (6:14—7:1)]
    1′. Recent events (7:4–16)
  B. The collection for Jerusalem (8—9)
    1. First appeal (8)
    2. Second appeal (9)
III. Part Two: The angry letter (10—13)
  A. Defense against accusations (10:1—11:15)
  B. Paul's foolish boasts (11:16—12:4)
  A′. Defense against accusations (12:5—13:10)
IV. Conclusion (13:11–13).

Our sequential look will follow the apparent chronological order of these letters. We will take a brief look at 6:14—7:1, then chapters 10–13 as perhaps a part of the earlier "letter in tears" written from Ephesus, then chapters 1–9 as Paul's last letter to the Corinthians written from Macedonia.

A. The Very Early Letter (2 Cor 6:14—7:1)

This letter, or letter fragment, in 6:14—7:1 reflects the separatism characteristic of pharisaic Judaism, a position that Paul himself once held (see Phil 3:5). The five rhetorical questions: "What partnership…? What fellowship…? What accord…? What in common…? What agreement…?" (6:14b–16a) all call for the answer, "None at all!" There is no compromise between good and evil.

The tone of this text is very Jewish. Beliar (or Beliel) was a Jewish name for the devil,[1] not otherwise used by Paul. "Cleansing oneself from defilement" is similar to expressions found in the

Jewish Dead Sea Scrolls[2] and reflects the general Jewish concern for ritual purity. The instruction, "Clear out the old yeast," refers to the Jewish ritual housecleaning of Passover. This last image is one Paul used for his instructions to expel the incestuous man in Corinth (1 Cor 5:6–8). On the other hand, the reference here to "the promises" of God in connection with a group of citations starting with Leviticus 26:12 is unusual for Paul. When Paul writes Galatians, "the promises" of God will refer to God's words to Abraham about progeny and be clearly distinguished from the law given to Moses (Gal 3:16–18). A strong argument, therefore, could be made that Paul did not write this text.

However, since the content of these lines corresponds at least somewhat to what Paul says he wrote in his first letter, we will consider the possibility that it reflects Paul's early thought. Whatever conclusion we come to regarding the origins of this text in 2 Corinthians, its "lumpy" appearance in the whole letter means we ought to read and understand the text apart from the situation in Corinth that Paul is now addressing and apart from the mentality Paul otherwise shows in 2 Corinthians.

B. The Angry Letter (2 Cor 10–13)

In this part of the letter, Paul speaks a great deal about himself and his relationship with the Corinthians. We find no explicit and developed theological expositions on Paul's favorite themes, but we do find important theological presuppositions in Paul's defense of himself.

Although Paul writes these chapters in an oral mode, freely moving from one topic to another, the whole section exhibits a well-organized chiastic structure:

A. Defense against accusations (10:1—11:15)
  B. Paul's foolish boasts (11:16—12:4)
A'. Defense against accusations (12:5—13:10)

In his defense against weakness, especially as he is compared with rival apostles, Paul begins and ends by reflections on "weakness" and "power" as perceived in faith (A—A′). Sandwiched between these defenses is what Paul calls his foolish boasting (B).

1. Weakness and Power (2 Cor 10:1—11:15; 12:5—13:10)

Paul starts by insisting on his strength. He speaks of the courage and confidence he could exercise if he wanted to as he stands up to opponents (10:2). He compares himself to an army with weapons that could demolish fortresses, take captives, and punish disobedience if he needed to (10:3–4). But Paul's mode of action is "gentleness" and "kindness" (10:1). In an allusion to Jeremiah, whose authority was both to tear down and to build up (Jer 24:6), Paul insists he wants only to build up (2 Cor 10:8; also 13:10). Paul, however, is warning his readers not to be fooled by what looks like weakness.

In the second half of this chiastic structure, Paul returns to the same theme but with a different approach, one that grows out of his **salvation trajectory**. He admits to weakness (12:5). He speaks of the humiliating "thorn in the flesh" (12:7–8). But now he sees this weakness as the place of God's power, what he also calls "the power of Christ" (12:9–10). The salvific character of this power in weakness is clearest when Paul brings up the theme of his weakness a third time (13:1–10). There he insists that his "apostolic weakness" may well bring about strength in the congregation: "We are weak but you are strong" (13:8).

The issue of Paul's weakness arose in an unfavorable comparison with some Christian opponents. Paul deals sharply with these adversaries. Somewhat disconcerting to the modern reader is Paul's characterization of his Christian adversaries, the "super-apostles" (11:5; 12:11), as "false apostles, deceitful workers, who masquerade as apostles of Christ," whom Paul then compares to Satan and his masquerades (11:13–15). We learn almost nothing at all about their teaching, which Paul finds so offensive. They seem to differ from Paul in accepting support from the Corinthians, an action Paul refused because of its implication of patronage (11:7–9). Since Paul insists he is in no way inferior as regards Judaism (11:22), perhaps these others are ministers of Jewish background preaching a Jewish-Christian approach.

The early church was by no means unified in its teaching. Issues of "territory" (*ho kanôn*) surface in this letter (10:12–18). Yet these adversaries were apparently Christians who left their families and possessions to preach a gospel message. Paul's anger is obviously fed by his anxiety for his Corinthian community. Sociologists will recognize here the technique of confrontation with outsiders by which the boundaries of a group can be established. Here, however, the "outsider" is a follower of Christ, although one who challenges Paul's authority. In school, Paul learned the rhetoric of rebuttal and refutation, which involved attacking the messenger not just the message, and he is using it here. Still it is disappointing to see Paul sucked into the passionate name-calling, so characteristic of family fights.

2. Paul's Foolish Boasts (11:16—12:4)

Sandwiched between the two defenses against accusations of weakness is something like a professional résumé, or list of qualifications. Actually Paul's résumé sounds like a parody on résumés. Instead of a long list of honors and accomplishments, Paul presents his moments of shame and his failures (11:22–33). He was beaten and jailed more than any of his rivals. He was hungry and cold more than others. While the Roman army gave a special honor to the attacking soldier who was the first up and over the wall of a besieged city, Paul finds "honor" in that he was lowered down the walls of Damascus in a basket (11:32–33).

Paul mentions his mystical experience some "fourteen years ago" (12:1–4). If this measurement of time is more a round number than an exact count, Paul may be referring to the experience of Christ that changed his life (Gal 1:15–16; see Acts 9:1–9). When his apostolic authority is questioned, Paul usually refers to this event (1 Cor 9:1; Gal 1:10–24; see 1 Cor 15:8–9). Paul says nothing about this experience here except to insist on its ineffable nature. It is almost as if it did not really happen to him!

C. The Letter of Reconciliation (2 Cor 1—9)

According to our hypothesis, the first nine chapters of our 2 Corinthians make up the next letter Paul wrote. It appears to be a letter of reconciliation written from Macedonia after the meeting with Titus (2 Cor 7:5–7).

1. The Greeting and Opening Prayer (1:1–14)

Paul's greeting is very similar to that in 1 Corinthians, except Timothy is now Paul's companion and "the holy ones" of the province of Achaia are greeted, apparently a reference to other Christians near Corinth (1:1–2).

The letter prayer in 2 Corinthians begins with the expression, "Blessed be the God and Father of our Lord Jesus Christ…" instead of "I give thanks to my God…" (1 Cor 1:4; see 1 Thess 1:2). The two expressions are similar in meaning as expressing "praise." However, in the "blessing [*eulogêtos*]" formula, Paul focuses entirely on God and omits mention of any good thing in the community. This shift may be deliberate.

Paul "blesses" God for the "encouragement [*paraklêsis*]" that he received "in our every affliction [*thlipsis*]" (1:4). Paul briefly mentions some grave affliction experienced in the province of Asia (1:8–11). He then continues describing the crisis that arose between himself and the Corinthians (1:12—2:13; 7:4–16).

In his reflection on these sufferings, Paul introduces two aspects that contribute to his **union with Christ trajectory** and his **salvation trajectory**. He speaks of his affliction as "the sufferings [*pathêmata*] of Christ which overflow to us" (1:5). He then sees the purpose of his suffering as "for your encouragement and salvation [*sôteria*]" (1:6). Finally, Paul sees the Corinthians also drawn into this drama as "sharers [*koinônoi*] of those sufferings [*pathêmata*]" so that they may "share in the encouragement" (1:7).

It is difficult to know where exactly Paul intended to conclude this letter prayer. Section 1:8–14 stands out as a development of Paul's "afflictions," closely connected in grammar to the preceding (*gar*). Although the section sounds like the beginning of a "newsy" section, Paul is clearly less interested in giving us details of the events than he is providing us with his understanding of his suffering and of the role of God in this suffering.

Developing his **God trajectory**, Paul describes how this suffering served to make him place his trust totally in God. It served to make Paul see God especially as the one "who raises the dead" (1:9). God "rescued [*errysato*]" Paul and will continue to rescue him (1:10). Placing oneself in the hands of God who raises the dead is an act Paul here calls "trusting [*peithein*]" (1:19). Later Paul will name "faith [*pistis*]" as this openness to the power of God raising Jesus (see Rom 10:9; Col 2:12). The resurrection of Jesus is the model of God's rescue. The section ends with a reference to "the day of our Lord Jesus" (1:14), ending much like the letter prayer of 1 Corinthians (1 Cor 1:8–9).

2. Recent Events (1:15—2:13; 7:4–16)

The details about events leading up to this letter are described in an inclusion beginning with 1:15—2:13 and then concluding with 7:5–16, each section woven in chiastic patterns with such strands as Paul's travel plans, his joy, the harsh letter, and the role of Titus, as well as God's faithfulness, and the offending member of the community. In these sections he is defending himself against the charge of fickleness.

Paul's defense in 1:15–24 falls into an A-B-A′ composition:

A. His travel plans (1:15–17),
  B. God's constancy and faithfulness (1:18–22)
A.′ His travel plans (1:23–24)

The interrelationship of these two topics is at the heart of Paul's defense. Instead of defending himself by describing his personal qualities, Paul returns to his **God trajectory** with the description, "God is faithful" (1:18). Tying into the **Jesus trajectory**, Paul insists that his mission is nothing less that the preaching of "the Son of God, Jesus Christ," described as the great "yes" of God (1:19). The content of this message should guarantee the firmness of Paul's preaching and that of his co-workers, Silvanus and Timothy, the team that went with Paul to Corinth on the second missionary journey (cf. 1 Thess 1:1; Acts 18:5). In effect, Paul argues that he is spending his life preaching Christ and the absolute faithfulness and constancy of God. How could he not be transformed by that message?

Here Paul includes the **Spirit trajectory**, describing "the Spirit" as a guarantee of God's faithfulness, like the deposit or down payment (*arrabôn*) in a financial transaction (2 Cor 1:22; cf. also 5:5). Here also is the first of many times where Paul describes the Spirit as "in our hearts." The experience of the Spirit in our hearts should be an experience of God's faithfulness and constancy, an experience of the great "Yes!" With the Spirit, Paul associates God's "seal" and God's "anointing," all vocabulary suggesting baptism (1 Cor 12:13; Eph1:13). Paul may be reminding the Corinthians of their baptism in his effort to reestablish this church on the firmness of God.

The second mention of his changed travel plans (1:23–24) flows into the beginning of a second chiasm, continuing the topic of his travels:

A. Paul's travels (2:1–2).
  B. The harsh letter he wrote (2:3–4)
    C. The person in the community who offended him (2:5–8)
  B'. The harsh letter (2:9–11)
A'. His travels (2:12–13)

The reprise of the newsy section in 7:4–16 is structured in a similar chiastic form:

A. Paul's joy (7:4)
  B. Titus (7:5–7)
    C. The harsh letter (7:8–13a)
  B'. Titus (7:13b–15)
A'. Paul's joy (7:16)

3. *Paul's Theology (2:14—7:4)*

The theological meat of this letter appears in the instructional section of the letter bracketed by the newsy sections. In this middle part, after an introductory defense of himself again

(2:14–17), Paul reflects on the "new covenant" of which he is a minister (3:1—4:6), on the afflictions and hopes of life (4:7—5:10), and on the ministry of reconciliation (5:11—7:4). These instructions are closely linked to the concrete experiences of both Paul and the community.

a. The New Covenant (2 Cor 3:1—4:6)

Paul's transition to the theme of the new covenant is particularly labored and involved (3:1–3). He starts by defending his lack of official letters of recommendation. Apparently, the early missionaries were to present these letters from established churches as a way of authorizing their work. Paul had no such letter.

He did not need any. His authority was not from any established church. It was directly from the Lord, as he will write later to the Galatians. Here Paul explains to the Corinthians how his credentials should be found in their hearts. A "letter of Christ" was written on the Corinthians' hearts with the "ink" of the Spirit (3:2–3). On a simple level, he is telling the Corinthians to look into their hearts to see the effect of his preaching, appealing to the evangelical principle, "By their fruits you will know them" (Matt 7:16).

On a deeper level, however, allusions here to Jeremiah and Ezekiel abound. Paul is confident that he is a minister of a "new covenant," apparently formed in the hearts of the Corinthians (3:4–6). This is "the ministry of the Spirit" (3:8). All of these details are important for Paul's **Spirit trajectory**.

In the remaining part of chapter 3, Paul then attempts his own midrash on Exodus 34:29–35, a free rendition of the biblical story of Moses and his veil, in an effort to connect with present issues. The images shift with awkward speed, but are important for Paul's **Spirit trajectory**, alluding to an "enlightening" role of the Spirit (3:12–18). The brief and somewhat surprising mention of "freedom" (3:17) in this context likewise adds a note that will become important for this trajectory in later letters.

Paul relates this theology of the Spirit and enlightenment to his own work (4:1–6). He admits his gospel might be "veiled" at least for "those being destroyed" (*hoi apollymenoi*) (4:3), the same word he used in 1 Corinthians to describe those for whom the cross is folly and weakness (1 Cor 1:18). This is a form of blindness that Satan, "the god of this age," inflicts on the "unbeliever" (*apistos*) to prevent him or her from seeing the light that God creates (2 Cor 4:3–4). Paul then relates this light to Christ as "the image of God" (4:4), on whose face appears the glory of God (4:6). The face of Christ is the mirror he refers to in 3:18, in which we see the glory of the Lord God.[3] Paul thus connects this issue of enlightenment also to his **salvation trajectory**, while at the same time adding an important note to his **Christ trajectory**.

b. Life after Death (4:7—5:10)

After expounding on the light and glory of the New Testament, Paul returns to the "real world" with its marks of darkness and death. He himself is an example of the pattern epitomized by the death and resurrection of Jesus.

Paul likes to list his afflictions and sufferings (4:8–11). He does so repeatedly in his Corinthian correspondence (1 Cor 4:9–13; 2 Cor 6:4–5; 11: 23–29; 12:10). At this point of the letter, however, he makes a remarkable contribution to the **union with Christ trajectory**, stating that these sufferings are in effect the way he is "carrying in his body the dying of Jesus so that the life of Jesus may shine forth in our bodies" (4:10). Paul attributes this new life to God's action. Through "the Spirit of faith" (4:13) he knows that "the one who raised the Lord Jesus will raise us also with Jesus and place us with you" (4:14), an allusion to Paul's typical future **eschatology** (1 Thess 4:14–15; 1 Cor 15).

As he continues to reflect on the present "working" of life and death, Paul slips in an interesting shift in this **eschatology trajectory**. At this point he begins to develop a view in which this resurrection is beginning now. What follows then is a series of contrasts that suggests a duality in human life. Each contrast is given as based on (*gar*) the next:

1. The "outer self," which is wasting away, with the "inner self," which is being renewed (4:16)
2. "Momentary light affliction" with "an eternal weight of glory" being produced in the present (4:17)

3. That which is "transitory" and "seen" with that which is "eternal" and "unseen" (4:18)
4. "Our earthly dwelling" with "a dwelling from God" (5:1)

The context of this last contrast is death, the dissolution of our earthly dwelling (5:1). Connected to our death is the reception of the "dwelling from God," described also as "being clothed again" (5:2), which he longs for (5:4, 7). Paul is not clear about the exact time of this dwelling or clothing change, except that it is linked to death, suggesting a reality that happens immediately after death. His expressions clearly designate a heavenly gift, quite distinct from the earthly body that is "taken off" at death. The note of Paul's longing here "to leave the body and go home to the Lord" (5:4, 7) for this new dwelling suggests something he wants the sooner the better, rather than something for which he and all others must wait for until the "day of the Lord."

The convergence of images here at least suggests something of a shift from the classical Jewish view of the human person as a breathing body to a more Greek view of the person as an enfleshed soul, capable of diverse types of existence. However, by associating "eternal" and "not made of hands" with the interior or unseen, Paul is focusing on the gift of God rather than the anthropological dimension.

Before moving on to the next theological topic, Paul makes an ethical reflection on his eschatology and in so doing presents his first scene of eschatological judgment, another important element in his **eschatology and soteriology trajectories**. "We must all be revealed before the judgment seat of Christ, so that each be recompensed according to what each has done in the body, either good or bad" (5:10; see Rom 14:10). Paul does not talk about eternal condemnation here as Matthew does (Matt 25:41, 46), but he does speak of a type of payment of salary (*komidzein*) that corresponds to good or bad actions in life, presumably rewards and punishments. Here Jesus is the judge, and the scene appears to be after death. This thought is intended to stimulate us to strive to be acceptable or pleasing (*heuarestoi*) to the Lord whether we are alive or dead (2 Cor 5:9).

c. The New Creation (5:11—6:13)

The third identifiable theme of this letter begins as if it were a logical conclusion to the preceding, "therefore" (*oun*), where the transition moves once again through the problem of Paul's credentials, "I hope, we are also apparent to your conscience" (6:11). Again Paul appeals to "the heart" rather than "external appearance" (6:12). Then, very quickly Paul moves to the topic of Christ and God's work through Christ, in an important development of Paul's **salvation trajectory**.

In this section Paul describes God reconciling the world (*kosmos*) to himself, overcoming the hatred that separated God from his own creation. The action is described as now and ongoing, not eschatological. The action is all-encompassing, at once directed toward us people (5:18) and all of reality (5:19). The action is that of God, the Father. Christ appears as the medium through whom and in whom the reconciliation takes place (5:18–19). The action nullifies "transgressions" (*paraptomata*) (5:19).

Paul starts by pointing out that the reconciliation begins by Christ's death, a particular historical death that in some way involved us all. "Because one died for all, all died" (5:14). Paul explains this as the way people can now live "for him" not "for themselves" (5:15). What happened in the concrete person of Jesus somehow happens in those united to him. If Christ died then we all have died, an intense expression of the **union with Christ trajectory**.

Thus for Paul the reconciliation effected by God through Christ is more than a change of attitudes. It is more than God simply changing his mind about us. It is more than even his forgiving our sins. As Paul goes on to describe, the reconciliation is in effect God re-creating his creation. "So that if anyone is in Christ, there is a new creation. The old has passed away, behold all is new" (5:17).[4]

Paul is quite aware that sin and death continue in the world. Thus Paul qualifies the cosmic drama with the words, "if anyone is in Christ." Here we see an important tension running through the whole of Paul's vision of salvation. In some way, God's saving activity changes all of reality. In another way, this activity occurs only by **union with Christ**. This is a tension between universality and particularity in matters of salvation, the tension of two vectors operating simultaneously.

The role of Paul and of the readers of this letter links to the particularity involved in this salvation. Paul describes himself as "an ambassador for Christ" and explains this role as one of "handing on" the reconciliation and "appealing" to others to be reconciled (2 Cor 5:18–20). He sees himself as a channel through (*dia*) whom God appeals to his creation. The readers are the object of the appeal, "Be reconciled to God!" (5:20). Presupposed in this appeal is the ability of the readers to accept or reject this reconciliation. Human beings are therefore drawn by God into this divine action in a way that calls for their conscious acceptance.

The role of Christ is under God, who is the one actively reconciling the world. This role of Christ appears in the following verse that has the form perhaps a type of a Christian formula, "The one [Christ] not knowing sin, he [God] made to be sin, so that we might become the justice of God in him" (5:21).

This description of Christ is striking. It is crucial for understanding Paul's **soteriology trajectory**. The expression "made to be sin" could refer to a "sin offering," which in the Old Testament was sometimes called simply a "sin" (Lev 4:3, 8, 14).[5] This sense of a sacrifice for sin might echo in Paul's statement and should not be ruled out entirely. However, the contrast between "sin" and "justice of God" strongly suggests that Paul wants to describe Christ as somehow entering into our sinfulness itself and by that solidarity bringing about our justification. The sense of "sin" here corresponds more to the Jewish apocalyptic sense of a cosmic power in itself rather than that of a human moral deviation. Ultimately, Paul is talking about categories of reality, not ethics.

4. The Collection for Jerusalem (8—9)

After the reprise of the newsy section (7:4–16), Paul appeals to the Corinthians to give toward a relief effort for the Jewish-Christian church ("the holy ones") in Jerusalem (chapters 8–9; see 1 Cor 16:1–4). Paul tries to motivate his readers by moral exhortations from scripture (9:6–10).

However, Paul draws on his **Christ trajectory** and his **salvation trajectory** to explain his practical exhortations. He evokes the example of Christ, who though rich became poor for us (2 Cor 8:9). The saying parallels in grammatical structure the statement Paul made about Christ regarding sin and justice:

2 Cor 8:9	*2 Cor 5:21*
Being rich [present Participle]	Not knowing sin [present participle]
He made himself poor for you [aorist]	God made him sin for us [aorist]
so that [*hina*] you might be enriched by his poverty.	so that [*hina*] we might become the justice of God in him.

Both statements affirm (with a participle) an existence of Jesus that then leads to a reversal (expressed by aorist finite verb) where Jesus becomes "poor" or "sin." The purpose or intention (*hina*) of this reversal is our enrichment or justification. Taken together, these texts contribute enormously to Paul's **Christology trajectory**. In 1 Corinthians Paul used the same structure to describe how he himself functions in his ministry: "Being free...I made myself a slave to all...so that I might gain a good number" (1 Cor 9:19–22).

5. Conclusion of Letter (13:11–13)

The final form of 2 Corinthians as we have it ends with a series of injunctions regarding authentic Christian community, "Rejoice...live in peace," adding a greeting from the community Paul is with ("the holy ones") and encouraging mutual greeting among the Corinthians (13:11–12). None of this is clearly related to the immediately preceding "harsh letter" and may have been placed here from "the letter of reconciliation" by the editor to conclude the present form of the letter.

The striking "trinitarian" blessing in the last verse picks up the parallel association of Jesus, God, and the Holy Spirit, first introduced in 1 Corinthians 12:4–6 in the discussion of the origin of the "spiritual gifts." Here in 2 Corinthians Paul connects each of this triad with a distinguishing gift to the community

(13:13). This final blessing stands out all the more when compared to the consistently christological blessing concluding Paul's earlier and later letters (1 Thess 5:28; 1 Cor 16:23; Gal 5:18; Rom 16:2; Phil 4:23).

III. The Thematic Summary of the Letter

A. God

Much of Paul's view of God found in 1 Corinthians is repeated in 2 Corinthians. Paul is "an apostle by the will of God" and is writing to "the church of God" (2 Cor 1:1; see 1 Cor 1:1–2). This is the "faithful God" (2 Cor 1:18; see 1 Cor 1:9), "the God and Father of the Lord Jesus" (2 Cor 11:31; see 1 Cor 15:21). He is also the "God of peace" (2 Cor 13:11, 13; see 1 Cor 14:33).

1. God as Present and Supporting Paul

Paul here also continues an emphasis he began in 1 Thessalonians with the theme of God as always present. As he says in 2 Corinthians, God is Paul's witness (1:23). Paul acts "in the presence of God" (2:17; 12:19) and "before God" (4:2; 7:12); Paul is "transparent" to God (5:11); "God knows" that Paul loves the Corinthians (11:11) and is not lying (11:31).

Perhaps because of the attack on his authority, Paul develops in this letter far more the role of God in his ministry. God strengthens Paul and anoints him (1:21), makes Paul qualified (3:5), gives Paul his "territory" (10:13). In effect, God's "faithfulness" guarantees Paul's firmness despite his irritating changes in travel plans (1:15–24). Paul stresses the description of "the God of all encouragement" who supports Paul in his suffering and thus allows him to help this church (1:3–4, 21; 7:6). Paul can act and live with the "power of God" (13:4; see 10:1–6). In this letter more than any other, God is named "the Lord" (3:16–18; 6:17–18 [the early letter]; 10:17–18).

2. *God's Initiative in Salvation*

Paul continues the theme of God's initiative in matters relating to salvation. God put his seal on us and gives the Spirit in our hearts (1:22). This God is the God described in the Torah, the God who said "let light shine out of darkness," who now "shines in our hearts" providing us with knowledge of his glory on the face of Christ (4:6). This God raises the dead (1:9, 18) and provides a new "dwelling" at death and prepares us for immortality (5:1, 5). This God initiates the reconciliation of the world to himself (5:19), from whom comes "the new creation" (5:17–18), who makes Christ to be sin, so that we may share in his own justice (5:21).

B. Christ Jesus

1. *The Lord*

Paul's use of the title "the Lord" for Jesus appears in this letter much as it did in 1 Thessalonians and 1 Corinthians, in parallel with "God, the Father" (2 Cor 1:2–3; 11:31; 13:13), as part of a general reference to Jesus often as a title accompanied by the proper name (4:5; 5:6, 8; 8:9), as naming the eschatological event of "the day of the Lord" (1:14), or as specifying the condition "in the Lord" (2:12; 10:17).

2. *The Medium of Divine Action*

In 1 Corinthians Paul had introduced the concept of Christ as the medium through whom God creates (1 Cor 8:6). In this letter he is even more emphatic about Christ as the medium through whom God works. In the letter prayer using the title "Son of God," the only time in this letter, Paul describes Jesus Christ as the great "yes" of God the Father (2 Cor 1:19). The promises of God are firm in Christ (1:20). God reconciles the world to himself through Christ. And for those "in Christ" the "new creation" takes place (2 Cor 5:17–19).

3. The Wisdom of God

For the first time Paul will describe Jesus as an "image of God" (4:4). The light of God's glory shines on Christ's face (4:6) and in that way Jesus functions as the mirror of God (3:18). While Paul earlier described male human beings as an "image of God" (1 Cor 11:7; see also 15:49), suggesting a link to "Adam theology," the language here suggests a more intense relationship to God. Actually, Paul's description in 2 Corinthians here suggests a more emphatic identification of Jesus with divine wisdom. The Wisdom of Solomon describes divine wisdom:

> She is a refulgence of eternal light,
> a spotless *mirror* of the power of God,
> an *image* of his goodness. (Wis 7:26)

Thus Paul seems here to be developing the wisdom Christology he briefly alluded to in 1 Corinthians where he described the crucified Christ as "the power of God and the wisdom of God" (1 Cor 1:24).

Preexistence appeared as a hint in 1 Corinthians where Christ is the medium of creation (8:6). The hint strengthens in 2 Corinthians where Paul describes Christ moving from a state of "not knowing sin" to being "made sin" by God (2 Cor 5:21) or from "being rich" to "he became poor" (8:9). In the first of this pair of formulas, the state of "not knowing sin" might possibly refer to the earthly Jesus in a kind of Johannine insistence on the innocence of the one being condemned to death. However, it is difficult to find any earthly period of Jesus' life that Paul could consider "being rich." Furthermore, nowhere else does Paul distinguish between a rich or innocent phase of Jesus' life and a poor or condemned phase. Generally in his letters, Paul's interest in the earthly life of Jesus is focused almost exclusively on Jesus' crucifixion and death. Most likely, Paul intends to describe Jesus "being rich" (8:9) in reference to Jesus before his earthly existence. Most likely, then, not knowing sin" (5:21) also refers to a preearthly existence. The texts are significant because they attribute personal actions ("knowing," "made himself") to the presumably preexistent Christ. From this preexistent state Jesus actively "made himself poor," just as Wisdom in Jewish literature actively descends to earth.[6] This personal activity suggests the existence of Jesus as a conscious personal agent before he becomes human. Both texts of 2 Corinthians appear as Paul's earliest real commitment to speaking of an existence of Jesus before he becomes human.

4. *Eschatological Judge*

Paul suggests the role of Jesus as eschatological judge in 1 Corinthians, where he describes how Jesus' coming will manifest motives and lead to praise from God (1 Cor 4:5). This letter explicitly refers to Jesus before whose "tribunal" (*bêma*) we must all appear (5:10). Later, Paul will refer to the "tribunal of God" (Rom 14:10).

Apocalyptic Judaism consistently sees God as the eschatological judge.[7] The eschatological Messiah in this literature often has a conquering function but is rarely described explicitly as the eschatological judge in any forensic sense. Only in *2 Baruch* do we find the Messiah coming as judge (72:2; see 70:9–10). *First Enoch* describes the Elect One or Son of man in this function (45:3; see 55:4; 61:8).

C. The Spirit of God

1. *Anticipated Eschatology*

While Paul had described Jesus as the "firstfruits" (*aparchê*) of the resurrection (1 Cor 15:23), in 2 Corinthians he twice refers to the present gift of the Spirit in our hearts as the "down payment" (*arrabôn*) of life after death (2 Cor 1:22; 5:5). The action of God giving "security" or "firmness" to our faith works both through Jesus experienced as risen from the dead, the beginning of a larger series, and also through the gift of the Spirit, the promise of more to come. This is the Spirit experienced in our hearts (1:22) as an interior gift complementing the objective saving work of God.

The Spirit functions in the hearts of believers. It is life-giving (2 Cor 3:6). It now brings about "glory" (3:7–11), just as it will do for the risen body (1 Cor 15:42–44). The transforming action of the Spirit is realized in the present, not just in the last days, as Joel

3:1–5 had described. The heart transformed by the Spirit thus becomes a sort of anticipation of the *eschaton* with its bodily resurrection and transformation.

2. The New Covenant

In this letter, Paul develops the interior action of the Spirit by linking it to the prophetic promises of a "new covenant." Paul develops an elaborate picture of God writing in the hearts of the Corinthians with the ink of the Spirit. This is the "letter of Christ" (3:2–3). This action of God qualifies Paul as a "minister of the Spirit," which is also to be a "minister of the new covenant" (2 Cor 3:6).

The connection between "the new covenant" and the heart as writing material is one that Jeremiah made some five centuries earlier. Shortly after the Babylonian devastation of 587 BC, Jeremiah promised that God would save his people through an internal renewal, the law written in their hearts. "Deep within them I will plant my law, writing it on their hearts. Then I will be their God and they shall be my people" (Jer 31:33). All this is a description of the "new covenant" that God will make with his people (31:31).

It is from the prophet Ezekiel, however, that Paul draws the image of the Spirit in the context of a new covenant. Writing during the same disastrous period of history in which Jeremiah lived, the prophet Ezekiel likewise conveys a divine promise of restoration. The words of Ezekiel sound almost like a commentary on Jeremiah's promise, but Ezekiel adds the element of "spirit."

> I shall give you a new heart, and put a new spirit in you;
> I shall remove the heart of stone from your bodies and
> give you a heart of flesh instead. I shall put my spirit in
> you, and make you keep my laws and sincerely respect
> my observances. (Ezek 36:26–28)

In a clever combination of images, Paul takes Jeremiah's vision of a new covenant as one where the law is written in the heart and adds Ezekiel's promise of the divine Spirit to identify the means by which God writes in the heart. The combination of the law and the Spirit creates a subtle allusion to the role of the

Spirit in the observance of the law in the heart of the believer, which Paul will develop in his next letter to the Galatians. It is in 2 Corinthians, however, that "the heart" takes on important theological significance. Paul sees the interior as the essential.

3. Prophetic Enlightenment and Continuity

In the context of new covenant, Paul suggests a role of the Spirit in "reading" or understanding the texts of Moses (3:15). In his midrash on Exodus 34:29–35, Paul speaks of the person of Moses and the veil over his face (3:12–13). Paul then shifts the images to the books of Moses and the veil over the hearts of unenlightened readers (3:14–15) to describe any reading that cannot see Christ in those texts.

Enlightenment occurs by a kind of "turning to the Spirit." Paul here cites the Exodus description of Moses, who would remove the veil when he turned toward the Lord.

> When Moses went before the Lord to speak to him, he removed the veil until he went out. (Exod 34:34)

Paul modifies the citation, however, so as to generalize the description as applying to anyone at anytime:

> Whenever one turns to the Lord, the veil is removed. (3:16)

He then adds the line, "Now the Lord is the Spirit" (3:17).

Although the expression "the Lord" as used by Paul normally refers to Jesus, one major exception to this rule arises when Paul is citing the Old Testament, as he is doing here in a rather free manner. The expression "the Lord" here in 2 Corinthians does not mean Christ, but rather "Yahweh," as it does in the Exodus text. When Paul identifies "the Lord" with "the Spirit" (3:17), Paul is not identifying the Spirit with Christ but with "the Lord" he had just mentioned. Paul is insisting that the Spirit he has been speaking of was in some way present in those events of the Old Testament. Moses' physical movement into the Lord's presence becomes the model for a believer's enlightenment by the

Spirit. For Paul, the presence of Yahweh was the presence of the same Spirit who enables us today to understand the true meaning of the Old Testament.

The veil preventing vision of the glory is taken away when one turns to the Lord God who is the Spirit (3:16–18). Paul appears to be articulating an enlightening or prophetic role of the Spirit. If the texts of the Old Testament are read in the light of that same Spirit, the reader finds Christ, and the reader also finds "the new covenant" with its unfading glory, the Spirit that brings life (3:6). If the texts of Moses are read without that light, if they are read with the blinding veil over the heart, the reader finds only the written document (*to gramma*), the stone tablet, which brings death (3:6).

By linking the action of Moses to that of the believer turning to the Spirit, Paul again suggests the continuity between the old and the new, a way in which the new was already present in the old. He hinted at that continuity in 1 Corinthians when he described Jesus as the "spiritual rock" that gave water to the Israelites in the Exodus story (1 Cor 10:3–4). What is "spiritual" is the "prophetic" glue that binds the epochs of God's action into a whole. Writing a year or so later to the Romans, Paul will express the same idea with different images (Rom 16:25–26).

The identification of "the Spirit" with "Yahweh," creates an interesting tension with the "trinitarian" blessing of the last verse of the letter (2 Cor 13:13). This blessing in the last verse of 2 Corinthians emphasizes again the association of the Holy Spirit with the Lord Jesus Christ and with God (13:13). The three are placed in parallel positions. The Spirit that Paul earlier described as God's inner consciousness (1 Cor 2:10–12), then as the ink of God's writing (2 Cor 3:3), and then identified with God himself in the Old Testament (3:17), now seems more like a person along with Jesus and the Father.

D. Salvation

1. Scope of Salvation

One strand of thought running throughout 2 Corinthians seems to insist on an exclusivist view of salvation in the style of

4 Ezra. As in 1 Corinthians so also in 2 Corinthians, Paul distinguishes "those being destroyed" and those "those being saved." These are the same categories he used in 1 Corinthians to describe those for whom the cross is folly and weakness (1 Cor 1:18). He uses the categories in his "letter of reconciliation" to describe the difference between those who find in Paul's work "an odor of death" and those who find there "an odor of life" (2 Cor 2:15–16). Paul's gospel is veiled for "those being destroyed," those "unbelievers" blinded by "the god of this age" (4:3–4).

In the "earlier letter" (2 Cor 6:14—7:1), Paul sounds even more pessimistic about the "unbeliever" (*apistos*). He places the contrast between "believer" and "unbeliever" in parallel with the contrast between righteousness and lawlessness, light and darkness, Christ and the devil. Later, writing 1 Corinthians, Paul seems to soften this absolute opposition between "believer" and "unbeliever" (*apistos*) at least in marriage (1 Cor 7:12–14). Then in his later "harsh letter" (2 Cor 10—13), he refers to the bleak "end" of the "false apostles" described as ministers of Satan (11:13–15).

As we saw in 1 Corinthians, the contrast between "those being destroyed" and "those being saved" fits into his apocalyptic theology of two ages and, at the same time, serves to establish the boundaries of the believing group by which the group can define itself. Paul's insistence in the "earlier letter" on a hostile confrontation with outsiders functions exactly the same way. It is an exhortation to maintain the boundary, not to be "yoked" with "those who are different" (2 Cor 6:14), to maintain the purity of the group (7:1). When in his "harsh letter" Paul demonizes his Christian opponents as "deceitful workers" and "Satan's ministers" (11:13–15), he is first and foremost trying to discredit their teaching as coming from outside the boundaries of legitimate teaching.

Throughout all this boundary drawing, Paul is describing two diametrically contrasting human reactions to the gospel and is explaining how the rejection and revulsion that outsiders show for Paul's gospel is not a reason for believers to falter. In fact, this rejection and revulsion show that the insiders are indeed on the right track toward salvation.

As he aims his rhetorical weapons at his Christian opponents, Paul is in fact drawing boundaries through the middle of the Christian community. Despite his harsh description of them and "their end" (11:15), it would seem unlikely that Paul would condemn to hell those outside these boundaries for their theological positions. Here the sociological function of the statement—not the soteriological or eschatological content—seems paramount, although Paul connects the two. From this sociological point of view, it is striking to see how divisions within a family are often the most bitter.

2. God's Cosmic Salvation

On the other hand, Paul introduces in the letter of reconciliation a universal or cosmic sense of salvation. Paul's "ministry of reconciliation" is defined as "God is in Christ reconciling the world [*kosmos*] to himself not counting their trespasses" (5:19). The action is all-encompassing, at once directed toward us people and all of reality. This for Paul is a "new act of creation [*kainê ktisis*]. The old realities have passed away, behold the new have come to be" (5:17). Paul emphatically places this description in the present. "New things have come" (5:18). "Now is the day of salvation" (6:2). The descriptions ring with Johannine tones of realized eschatology (John 3:17; 4:42).

The description also rings of apocalyptic tones in the sense of a salvation that is not just a matter of "getting souls to heaven" but a renewal of all reality, including material reality. In apocalyptic writing, the image of a "new creation" is an expression of the universal and final triumph of good over evil at the end of time (see Rev 21:1–8). Paul, however, is speaking of something present now.

By describing the transformation as "a new creation" (5:17), Paul is tying into the Deutero- and Trito-Isaian sense of salvation as an engagement of God's creative power (Isa 65:17; see 51:9–16). In Trito-Isaiah the context is the restoration of Israel after the Babylonian Captivity:

> Past troubles will be forgotten and hidden from my eyes. For now I create new heavens and a new earth,

> and the past will not be remembered and will come no more to men's minds. (Isa 65:17)

Paul starts his description of a cosmic transformation with the phrase, "If anyone [*tis*] is in Christ..." (5:17). We could read this as a restrictive condition according to the normal function of an "if" clause. On the other hand, Paul does not add any note of exclusion from this transformation, leaving the matter rather indeterminate ("if anyone"). The center of importance is not on human activity.

The focus is on Christ. Christ is the medium. God reconciles the cosmos to himself in Christ and reconciles us through him. The new creation must also occur in Christ. If the new creation happens "if someone is in Christ," then in effect the new creation occurs fully in the risen humanity of Christ. This risen Christ is, in the fullest sense of the word, "the new creation." To look at this reality is to see the full meaning of salvation. The rest of God's creation can take part in this salvation only to the extent they are a part of Christ raised from the dead, only to the extent they are "in Christ."

The magnitude of this saving action seems to preclude the vision that it in any way depends on human decisions. Creation is in a sense being restarted, and the cosmos is being reconciled by God to himself. In the Pauline view, we can no more reconcile ourselves to God than we could create ourselves. Here Paul is laying the basis for his later thought that all justification comes not by works of the law but by grace (Rom 3:21–31).

3. Salvation through Christ's Death and Weakness

In 2 Corinthians, Paul picks up with emphasis what he stated briefly in 1 Thessalonians (5:10) and what he passed on as an element of apostolic tradition in 1 Corinthians (15:3), namely, that Christ died for us. In this letter the emphasis appears in the repetition and with the universal scope added, "One [Christ] died for all...he indeed died for all" (2 Cor 5:14–15). The crucifixion was an atoning death through which God rescues the world. Paul is tying into the theology of the suffering servant who suffered and died for the people (Isa 53:8–9).

Referring certainly to the crucifixion—and probably to the whole human life of Jesus—Paul identifies Christ with the reality from which salvation is necessary: "Not knowing sin, God made him to be sin so that we might become the righteousness of God in him" (5:21). Again like the suffering servant "who was assigned a grave among the wicked" (Isa 53:9), Christ needed the saving action of God. The expression in Paul appears to be a formula that appears again in the parallel description of Christ becoming poor so that we might become rich (8:9). The constant in both expressions is a description of God's saving action in Christ that functions to eliminate sin by an engagement with sin, as it were, on its own level, by Christ's solidarity with sin. Both formulas express God's actions. God's action is through some form of destruction suffered by Christ.

Thus the crucifixion is atoning because the crucified one enters into our sinful condition. Paul had said in 1 Corinthians that the saving strength of God looks like weakness (1 Cor 1:18–25). Here he insists that this weakness is in fact the means of salvation. Jesus functions not as the powerful agent who communicates salvation through his power and substance, but rather as a model of the need for salvation, "poor" and "sinful." These deficient conditions become means of our blessing. He will return to this theme again in future letters (Gal 3:13; Rom 8:3).

This paradoxical plan of salvation appears also in Paul's conception of his own work. In 1 Corinthians he described how his apostolic arrival manifested "weakness, fear, and trembling" (1 Cor 2:1–5). In his "harsh letter," he insists again that the "power of Christ," which is the power of the crucifixion, is expressed in this weakness (2 Cor 12:9; 13:4). He defends his apostolate by boasting in his weakness (11:30; 12:5, 9). "For power is made perfect in weakness" (12:9). Just as Christ's becoming poor leads to the enrichment and justice of sinners, so Paul sees his weakness and other "workings of death" as leading to the life of his congregation:

> We are afflicted in every way, but not constrained.... So death is at work in us, but life in you. (2 Cor 4:10–12)

> We are weak but you are strong. (13:8)

These lines have a caustic tone—even one of sarcasm—but down deep Paul sees something at the core of his ministry, based precisely on the paradoxical character of the power of the crucifixion. Christ's power arises from the weakness of his death on the cross and this power is "for you [*eis hymas*]" (13:3). The same pattern describes the power of Paul for the Corinthians. "So likewise we are weak in him, but we live with him by the power of God for you [*eis hymas*]" (13:4). In 1 Corinthians Paul had addressed his congregation in similar words (1 Cor 4:10). Paul humbles himself so that the Corinthians might be exalted (2 Cor 11:7). For all his grumpiness here, Paul sees saving goodness coming from his suffering.

E. Union of Life with Christ

Paul's paradoxical form of ministry is not just an external imitation of the conduct of Christ. It is arises out of a profound sharing of that life, a concept that has no parallel in Judaism. The workings of death in Paul lead to the life of his community because that death at work in him is the death of Christ:

> We are afflicted in every way, but not constrained... always carrying about in the body the dying of Jesus, so that the life of Jesus may also be manifested in our body.... So death is at work in us, but life in you. (2 Cor 4:10–12)

In 1 Corinthians, Paul developed the theme of union of life with Christ, especially with the image of the body and its members in order to stress the social coherence of the church. In 2 Corinthians union of life with Christ functions especially to describe how Christ continues to function through Paul's ministry. As he says in his letter prayer, "The sufferings [*pathêmata*] of Christ overflow to us" (1:5), sufferings that lead to "your encouragement and salvation [*sôteria*]" (1:6). In effect, Paul sees himself drawn into the atoning sufferings of Jesus. For Paul, the Corinthians are also drawn into this drama and form a "community [*koinônoi*] of those sufferings [*pathêmata*]" and thus also a community of "encouragement [*paraklêsis*]" (1:7).

It is in the "harsh letter" that Paul multiplies the references to his union with Christ. Not only that he is "of Christ" (10:7) but he is speaking "in Christ" (12:19; also 2:17) and conversely he will say, "Christ speaking in me" (13:3). He insists that the power of Christ dwells in him (12:9).

Because the power of Christ dwells in him, the "weaknesses, insults, hardships, persecutions, and constraints" that Paul suffers are suffered "for Christ" (*hyper Christou*) (12:10). Paul does not explain what he means by suffering "for Christ." In the letter of reconciliation, Paul refers to his sufferings ("being handed over to death") as "because of Jesus" (*dia Iêsoun*) (4:11), a reference mostly likely to the reason for his suffering. The description of suffering "for Christ" may actually mean "on behalf of Christ" or even "for the benefit of Christ" since this expression parallels Paul's description of Christ's sufferings and death "for us" (1 Thess 5:10; 1 Cor 11:24; see 1:13; 2 Cor 5:14–15; 5:21).

Paul is not claiming this union with Christ as a special apostolic privilege. It is part of the life of faith of any believer. He admonishes the Corinthians, "Examine yourselves to see whether you are living in faith.... Do you not realize that Jesus Christ is in you?" (13:5). Here "living in faith" is directly parallel to "Jesus Christ in you." As he begins to describe the cosmic reconciliation accomplished by God in Christ, Paul asserts, "One died for all, therefore all died" (5:14). Paul here is picturing a solidarity of all people with Christ on the cross.

F. Eschatology

1. *Future Eschatology*

Although reconciliation with God and salvation in this letter seem to be a present reality, Paul maintains a sense of future eschatology. His trust is in God "who raises the dead" (1:9), which has begun in Christ but will occur for the rest of humanity only in the future. He speaks of the "judgment seat of Christ" before which we must all appear in the future (5:10; see Rom 14:10).

2. Eschatology at Death

However, new in this letter is a sense of some form of eschatological life immediately at death. Paul introduces here the image of the eternal and heavenly dwelling or building from God, which we receive "should this tent be destroyed" (5:1). He seems to be describing an action of God that he expects to occur at his death.

Paul does not have an image of a "spiritual soul" in a spiritual heaven. He sees the need for some form of building or clothing, "not made by human hands" (*acheiropoiêtos*), which in the religious jargon of the time meant something from God (Col 2:11; Mark 14:45), here a reality that would complete the human person or at least eliminate the sense of "nakedness" (5:4). Nevertheless the general thrust of this description seems to be an affirmation of a personal existence immediately after death. If this is correct, then Paul is beginning to follow a Hellenized trend in Judaism that pictured such existence.[8]

On the other hand, the clothing imagery and the result of this new clothing as death being "swallowed up" is the same as that described in 1 Corinthians for the general resurrection of the dead (5:4; see 1 Cor 15:54). Hence, Paul may be probing in this direction but at this point is not clear that he has something in mind different from the final resurrection of the dead. Again, we see two vectors set up, perhaps one to correct the other.

3. Eschatology Now

The Spirit as "down payment" of the heavenly life (5:5; see 1:22) is another image in this letter for eschatological anticipation. The Spirit characterizes the risen body (1 Cor 15:44) but is given in some form now as a pledge of the future payment in full. The Spirit anticipates the eschatological "glory" of the risen body (see 3:7–11; 1 Cor 15:43). This transformation is now, but it is only in the heart, not in the present corruptible body.

Paul can likewise speak about the "new creation" in Christ that is now. "The old passed away [aorist tense], behold the new has arrived [perfect tense]" (5:17). We are not just waiting for the day of the Lord. This new creation is all part of God in the process of reconciling the world to himself (5:18–19).

IV. The Message of the Letter

The worry of Paul for his church has taken on a dire tone. Things appear to have gotten much worse than what Paul envisioned in 1 Corinthians. Because of the geographical distance, because of his "infirmities," because of his fear of having to face the trouble in anger, Paul does not seem to be able to handle the situation. In no other letter does Paul write so much about himself and his worries.

The ministry of Christ, however, reminds Paul that God's salvation operates through apparent weakness. God raises from the dead. "Church" success does not come by human accomplishment but by God's action in the resurrection.

The same pattern of power in weakness must therefore characterize any minister of Christ. That power and effectiveness of Christ operates through weakness. The life of Christ is communicated through death. Paul cannot come to his community as some sort of superior member of the community, dealing with sin by the direct exercise of power. Rather, like Christ Paul himself can enrich his community by being "utterly spent" for them, by becoming poor. He can empower them by becoming weak.

Like the prophets of old, Paul could not do the work of God without being drawn personally into the pathos of God. Like the prophets of old, Paul ran into failure during his lifetime. The power of the prophets rose from their writings read long after their deaths. If we look at it from a long-term historical perspective, Paul's success in establishing a vibrant Christianity is astounding. In his time, however, he could not see it. Success in any matter of faith is a matter of God's time. The resurrection is an eschatological event. It is the Spirit in his heart, the "down payment" of the resurrection, however, that allowed Paul to continue working. In the end he was not discouraged.

8
Galatians

In the third century BC, a Celtic tribe migrated from Gaul across the Bosporus to the north-central part of modern-day Turkey. Their new territory became known as "Gallo-Graecia," eventually corrupted to "Galatia." Their main cities were Ancyra, Pessinus, and Tavium. Intimidated by the Roman armies in their wars of expansion, the last of the Galatian kings, Amyntas, in 25 BC bequeathed his kingdom to the Romans. In response, the Romans made Ancyra the capital of the new province and enlarged it to include parts of Paphlagonia and Pontus to the north and Pisidia, and parts of Lycaonia and Phrygia, to the south.

I. Background for the Letter

A. The Time and Place of Writing of the Letter

Understanding the background of Paul's Letter to the Galatians poses a challenge. As he writes this letter, Paul does not say where he is. Apparently he has been to Galatia more than once (Gal 4:13 "the first visit"). However, a long time has not lapsed since he was there or at least since he had some report from the church there: "I am amazed at how fast you have fallen away" (1:6). Hence, many commentators today see this as a relatively early letter, perhaps preceding even 1 Corinthians, written from Ephesus.

A careful comparison of this letter with Romans, however, suggests that these two letters were written close to each other. Common expressions, common images, common concerns link these two writings. In both letters Abraham plays a dominant role. Both develop toward a type of climax with the "Abba" prayer that issues from the presence of that Spirit in our hearts.

Hence, another hypothesis comes to mind. As we will see in the next chapter, Paul carefully developed his thoughts for the Romans. During this period of intense reflection, he could have heard of a crisis in the church of Galatia. He saw that the root of the problem for the Galatians lay precisely in their concept of the law, on which he was already reflecting in his developing letter to the Romans. He takes his reflections, adds descriptions of his concerns for the Galatians, and develops a response specifically geared for Galatia.

Romans, as we will see, is easy to situate. Paul is in Cenchreae, just outside of Corinth (Rom 16:1). He now has the collection of money that he planned in 1 Corinthians and expected to collect in 2 Corinthians. If we correlate Romans with the story of Paul in Acts, we would situate Romans at the end of his third journey, around AD 58, when Acts describes him making a brief journey to "Greece" (Acts 20:2–3).

In Corinth Paul would have been almost as close to Galatia as he would have been in Ephesus. The Aegean Sea was itself a link for the cities on its shores rather than a barrier. Locating this writing in Corinth at the end of this third journey would place it about three years after his last visit to Galatia. This is the hypothesis we will follow in this study.

B. The Readers

Another difficulty arises when we want to identify those whom Paul expected to read this letter. Galatia was both a territory in the north-central part of Turkey as well as an official province including that territory but extending far to the south. Was Paul writing to the Galatian people of the north part of the province, or was he writing to the cities of the south part of the province mentioned in Acts?

An identification of the readers with those living in the southern part of the province has one advantage. It allows us to correlate better the description of Paul in Acts with his letter writing. Acts 13—14 describes Paul founding churches in Antioch,

Iconium, Lystra, and Derbe—all cities within the southern part of the province of Galatia. To see the inhabitants of these cities as "the Galatians" to whom Paul addresses his letter is to provide a tighter link between Luke and Paul. These cities are otherwise not mentioned by Paul.

Serious difficulties arise, however, with seeing the recipients of this letter as inhabitants of southern Galatia:

1. Paul addresses the readers, "You stupid Galatians!" (3:1). Such a blast would have no effect unless the readers clearly and consistently identified themselves as "Galatians." Paul thus seems to be identifying an ethnic group.
2. An attempt to correlate Paul's epistles with the Acts by identifying the recipients of his Letter to the Galatians with the churches he founded on his first journey causes as many problems as it solves. Presumably, this first journey would correspond to the fourteen years Paul describes as spent in the region of Syria and Cilicia (Gal 1:21). Yet Paul writing to the Galatians about these fourteen years does not at all refer to this visit as he talks about the fourteen years.
3. A correlation between the epistles and Acts could be done simply by noting the ambiguity in Acts 16:6 and 18:23, where Luke could be distinguishing Phrygia from the Galatian country, suggesting in fact a trip up north to the territory of the ethnic Galatians.
4. Paul has no particular habit of referring to places only under their official Roman names. He speaks of traveling from Jerusalem to Syria (Gal 1:18–21). In fact, the province of Syria included Jerusalem. Similarly, he refers to Judea (1 Thess 2:14) and Arabia (Gal 1:17), neither of which were official province names.

For these reasons, Paul appears to be writing to the inhabitants of northern Galatia, that is, the ethnic Galatians perhaps in the area of Ancyra, modern day Ankara, capital of the Republic of Turkey.

C. The Crisis in Galatia

An examination of this Letter to the Galatians reveals a complex situation that provokes Paul to send this harsh letter. The situation seems to involve several aspects:

First, Paul refers to the Galatians coming from a "bondage to beings that by nature are not gods" and of now wanting "to turn back again to the weak and poor elements [*stoicheia*]" (4:8–9), which are presumably "the elements of the world" (4:3). This sounds like a relapse into some form of paganism, although Paul speaks of these "elements" in the context of the law. Perhaps his elaborate warnings against the "cravings of the flesh" (5:16–21) reflect the recurrence of pagan immorality, although again Paul speaks of these cravings in his discussion of the law.

Second, Paul describes the Galatians as wanting "to be under the law" (4:21). A Judaizing movement appears to have taken root in Galatia. Despite Paul's reference to his earlier difficulty with the "people from James" (2:12), the Judaizers now in Galatia do not appear to be full-blown Jewish Christians, much less missionaries from the Jerusalem church. Paul, in fact, insists that the Jerusalem church supports his work (see 1:9). Paul in effect ridicules the Galatian attempt to adopt the law as dilettantes, picking and choosing only parts of the law to observe. "Tell me, you who desire to be under the law, do you not hear the law?" (4:21). "I testify again to every one who receives circumcision that he is bound to keep the whole law" (5:3). The Judaizers, at least as Paul sees them, appear to be Gentiles who learned about circumcision and now want to press this onto the community as a condition for salvation. Some fifty years later Ignatius of Antioch also warned about Gentiles in Asia Minor preaching the Jewish law (*Phila* 6:1).

Third, the Galatians are apparently ready to reject Paul as a "Johnny-come-lately" without the qualifications of a "real" apostle and dependent on the Jerusalem authorities to start with. The accusation against Paul also seems to describe him as opposing the mother church of Jerusalem. Paul's vigorous defense insists that he has his apostolic call directly from Jesus. He was never simply a delegate from Jerusalem.

II. The Sequential Study of the Letter

A. The Outline of the Letter

For all its anger, this letter involves an intricate and carefully worked out structure, especially after the opening autobiographical apologia:

I. Opening (1:1–10)
  A. Address (1–5)
  B. Expression of astonishment (6–10)
II. Autobiographical apologia (1:11—2:16)
III. Instruction: Justification through faith (2:17—4:31)
  A. Summary (2:17–21)
    —Personal concerns for the Galatians (3:1–5)
  B. Abraham and the Old Testament (3:6–22)—rabbinic style homily?
    1. 1st cycle (3:6–14)
      a. positive: the blessing (6–9)—Gen 15:6; Gen 12:3
      b. negative: the curse (10–12)—Deut 27:26; Hab 2:4
      c. Christ: blessing and curse (13–14)—Deut 21:23
    2. 2nd cycle (3:15–22)
      a. positive: the promise (15–16)—Gen 12:7
      b. negative: the law (17–21)
      c. Christ (22)
  C. Before and after (3:23—4:31)
    1. 1st cycle (3:23–29)
      a. before: the law pedagogue (23–24)
      b. after: Christ (25–29)
    2. 2nd cycle (4:1–7)
      a. before: *nepios* (1–3)
      b. after: *hyios* (4–7)
    3. 3rd cycle (4:21–31)
      —Personal concerns for Galatians (4:8–20)
      a. before: Abraham's two sons (21–27)—Gen 16; 21:1–21; Isa 4:1
      b. after: the two children now (28–31)—Gen 21:9

IV. Christian living (5:1—6:10)
  A. Freedom, not slavery, freedom (5:1–13)
  B. The law of love, flesh/spirit antithesis, the law of Christ (5:14—6:2)
  C. Maxims (6:3–10)
V. Conclusion (6:11–18)

B. The Greeting (1:1–10)

Paul comes on strong. His authority as an apostle is directly from "Jesus Christ and God the Father who raises him from the dead" (1:1). After his typical greeting, Paul gets directly into his **salvation and eschatology trajectory**, with a description of Jesus, "who gave himself for our sins that he might extract us from the present evil age [*aiôn*] in accord with the will of our God and Father" (1:4). We see here a reference to the atoning death of Jesus ("who gave himself for our sins"), the apocalyptic sense of sin as cosmic ("the present evil age"), and the initiative of God the Father, according to whose will this whole process takes place.

In place of a thanksgiving prayer, Paul starts with an abrupt admonition, "I am amazed" (1:6). The unkind words that follow (1:6–9) for the opposition missionaries ring much like those for the "false apostles" in 2 Corinthians (2 Cor 11:13–15).

C. Paul's Defense of His Ministry (1:11—2:16)

Instead of a "newsy" section as normal in other letters following the greeting, Paul recalls events some twenty years earlier in order basically to describe his role in the new church. He speaks of his encounter with the risen Jesus, an encounter that changed his life (1:11–17), along with a brief description of his early contacts with the Jerusalem church (1:18–24). The verses can be compared with Acts 9:1–30. The allusions Paul makes (Gal 1:15–16) to the vocation of Jeremiah are subtle (Jer 1:5) but show that Paul saw his encounter with "the Son" as more of a prophetic vocation than a religious conversion. The title for Jesus here is important for Paul's **Christology trajectory**.

The description of Paul's second meeting with the leaders of the Jerusalem church (2:1–10) again emphasizes his harmony with them, despite Paul's ambivalence about their "reputation" (2:6). The only stipulation was to "be mindful of the poor" (2:10), which if interpreted ecclesiologically would express the importance of remembering the "mother church" of Jerusalem. The verses can be compared with Acts 15:1–35.

Paul is first to express the tenuous nature of this harmony. He goes on to describe the conflict with Cephas (Peter) in Antioch, implicating James, the apparent leader of the church of Jerusalem, and even Barnabas, Paul's companion up to that point (2:11–14; see Acts 15:36–39).

Verse 15 starts with a continuation of the conversation between Paul and Peter. By the end of 16, however, Paul is speaking to the Galatians. It is difficult to say exactly where in these two verses Paul makes the shift. In any case, his main thought, both to Peter and to the Galatians, is expressed in verse 16, in a chiastic construction:

a. A person is not justified [*dikaioutai*] by the works of the law
   b. but through the faith of Christ [*pisteôs Christou*].
      c. And we have come to faith in Christ Jesus [*eis Christon Iêsoun episteusamen*]
   b.' so that we might be justified by the faith of Christ
a.' not by works of the law, since by works of the law no one is justified.

In a shift of vocabulary that will become dominant in both Galatians and Romans, Paul speaks of being "justified." The word is borrowed from forensic language and perhaps could refer in a Jewish context to the action of God expected when he comes as the just judge (Isa 46:13; 62:1–2). Paul here speaks of it as a present reality and as accomplished by "the faith of Christ" in contrast to "works of the law." The rest of his letter will be an attempt to explain this thought crucial to Paul's **salvation trajectory**.

In both Galatians and Romans, Paul will focus on the role of faith as key to this justification. The expression he uses to designate the reality through which and by which one is justified is "the faith of Christ." It is not clear what he means. This genitive construction could range from designating the matter that characterizes something (as in "the cup of gold") to designating the owner (as in "the cup of John"). Here it is contrasted with human performance in regard's to God's commands ("works of the law"), but still it is associated with the human action of coming to faith ("we have come to faith") directed to Christ Jesus (*eis Christon*). Because of this contrast with human performance, it would seem to be incorrect to translate *pistis Christou* as "faith in Christ" as if Christ were the object to which the human act is directed. When Paul wants to speak about faith as a human action directed to Christ, he shifts to the verb form *episteusamen,* and uses a specific preposition, *eis Christon*.

D. The Opening Summary (2:17–21)

The next five verses (2:17–21) continue a dense summary of doctrine for the whole letter. It is Paul's first attempt at explaining the meaning of a life of faith, but this time in the context of the **union with Christ trajectory**. The composition consists of lines alternating more or less between descriptions of what "I" did and descriptions involving Christ:

> It is through the law that *I died* to the law, to live for God.
> I have been crucified *with Christ,*
> The life, however, *I live* now is not my own;
> **Christ lives** in me.
> *I now live* in the flesh;
> I live in faith [*en pistei*], that of the **Son of God**,
> who loved me and gave himself for me. (2:19–20)

This summary combines several of the major trajectory themes we have been following. The **salvation trajectory** again here stresses salvation through death. Christ "gave himself" in his love for Paul. Paul dies in order to live for God. The law, somehow, is part of the picture of destruction. Paul dies "through the law" and "to the law" by being "crucified with Christ." The result is such an intense union that Paul can say that his life is more that of Christ than of himself!

Paul explicitly describes this union as a life "in faith." Faith is the mode or way in which he now in his human life (*en sarki*) becomes part of this divine drama which occurs in Christ.

E. Justification through Faith: Lessons from the Old Testament (3:6–22)

After expressing his intense concern for the Galatians where he introduces his "Spirit/flesh" antithesis (3:1–5), Paul begins a rabbinic-type homily. The subject is Abraham and his justification. The structure is a typical rabbinic concatenation of Old Testament texts, linked by developments around key words from the text. As it now exists in this letter, the homiletic development moves in two cycles, 3:6–14 and 3:15–22, each with an important contrast, each ending with a reference to Christ, thus adding to the **Christ trajectory**.

1. The First Cycle (3:6–14)

The first cycle contrasts the blessing stemming from Abraham with the curse stemming from the law. It is also a contrast between "faith" and "doing these things," referring to an observance described in Leviticus (3:12).[1] Abraham becomes a model of believing. Therefore, those "of faith" (*ek pisteôs*) are connected to Abraham and "the faith of Abraham" (3:9).

In a rather shocking conclusion, Paul refers to **Christ** as directly involved in the curse of the law: "Christ bought us back from the law's curse by himself becoming a curse for us" (3:13). The line parallels in content the description of Christ in Paul's previous letter: "For our sakes God made him who did not know sin, to be sin" (2 Cor 5:21). Again, Paul stresses the deep involvement of Christ in the sinfulness from which he redeems humanity. And again, he stresses that salvation comes from destruction, a destruction suffered by Christ. In this **salvation trajectory** Paul returns to the image of salvation as a purchase (3:13; see 1 Cor 6:20; 7:23). Here Jesus is the agent of the transaction.

Paul then connects this destruction with the law. Through the law Christ becomes "a curse." Through the law Christ dies. However, through that death "comes the promise of the Spirit," which for Paul means an extension of blessings to those outside the law, the Gentiles of the world. Implied here is the thought that through the death of Christ the law in its exclusiveness dies.

2. The Second Cycle (3:15–22)

The second cycle contrasts the promises given to Abraham, which Paul calls the "previous covenant," with the law that came some 430 years later. Tagged on to the description of the promises is a smidgen of rabbinic exegesis on the word *seed*, referring to the posterity of Abraham. Like a good rabbi of his day, Paul focuses on the grammar of the word and sees here a singular noun. He then attaches a theology to that singular form. A modern philologist would cringe at Paul's reasoning. The word *seed* is a collective noun, referring to a group even in its singular form. Once again we are reminded that Paul thought in the literary forms of his day—not ours—and that his use of the Old Testament consists of finding hooks on which to hang his theology, not to probe the theology and intentions of the historical author.

Paul's reference to the covenant made with Abraham probably alludes to Genesis 15 (the J or E tradition?), which describes a divine covenant between God and Abram (later Abraham), one promising progeny with no mention of either land or circumcision.[2] The point of the antithesis is to show the priority and superiority of the promises over the law.[3] In this way Paul can show how the promises can be fulfilled without the law. "The faith of Jesus Christ" is the key to this fulfillment. Through this faith as an opening to new life, the "restriction of all things under sin" is broken and "the promises are given to those who believe" (3:22).

F. Justification through Faith: The Fullness of Time (3:23—4:7)

The next part of the letter tries a new approach on the same subject with another double cycle, 3:23–29 and 3:23—4:7. Each cycle contrasts the epoch before Christ with the epoch after Christ. These contrasts allow us to understand Paul's vision of history, the continuities and discontinuities between the old and the new.

1. The First Cycle (3:23–29)

The first cycle contrasts the epoch "before faith" (3:23) with "the coming of faith" (3:25). The focus is on the individual, although the thought is epochal not psychological. "Faith" is not so much an action of individuals as rather a gift of God that "comes," much like the epochal coming of "the mature/perfect" (*to teleion*) associated with the gift of "love" (*agapê*) when one puts aside the things of a child (*nêpios*) (see 1 Cor 13:10–11). In the first epoch, we were under the rule of a *pedagôgos*, a household slave in charge of the children, not so much the teacher, but rather the "babysitter" who would drag the children by the ear to school and back. Paul identifies that *pedagôgos* with the law.

With "the coming of faith," the relationship to the pedagogue changes radically. We are no longer under this babysitter because "all have become sons [*hyioi*] of God because of your faith in Christ Jesus" (3:27). We have entered fully into the household of God, not in the restricted form of a child in the house but as a fully entitled "son." Paul is thinking of the transition from minority to adulthood. Paul is not focusing on maleness of a son as contrasted with a daughter. In the next sentence Paul will throw out any considerations of gender. However, the term "son" reflects the privileged position of the adult male child in a family of Paul's culture. The term reflects also the relationship of Christ to his Father. As Paul insists again, it is only by our participation in Christ, our being "in Christ," that we possess this status of fully entitled members of God's family (3:27).

Paul draws two immediate consequences of this epochal change. First, all the distinctions important in Paul's day for dividing humanity are meaningless (3:28). The divisions between "slave and freeman, male and female" were considered absolutely essential for contemporary society. The division between "Jew and Greek" was fundamental for Jews. Paul describes the new unity of humanity in Christ that overcomes these cultural divisions. The reference to baptism (3:27) may suggest that these lines in fact came from a baptismal formula that Paul knew.

Second, Paul points out how this participation in the full status of Jesus' Sonship means also sharing in Jesus' rights to the promises made to Abraham (3:29), promises that are independent of the law because they were prior to the law.

2. *The Second Cycle (4:1–6)*

In the second cycle of this literary development, Paul expresses the same ideas with new terms and images. Like the first, the second cycle also involves a "before" and an "after," without, however, Paul explicitly using those terms. He focuses intensely on the temporal categories as one replaces the other but here shows even more clearly how these epochal changes involve us personally.

The "before" is described at 4:1–3. The situation is that of an "infant" or "child" (*nepios*), the same term Paul used to describe the Corinthians when they did not exhibit the full spiritual existence of the faithful (1 Cor 3:1–4) and to describe the imperfect realities that are put aside "when the perfect comes" (1 Cor 13:11). Here Paul likens the situation to that of a slave, a member of the household but one without any real rights. Here Paul envisions an end to this epoch in the phrase, "until the time set by the Father" (4:2).

The "after" epoch appears in detail in 4:4–7, where almost every word packs an important theme about living in faith. Paul sets the whole description in the context of an epoch, "when the fullness of time came" (4:4). This fullness appears as the equivalent of adulthood for the individual in contrast to being a child. Paul describes the essence of that epoch as the sending of the Son of God, applying here what appears to be an early Christian formula.[4]

Paul's particular rendition of this "God-sending-the-Son" formula is complex and dense. To this formula, Paul adds two conditions that characterize Christ as sent and then two conditions that characterize our salvation intended by this sending. The two pairs, in fact, show an interesting correlation. The correlation is in an inverted or "chiastic" form:

God sent forth his Son
a. born of woman
b. born under the law
b.' in order that he might buy back those under the law
a.' in order that we might receive adoptive sonship.(4:4–5)

The two conditions to which Christ submitted as sent by God are fundamentally negative, being born of a woman[5] and being subjected to the law. From these two negative conditions arise two major blessings for us. Christ's subjection to the law leads to our freedom from the law. Christ's condition as a human child leads to our condition as a son of God. Paul is developing his **salvation trajectory** and reflecting also his **Christ trajectory**, focusing on something suffered by Christ, without, however, referring here to the death of Jesus. Alluding to Jesus' birth, Paul makes one of his few references to an aspect of the mortal Jesus other than his death as having saving significance.

To develop further his description of what happens after "the fullness of time," Paul adds a second sending by the Father, this time, the sending of **the Spirit** (4:6). It is the Spirit in our hearts that drives home our status as sons of God. It is the Spirit from our hearts that generates the prayer to God as "Abba." The Aramaic term, possibly used to address one's father in a familiar and intimate way, may well have been the word Jesus historically used to refer to God as his Father (see Mark 14:36). It might well have been the term Jesus used to teach his disciples to pray (see Luke 11:2). For Paul, it is the Spirit who allows an internal correspondence of the heart to the objective, epochal transformation of time. This is the time of adult sonship. The Spirit in our hearts directs us individually to God as intimate Father.

The description here of Christ's negative condition, the resulting benefit for humanity and the gift of the Spirit, echoes an earlier statement of Paul in the letter, "Christ bought us back from the power of the law's curse by becoming a curse for us...in order that the nations might become the blessing of Abraham in Jesus

Christ, in order that we might receive the promise of the Spirit through faith" (3:13–14).

G. Freedom (4:8–31)

Up to this point, Paul is explaining what it means to be justified by the "faith of Christ." Paul starts again with a new angle on the same topic. The theme now is freedom (*eleutheria*) and includes a third "before" and "after" cycle.

The concept of freedom as an interior quality is foreign to the Old Testament and in general is not a Jewish concept. Here Paul is apparently introducing the Stoic ideal of *eleutheria* into this discussion of the law, shifting, however, from the Greek nuance of self-sufficiency to stress the attitude that acts out of a loving relationship to God. Paul ties the ideal to the action of God rather than to human accomplishment.

Again he addresses the Galatians and expresses his concern for them (4:8–20). Again he returns to the Old Testament and the example of Abraham, in a rather loose allegorization of Genesis texts (Gen 16 and 21) not unlike those of the rabbis of his day. Using social categories of his day, Paul then describes Sarah as the "free woman [*eleutheras*]" in contrast to Hagar, the "slave woman [*paidiskê*]" (4:21–27). All of this development leads to the declaration of the believer now as a free person, a child according to the Spirit (*kata pneuma*), a child of the promise and of the free mother (4:28–31).

H. Exhortations to Christian Living (5:1—6:10)

Now in the second half of this letter, Paul shifts from explanation to exhortation. He urges the Galatians to hold on to the freedom to which God calls them, a freedom that is inseparable from love and the Spirit. By drawing on images and themes from his **trajectories** concerning **the Spirit**, **union with Christ**, and **salvation**, he develops his instruction regarding the Mosaic law, particularly the law of circumcision.

Paul first expresses his concerns for the Galatians. He seems to contradict himself when he warns, "If you have yourselves circumcised, Christ will be of no benefit to you" (5:2), and then asserts, "Neither circumcision nor having a foreskin counts for anything" (5:6; see also 6:15). As he seems to wish for a divine judgment against his adversaries (5:10), Paul is certainly trying to draw borders around the community and protect the inner circle. In Galatians, Paul still imputes evil motives to the "false brothers" in Jerusalem (2:4) and describes the action of the Jewish Christians in Antioch as "hypocrisy" (2:11–13). A certain meanness appears here in his wish that those pushing circumcision would slip and castrate themselves (5:12).

Then drastically changing his tone, Paul explains the connection of freedom, love, and Spirit beginning at 5:13, where he warns about a false freedom and points out how authentic freedom leads to a new and good kind of slavery. "You, brothers, have been called to freedom, not the freedom as a pretext for the flesh; rather be a slave [*douleuete*] to one another through love" (5:13). Paul is speaking in the language of paradox.

The key to this paradox is love. Love allows service to be an exercise of freedom. Love distinguishes authentic freedom from a false freedom. Love is also, as Paul explains in the next verse, the key to observing the law. "The whole law has found its fulfillment in one command, 'Love your neighbor as yourself'" (5:14).

Here Paul shows how far he has come from his pharisaic past, where living a just life was a matter of obedience to a multitude of prescriptions. The ideal of the Pharisees was to see everything they did as an act of obedience, to see everything they did as regulated by a divine ordinance, and hence everything they did as an act of religion. The intention was noble, but the results usually enslaving. Individuals lived their day in constant concern about breaking a rule, preoccupied about their conduct, preoccupied about themselves.

Paul takes the exact opposite approach, focusing on love as the fulfillment of the law. This instruction provides an unusual testimony of Paul's contact with gospel traditions. A decade or so later, the gospels will record Jesus' similar instruction, "The first commandment is, 'Hear, O Israel: The Lord our God, the Lord is one; and you shall love the Lord your God with all your heart....' The second is this, 'You shall love your neighbor as yourself'"

(Mark 12:29–30, and parallels). Citing Deuteronomy 6:5 and Leviticus 19:18, Jesus insisted on this internal law of the heart (see also Mark 7:1–23). Paul's insistence here reflects very probably his dependence on the oral teachings passed down in the Christian communities stemming from Jesus himself.

Earlier in 2 Corinthians, Paul spoke of the law written in the heart and connected that law with the Spirit. There Paul played with the antithesis of "letter" and "Spirit." Here in Galatians he connects this law of love with the Spirit and plays with the antithesis of "flesh" and "Spirit." He does so by means of an elaborate chiastic structure, 5:14—6:2, a structure that begins and ends with explicit references to the new law in the life of the believer. The chiastic structure itself consists of alternations between positive and negative statements, working up to the pivotal contrast between the works of the flesh (5:19–21) and the fruit of the Spirit (5:22–23a). The alternations between positive and negative statements for the most part throughout this chiasm follow the antithesis between Spirit and flesh:

A. The law of love (5:14)—positive
 B. Harming one another (5:14)—negative
  C. Walking in the Spirit (16a)—positive
   D. Lusts of the flesh (16b–17)—negative
    E. Not under the law (18)—positive
     F. Works of the flesh (19–21)—negative
     F'. Fruit of the Spirit (22–23a)—positive
    E'. Not under the law (23b)—positive
   D'. Lusts of the flesh (24)—negative
  C'. Walking in the Spirit (25)—positive
 B'. Harming one another (26)—negative
A'. The law of Christ (6:1–2)—positive

This chiasm is important for understanding Paul's concept of "flesh." Earlier (1 Cor 15) we saw Paul's distinction between "body" (*sôma*) and "flesh" (*sarx*), where "flesh" as such is excluded from the kingdom of God (1 Cor 15:50). Here we see "flesh" as a dimension or sphere of power, with its own "cravings" and "works." "Flesh" appears precisely as the "anti-Spirit" dimension of life. "The flesh lusts against the Spirit; the Spirit, against the flesh. The two are directly opposed" (5:17). Furthermore, as the list of the "works of the flesh" clearly indicates, Paul has in mind something far more comprehensive than sex or sensuality. Idolatry, sorcery, jealousy are not what we would consider "sins of the flesh." In fact, the general opposition Paul makes between flesh and Spirit tells us that he is thinking of something more than any anthropological element. This is apocalyptic language. Paul lists the "works of the flesh" and insists on the utter incompatibility of this dimension with the kingdom of God (5:19–21). As he said in similar words to the Corinthians, "Those doing these things will not inherit the kingdom of God" (5:21; see 1 Cor 6:9).

In contrast, Paul then describes the "fruit of the Spirit" and names "love" first (5:22–23). Although Paul speaks of a plural "works" of the flesh, he names a singular "fruit" of the Spirit. The list that describes this "fruit," does not give us a multitude of things, but really one reality with many names.

Bracketing this contrast between the "works" and the "fruit" in the present chiastic structure is Paul's insistence on freedom from the law. He says the same thing twice, before and after: "If you are guided by the Spirit, you are not under the law" (5:18). "Against such [fruit] there is no law" (6:23b).

In this way again Paul weaves freedom, love, and Spirit together into a tight fabric. He is saying in effect that the law, including the Ten Commandments, does not exist as an authority for a person filled with love and the Spirit. The qualification of being filled with love and the Spirit is a big one, but the conclusion of freedom from the law marks the high point of Paul's instructions about the role of the law. He will summarize the same points with a softening of the tone in Romans 13:8–10.

In a wider bracket of the whole chiasm (5:14 and 6:2), Paul emphasizes the theme of the new law. He described it first simply as love fulfilling the whole law (5:14). At the end, he describes it as "the law of Christ" (6:2), where he gives greater concreteness to this new law. In 1 Corinthians Paul described himself as under "the law of Christ" to indicate how he is not really "outside God's law" in his comportment with Gentiles (1 Cor 9:21). In Galatians he applies it precisely to the situation of an imperfect community, to a community where members see each other in their sinfulness. Paul sums up the new law in this situation as simply, "Carry one another's burdens." He has in mind the image of Christ, who "became a curse for us" (Gal 3:13), who became "sin" for us (2 Cor 5:21), who redeemed us by sharing our burden of sinfulness. Hence, Paul can call this new law simply "the law of Christ." The striking expression reflects on the role of Christ as the key to understanding the law.

I. Maxims and Conclusion (6:3–18)

Paul follows with a series of short but unrelated instructions (6:3–10). With a final jab at his opponents (6:11–13), he makes a final contrast between a life based on circumcision and one based on the "new creation" (6:14–16) and concludes with his typical christological blessing (6:18).

III. The Thematic Summary of the Letter

A. God

Off the starting block, Paul identifies God as "Father" and "our Father" (1:1, 3–4). Judaism had taught Paul to address God in prayer as "Father."[6] The late wisdom traditions in which Paul grew up addressed God this way (Wis 14:3; Sir 23:1, 4). The Aramaic form that Paul uses here, "Abba" (Gal 4:6), however, suggests that he had received this name for God from the early Jerusalem church, to be conserved in its original form perhaps because Jesus used that term (see Mark 14:36; Luke 11:2 [Q]). Paul identifies the Spirit of God in our hearts as the one who actually addresses God as "Abba." This Spirit, as Paul insists, is precisely the Spirit of God's Son (Gal 4:6).

Paul is also very clear in the letter that this God is the God we know from the Old Testament. This is the God in whom Abraham placed his faith (3:6; referring to Gen 15:6) and who ratified a covenant with Abraham (3:17; see Gen 15:18).

Probably because of its polemic nature, this letter is the clearest about the role of God in the vocation and apostolate of Paul. Paul sees himself as an "apostle through Jesus and God the Father" (1:1). However, Paul then insists on the agency of this God as he describes how God set him apart, called him, and revealed his Son to him (2:15–16).

Paul also focuses on God the Father as principal agent of salvation. In order to redeem us from the law and to give us a status of adoptive members of his family, God sends his Son to be born of a woman (3:4). It is God who raised Jesus from the dead (1:1). Finally, God completes this mission of Jesus by sending the Spirit of his Son into our hearts by which the loving relationship to God as "Abba" can be experienced (3:6).

Paul tries to place God in the central focus of the Galatians as he speaks of their new situation. "Now" they are characterized as "knowing God" (4:9), a statement that Paul then corrects to insist even more on the agency of God, "rather being known by God" (4:9). This knowledge of God is an intimate experience of God. In Paul's Jewish faith, the knowledge of God meant accepting God's will.

B. Christ Jesus

1. Human Being and Son of God

More than in any previous letter, Paul stresses the flesh-and-blood life of Jesus. He is Jewish as subject to the law and as "the seed" of Abraham. As such he becomes the heir to the promises (3:16). Paul insists again on the crucifixion (3:1), where Jesus enters into the "cursed" situation of those under the law (3:13). In fact, the whole mission of Jesus from God is summed up as "born of a woman, born under the law" (4:4).

This letter also stands out by the frequency with which Paul calls Jesus "the Son" or "his [God's] Son." Paul starts the series with the description of his own vocation, with God revealing "his Son" to him (1:16). Paul lives "by faith in the Son of God" (2:20). God sent both "his Son" to be born of a woman and "the Spirit of his Son" into our hearts (4:4–5).

Paul is carrying on the trajectory he began in 1 Thessalonians where he described believers as waiting for "the Son from heaven" (1 Thess 1:10). He continued this trajectory in his Corinthian correspondence where he again wrote of "the Son" as an eschatological reality (1 Cor 15:28), but also as a present reality with whom believers form a community (1 Cor 1:9). In 2 Corinthians, Jesus as "Son of God" is the great affirmation of God (2 Cor 1:19). Here in Galatians the title becomes an image consistently associated with the way God intervenes in the life of believers.

2. The Preexistent Son?

By using the sending formula in Galatians, "God sent his Son born of a woman..." (Gal 4:4), is Paul alluding to an existence of Christ before his birth? The description of God sending his Son is ambiguous. Does God have a Son before he sends him? The sending of the Son could be like that of the sending of the prophets (Isa 6:8; Jer 1:7). On the other hand, this mission of the Son seems to include his being born of a woman. Yet if this were a "prenatal" vocation, we would expect a reference to the womb, as Paul does in regard his own vocation (Gal 1:15).

Again Paul seems to be dangling the possibility that Jesus preexisted as God's Son. Yet the suggestion remains vague. Nothing is said here about a personal attitude of Jesus so as to distinguish personal preexistence from a general plan of God where the Son could exist as an idea.

If, however, we place this sending formula in the trajectory begun in the Corinthian correspondence, the suggestion becomes louder. In that correspondence, Paul made an effort to identify Jesus as the wisdom of God (2 Cor 3:18; 4:4–6) and referred to the role of Jesus in creation (1 Cor 8:6). In that correspondence, the contrast formulas describing Jesus as moving from "being rich" to "he made himself poor" (2 Cor 8:9) and as "not knowing sin" to being "made sin" by God (5:21) appear to refer to an active and personal phase prior to the flesh-and-blood career of Jesus. In this trajectory, the sending formula in Galatians begins to ring with the suggestion that God had his Son before he sent him—that Jesus preexisted before becoming human.

3. *Christ and the Spirit*

As regards the relationship between Christ and the Spirit, Paul in Galatians stresses continuity between the two. This continuity is clear from the parallel missions of Christ and the Spirit (Gal 3:6–7). This continuity appears also in Paul's theology of the law that usually revolves around the Spirit but in Galatians is summarized by "the law of Christ" (6:2). In his Corinthian correspondence, Paul's allusion to Jeremiah's law written in the heart involves both the "ink" of the Spirit and the "letter of Christ" (2 Cor 3:3).

C. The Spirit of God

1. *The Spirit/Flesh Antithesis*

In 1 Corinthians, Paul used the "spiritual/natural" antithesis to distinguish the risen body from the mortal body (1 Cor 15:42–44) as well as to distinguish those who have received the Spirit from the members of "this eon" (1:18—2:16). In 2 Corinthians, Paul played with a "Spirit/letter" antithesis to explain the ambivalent character of the Old Testament law. Now in Galatians, Paul orchestrates a much more developed "Spirit/flesh" antithesis to describe the morality of a believer freed from the law (Gal 5:13—6:2).

The word *flesh* (*sarx*) in Paul's vocabulary must be distinguished from the word *body* (*sôma*). In 1 Corinthians, Paul uses the term *body* to describe what will rise as a spiritual reality at the general resurrection (1 Cor 15:42–44). The "body" is for the Lord and is capable of being a temple of the Spirit (6:13–19). On the other hand "flesh and blood" cannot inherit the kingdom of God (15:50). This distinction between "body" and "flesh" seems original with Paul.

Here in Galatians, the "flesh/Spirit" antithesis appears as the Jewish apocalyptic clash of cosmic fields of power, which pervade the human person and somehow link to anthropological parts, namely, human flesh and spirit, yet which are far greater than the human person. The Spirit here is above all the Spirit of God.

With the word *flesh* Paul appears to be trying to express the apocalyptic notion of an evil eon, in which humanity exists, that is manifested in a human mode of existence, and that illustrates the enormity and power of sin. "The works of the flesh" are a whole range of sins (Gal 5:19). "Sowing in the flesh" leads to harvesting corruption, in contrast to "sowing in the Spirit," which leads to harvesting "eternal life from the Spirit" (6:8). This cosmic sense of "flesh," then, is not simply the soft tissue of the human body. However, this soft tissue, with its vulnerability and with its corruptibility, may for Paul symbolize the cosmic dimension of weakness and corruption. This is not the typical Hellenistic concept of body or flesh as the tomb of the soul, nor is it the Old Testament view of flesh as the person himself or herself, especially in his or her weakness before God. In the way Paul uses it, this flesh/Spirit antithesis has no real parallel in Jewish writing.

2. The Spirit and Freedom from the Law

As he develops this antithesis between Spirit and flesh, Paul stresses the role of the Spirit in freedom from the law. "If you are guided by the Spirit you are not under the law" (Gal 5:18). He explains this extraordinary statement by describing the fruit of the Spirit, beginning with love, and then declares, "Against such there is no law" (5:23).

Paul is of course advocating moral living. As he says, "If we live by the Spirit, let us follow in the line of the Spirit" (5:25). Paul's insistence is on the priority of life over conduct, the priority of love over rules and laws (5:14; see Mark 7:15–23; 12:28–34).

The Spirit is a natural image for this freedom precisely because the Spirit for Paul is sent "into our hearts" (Gal 4:6). In 1 Corinthians, Paul had insisted "the Spirit of God dwells in you" (1 Cor 3:16). In 2 Corinthians, Paul made the "heart" connection explicit (2 Cor 1:22; 3:3). Here in Galatians, he associates the human heart with the very mission of the Spirit.

Because of this close connection between the Spirit and freedom from the law, Paul accuses the Galatians of beginning in the Spirit but now ending in the flesh (3:3). They are moving from this freedom toward a sense of obligation, toward the rule of circumcision. With the image of a foreskin hanging in front of him, Paul has a great play on words. In this sense, the religion of the circumcision is a religion of the flesh.

Although love and interiority remain major themes in the Old Testament (Deut 6:4–6; 10:12; Ezek 11;19; 36:26–27), and although Jeremiah connected this interiority with the law (Jer 31:33), no Old Testament or Jewish text comes close to Paul's theme of freedom from the law through the action of the Spirit.

3. The Spirit and the Abba Prayer

The immediate result of the mission of the Spirit into our hearts is the "Abba prayer." In this letter Paul describes the Spirit crying "Abba," thus establishing the relationship of loving child to caring Father. Paul's insistence on the Spirit's prayer as taking place in the heart might also suggest the interior experience of this loving relationship by the believer. In this sense, the mission and the prayer of the Spirit become a type of demonstration "that indeed you are [*hoti de este*]" of our adoption into the family of God.

Conversely, this prayer of the Spirit colors the Spirit clearly as a person. No longer simply the ink on the heart, this Spirit closely parallels the personal mission of the Son, both sent by the Father, both involved in personal activity (3:6–7).

D. Salvation

Although this letter is intended as an explanation of God's saving activity through Christ apart from the law, the words *salvation* (*sôteria*) and *to save* (*sôdzein*) are notably absent in this letter. Instead, the idea appears with a variety of other words and images that Paul uses to describe this basic good thing God is doing for us.

1. Being Justified

Opening the instructional part of this letter at 2:16, Paul uses the verb "to be justified" (*dikaiousthai)* three times to describe the result of the action of God in the present or in the past benefiting human beings. In this verse, Paul insists that this result takes place not through observance of the law but by "the faith of Christ." It is the blessing or benefit for which Christ died (2:21).

In the Septuagint Bible (LXX), the Greek verb in the active voice translates *hizdiq*, the hiphil (or causative) form of the Hebrew verb *zadaq*, meaning to make or declare someone to be just or righteous (Deut 25:1; Isa 50:8), to deliver from oppression (Ps 82:3; Isa 50:8), or somehow make someone to be in good standing with God (Isa 53:11; Dan 12:3). The basic idea appears in Paul's citation of Genesis 15:6 where Paul uses the noun *justice* (*dikaiosynê*), describing Abraham as believing God, "and it was credited to him as justice" (Gal 3:6).

Paul introduced this concept in his Corinthian correspondence. In 1 Corinthians Paul briefly mentioned how his readers were "now justified [*edikaiôthête*] in the name of the Lord Jesus Christ and in the Spirit of our God," citing perhaps a baptismal formula in which "justified" is in parallel with "washed" and "sanctified" (1 Cor 6:11). There Paul was contrasting the present situation of his readers with a life of sinfulness, which cannot inherit the kingdom of God (6:9–11). In 2 Corinthians Paul briefly declared that God made Christ "to be sin so that we might become the justice of God in him" (2 Cor 5:21).

In Galatians as in the Corinthian correspondence, Paul describes "justice" or "justification" mostly as a past or present reality. He does, however, speak of it here also as a future hope. "By the Spirit from faith we await the hope of justification" (Gal 5:5). This future reality looks like the "eternal life" one reaps from the Spirit (6:8).

2. Being Purchased

In 1 Corinthians, Paul used the image of the purchase to explain some form of rescue. "You have been purchased [*êgorasthête*] at a great price" (1 Cor 6:20; 7:23). In Galatians Paul elaborates: "Christ purchased [*exêgorasen*][7] us from the curse of the law becoming a curse for us" (3:13). Here Christ is the agent of the transaction. Later in the letter describing God's sending of his Son, the purpose of the sending is disclosed as "that he might purchase [*exagorasê*] those under the law" (4:5). Although the agent of the action is not explicit, the grammar of the sentence would suggest that it is "his Son."

While Paul insists that the fundamental agency of salvation lies with God the Father, Paul is speaking of Jesus as the one who actively brings about salvation. This imagery is not new. In 1 Thessalonians, it is Jesus who "rescues us from the coming wrath" (1 Thess 1:10). Also in Galatians, Jesus is the one "giving himself for our sins so that he might extract us [*exelêtai*] from this present evil age" (1:4). The image of the purchase or redemption allows Paul to focus even more on the specific activity of Jesus bringing about salvation. Of course, Jesus "purchased those under the law" in his role of Son being sent by God. (Gal 4:4–5). Thus, God the Father remains the fundamental agent of salvation.

Paul never suggests anyone to whom the price is ever paid. The involvement of God the Father in the sending of his Son precludes here a sense that some ransom had to be paid to God—and Satan is never mentioned in this letter. Perhaps the best handling of the issue is not to ask the question at all. The price of the purchase is not paid to anyone. It is just paid, and it is paid by Christ, presumably by his whole mission to suffer as the curse "on the tree" (3:13), "publicly crucified" (3:1). As is clear in 1 Corinthians 7:23, the result is a form of freedom as in the case of the ransom of slaves.

3. *The Fullness of Time*

What stands out in Galatians is Paul's attempt to depict salvation in terms of historical epochs. This gift of God appears as the transformation of history much like the transformation of the cosmos found in the apocalyptic portrayal of salvation, especially in the portrayal of the "two ages."[8] Paul, however, is not looking to an eschatological future. He develops this depiction by the contrast "before faith" and "now" (3:23–29). He repeats this contrast with that between the period of the "child [*nêpios*]" and what he calls "the fullness of time [*to plêroma tou chronou*]," which is also the age of "adoptive sonship [*hyiothesia*]," which God accomplishes by sending his Son and the Spirit of his Son (4:1–7).

In 2 Corinthians, Paul spoke of "the new covenant" transforming the law of the "old covenant" into the ministry of the Spirit (2 Cor 3:4–18). Somehow history has changed. Second Corinthians also described the act of God "reconciling the world to himself" (2 Cor 5:18–19), transforming the world by a "new creation" (5:17). The personal action of believers, however, is not excluded in 2 Corinthians, where Paul also refers to the personal action of "turning to the Lord" (3:16) and appeals to the individual readers to "be reconciled to God" (5:20).

So, likewise, in Galatians, Paul interweaves the cosmic and the personal as he the "fullness of time" and the "Spirit sent into our hearts." God is "saving history," as it were, and individuals are drawn into this salvation to the degree they are drawn into this fullness of time.

Although Paul is speaking of a present reality and the action of God, he heads off the objection that the whole matter of salvation is automatic, as if it makes no difference how we live. People are capable of rejecting the Spirit and "turning back to the weak and poor elements" (Gal 4:9). Christ is not a minister of sin (2:17). Paul lists the "works of the flesh" as present realities and insists as he did in 1 Corinthians that those who do these things "will not inherit the kingdom of God" (Gal 5:21; 1 Cor 6:8–10). There can be no "inheriting the kingdom" until such works are replaced by the fruit of the Spirit. Conduct is important as a consequence of living by the Spirit (Gal 5:25).

E. Union of Life with Christ

1. *Life by Faith*

The way in which Paul begins his whole theological reflection in this letter in chapter 2 points out the intense sense in which Paul sees a union of life with Christ as the key element by which believers are justified, freed from the law, and drawn into maturity in the family of God. Paul declares "he died to the law" and explains by saying, "I have been co-crucified [*synestaurômai*] with Christ" (2:19). He insists, "Christ lives in me" (2:20).

Continuing this thought, Paul then describes his situation, "I live by faith" (2:20). Living by faith thus means Christ living in you. Paul implied this equivalence in 2 Corinthians when he admonished his readers to examine "whether you are living in faith" and then asked the question, "Do you know that Christ Jesus is in you?" (2 Cor 13:5). If now writing to the Galatians, Paul insists that we are justified "by faith," or more specifically, "by the faith of Christ," in contrast to works of the law (Gal 2:16), he would almost certainly see this justification as occurring by the union of life between the believer and Christ, rather than by some good action, a human act of faith, a human decision by which we bring about justification. Faith is the human side of living in union with the death and risen life of Christ. It is not so much a human action, or even a mental action of a human being, as far more an opening to the life of Christ and a reception of that life. It is essentially the act of God viewed from the human side, viewed as received in this life.

In 2 Corinthians, Paul showed how the great drama of salvation or reconciliation occurs first in Christ. He is the new creation, in whom the old has passed away and in whom all is new. This new creation occurs if anyone is "in Christ" (2 Cor 5:17–18). There he also insisted that he was carrying "the dying Jesus about in the body, so that the life of Jesus may be manifest in our body...constantly being given up to death so that the life of Jesus may be manifest in our mortal flesh" (2 Cor 4:10–11).

Galatians focuses on union with Christ as the way by which the power of God active in Christ then flows into our individual lives. Paul sees his whole ministry with the Galatians as labor pains "until Christ be formed in you" (Gal 4:19). "Faith" is more the way in which this union appears in our life rather than the thing we must do for God to justify us.

2. *Human Agency*

In his description of Abraham, however, Paul uses the verb form to indicate an action of a human being, "Abraham believed [*episteusen*] God and it was credited to him a justice" (3:6). This is a citation of Genesis 15:6, but Paul uses it as an illustration of

God justifying the Gentiles by faith (*ek pisteôs*) (3:8). In Genesis, the focus is on Abram's (Abraham's) action as somehow meriting divine blessing.

Actually, Paul used very similar vocabulary about himself, sandwiching a description of his "coming to faith [*episteusamen*] in Christ Jesus" between two statements about "being justified by the faith of Christ" (2:16). It is in the next breath that Paul speaks so emphatically about Christ living in him (2:20). It would appear that Paul wants to maintain human agency in the faith that justifies, yet he insists that the power of God comes not from his choices but from his union with Christ.

He could see this combination of human agency and divine power even with Abraham, who somehow was living the life of Christ, a union that manifested itself by a coming to believe. It would appear then that this synergy of the human and the divine may be simply another case where Paul insists on human response to the gift of God: "If we live by the Spirit we should follow the Spirit" (5:25). This is the normal situation. The "faith of Christ" should manifest itself in a personal act of believing.

The union with Christ theme in this letter is also associated with baptism, as "clothing yourselves with Christ" (3:27). The result is the elimination of major social distinctions and "being one in Christ" and "belonging to Christ" (3:28–29). The stress here is social unity among believers. The presupposition is union with Christ.

We can find some similarity of Paul's thoughts about union with Christ in the presentation of the "suffering servant," in solidarity with whom others are healed (Isa 52:13—53:12). Nothing, however, in Paul's Jewish theological background comes close to the intensity with which he sees this union of life as the key to sharing in the saving power of God.

F. Eschatology

This letter is not rich in eschatology. Galatians focuses far more on the "now" and the present "fullness of time." The apocalyptic view appears with reference to the "present evil age" from which Jesus rescues us (1:4). The gift of the Spirit in our hearts along with the "fruit" of the Spirit allows us to live the "kingdom of God" (5:21) now with the freedom of that kingdom, just as the "works of the flesh" now set a person up to be disqualified from the kingdom (5:16–26).

The "sowing" and "reaping" imagery of eschatological judgment appears briefly in the final admonitions of the letter, and sowing in the Spirit means reaping "eternal life from the Spirit" (6:7–8). "In due time we shall reap our harvest" (6:9).

IV. The Message of the Letter

In Galatians, Paul urges the reader to regain the perspective of "the fullness of time." Despite his exaggerated indignation with those who disagree with him, Paul is on target admonishing people not to worry about circumcision or other matters that "do not count for anything." What counts is Christ living in us, drawing us as adult members into the family of God.

The Spirit in our hearts gives us the appropriate sense of ethics, not by enlarging a list of rules but by guiding us instinctively by love. The Spirit in our hearts gives us a sense of God's tender love, which draws us freely to avoid the works of the flesh.

This fullness of time is the time when God sends both his Son and the Spirit of his Son to free us from the law. Yet this mission does not separate us from our Jewish past. In this regard, Paul insists on our insertion in a tradition that extends back to Abraham. Of course, this is the Abram of Genesis 15, where there is no mention of circumcision, not the Abram of Genesis 17, where circumcision is insisted upon. Paul seems quite convinced of his freedom to interpret the scriptures, as he explained in 2 Corinthians 3. All this is because of Jesus, born of a woman, the seed of Abraham, who shares his life and his inheritance with us.

9
Romans

Rome was the capital of the empire, the hub of a network of roads that connected the whole Mediterranean world. At the time of Paul, the population of "The City" was about one million people, mostly lower class or plebeian, freedmen and slaves. In some ways the city was a miniature of the empire, including samples of the diverse nations.

Among this cosmopolitan population, Jews formed a numerous and influential group through most of the first century. Under Claudius, however, Jews were banned from the city for about five years. This event, generally dated as lasting from AD 49 to 54, is described by Suetonius, according to whom the expulsion took place because of disturbances within the Jewish community stemming from "Chrestus as instigator."[1]

I. Background for the Letter

A. Origins of the Roman Church

Writing to the Christians in Rome, Paul admits he did not found their church (15:20). Most likely that founding occurred several years earlier. Paul speaks of his repeated intention of visiting them "for many years" (1:13).

If Suetonius's description of the disturbances within the Jewish community with its reference to "Chrestus" is in fact a garbled version of fights within the Jewish community over faith in "Christus," we can see the existence of a significant Jewish-Christian community already in AD 49. Such an early beginning is confirmed by the recent discovery of a Christian funerary inscription now dated AD 47.

A postbiblical tradition and some archeological evidence places Peter in Rome in the mid-60s. Eusebius cites a Gaius [Caius] of Rome (c. 200) and a Dionysus of Corinth (c. 165) as testimonies of Peter's work and death in Rome.[2] These testimonies contain some internal difficulties but are strengthened by archeological traces of first-century Roman Christian devotion to both Paul and Peter in the catacombs as well as traces of what appears to be the venerated tomb of Peter on the Vatican hill. Writing to the Romans, however, Paul indicates no awareness of Peter's presence in that community.

B. Problems within the Community?

Paul is not writing to the Romans to correct any major problems. Nevertheless, a good part of this letter deals with the relationship between Jews and Gentiles, both within and outside the Christian community. Paul may be aware of difficulties in the Roman church between Jew and Gentile that he is trying to address in a delicate manner.

The expulsion by Claudius of all Jews from the city and the subsequent revocation of that edict after the death of Claudius could easily have set up a tense situation for Roman Christians. We can assume that the early leadership of the Roman church was Jewish. This leadership would have been expelled from the city under Claudius. When the Jews returned in AD 54, the original Jewish leaders of the Christian community may well have sought their former prominence within the community, with the result that a Jewish-Gentile rivalry arose within that community.

C. Events Leading to the Letter

Paul gives us a rather precise setting for the writing of this letter. He speaks of having completed his work in the Near East ("from Jerusalem to Illyricum") and of his new plans to go to Spain (15:19, 24). First, however, he is going to Jerusalem to bring the collection of money he has gathered from the Gentile churches (15:26–27). Apparently he is writing from Cenchreae, the eastern port of Corinth (16:1).

The reference to the completed collection from Macedonia and Achaia ready to be taken to Jerusalem (15:25–29) clearly places Romans after the Corinthian correspondence. His presence near Corinth corresponds to his travel plans described in 2 Corinthians (1:15–16; 9:1–4). This letter fits well into the end of "the third journey" described in Acts 20:1–3. A probable date, therefore, for the writing of this letter would be around AD 58.

D. Paul's Purpose in Writing

Paul is preparing his intended trip to Rome. The letter appears to be an attempt to establish some rapport with the Roman community. He is coming, not as a founding missionary, but as a guest traveling through to points further west, travels that would have required enormous logistic support, which the Roman community possibly could provide.

Given the extended theological development of this letter, we can conclude that Paul wanted especially to introduce his teaching to this community. Perhaps he felt the need to refute accusations that distorted his teaching. The letter, for instance, goes to great pains to insist that Paul is not advocating libertinism in his preaching freedom from the law. He insists on the value of being a Jew, yet insists that all peoples, Jews and Gentiles, stand as sinners before God. He also insists that all peoples, Jews and Gentiles, are offered the power of salvation. We find here basically the same ideas as those seen in Galatians, without the polemic barbs and with a more moderate view of the law in the historical plan of God's salvation. As in Galatians, Abraham again appears as a model of faith. However, far less is said to downplay the role of Moses and the law in God's historical plan.

Given this intention on the part of Paul, we can expect in this letter a rich and balanced source of Pauline theology. This is not to say that Romans gives us a systematic treatise. Romans still retains the character more or less of a letter, geared toward a specific occasion and concrete needs. However, since one of the needs is precisely to express a comprehensive picture of his theology and since a principle focus concerning the Romans is God's overall plan of salvation for both Jews and Gentiles, Romans shows a care and a comprehensiveness unsurpassed in Paul's other letters, giving up perhaps a good example of an "epistle."[3]

E. Influence of the Diatribe

Of all Paul's letters, Romans shows the closest adherence to the techniques of the Stoic diatribe. We see an abundance of questions objecting to Paul's teaching and Paul's answers to those questions:

> What, then, are we to say? Let us continue in sin that grace may abound? Certainly not!
> (6:1–2; see 6:15; 7:7; 7:13)

Paul personifies the position of unredeemed humanity:

> What a wretched man I am! Who can free me from this body under the power of death? (7:24)

In general, the letter is written in dialogue form, not so much with the readers in Rome, but with an imaginary interlocutor off whom Paul bounces his ideas.

F. The Integrity of the Letter: The Special Problem of Chapter 16

A small number of manuscripts do not include chapter 16 in their copy of Romans. One very important manuscript that does include chapter 16 places the solemn ending of the letter, 16:25–27, right after chapter 15, thus suggesting an original ending to which something was later added. This chapter, furthermore, is puzzling by its long list of names to whom Paul sends special greetings, including "Epaenetus, the firstfruits of Asia for Christ" (16:5), and "Prisca and Aquila" (16:3), whom we last saw in Ephesus (l Cor l6:19). It is surprising to see so many personal acquaintances in a church Paul has never even visited.

The manuscript variants along with the unusual character of this chapter at least suggest the possibility that this chapter was not part of the original letter sent to Rome. It has been suggested that Paul added this chapter in a second edition of this letter intended for Ephesus. Strengthening this suggestion is the lack of the expression "in Rome" at 1:7 in a very small group of manuscripts.

On the other hand, the manuscript variants could testify to the possibility that later copyists wanted to give this letter more universal appeal by dropping the personal remarks that linked the letter to the church of Rome. The tendency in the later first century was to read, copy, and collect the letters of Paul as if they were originally directed to all Christians. Furthermore, Paul would need to do a bit of "name-dropping" if he were trying to drum up support among the Roman Christians. Many of the names listed in chapter 16 appear to be Jewish Christians, like Prisca and Aquila, who may well have returned to Rome after the death of Claudius. Seeing chapter 16 as belonging to Paul's original letter and then later dropped in some copies is a hypothesis that explains the manuscript evidence and has the advantage of being a simpler explanation.

II. The Sequential Study of the Letter

A. Outline of the Letter

Like Galatians, Romans falls into a doctrinal section (chapters 1–11) and an exhortatory section (chapters 12–15). The doctrinal section likewise follows the cyclical pattern of Galatians. The first cycle (l:16—4:25) is dominated with the word *justification,* describing a present gift. The second cycle (5:1—11:36) is dominated by the word *salvation,* describing an eschatological fulfillment.

The cycle of each doctrinal part appears in a pattern of four elements. Each begins with a summary proclamation of the main idea, justice or salvation. This is followed by a development of the need for this gift, hence a development stressing sinfulness. After this somber development comes a positive exposition of the gift. This exposition in turn leads to a consideration of Jewish salvation history.

The outline of Romans appears as follows:

I. Opening (1:1–15)
  A. Address (1:1–7)
  B. Thanksgiving and prayer (1:8–15)
II. Part One: Justification (1:16—4:25)
  A. Theme announced (1:16–17)
  B. The need: humankind as the object of God's anger (1:18—3:20)
  C. Justification by faith (3:21–31)
  D. Example from Israel—Abraham (4)
III. Part Two: Salvation (5—11)
  A. Theme announced (5:1–11)
  B. The need: sin, death, and the law (5:12—7:25)
  C. Life in the Spirit (8)
  D. Example from Israel—the role of contemporary Israel (9—11)
IV. Exhortations (12:1—15:13)
V. Conclusion (15:14—16:27)

B. The Opening Greeting and Prayer (1:1–15)

Paul begins his letter describing himself as both a "slave" and an "apostle," without associating any other co-worker with him in the writing of this letter. He describes the object of his work as "the gospel of God," a description that then gives him the opportunity for a summary of his theology, with a particular focus on his **Christ trajectory**.

In this trajectory, Jesus is "from the seed of David according to the flesh" and the "Son of God established in power by the resurrection according to the Spirit of holiness" (1:3–4). Connecting the divine Sonship of Jesus with the resurrection might reflect an early Christian theology, whereby Jesus was seen to be "adopted" by God as his Son at the moment of the resurrection.[4] Paul, however, focuses more on the "power" aspect of the Sonship as begun at the moment of the resurrection. The play on "flesh" and "Spirit" clearly refers to the combined human descent and divine role of Jesus. Yet after Galatians, the "flesh/Spirit" antithesis in

Paul's **Spirit trajectory** necessarily rings with at least an echo of the duality of "this age/age to come" in the apocalyptic view.

The term "Spirit of holiness" (1:4), instead of the more usual Pauline expression, "Holy Spirit," has a Semitic ring to it. The "of" expression as used here is a Semitic way of expressing an adjective. A "throne of holiness" is basically "holy throne"; a "crown of glory," basically a "glorious crown." Although occasionally Paul uses such Semitic genitives (for example, "newness of life" at 6:4), the general ring of this text suggests Paul is building on a formula he inherited from the early Jewish church.

Paul names the readers in Rome as "called to belong to Jesus Christ," "beloved of God," and "called to be holy," (1:6–7) without calling them a "church," as he has done in his letters up to this time. Perhaps this is a deliberate choice in the light of the Jewish/Gentile split that Paul perceives to be dividing Rome.

The thanksgiving prayer focuses on the "faith" of the readers (1:8), with no mention of their love. Paul's petition is for himself and the trip he hopes to make (1:10). In this petition, Paul delicately sees his role as "sharing spiritual gifts" to achieve "mutual encouragement from one another's faith" (1:11–12).

C. The Opening Summary 1:16–17

In a way, the whole message of Romans is contained in the opening summary of 1:16–17, which immediately introduces Paul's **salvation** and **God trajectories** :

> I am not ashamed of the gospel. It is the power of God leading everyone who believes in it to salvation, the Jew first, then the Greek. For in the gospel is revealed the justice of God which begins and ends with faith; as Scripture says, "The just man shall live by faith."

Paul first announces the theme of "salvation" (*sôteria*), which he will develop in the second part of the doctrinal section, and which generally will have an eschatological color in this letter. Here he insists on the universality of this salvation. It is for both Jew and Greek (Gentile). Yet he also insists on a priority here. Salvation is first for the Jew. At once Paul is refuting Jewish claims to exclusivity as a people of God as well as any Gentile sense of superiority over the Jews. Both Jew and Gentile stand as humble recipients and beneficiaries of God's power, a power expressed in "the gospel."

Paul is not thinking of our four gospels. They have not yet been written. The term *gospel* is new in Christian vocabulary. Paul used the term without explanation several times in all his earlier letters. It was the object of his preaching and discourse (1 Thess 2:2; 1 Cor 9:14.18; and so on). It is life-giving, like the begetting power of a father (1 Cor 4:15). It is the "gospel of God" (1 Thess 2:2; 2 Cor 11:4; Rom 1:1) but especially "the gospel of Christ" (1 Cor 9:12; 2 Cor 2:12; Gal 1:7; Rom 15:19; and so on). As he introduces the theme here in Romans, he insists on the gospel as a power. This preaching and discourse convey the very power of God saving his creatures. The rest of Romans in effect appears to be a development of how Paul understands this gospel and power.

The second statement of Paul in this summary introduces the theme of "the justice [*dikaiosynê*] of God," which he will develop in the first cycle of the doctrinal section. As is clear from its connection here with God's salvation, this justice is not the justice opposed to mercy. Rather, this is the justice whose revelation brings about salvation. This is the justice that justifies. All this is the work of God.

To introduce the full scope of the letter, this summary then alludes to another element in this drama of **salvation** as it engages human life. This is the element of faith (*pistis*). This justifying justice of God begins and ends with faith. As Paul states, this faith is a principle of life. The just person lives by it. Paul will explain what he means in the rest of the letter.

D. The Need for Justification (1:18—3:20)

Much of what Paul wrote in Galatians could be thrown back in his face as evidence of his being "soft on sin." He told his readers that as guided by the Spirit they are not under the law (Gal 5:18). All they need to do is love (5:14). For many, however, the reality of the Greco-Roman culture was one of brutality and selfish cruelty. Preaching love without the rules of the law seemed like words of a person who had never confronted evil. Proclaiming that our hope lay in grace and faith rather than in our good works (2:16) sounded like a trivialization of evil works. As noted above, Paul hears the objection quite clearly: "What then? Shall we sin because we are not under the law but under grace?" (Rom 6:14).

Paul answers this imaginary objector, "By no means!" The foundation for this answer is a section that runs from Romans 1:18 to 3:20. There Paul describes the seriousness of sin the way the prophets of old did. He describes the destructive "anger [*orgê*] of God" against sin (1:18; 2:5; and so on). For Isaiah, Jeremiah, and Ezekiel, the anger of God blazed like a consuming fire (Isa 30:27; 65:5; Jer 17:4; Ezek 21:36) or as a raging storm (Isa 30:30; Jer 30:23; see Ps 83:16). With great emphasis Paul adds this note of divine anger into his **God trajectory**.

Paul's portrayal of divine anger against sin falls into two parts, one describing the sinfulness of the Gentiles, a second describing that of the Jews. The sins of the Gentiles come under scrutiny especially in 1:18–32. Paul points out the "original sin" of the Gentiles and then the "secondary sins" that result. The secondary sins are those most obvious to his eyes: idolatry (1:23) and sexual immorality, particularly homosexuality (1:24–27). These visible sins, however, are the result of a deeper problem: the dulling of the mind and heart (1:21b–22). At the origin of it all is a sin that Paul describes as the failure to glorify and praise God, who should have been recognized in his creation, known in the revelation of himself to the Gentiles through the visible works of his hands (1:19–21a).

Paul describes the sins of the Jews especially in 2:17—3:8. These sins seem to have the form of hypocrisy:

> Now then, teacher of others, are you failing to teach yourself?
> You who preach against stealing, do you steal?
> You who forbid adultery, do you commit adultery?
> You who abhor idols, do you rob temples?
> You who pride yourself on the law, do you dishonor God by breaking the law? (2:21–23)

Paul's indictment here is not at all clear. Such blatant transgressions were not characteristic of the Jewish people of that time—much less the Jews whom Paul knew. A few lines later, however, Paul explains what he means, indicating perhaps the "original sin" for Jews:

> Appearance does not make a Jew. True circumcision is not a sign in the flesh. He is a real Jew who is one inwardly, and true circumcision is of the heart; its source is the Spirit, not the letter. (2:28–29)

With the "Spirit/letter" antithesis that he introduced in 2 Corinthians 3:6, Paul picks up his **Spirit trajectory** to describe an interior conformity with the law, the law of the Spirit and the heart. Presumably for Paul, the universal sinfulness of the Jews stems from the lack of any transformation in their hearts.

Following the cue of the prophets (Jer 1:15–16; Ezek 7:3–9; 16:38), Paul adds the theme of a punishing judgment (*krima*) to that of divine anger, adding to his **eschatology trajectory**. In a phrase reminiscent of Zephaniah 1:15, Paul speaks of "the day of anger" (*dies irae*) with future "repayments" that cut across the division of Jews and Gentiles.

> In your hard and unrepentant heart you are storing up anger for yourself on the day of anger and revelation of the just judgment of God, who will repay [*apodôsei*] each according to his work,
>
> on the one hand, eternal life to those seeking glory and
> honor and incorruption by constancy in good works,
> on the other hand, anger and rage to those who in selfish
> ambition
> disobey the truth and obey wickedness, affliction and
> distress upon every human being who does evil,
> Jew first and then Greek,
> but glory, honor, and peace for everyone who does good,
> Jew first and then Greek. (Rom 2:5–10)

This is the text that comes closest to the kind of "last judgment" scenes that we see in Matthew and other Jewish writings where the restriction of salvation is stressed by the depiction of all those who are condemned to hell (Matt 28:31–46; Dan 12:2; *2 Baruch* 59:2; *4 Ezra* 7:35–48).

Paul, however, starts this whole topic by a description of the *present* anger of God now being "revealed" or set into action (Rom 1:18). What Paul earlier saw as a future eschatological judgment (see 1 Thess 2:10; 5:9), he now pictures as a present or realized eschatology. The future tense of the verb "he will repay" in Romans 2:6 appears to be the result of an almost direct quotation from Psalm 61[62]:13, "You will repay [*apodôseis*] each according to his work."

E. Justification (3:21–31)

Paul's conclusion in Romans about universal sinfulness leads to the proclamation of God's justification for all. This is a major presentation of Paul's **soteriology**. The present revelation of God's anger leads immediately to a description of the present manifestation now of God's justice (*dikaiosynê,* 3:21). However, instead of speaking of some form of severe punishment, Paul describes gift and grace.

The tight interlacing of ideas in this summary section can be seen by the chiastic structure of the section:

a. But now the justice of God has been *manifested* apart from the law, witnessed by the law and the prophets,
  b. The justice of God through the faith of Jesus Christ,
    c. for all believers, without distinction, because all have sinned and are deprived of the glory of God.
  b'. [They are] justified freely in his grace through the redemption in Christ Jesus,
a'. Whom God *set forth* as a propitiatory through faith, in his blood, for *the showing* of his justice...(3:21–25)

The correlation of b–b' shows that the justice of God that operates "through the faith of Christ" (3:22) also operates "freely in his grace" (3:24). "Through faith" here is the same as "freely" as a "grace." It is not a description of the one good act we need to do to get God acting. Above all, as the correlation points out, it is "the justice of God" (3:22) that makes people just (3:24).

The correlation a–a' focuses on God's action, manifesting or showing his justice. The common element in this correlation is God's action. This is a justification that is the work of God. It is apart from the law, although it is witnessed by the law and operates in the echo of a cultic procedure for sin (3:21). The words *redemption, propitiatory,* and *blood* all reflect the vocabulary of the Temple, where bloody sacrifices were offered to God. The "propitiatory" was the golden plate on top of the ark of the covenant, which the high priest sprinkled with blood on the Day of Atonement. The ritual was believed to take away sins. Paul is clearly comparing the death of Jesus to that ritual.

The central item, c, stresses the universality (*pantes*) of this justifying action of God. The gift of God is "without distinction" precisely because (*gar*) "all have sinned," as Paul explained in the preceding chapters.

As in Galatians, the concept of divine justice is rooted in the covenantal *zedek* of God. The theme derives from the Old Testament prophets, who described this justice as taking place especially on "the day of the Lord," a final day climaxing history and establishing the rule of God over creation. The prophets believed that God would someday come as judge and set things right. Paul changes the timing of this divine intervention. Here this justification has already taken place. "Now…the justice of God has been manifested" (3:21). This "now" represents the new epoch of justice, formerly thought of as part of the end of time.

This bloody death of Jesus is for Paul the way God manifests his justice. This is how God shows his power "to justify the [one justified] by the faith of Jesus [*ek pisteôs Iêsou*]" (3:26). Paul's theocentric stress appears again. God is the one who justifies. Jesus and his death become the means through which God acts.

Paul then continues the development of the last part of the chiastic structure (a'), describing the role of the bloody death of Jesus by a rhythmic series of prepositional phrases, possibly taken from an early Christian hymn and adapted by Paul:

for [*eis*] a manifestation of his justice
through [*dia*]the overlooking of past sins
in [*en*]the patience of God
toward [*pros*] the manifestation of his justice
in [*en*] the present time
for [eis] him to be just and justifying the [one justified]
by [*ek*] the faith of Jesus. (3:25–26)

The ideas here develop around the manifestation of God's justice, related to both the past and the present, and climaxing in the justifying nature of that justice. God is both just and justifying. God's justice makes things right.

F. An Example from the Salvation History—Abraham (4:1–25)

Paul then brings this cycle to a conclusion by the illustration of Abraham (chapter 4). A comparison with Galatians 3:6–22, particularly with the scriptural quotations Paul uses there, shows the close relationship of the two letters. The comparison also shows the freedom with which Paul rethinks his thoughts as he moves from one situation to another.

Paul is a bit more careful to say he is referring to Abraham (Abram) not yet circumcised (4:15), the figure who shows up in Genesis 15. The ritual of circumcision depicted in Genesis 17, therefore, looks like a later "seal" on the justice Abraham (4:11), with which he was already "credited" two chapters earlier. For Paul the upshot of all this is the way Abraham becomes the "father" of both the circumcised and the uncircumcised (4:12). The comparison of the promises to Abraham with the law of Moses (4:13–17) is a reprise of Galatians 3:15–21.

Finally, Paul goes on to depict old Abraham and sterile Sarah as examples of the dead, to whom God gives new life (4:17–19). In parallel descriptions of Abraham's faith, Paul states, "He believed [*episteusen*], hoping against hope" (4:18); "he did not doubt God's promise" (4:20); "he was fully convinced" (4:21). This act of believing is clearly a human attitude of trust in God's power.

The object of Abraham's trusting faith, as Paul specifies, is the God "who gives life to the dead and calls nonbeing into being" (4:17). Similarly, Paul describes the object of our faith as "the one who raised Jesus our Lord from the dead" (4:24). The trusting openness to God is an openness specifically to the creative and resurrecting power of God. This is the specific meaning of faith for Paul.

As a consequence, Abraham can be described as "empowered by faith" (4:20). Moreover, the "faith of Abraham" (*pistis autou*, 4:5) is "also for us to whom it will be credited" (4:24). This is a vicarious "crediting" already mentioned earlier (4:11). Paul's portrayal of Abraham here becomes a possible parallel and explanation of the "faith of Christ" that Paul spoke of so much in Galatians and appears again in the summary introduction of this part of this letter (Rom 3:22, 26) as the basis of our justification.

G. Salvation (5:1–11)

Beginning the second major cycle of his instructions, Paul again gives a summary statement (5:1–11), which will be followed by a lengthy description of the need (5:12—7:25), a development of the new theme (8:1–27), and an application to salvation history (9:1—11:36).

The summary statement of the new theme climaxes with the proclamation:

Now that we have been justified
  by his blood,
  all the more will we be saved by him from God's wrath.
For if, when we were God's enemies, we were reconciled to
    him
  by the death of his Son,
  all the more as reconciled will we be saved by his life.
(5:9–10)

As distinguished here from justification, **salvation** appears clearly as a future **eschatological** reality. For Paul in Romans, we are not yet saved. We are justified. We will be saved. At the same time, Paul insists on having full confidence in this salvation.

Paul works up to this proclamation by an extremely involved statement that weaves together the double triad of (a) faith, hope, and love,[5] as well as (b) **God, the Lord Jesus**, and **the Holy Spirit** (5:1–5). Consistent with his **salvation trajectory**, Paul insists that we are saved by Christ's blood (5:9).

Most important, as Paul points out, the death of Christ not only tells us about Jesus, it proves the love that **God** himself has for us (5:8). This detail maintains the theocentric character of justification and salvation. Behind the whole drama is the love of God for us.

H. The Need for Salvation (5:12—7:25)

As in the first cycle of his instructions, Paul again presents the negative backdrop for the gift of salvation. He returns again to the theme of sin. This development will continue through chapter 7. However, unlike the first cycle, this negative development contains several digressions. Paul develops some thoughts on baptism (6:1–14), on the new freedom and slavery (6:15–23), and on freedom from the law (7:1–6), before returning to the theme of sin and death (7:7–25).

The key to understanding Paul's notion of sin consists in grasping the tension within this concept. Following one vector of this tension, Paul insists that sin is a human reality: "Through one man sin entered the world" (5:12). Sin is above all an act of the human heart. It is not some physical reality or aspect of reality such as the Gnostic dualist would conceive it. Paul is too good a Jew to hold that anything of creation is evil by its nature or structure.

Following a second vector, Paul insists that sin, once it is in the world, becomes a power greater than human beings. Sin becomes an enslaving power that imprisons the human person and dwells in him or her: "I am weak flesh sold into the slavery of sin" (7:14). Here we see the apocalyptic Paul dealing with the problem of good and evil on the level of cosmic powers. Thus "sin," "death," "flesh," and "the law" as enslaving powers dominate this section of the letter where Paul again prepares for his treatment of salvation.

The image that captures this tension between personal and cosmic evil is that of death. Death is a reality we all carry with us. On one level, it appears as simply the personal end of earthly existence. On another level, it appears as the scourge of sin: "Sin entered the world and with sin death" (5:12). "Sin reigned through death" (5:21). We thus speak of the power of death. Before its inevitability we are all helpless.

The connection between sin and death is brought out in the text about Adam, through whom sin and death enter the world (5:12), a theme that Paul received from late Jewish wisdom literature (see Wis 2:24). Paul earlier said that sin as a "transgression" did not exist before the law (4:15), but here he insists that even before the law, "sin was in the world" (5:13). He must say this because death "reigned" in the world even during the period from Adam to Moses, and "sin reigns in death" (5:21). Paul then specifies that this sin was a form of sin other than "the transgression" of Adam (5:14). Sin was in the world and reigned over all precisely through their mortality. Any **salvation** from sin must be a salvation from mortality.

Since the crucifixion and resurrection of Christ, however, death has another side. Through death Christ was freed from death's power (6:9). Because Christ died and was raised, "death no longer reigns [*ouketi kyrieuei*] over him" (6:11). Implied here is the idea that death and therefore sin did reign over him. He needed rescue. That rescue occurred through Jesus' death and resurrection, an important element of Paul's **Christ trajectory**. Through death and resurrection, likewise, we are "no longer in slavery to sin" if indeed "our old self is co-crucified" with Christ (6:6). Paul's **union with Christ trajectory** merges with the **salvation trajectory**.

Very important for understanding this theology of **salvation** is the line that is meant to explain the basis (*gar*) of his position: "For the dying person [*apothanôn*] is absolved [*dedikaiôtai*] from sin" (6:7). Death itself becomes a means of freedom from sin. Paul presents this judgment as the basis for understanding why a person through baptism can be justified or freed from the slavery to sin now. In baptism we can anticipate our death by being "co-crucified."

This thought is part of a digression into a consideration of baptism as a way in which we are "co-crucified." Baptism is a way in which we share in Christ's death:

> Through baptism into his death we were co-buried with him,
> so that, just as Christ was raised from the dead by the glory of the Father,
> we too might conduct ourselves in a new life.
> If we have been united with him through likeness to his death,
> so shall we be [through a likeness] to the resurrection.
> (6:4–5)

The time categories of this description are of significance. Paul places the baptized person in the tomb. Death and burial are in some way already past. The resurrection of the body is clearly future. At present, however, is a new way of life.

Paul therefore sees some anticipation of the resurrection to new life. He concludes, "Consequently you too must think of yourselves as dead to sin and living for God in Christ Jesus" (6:11). "Present yourselves to God as raised from the dead to life" (6:13). Colossians will pick up this thought of realized resurrection (Col 2:12).

Such an optimistic view of God's dealing with sin in our lives could lead to the presumption that sin in our lives is of little import, an objection formulated by the imaginary interlocutor of 6:15, "Shall we sin because we are not under the law but under grace?" Paul answers with the image of becoming "slaves of God," which involves intense sanctification and ends in eternal life (6:22).

I. The Power of Sin (7:1–25)

Paul now introduces a discussion about the law. Essentially, as he did in Galatians, Paul discusses the power of the law in terms of some epochal "before" and "after." Paul contrasts two times, "when we were in the flesh...but now..." and then adds the Spirit/letter antithesis he developed in 2 Corinthians 3. "Now" we are freed from the law as "letter" to serve in the "newness of the Spirit" (7:5–6).

This freedom takes place because "you were put to death to the law through the body of Christ" (7:4). The connection between freedom and death is illustrated by the freedom of the widow (7:1–3). Unfortunately in this illustration, it is not clear who is supposed to have died. The widow is freed when her husband dies, not when she dies. The death of Christ would be liberating if somehow Christ in his flesh and blood existence was identified with the law and its enslaving power, like the demanding husband. The death of the believer could be a part of the picture perhaps in the light of Paul's sense of the believer's union of death and life with Christ. The analogy remains muddled except to show how freedom can come from death.

Paul then discusses sin as a power to possess, enslave, and divide the human person (7:7–25). In this discussion, the pronoun *I* probably is Paul's rhetorical way of personifying unredeemed humanity, a rhetorical device he would have learned from Stoic teachers. He is most probably not giving us autobiographical information about his life before Christ.

In this discussion, unlike that in Galatians, however, he takes pains to present the law as "spiritual" (*pneumatikos*). The problem lies in the "fleshy" (*sarkinos*) character of human existence without Christ (7:14). Given to a fleshy human being, the law leads to slavery and a division in the personality between some "inner self" and the "members" (7:22), a condition Paul sees as "miserable" (7:24).[6]

J. Life in the Spirit (8:1–39)

Chapter 8 is the high point of the letter to the Romans. Perhaps no other chapter in Paul's writings contains such density of insight, such a concentration of key thoughts and images for Paul's theology. Here Paul will weave together key thoughts for his **Spirit trajectory, salvation trajectory, union with Christ trajectory**, and even his **eschatology trajectory**.

The chapter begins with an upbeat proclamation of the new epoch: "Now there is no condemnation for those in Christ Jesus" (8:1). This "now" is characterized by "the law of the Spirit," by "life in Christ Jesus," and by freedom from "the law of sin and death" (8:2). The following verses in this chapter attempt to explain what Paul means by this new epoch of life and freedom.

1. God Condemning Sin in the Flesh (8:3–4)

In Romans 8:3 Paul portrays Christ sent into our sinfulness, a crucial element in both Paul's **Christ** and **salvation trajectories**. As he did in Galatians, he uses the "God-sending-Son" formula to describe the action of God and the role of Jesus bringing about this new epoch. The text forms a close parallel with Gal 4:4:

Rom 8:3–4	*Gal 4:4*
God sending his Son	God sent his Son
in the likeness of sinful flesh	born of a woman
and concerning sin	born under the law
condemned sin in the flesh	
in order that the just demands of	in order to redeem those
the law be fulfilled in us who	under the law,
walk not according to flesh	in order that we might
but according to the Spirit.	receive adoption

The translation "in the likeness of" in Romans can be misleading. We generally understand the expression to mean "somewhat like but not quite the same as." The Greek word for *likeness* Paul uses here is *homoioma,* which in the literature of the time never meant merely an approximation or limited resemblance to some reality. In the Greek Old Testament, the word, *homoioma,* describes a fully adequate and perceptible expression of some reality, in some sense the very model of some reality (4 Kgs 16:10; Josh 22:28; Sir 38:28; Ezek 2:1). Paul's use of the term stresses a profound similarity among diverse realities, a repeated pattern that creates a dynamic solidarity (see especially Rom 6:5; Phil 2:7). Here Paul is describing the humanity of Christ in its solidarity with sin, the humanity of Christ as "a model of sinful flesh."

2. Life in the Spirit (8:5–13)

The antithesis between flesh and Spirit appears nowhere in Paul clearer than in the next verses of this chapter. Here Paul comes as close as he ever does to sounding like a Gnostic dualist, except that Paul distinguishes between "flesh," which is hostile to God (8:7) and "body," which awaits redemption (8:23).

> The mentality of the flesh is toward death
> but that of the Spirit toward life and peace.
> The flesh in its mentality is at enmity with God.
> It does not submit to the law of God; indeed it cannot.
> Those who are in the flesh cannot please God. (8:6–8)

Paul is describing the two cosmic powers or spheres in diametric opposition to each other, two powers that are also two possibilities of life.

> But you are not in the flesh; you are in the Spirit,
> since the Spirit of God dwells in you. (8:9)

The key element is the Spirit of God, either dwelling or not dwelling in us. Being "in the flesh" or "in the Spirit" results from whether or not the Spirit dwells in us. Paul here merges the **Spirit** and the **salvation trajectories**.

The imagery here becomes a bit confusing. Who is in whom? Paul's usual terminology describes the Spirit in our hearts and us existing in Christ. Here, however, Paul is insisting on the cosmic dimension, that is, the more than human dimension of both "flesh" and "Spirit." Hence, he expresses life as being contained in these spheres. Paul is stressing not just an external measure of conduct but a mode of existence. That mode of existence must change, and it does change "if the Spirit of God dwells in you." Just as "sin dwelling in" a person (7:20) enslaves that person, so "the Spirit dwelling in" a person frees that person for a new life, changing the very internal principle of existence for that person. Paul's intention here is to express the intense involvement of the believer in the Spirit, an involvement that entails "belonging to Christ" (8:9) and a future resurrection of the body (8:11).

3. *The "Abba" Prayer and the Resurrection (8:14–26)*

Paul returns to the idea of the resurrection of the body, associating this future gift with a present prayer, associating **Spirit** now with **eschatology**. Verses 14–26 form a chiastic structure beginning and ending with prayer through the Spirit, dealing with eschatological glory, and centered on the involvement of all material creation in this freedom of believers:

A. The "Abba" prayer through the Spirit (8:14–15)
  B. Our inheritance of glory (8:17–18)
    C. The liberation of all creation including our bodies (8:19–23)
  B'. Our hope of an unseen reality (8:24–25)
A'. The ineffable prayer of the Spirit (8:26–27)

A–A' focuses on prayer. Paul had written of this Abba prayer in the parallel text of Galatians (4:6). In Galatians it is the Spirit in our hearts who cries "Abba." Here in Romans Paul insists more on our part in this prayer. Here it is we who cry "Abba." Paul also insists on a conjoint action. He describes the united witness of both "our spirit" and God's Spirit that we are children of God.

Thus in A' Paul can return to the image of the Spirit's own prayer, which exceeds our ability to express. These "ineffable groanings" (*stenagmoi*, 8:26) are related to the Abba prayer. This is the prayer that arises from the "Spirit of adoption," the Spirit that Paul in Galatians called "the Spirit of God's Son," expressing the relationship to God that it produces in the heart of the believer, a relationship struggling to attain its completion. As expressing struggle, "the groanings" of the Spirit become the Spirit's part in apocalyptic suffering involving all of creation in its "groanings" (8:22) and our eschatological "groanings" (8:23).

B–B' focuses on **eschatology**. Both describe a future orientation caused by the Spirit, on the one side, an inheritance, on the other, a hope. Both allude to a present difficulty in this orientation by referring to suffering and endurance.

At the focal point of the chiasm, C, is a description of the involvement of all reality in the struggle to attain the completion of God's liberating salvation. For Paul **eschatological salvation** is far more than a matter of saving souls. Rather, this salvation consists of God recreating his universe (2 Cor 5:17). All nature, all creation, is a part of this picture. Paul pictures this involvement as a kind of suffering. Nature "groans [*systenadzei*] in labor pains" (8:22), the common image of apocalyptic suffering as the end approaches. As part of this cosmic involvement, Paul sees the human body and its future resurrection from the dead. We join in nature's labor pains (*stenadzomen*) as we await "the redemption of our bodies" (8:23).

In anticipation of the final triumph, however, we and all of creation can live in joyful hope. **The Spirit** has been given to us. That Spirit is the beginning of the resurrection (8:11), the "firstfruits" (8:23; see "down payment" in 2 Cor 1:22). The groanings of creation are supported by the ineffable groanings of the Spirit.

In the remaining part of chapter 8, Paul expresses again his absolute confidence in God's love. "If God is for us, who can be against us?" (8:31). **God** is in complete control of salvation, having "foreknown," "predestined," "called," "justified," and "glorified" those who love God (8:28–30). Paul describes all these actions with the past (aorist) tense, using the style of the prophets to describe even future events that are certain.

Paul must still live with trial and distress, danger and the sword. However, he is confident:

> Neither death nor life, neither angels nor principalities, neither the present nor the future, nor powers, neither height nor depth nor any other creature will be able to separate us from the love of God that comes to us in Christ Jesus, our Lord. (8:38–39)

K. The Place of Israel (9:1—11:36)

In the next three chapters, Paul focuses on **salvation** with an occasional glance at **eschatology**. Here Paul attempts to incorporate these insights concerning the love of God into his understanding of salvation history, and, in particular, into his understanding of the role of Israel. Throughout Romans, Paul insists on the basic commonality of Jew and Gentile both in sin and in justification by faith. Yet Paul is unique in the New Testament for his passionate concern for the Jews. He alone insists on their continuing positive role in God's plan. He insists on their enduring priority.

Working up to this question, Paul sets out a series of his basic positions. He begins with a focus on **God**, and then draws in a combination of **Christology** and **soteriology**. In this theological focus, Paul recalls the free choices of God in this history of Israel (9:6–14) and concludes with the sovereign power of God's will: "So it depends not upon someone's will or exertion, but upon God, showing mercy" (9:16).

Working up to the issue of the Jewish rejection of Jesus, Paul brings in the negative side of God's freedom: "He shows mercy on whom he wills, and he hardens those whom he wills" (9:18). Paul counters the objector's complaint about unfairness with God's "potter's rights." Drawing on the imagery of Jeremiah 18:1–12, Paul declares God's right to make both "vessels of wrath made for destruction [*apôleia*]" and "vessels of mercy prepared beforehand for glory" from the same lump of clay (Rom 9:19–24). This distinction is meant to cut across Jewish-Gentile distinctions and apparently refer to the absence or presence of faith in one's life (9:30–32).

In Jeremiah, the parable about the potter and his clay stresses the way the potter can change his or her mind and redo the clay, an illustration of God's freedom in dealing with Israel:

> Whenever the object of clay which he was making turned out badly in his hand, he tried again, making the clay another object of whatever sort he pleased. Then the word of the Lord came to me, "Can I not do to you, house of Israel, as the potter has done?" (Jer 18:4–5)

Thus, God's work is sometimes destructive and at other times constructive (18:7–10). It is, however, always toward a final product that is pleasing to God. Jeremiah avoids any impression of capricious action by focusing on the end product. By insisting on the potter trying again and again until he has an object that he likes,

Jeremiah makes God's action a bit more understandable. The clay, the forming work, and the potter are seen as an integrated whole.[7]

Leaving out the elements of changing and reforming the clay, Paul takes a more in-your-face approach insisting on the freedom of the potter, where the creature simply does not talk back to God (Rom 9:19). Yet the reversal of Israel's destiny for salvation that Paul describes later in this discussion (11:25) could well indicate that Paul has understood and is using Jeremiah contextually.

Paul, however, refuses to trivialize personal faith in Christ. He reminds his readers, "Christ is the end [*telos*] of the law for the justification of everyone having faith [*pisteuôn*]" (10:4), where the Greek word *telos* could mean the end as temporal termination or the end as purpose. Whatever is involved, it works for those "having faith." Then Paul roots "having faith" in personal action:

> If you **confess with your mouth** that Jesus is Lord
> and *believe [pisteuês] in your heart* that God raised
> him from the dead,
> you will be saved.
> For one *believes with the heart* unto justification,
> and one **confesses with the mouth** unto salvation.
> (10:9–10)

In this chiastic structure, "justification" and "salvation" appear the same, although one is related to the heart and the other to the mouth. Once again, having faith or believing is oriented toward God raising Jesus. The key or central thought is expressed, "You will be saved."

Dealing with the question of Israel, Paul is faced with a dilemma. On the one hand, he sees the evidence of Jewish resistance to the gospel. They are not people who believed that God raised Jesus from the dead. On the other hand, he is convinced of the principle, "God's gifts and his call are irrevocable" (Rom 11:29). To the question, then, "Has God rejected his people?" Paul answers, "Of course not!" (11:1). Where then is Israel in God's saving plan? Paul answers in two ways. The first way deals with the present reality; the second, with an eschatological reality.

1. First Answer: The Chosen Remnant among Israel

Paul's first answer uses the Old Testament image of "a chosen remnant" (11:2–5). He refers to the story of Elijah, confronted with the almost total failure of the people to worship Yahweh (1 Kgs 19) as well as to numerous texts in the prophets referring to a "remnant" (Isa 10:20–22; 11:11; Ezek 14:22; Joel 3:5). As then so now, the answer to the prophet's discouragement consists in avoiding quantitative reckoning. Paul sees the plan of God succeeding through a minority, a representative remnant of the people.

Presumably for Paul, this chosen remnant consists of the Jews who accepted the gospel, the Jewish Christians represented especially by the Jerusalem church. This church, then, forms a key element in Paul's understanding of salvation history. This church is the guarantee that God's gifts are irrevocable. This church is the link between God's covenant to Israel and the churches of the Gentiles.

2. Second Answer: The Eschatological Salvation of the Jews

Paul then faces the real issue, the role of the nonbelieving Jews. After acknowledging the mystery of spiritual blindness (11:7–10; see also Matt 13:14–15), Paul ventures an explanation tied into his vision of the ultimate triumph of God (11:11–29). Paul is convinced that Israel's present refusal of the gospel is part of God's saving plan. The answer he gives here becomes an important element in Paul's **salvation trajectory**.

Paul admits that his first concern remains Israel. His hope is to show Israel what it is missing by demonstrating the grace of God operating in the Gentiles. "I glory in my ministry, trying to rouse my fellow Jews to envy" (11:14). He sees the Gentile churches as foreign branches grafted onto "a holy root," grafted on to manifest the vitality of that root (11:17), an action that will eventually lead to "the full number [*to plêroma*] of Gentiles coming in" (11:26).

At this point, Paul makes an extraordinary statement about God's salvation: "And thus all of Israel will be saved" (11:26). Paul is probably not thinking of individual Jews converting to and being absorbed by a Gentile Christian church. He is writing about the salvation of the Jews as a people. In fact, Paul does not speak about Israel "converting" in any way, although he previously described their being "grafted back on" to the olive tree only "if they do not remain in unbelief" (11:23). Paul is convinced of a universal salvation of the Jews that happens through the Gentiles' acceptance of the gospel.

The point here is not what Israel must do in order to be saved, but how God's plan will infallibly include "all Israel" along with and by means of the "full number of the Gentiles." The presently unbelieving Jews, then, are not unaffected by the grace of God manifested in Christ. By that grace the Jewish people as a whole are already consecrated: "If the first fruits are consecrated, so too is the whole mass of dough. If the root is consecrated, so too are the branches" (11:16).

Recalling (somewhat freely) the words of the Book of Isaiah (40:13–14), Paul concludes with an expression of wonder and praise:

> How deep are the riches and the wisdom and the
> knowledge of God!
> How inscrutable his judgments, how unsearchable his ways!
> For "who has known the mind of the Lord?
> Or who has been his counselor?
> Who has given him anything so as to deserve return?"
> For from him and through him and for him all things are.
> To him be glory forever. Amen. (11:33–36)

L. Various Exhortations (12:1—15:13)

In the last major part of this letter, Paul exhorts the readers on a variety of topics. Except for a brief reflection on eschatology, the major theological trajectories seem to move out of the spotlight:

a. Introduction: the renewal of the mind and mental worship (12:1–2). Paul presents a Jewish Diaspora view of worship where access to the Temple in Jerusalem was impossible. He suggests "mental [*logikê*] worship," and explains it as an "offering of your bodies" (12:1) and a "renewal of your minds" (12:2). This action is further defined by contrast with "this age" [*ho aiôn houtos*], which for Paul remains evil.

b. Humility and charity within the community (12:3–8). Paul urges humility, "not thinking of oneself more highly than one ought to think" (12:3), which as expressed here is a very Hellenistic virtue where everyone should know "their station." Paul, however, "Christianizes" this thought by the comparison with being "one body in Christ" (12:5). The "members" differ from those described in 1 Corinthians 12, where Paul first used the body metaphor for the community. In Romans the roles are less "charismatic," more practical with the listing of "ministers," "sharers," "presiders," and those who support others by "eleemosynary" (mercy) activities. No mention of "prophets" or "speakers in tongues."

c. Charity to all, even to enemies (12:9–21). The exhortation then continues regarding love and friendship (*agapê* and *philadelphia*) in general. Paul starts with the need for a warm affection for one another, one that involves helping others especially by hospitality (12:9–13), the virtue that allowed the missionaries to travel and work. Paul then turns toward the need to love and bless "those who persecute you" (12:14), citing a Jesus tradition that shows up now in Luke 6:28. Cycling through the same sequence again, Paul advises rejoicing with one another (12:15–16) and then doing good to your enemies (12:17–21), again citing Jesus traditions known now in Luke 6:27, 29, and 35.

d. Submission to civil authority (13:1–7). Paul is writing this exhortation apparently at a time outside any major persecution by the Roman authorities. Things will change quickly and we will see the opposite attitude in the Book of Revelation. The advice sounds close to the Jesus traditions about paying taxes, which we have in Mark 12:17 and parallels 1 Peter 2:13–17.

e. Love fulfills the law (13:8–10). Paul then repeats what he wrote in Galatians 5:14, about love being the fulfillment of the law. However, instead of concluding that those with the Spirit are not under the law (Gal 5:18), Paul here lists some of the Ten Commandments and speaks of love as "summing them up" (Rom 13:9). The point here is to show how the law still exists but in a deeper way for those who love.

f. Approach of the day (13:11–14). Paul alludes briefly to **eschatology**, reminding the readers of the nearness of "the day," "Our salvation is nearer now then when we first believed. The night is advanced, the day is at hand" (13:11). Paul then shifts the issue to moral life, conducting one's self properly, "as in the day."

g. Charity toward the weak, especially in food matters (14:1—15:6). In a more developed treatment, Paul returns to the topic of food and possible restrictions on eating, in a development reminiscent of 1 Corinthians 8:1–13 and 10:23–33. Here Paul insists that "the kingdom of God is not a matter of food and drink, but of justice, peace, and joy in the Holy Spirit" (14:17). As he wrote to the Corinthians, he also insists in not harming the weaker member of the community. In Galatians he described the "law of Christ" as bearing one another's burdens (Gal 6:2). Here he repeats the same thought: "We who are strong ought to carry the failings of the weak and not to please ourselves" (Rom 15:1). Somewhat buried in this exhortation is another **eschatological** note: "We shall all stand before the tribunal of God.... Each of us shall give an account of himself to God" (14:10–12).

h. Conclusion: the gospel for Jews and Gentiles alike (15:7–13). Perhaps using a "testamonia" or list of favorite scripture texts, Paul seeks to show the place of both "the circumcised" and "the Gentiles" in the work of Christ. He ends the section with a prayer that weaves together thoughts about **God**, the power of the **Holy Spirit**, hope, joy, peace, and having faith (15:13).

M. Conclusion of the Letter (15:14—16:27)

The remaining verses of the letter appear as a long rambling conclusion. Paul speaks of the writing of this letter (15:14), his sense of finishing his ministry in the East (15:19), his hopes of traveling to Rome on his way to Spain (15:24, 28–29), and his present task of bringing the monetary collection from Corinth to Jerusalem (15:25–27).

Writing here something like a "letter of recommendation," he commends Phoebe to the Romans. This apparently is the kind of "letter of recommendation" that the Corinthians wanted someone to write for Paul (2 Cor 3:1–3). Described as a "deacon" (*diakonos*) and a "patroness" (*prostatis*) in the "church at Cenchreae," the role of this woman is very important for understanding the developing structures of the Pauline churches (Rom 16:1–2). Then Paul adds a long list of names of believers in Rome whom he wants to greet (16:3–20), with greetings from Corinth to the Romans (16:21–23), providing us with more insight into the personalities and roles in the early Pauline churches.

The letter as we have it now[8] ends with a doxology (a prayer of praise), which describes the gospel as "the revelation of the mystery kept secret for long ages, now manifested through the prophetic writings, and...made known to all nations" (16.25–27). The pattern of stages "held secret," "now manifested," and "made known" describes the gospel not so much as an absolutely new thing, but as a reality that has been there all along, connecting the past and the present. The difference in the epochs lies not so much in terms of some new thing added as rather by the manifestation of what was always there. This way of picturing God's action shows how Paul has little difficulty bringing Abraham into the picture of faith.

III. The Thematic Summary of the Letter

A. God

1. Agent of Salvation

Perhaps no other letter of Paul focuses so intently on God the Father as the principal agent of salvation. Paul is preaching "the gospel of God" (1:1). This is the "power of God" for salvation and reveals God's justice (1:16–17). This is the God who "predestined" those he "foreknew," those he "justified" and "glorified" (8:29–30). These saving actions are described as anticipating human decisions. It is God who "overlooks" sins (3:25) and as such manifests his "justice," a concept at the center of Paul's thought in this letter (see 3:21–31) and closely related to the brief mention of God's faith or fidelity (*hê pistis tou theou*, 3:3).

2. The Anger and Judgment of God

In no other letter do we find the insistence that Paul makes in Romans on the role of God as the final judge (2:5–11, 16; 3:6; 14:10–12), following the constant Old Testament (Isa 3:13–15; Hos 4:1; 5:1; Mic 6:1–5; Zeph 3:8) and Jewish theme (*1 Enoch* 47:31; 90:15–27; *4 Ezra* 7:33–44). Likewise, no other letter of Paul contains the extensive portrayal of "the wrath of God" (*orgê theou*) that we have here in Romans. In 1 Thessalonians, Paul had briefly alluded to the "the wrath to come" from which Jesus rescues us (1 Thess 1:10; also 5:9), but this theme dominates the opening chapters of Romans. It is obviously important for Paul. In these opening chapters, "the wrath" is also a present reality, a "wrath" that is now revealed or set in motion—although a future "wrath" is again mentioned in Romans 8:9. The themes of judgment and divine wrath are both drawn especially from the Old Testament prophets, and function in this letter to establish the seriousness of sin, and, in general, the need for divine justification and salvation. At the same time, it evokes the problematic picture of God saving from God.

3. The Love of God

Paul balances his comments about the "wrath of God" with an important description of the "love of God" (*agapê tou theou*) in chapter 5 (5:5; also 8:39). In Romans, for the first time, Paul explains what he means by this term, which he briefly mentioned without explanation in the concluding blessing of 2 Corinthians (2 Cor 13:11, 13). As he had said regarding the "love of Christ,"[9] the "love of God" is a power from which no creature can separate Paul (Rom 8:39). It is poured out into our hearts through the holy Spirit (5:5). Also for the first time, Paul addresses his readers as "beloved of God" (Rom 1:7).

In Romans 5 this love of God is related to human sinfulness and becomes clear in the death of Christ. "God demonstrates his love for us that while we were still sinners Christ died for us" (Rom 5:8). This love precedes the death of Christ and in some way is behind the whole drama of the crucifixion. Whatever Paul means by the "wrath of God" in the opening chapters of this letter or in 8:9, this insistence on the love of God in verse 8 prevents us from wrongly thinking of a God who started out angry at us and needed to be appeased by the death of Jesus. The death of Christ does not bring about God's love. Rather, the love of God is always already there and is manifested in this death. God's love is now seen as the suffering love of a vulnerable God.

4. The Constancy and Mystery of God

As he reflects on the continuing role of Israel in God's plan, Paul develops other traits of God, traits without clear parallel in earlier letters. Using the imagery of Jeremiah, Paul insists on the "potter's rights" of God over his objects of clay that cannot be challenged (9:19–22; see Jer 18:1–12). The "kindness and severity" of God (11:22) describe God's diverse ways of dealing with human beings, ways that again perhaps elicit human perplexity but cannot really be challenged. Alluding to the fidelity of God again (Rom 3:3) against a charge of caprice, Paul then speaks of God's constancy: "The gifts and call of God are irrevocable" (11:29).

Concluding the section on Israel is a reflection on the mystery of God's judgments and ways (11:33–35). Here Paul ties into a thought he had written to the Corinthians using the text of Isaiah 40:13 (see also 1 Cor 2:6). The thought reflects Jewish wisdom traditions (Job 11:7–8; Psalm 139:17–18; Wis 17:1) as well as the special prophetic traditions of the line of Isaiah (Isa 40:13; 55:8–9).

The appropriate human reaction to this mystery is praise: "To him be glory forever" (15:7; 16:27), a praise directed to "the God and Father of our Lord Jesus Christ" (15:6), an expression Paul used in this Corinthian correspondence (2 Cor 1:3; 11:31).

B. Christ Jesus

1. Mortal Human

Paul continues the stress that he began in Galatians describing the humanity of Jesus. There Jesus was the "seed" of Abraham (Gal 3:16), sent as Son of God to be born of a woman (4:4). In Romans, Jesus is quickly identified as "of the seed of David" (Rom

1:3). Paul twice explicitly describes Jesus "according to the flesh" (1:3 and 9:5), saying little about the activity of Christ during this existence "according to the flesh," except that "he died," a death that is usually described as atoning for others (5:6, 8; 14:9, 15). With this death in mind, Paul in Romans describes Jesus sent as Son of God "in the likeness of sinful flesh" (8:5). In no other writing does Paul insist as intensely on the solidarity of Jesus with human earthly sinfulness.

2. Son of God Raised from the Dead

Paul maintains his focus on the resurrection of Jesus. As he insisted in his previous letters (1 Cor 6;14; 2 Cor 4:14; Gal 1:1), Jesus "was raised" by God (4:24, 25; 6:4, 9; 7:4; 8:11, 34; 10:9). The one exception in Romans to the passive role of Jesus in his resurrection is a brief discussion of life and death along with the role of Jesus as Lord of the dead and the living, because "Christ died and came to life [*edzêsen*]" (14:9).

At the beginning of the letter, Paul adds an aspect of this resurrection by which Jesus becomes Son of God in a way that he was not at his sending. At the resurrection, Jesus is "Son of God established in power...according to the Spirit of holiness" (1:4). Paul is focused on the transformation that Jesus underwent at the resurrection. The idea of the profound transformation of Jesus at the resurrection appears in the earlier descriptions of Jesus, who was "crucified out of weakness" but who "lives by the power of God" (2 Cor 13:4). The idea also correlates with what Paul thought about the transformation of the body in the general resurrection (1 Cor 15:42–44) and about the sense that Paul had of divine reconciliation as "a new creation" in Christ (2 Cor 5:17), as well as Paul's general position on the "flesh/Spirit" antithesis (Gal 5:16–25).

Paul affirms the status of Jesus as Son of God prior to the resurrection in another use of the sending formula, "God by sending his Son in the likeness of sinful flesh...condemned sin" (Rom 8:3). Like its parallel in Galatians 4:4, the formula suggests that God had his Son before the Son enters into "sinful flesh." The sending appears to involve the entire earthly career of Jesus. The agency here as in Galatians, however, is entirely that of God, and Jesus is not pictured as making a decision or having an attitude.

3. Medium of God's Action

In Romans, Paul likewise maintains the role of Jesus as a medium of God's action on behalf of humanity. Paul develops that role by specifying additional divine actions. "God will judge... through Christ Jesus" (2:16). The justice of God works "through the faith of Jesus Christ" (3:22). "We have peace with God through our Lord Jesus Christ" (5:1). We will "reign in life through...Jesus Christ" (5:17), and "grace reigns...through Jesus Christ" (6:21). No one can separate us from "the love of God which is in Christ Jesus our Lord" (8:39). However, Paul avoids the term "mediator" (*mesitês)* for Jesus, a term he seems to reject in Galatians 3:19–20 for the relationship established between God and human beings through faith.

C. The Spirit of God

1. The Spirit/Letter Antithesis and Religious Observance

Early in Romans Paul alludes to the "Spirit/letter" antithesis in his discussion of who the true Jew is. "One is a Jew inwardly, and circumcision is of the heart, in the Spirit, not the letter" (Rom 2:29). Thus, real circumcision is not the outward sign. It is not "in the flesh" but "of the heart" (2:29). Paul is repeating the imagery of Jeremiah (4:4; 9:25).[10] In 2 Corinthians the Spirit/letter antithesis is used in the description of the nature of the "new covenant" (2 Cor 3:6–8). As in his earlier letter, Paul in Romans is thinking of interior conformity with the law—the law of the Spirit and the heart.

The Spirit is thus the key to freedom from the law and especially the law of circumcision. Paul can deal with the provision of Genesis 17 that the circumcision covenant is God's "covenant with you and your descendants after you throughout the ages as an everlasting pact" (Gen 17:7). For Paul, circumcision is observed interiorly by the Spirit in our hearts. The religious observance and "offerings of the Gentiles" are thus "sanctified by the

Holy Spirit" (Rom 15:16) and made part of the "worship, holy and pleasing to God" (12:1).

2. The Spirit and Salvation

Romans 8 is, in effect, an extensive reflection on the role of the Spirit in salvation. This chapter is dominated by the "Spirit/flesh" antithesis, an original concept in Paul based on Jewish apocalyptic categories. The antithesis appeared first in Galatians. Here Paul stresses the way in which one is liberated from "the flesh" to live in "the Spirit." "The law of the Spirit of life in Christ Jesus has freed you from the law of sin and death" (8:2). Redemption or liberation necessarily requires a shift and transformation from an existence "in the flesh" and "according to the flesh" to an existence "in the Spirit" and "according to the Spirit." This transformation occurs if the "Spirit of God dwells in you" (8:9).

Furthermore, such an existence "in the Spirit" orients us to the eschatological resurrection of the body. "If the Spirit of the one who raised Jesus from the dead dwells in you, the one who raised Christ from the dead will give life to your mortal bodies also, through the Spirit that dwells in you" (8:11). Paul is careful to maintain principal agency of the resurrection with God, but he insists that God acts through the Spirit already dwelling in the human being.

Furthermore, that Spirit establishes continuity between the resurrection of Jesus and that of other human beings. We have "the Spirit of the one who raised Jesus." Likewise, Paul had earlier described Jesus as the Son of God established in power at his resurrection, "according to the Spirit of holiness" (1:4). This is "the power of the Holy Spirit," which establishes hope (15:13).

In 1 Corinthians, Paul insisted on the "spiritual" transformation of the body at the resurrection (1 Cor 15:44). There he had also insisted on the "spiritual" transformation of the person who had received the Spirit from God to know the gifts of God (2:13–15). In 2 Corinthians, he had also named the Spirit in our hearts as the "down payment" of life after death (2 Cor 1:22; 5:5). In Galatians, Paul presented the Spirit as the guide and principle of moral life (Gal 5:16–25), briefly mentioning the eschatological effects of "sowing in the Spirit" (6:8). Romans 8 appears to be Paul's attempt to pull together and develop these initial insights.

3. *The Spirit and Prayer*

To be led by the Spirit of God is to be an adult child (*hyios*) of God, because this Spirit is the Spirit of adoption (*hyiothesia*) (8:14–15). Hence, as he wrote in Galatians 4:6, this is the Spirit that enables us to pray *Abba*, the endearment form of addressing a father. The Spirit "bears witness with our spirit"[11] that we are now adult children (*hyioi*) of God (Rom 8:16). All this is part of the "inexpressible groanings" that are also the Spirit "interceding for the holy ones" (Rom 8:26–27). In this way, the Spirit comes to the aid of our present weakness and our inability to pray.

Paul insists that God understands these prayers, which might be unintelligible to us. "God knows the intentions of the Spirit" (8:27). In 1 Corinthians, Paul had speculated on how the Spirit of God alone knows the depths of God (1 Cor 2:11). Here Paul reverses the familiarity, in effect describing how the Spirit in our hearts, interceding for us, draws us into the intimacy of God's life.

Nothing in Stoicism approaches this view of the Spirit in prayer. Although in the later Old Testament and Judaism, the Spirit functioned in prophecy, I likewise can find nothing close in his Jewish background or in parallel Christian tradition[12] to Paul's view of the Spirit praying in the believer's heart.

D. Salvation

1. *Present and Future*

Paul has many terms for the fundamental grace of God meant to bring human existence to a successful conclusion. Some are basically synonymous; others have somewhat different nuances. At one point, he clearly distinguishes a present reality, "being justified" (*dikaiousthai*), from a future gift, "being saved" (*sôthêsthai*). Along with present justification, Paul also associates "being at peace" with God (5:1; see Gal 5:22), having "access" to God (5:2), and "being reconciled" with God (5:10–11; 2 Cor 5:18–19). Paul associated "the overlooking of sins" with justification (Rom 3:25). Salvation, on the other hand, appears here as an eschatological reality, an object of hope (Rom 5:9). The resurrection of the dead, or as Paul says, "the redemption of our bodies," is central to our hope of salvation (8:23–24).

In the theology of Paul, the Spirit brings together present justification and future salvation. God will raise us from the dead by his Spirit who already dwells in us (8:11; 1 Cor 3:16; Gal 4:6) as the "firstfruits" (8:23), for we are no longer "in the flesh" but "in the Spirit" (8:9). The dwelling of the Spirit in us now appears to be a way in which the resurrection is anticipated at least in some "spiritual" way, providing thus "the firstfruits of the Spirit" (8:23).

The continuity guaranteed by the presence of the Spirit between bodily resurrection and the present life of faith was hinted at by Paul earlier when he described the transformed believer and the risen body as "spiritual" (*pneumatikos*, 1 Cor 2:15 and 15:44) and when he described the gift of the Spirit as the "down payment" (*arrabon*, 2 Cor 1:22; 5:5). As Paul says in Galatians, "eternal life" is part of the harvest "from the Spirit" that comes from "sowing in the Spirit" (Gal 6:8).

2. Sin and the Spirit/Flesh Antithesis

What perhaps distinguishes Paul's soteriological views in Romans lies in two correlated themes, his intense concentration on sin and his use of the Spirit/flesh antithesis.

In line with the exilic prophets, Paul focuses on individual lives rather than the nation when he describes God saving from sin. Previously, Paul had connected sin with the redeeming death of Christ, especially by describing Christ dying "for our sins" (1 Cor 15:3; Gal 1:4; see also Rom 5:8; 1 Thess 5:10). In Romans, however, we have for the first time a description of God "overlooking" sins (Rom 3:25). This follows the lengthy presentation of the sins of both Gentiles and Jews (1:18—3:20).

Here, however, Paul maintains an apocalyptic perspective in this matter of God dealing with sin. He is not talking simply about external personal relationships and moral reform. Paul does not speak of God "forgiving" sin like some debt. Nor does he use the psalmist's language of "washing" or "cleansing" from sin (Ps 51:3–4). In this perspective, evil is a cosmic power of some form. Earlier, Paul had used eon or epoch language to describe the sinful condition of the world (1 Cor 1:20; 2:6, 8; 2 Cor 4:4) and the rescue that God effects (Gal 1:4).

In Romans, Paul shifts from eon language to categories more closely connected to human existence, "flesh" and "Spirit," without, however, losing the note of cosmic power where the real issue lies in a picture of God dealing with sin. Paul is continuing the language of Galatians, which associates the power of sin with "flesh" (*sarx*) in its antithesis with "Spirit" (Gal 5:16–25). In Galatians, the imagery functions mostly to describe the importance of moral conduct and freedom from the law. Chapter 8 of Romans picks up the same antithesis to describe the work of God dealing with sin and the transformation effected in the life of the believer by that work.

3. The Scope of Salvation

It is not easy to determine how Paul envisioned the scope of those included in this fundamental grace of God. Who is to be saved? We can find two conflicting positions or vectors in Romans. On the one hand, Paul insists on judgment and responsibility to God for evil behavior. On the other hand, Paul speaks of justification and salvation as effectively enveloping all.

As we will see below in Paul's eschatology, Romans stands out by its frequent and emphasized references to final judgment (2:5–11, 16; 3:6; 14:10–12). Paul describes here a responsibility or accountability, apparently after death, to God for one's sins. In this way Paul links up with typical apocalyptic theology (see Dan 12:1–3; *4 Ezra* 7:36; 8:41; Matt 25:31–46).

Romans, especially in the first section on sin (1:18—3:20), also stands out by its dramatic insistence on a kind of universal condemnation. Not unlike the accusations of the Old Testament prophets is the conclusion of this section: "There is no just man, not even one" (3:10). "The whole world stands convicted before God" (3:19). Everyone stands condemned before God. Everyone has become the object of God's wrath.

Paul's point here, of course, is the universal need for God's justification and salvation. Paul then moves on to describe that "justification" (3:21–31). The sequence of thought in these chapters of Romans is similar to that in 1 Corinthians 15. There Paul excludes all "flesh and blood" from "the kingdom of God" (1 Cor 15:50). Then immediately he describes confidence in a universal transformation (15:51–57). Later in Romans, Paul issues a similar apparent exclusion of all human beings from God's graces: "Those who are in the flesh cannot please God" (Rom 8:8), following immediately with the upbeat statement, "but you are not in the flesh…you are in the Spirit" (8:9).

In fact, the rest of chapter 8 expresses great optimism about the scope of salvation. God handed his Son over for "us all" and will give us everything. "If God is for us, who is against us?" (8:31). Of course, one could respond that God is universal in his initial offer of salvation, but we have to toe the line or the deal is off.

There are, however, two places in Romans where Paul suggests that personal behavior is not the issue of salvation. The first deals with Paul's reflections on death as anticipated by baptism. As seen below in the study of Paul's trajectory of union with Christ, baptism for Paul is a way of being "co-crucified" with Christ and in this way freed from the slavery to sin (6:4–6). The importance of baptism for salvation is very clear. However, in the light of Paul's earlier polemic in Galatians about salvation through works of the law and particularly circumcision (Gal 2:16–21; 5:2–6; also in less intensity at Rom 3:28), it would seem unlikely that Paul is here promulgating a new rule or work of the law to follow in order to gain salvation, as if now baptism were the new circumcision.

The significance Paul sees in baptism lies not in the way it becomes the new legal hoop through which good guys can jump and distinguish themselves, but in the way it effectively anticipates death. He then explains, "For the dying person [*apothanôn*] is absolved [*dedikaiôtai*] from sin" (6:7). The importance of baptism lies in the way a person can be justified or freed from the slavery to sin now. The connection between baptism and freedom from sin lies in the way we can anticipate our death by being "co-crucified." The implicit suggestion here is that physical death is the fundamental way in which God liberates from sin. This way would be applicable to all humanity.

The second place in Romans where Paul suggests a salvation not limited to good people is in his discussion of the Jewish people, where he declares, "And thus all of Israel will be saved" (11:26). The link back ("thus") refers not to some conversion or good action on the part of the Jewish people, but to the "full number of the Gentiles entering" (11:25). The focus here is on God's saving action, first of Gentiles and then of Jews. Paul does not speak here about Israel converting—although that is not ruled out.

The conviction of Paul is striking. He is not saying that he hopes this will take place. He is convinced it will. Paul is quite aware of the "sins of the Jews" just as he is aware of the "sins of the Gentiles" (Rom 1—3). His conviction lies in his understanding of God and God's way of dealing with sin. Earlier he had suggested that the unbelieving Jews and Gentiles were "vessels of wrath made for destruction [*apôleia*]" (9:22). The Greek word, *apôleia*, often describes eschatological condemnation (Matt 7:13; 2 Pet 3:7; Rev 17:8, 11). In Paul's view here, however, this "destruction" is not the last word in God's dealing with sin. In the end "all of Israel will be saved" (11:26). Jeremiah's imagery of the potter and the clay (Jer 18:1–12), which Paul drew on to construct his own image of "vessels of wrath" (Rom 9:21–24), stressed the potter's action of smashing the clay that turned out badly and refashioning it until it is what the potter wants. Destruction (*apôleia*) appears as an intermediate stage.

Ultimately, God will show his greatness by a form of universal salvation. Paul sees this ultimate inclusion of Israel as the signal for the ultimate triumph of God, the liberation of the material universe from death and corruption. This ultimate inclusion will be the signal for the resurrection of the dead (11:15), which for Paul in 1 Corinthians was also the sign of the destruction of the "last enemy" (1 Cor 15:26).

4. The Role of Christ

Although in Romans he emphasizes the saving role of God the Father, Paul does not back off from the place of Christ in this drama. While ultimate agency for salvation is firmly in God's hands, Christ becomes an inseparable element in this picture. As in some way a medium of justification and salvation, faith in Romans is clearly directed to the power of God raising Jesus. "If you confess with your mouth that Jesus is Lord and believe in your heart that God raised him from the dead, you will be saved" (10:9). The theme is announced earlier in the discussion of Abraham's faith. Abraham had faith in God, "who gives life to the dead" (4:17), a description Paul uses to explain why we "believe in the one who raised Jesus our Lord from the dead" (4:24). This specific of faith follows on Paul's earlier insistence on faith as part of Christ living in the believer (2 Cor 13:5; Gal 2:20).

In Romans, Paul again maintains the atoning death of Jesus: "While we were still sinners, Christ died for us" (Rom 5:8; see 1 Thess 5:10; 1 Cor 15:3; Gal 1:4;). Here in Romans, Paul stresses the physical death of Jesus as the key element. "We are justified by his blood" (Rom 5:9; see 3:25). Human death as God's way of dealing with sin remains central.

The thought in Romans 8:3, "God sending his Son in the likeness of sinful flesh," is also a continuation of the description of Christ "becoming a curse for us" (Gal 3:13) or "God made him to be sin" (2 Cor 5:21). Paul is insisting on the intense solidarity of Christ with us in our sinfulness. It is by this solidarity of Christ with our sinfulness that God rescues us from that condition. The only Jewish background that comes close to this insistence on redemption by solidarity in sinfulness is the fourth "suffering servant" hymn in Deutero-Isaiah (Isa 52:13—53:12).

By the death and resurrection of Christ, God condemns sin "in the flesh," that is, in the flesh of Christ. As Paul said earlier, "Death has no more power over him. His death was death to sin, once for all; his life is life for God" (Rom 6:9–10). We benefit from this transformation of Christ by our union with him.

E. The Union of Life with Christ

1. Various Images

The development of Paul's **union with Christ trajectory** in Romans involves the reusing of many images and expressions from earlier writings. Paul peppers this letter with his usual "in Christ" and "in Christ Jesus" expressions. Early on he speaks of "redemption in Christ Jesus" (3:24) and of "living for God in Christ Jesus" (6:11; see also 6:23). Toward the end of the letter, Paul uses this qualification often for himself, his work, and his co-workers. He speaks the truth "in Christ" (9:1; see 15:17–18; 16:3, 7, 9, 10).

Other familiar images in this letter include the "body" metaphor, describing the simultaneous union of believers with Christ and with each other: "Though many, we are one body in Christ" (12:5), picking up the theme from 1 Corinthians 12. Paul also uses the "clothing with Christ" image that he used in Galatians 3:27 in connection with baptism. In Romans, the exhortation is in connection with the morality appropriate for the approach of eschatological salvation: "Clothe yourselves with the Lord Jesus Christ and make no provision for the desires of the flesh" (Rom 13:14).

In two places in this letter, however, Paul adds a new development to the trajectory. One development connects this union with Christ with baptism, chapter 6. The second connects this union with the Spirit.

2. Through Baptism

In chapter 6, Paul speaks of baptism as being "baptized into Christ's death" and being "co-buried" with him (6:3–4). He continues, "Our old person was co-crucified…and we have died with him" (6:6–8). He repeats the thought in the next chapter: "You were put to death…through the body of Christ" (7:4). The consequence of this union with Christ in death is a union with him in life. We now "walk with him in a newness of life" (6:4) and we "will live with him" (6:8), since "we will be united through a likeness to his resurrection" (6:5). In effect, death and resurrection are as inseparable in the life of the believer as they are in the life of Christ. Baptism is in some way an entry into that drama of death and resurrection.

In Galatians, Paul had spoken of baptism as clothing oneself with Christ (Gal 3:28). Such a union with Christ, for Paul, led to freedom from the law as pedagogue, along with the end of social distinctions. Nothing was said about union with the death of Jesus. In a somewhat parallel way, writing 1 Corinthians, Paul saw the Lord's Supper as a "sharing" (*koinônia*) in the body and blood of Christ (1 Cor 10:16), a union with Christ that also had an important social consequence, becoming one body (10:17).

3. Through the Spirit

In chapter 8 of Romans, Paul adds a second new development to the **union with Christ trajectory**. Paul begins this chapter about salvation by speaking about "the law of the Spirit of life in Christ Jesus" (8:2), which assures that "now there is no condemnation for those in Christ Jesus" (8:1). In this chapter, this presence of Christ is described in clear parallel to the indwelling of the Spirit, which is the key to resurrection: "If Christ is in you...if the Spirit dwells in you" (8:10–11).

Before concluding the topic, Paul adds a note of confidence in the permanence of this Spirit of life in Christ Jesus. He lays down the challenge, "Who will separate us from the love of Christ?" (8:35). In the next lines as he finishes his answer to the rhetorical question, Paul connects that love of Christ to the love of God, declaring that there is no power that "will separate us from the love of God which is in Christ Jesus our Lord" (8:39). The loving power that unites us to Christ is ultimately the love of God, and God has "predestined" those who love God "to be conformed to the image of his Son, so that he might be the firstborn among many brothers and sisters" (8:29).

F. Eschatology

If anything, in Romans Paul moves away from future eschatology to a more realized or spiritualized interpretation of end-time events. Paul points out how the anger and the justice of God are now being manifested (1:18ff.; 3:21ff.). We are now co-crucified with Christ (6:6). Paul will even urge his readers, "Present yourselves to God as raised from the dead to life" (6:13). We are now no longer in the flesh but in the Spirit (8:9). The mystery held secret in past ages is now being revealed (16:25–26). In other words, "the kingdom of God is…a matter of justice, peace, and the Holy Spirit" (14:17).

Yet to the very end of the letter, Paul demands attention to the future. "Our salvation is nearer now then when we first believed. The night is advanced, the day is at hand" (13:11). The point Paul is making consists in the importance of present morality, conducting one's self properly, "as in the day." Still he is not collapsing eschatology into the present. He did the same jockeying between the future and the present in 1 Thessalonians (see 1 Thess 5:5–11).

Paul's trajectory of future eschatology develops here in a brief treatment of eternal life, in his extensive considerations of the general resurrection, and in his continued portrayal of a future judgment.

1. *Eternal Life*

Writing to the Galatians, Paul briefly introduced an image of salvation that suggests a contact with Johannine Christianity, "eternal life." In Galatians, "eternal life" is the eschatological (*zoê aiônios*) harvest of sowing in the Spirit, in contrast to corruption, which is the harvest of sowing in the flesh (Gal 6:8; see also the *oikia aionios* of 2 Cor 5:1). Paul is tying into the salvation concepts of apocalyptic Judaism.[13]

In Romans, Paul repeatedly refers to "eternal life" as an image of salvation, probably understood as eschatological. It is the recompense of God at the great judgment, "eternal life to those who seek glory, honor, and immortality through perseverance in good works" (Rom 2:7). Here it is contrasted with "wrath and fury" suffered by those who go the other way. Later, it is part of Paul's contrast between sin and grace: "As sin reigned in death, grace also might reign through justification for eternal life"

(5:21). Here it is the goal or term of justification. Similarly, as sanctification is the "fruit" of being a slave of God, so eternal life, the "spiritual gift" (*charisma*) of God, is the goal, just as death is the "salary" of sin (6:22–23).

2. The Future Resurrection

In his discussion about baptism, Paul maintains the future character of the resurrection. "If we have been united with him through likeness to his death, so shall we be [through a likeness] to the resurrection" (6:4). He refuses to spiritualize the resurrection in order to draw it into the present, the way he spiritualizes the death and co-crucifixion of the believer (6:3–4). The future is still important: "If we died with Christ, we believe that we will also live with him" (6:8).

Similarly in chapter 8, Paul describes the present role of the Spirit in our hearts now crying, *Abba* (8:15). This is the Spirit that now transforms us from living "in the flesh" to living "in the Spirit" (8:9). The result is a combination of realized death and life, "the body is dead" but "the Spirit is alive" (8:10). Yet Paul insists that the future hope remains that God "will give life to your mortal bodies also through his Spirit that dwells in you" (8:11).

As he continues in this chapter, Paul draws all of creation into this hope. "Creation awaits with eager expectation the revelation of the sons and daughters of God.... Creation is groaning in labor pains even until now" (8:19–22). Paul explicitly connects this expectation and groaning with the "redemption of our bodies" for which we also groan, "having the firstfruits of the Sprit" (8:23).

Paul's view is consistent with a Jewish apocalyptic vision of "a world to come," a type of re-creation that is more than a spiritual heaven. What is distinctive in Paul's view, however, is an element of continuity. This creation and our present bodies are groaning for transformation. The present world is not destroyed or banished (Rev 20:1; *4 Ezra* 6:7–20; 7:30) but raised to a new level.

In Paul's mind, the future resurrection of the body is not just an epilogue to the spiritual salvation of souls. In a mysterious way, salvation is not complete. To a large degree, creation is still subject to corruption. As Paul said to the Corinthians, "The last enemy to be destroyed is death" (1 Cor 15:26). Death is still reigning over us. Hence, Paul hears the groaning and the labor pains of material reality in a struggle, geared to last until the final day, when human beings will be part of this ultimate triumph of God through the resurrection of their bodies.

Paul had introduced the drama of the eschatological resurrection in 1 Thessalonians 4—5. In 1 Corinthians 15, he had insisted on integrating this drama into his vision of salvation. In 2 Corinthians 6, he had hinted at a cosmic scope of this salvation by portraying God as "reconciling the world [*kosmos*] to himself" in an act of a "new creation." Here in Romans 8, he moves from the hint to an explicit position.

3. The Future Judgment

For all the insistence on a kind of realized eschatology in Romans, this letter stands out with its references to a future judgment. In typical prophetic language, Paul threatens divine anger, which is being "stored up" by evildoers for a "just judgment of God" (2:5). Paul names this day as "the day when God will judge people's hidden works" (2:16).

Paul returns to the theme at the end of his letter when he refers to the tribunal of God. "We shall all stand before the tribunal of God.... Each of us shall give an account of himself to God" (14:10–12). In 2 Corinthians, Paul referred to a future "tribunal of Christ" before which we must all appear (2 Cor 5:10). In Romans, Paul returns to the more traditional Jewish view of God as judge.

In 1 Thessalonians, Paul had written about the divine eschatological anger to refer to how Jesus would rescue us from it (1 Thess 2:10; see 5:9[14]). That combination of themes occurs again in Romans. "Now that we have been justified by his [Jesus'] blood, all the more shall we be saved by him from God's wrath" (Rom 5:9).

In general, then, this picture of the future wrath of God functions much like the present wrath of God to show the seriousness of sin and the greatness of the rescue effected by Christ. The image of this dreadful judgment is drawn almost directly from Jewish apocalyptic categories. In Paul, however, judgment and wrath, whether future or present, need to be understood in the light of what Paul says about divine love "while we were still sinners" (Rom 5:8).

It is significant that the letter that insists the most on a kind of universal salvation is the same letter that insists the most on responsibility for one's sins. The two themes function like conflicting vectors pulling us in a direction not described by either.

IV. The Message of the Letter

The message this letter broadcasts is a powerful yet confusing message about God. Paul insists on a God who deals with sin, a God who demands accountability for sin, a God who judges and punishes in his anger. At the same time, this is a God who seems to be ready to forgive all sin in his love for humanity. These two attitudes of God seem impossible to reconcile, at least from a human perspective. Perhaps that is why Paul adds the message about the "inscrutable judgments and unsearchable ways" of God (11:33).

In that mystery of God, Paul can see the crucifixion of Christ as a manifestation of God's love (5:8). In fact, Christ, the beloved Son, becomes the focus of humanity's accountability for sin and therefore the focus of God's anger against sin. In this letter Paul focuses on God, but Christ is inseparable from God's saving actions.

The issue of the salvation of the Jews seems to be Paul's way of insisting on the ultimate triumph of God over sin. The sins of the Jews are very serious, as are the sins of the Gentiles, but God is greater than sin. The mystery of Israel's blindness forms a part of the mystery of sin and death's continuing influence in the universe. The present triumph of God over sin and death remains camouflaged behind the sign of the cross, behind weakness and suffering (1 Cor 1:18–25). However, sin and death along with the blindness of Israel are temporary anomalies. They do not belong. It is only a matter of time before these evils also are conquered.

In the meantime, believers face an inscrutable tangle of love, crucifixion, and resurrection. Perhaps the Abba prayer best captures this tangle. This prayer inspired by the Spirit is at once a prayer of joyful intimacy and still a prayer of agony (see Mark

14:36). We await the fullness of salvation that we see in the risen Christ. However, we do not wait alone. With the Spirit, we groan "Abba" in union with all creation. We unite with all nature in its longing for the full revelation or empowerment of God's children, liberation from death and corruption. Our longing, however, is joyful. We stand in hope, confident of the incomparable glory to be revealed in us (8:14–24).

10
Philippians

The city of Philippi was located about eight miles inland north of the Aegean Sea. It lay on the main highway running east-west through Macedonia, the Via Egnatia.

Philip II of Macedonia, the father of Alexander the Great, named it after himself in 356 BC. The city and its surrounding plains became famous as the site of the battle of Philippi (42 BC), when Octavius and Mark Anthony defeated the republican forces of Brutus and Cassius. Afterwards, the city became a Roman *colonia*, with a large population of Roman veterans. Acts 16:12 refers to the city as "the first city in the district of Macedonia." Thessalonica was the capital of the province of Macedonia. Philippi, therefore, appears here as the seat of government for a political subdivision within the province.

I. Background for the Letter

A. The Founding and Development of the Church

Paul makes no clear allusion to his founding of this community or to its early development, as he does in his other letters. This lack may be an indication of the late date of this letter. What we do learn from Paul's remarks is that the community is suffering from outside opponents (Phil 1:28–30) and is being bothered by Judaizers (3:2–3). This picture of difficulties is confirmed by remarks in other letters (see 1 Thess 2:2; 2 Cor 8:1–2).

This community has a warm relationship with Paul. Paul's words to the Philippians are very tender: "God himself can testify how much I long for all of you with the affection of Christ Jesus"

(1:8), "you whom I so love and long for" (4:1). This was the only community Paul trusted enough to accept money from, money that they twice sent to Paul in Thessalonica (4:16). Paul is probably referring to the Philippians when he writes to the Corinthians about the generosity of the "brothers in Macedonia" who not only contributed to the collection for Jerusalem (2 Cor 8:1–5) but also supported Paul in his own difficulties (2 Cor 11:9).

B. Circumstances Leading up to Writing

Paul is in prison. A hearing of his case has been held, and his situation could go either way, condemnation to death (1:20; 2:17) or release to return to Philippi (1:25). Paul feels optimistic about the outcome (2:24).

The Philippians had sent a community member by the name of Epaphroditus to help Paul. Epaphroditus became deathly sick, but was recovering by the time the Philippians had heard about the sickness (2:25–26). He will be returning shortly. Timothy is also with Paul (1:1), and Paul will shortly be sending Timothy to Philippi to fetch news about the church there (2:19).

Coming out of these circumstances, therefore, this letter appears to be one motivated principally by the need for personal communication. Paul wants to thank the Philippians for their help. He wants to reassure them of Epaphroditus's recovery and give news about himself. Unlike the letters to Corinth and Galatia, Paul is not addressing any major problems within the church. Only briefly does he allude to some bickering (4:2).

Nevertheless, Paul takes the opportunity to share his understanding about Christian living and about Christ. In this letter, Paul's understanding of both exhibits unparalleled depths and richness. This level of understanding strongly suggests a late date for this writing.

C. The Place and Timing of the Letter

Christian tradition has long situated the writing of Philippians in Rome, during the house arrest described in Acts 28:30–31.

References to "the praetorium" (1:13) and "the house of Caesar" (4:22) seem to confirm this tradition.

However, the principal difficulty with this view lies in the amount of communication presupposed in this letter between Paul and the Philippians. Philippians 2:25–26 alone presupposes four trips recently made between the two, a trip every time information passed between Paul and the Philippians. Other trips are planned. Travel between Philippi and Rome is estimated to have taken about a month.

On the other hand, travel between Philippi and any city around the Aegean basin like Ephesus would have required only a week to ten days. For this reason, scholars today suggest an imprisonment at Ephesus, where Paul, according to Acts, suffered life-threatening difficulties (Act 19:23–40). The "house of Caesar" as well as the "praetorium" existed also at Ephesus and other cities like Jerusalem (see Mark 15:16 and parallels).

If we select this city as the location of the letter writing, we have two probabilities for its timing: either early or very late. Paul was in Ephesus at the time of his writing 1 Corinthians (around AD 57). He could have been imprisoned there and have written to the Philippians at that time. The writing would have had to be before he even conceived the idea of a collection to be gathered from the Greek churches in favor of the Jerusalem church, hence, considerably before 1 Corinthians.

The other time slot possible for an Ephesian composition of this letter would be late, that is, perhaps after a Roman imprisonment or house arrest, as described in Acts, lasting two years (Acts 28:30–31), that is, until about AD 63. Tradition locates the death of Paul in Rome in AD 67. Such a chronology leaves three or four years for Paul to return to his ministry in the Near East. Philemon, a letter also very probably written either during or after his Roman captivity, indicates Paul's abandonment of his plans to travel to Spain (see verse 22). The Letter to the Philippians, like that to the Colossians, shows several distinctive features, particularly a maturity of thought and theological development, which are more understandable if we see these letters as late in Paul's career, a view we will use in this study.

D. The Integrity of the Letter

The mood of the letter shifts very abruptly after 3:1, which likewise shows some earmarks of a letter ending. This shift here and the less evident shifts at 2:18 and 4:9 suggest the possibility that our present letter is the result of editing, somewhat like 2 Corinthians. A hypothesis enjoying some popularity not long ago suggested that our present Philippians is really the final redaction of three shorter letters: (a) a note of thanks (1:1–2; 4:10–20), (b) a letter of personal news (1:3—3:1; 4:4–9, 21–23), and (c) a letter warning against Judaizers (3:2—4:3).

The change in moods, however, could be explained much more simply by the assumption of an extended period of time for the letter writing. Furthermore, the more complicated hypothesis of several letters edited together does not really help explain any other problems in the present form of the letter.

II. The Sequential Study of the Letter

A. The Outline of the Letter

In its present form, Philippians alternates in typical Pauline fashion between "newsy" sections, about Paul's situation and about his companions, and more theological sections, mostly in the form of exhortations. The structure forms an outline as follows:

- I. Opening (1:1–11)
  - A. Address (1:1–2)
  - B. Thanksgiving and prayer (1:3–11)
- II. News of Paul's situation (1:12–26)
- III. Exhortations (1:27—2:18)
  - A. Struggling for the faith (1:27–30)
  - B. Unity in humility (2:1–11)
    - —Christological hymn (2:6–11)
  - C. Working for salvation (2:12–18)
- IV. Plans concerning Timothy and Epaphroditus (2:19–30)
- V. Exhortations (3:1—4:9)
  - A. Warning against Judaizers (3:1–11)

B. Continuing the spiritual effort (3:12–16)
C. Warning against enemies of the cross and libertarians (3:17–21)
D. Recommendations to individuals and maxims (4:1–9)

VI. Paul's gratitude (4:10–20)

VII. Closing: greeting and blessing (4:21–23)

B. The Greeting and Thanksgiving (1:1–11)

For the first time since writing 1 Thessalonians, Paul omits calling himself an apostle, describing himself and Timothy as simply "slaves of Christ Jesus." He addresses his readers also not as "church" but as "the holy ones" (*hagioi*) in Philippi (1:1). In his greeting he also mentions officers in the community, "bishops and deacons" (1:1). This is the earliest reference in the New Testament to the office of bishop, which will become very important in later ecclesiastical development. Paul addresses both groups in the plural, however, indicating he is not addressing any "monarchical bishop" like that of second-century churches. Paul's greeting, furthermore, is to the community with their bishops and deacons, not simply to these officers and through them to the community according to the hierarchical structures of the next century.

In the opening letter prayer, Paul expresses both thanksgiving and petition. He thanks God for the way the Philippians have been "partners" (*koinônoi, sygkoinônoi,* 1:5, 7) with him in his work and in hardships. This relationship, not that of patron, may have been the one Paul wanted when he accepted material support from others. With a reference to **eschatology**, Paul sees this joint effort as rooted in **God**'s initiative. "I am confident of this, that the one who began a good work in you will continue to complete it until the day of Christ Jesus" (1:6).

Paul's petition in this prayer is for the growth of the Philippians' love, "so that your love may more and more abound in knowledge [*epignôsis*] and all experience [*aisthêsis*]" (1:9). Love is to grow and become perfect in knowledge. Again Paul alludes to "the day of Christ" (1:11). In his earlier correspondence to the Corinthians, Paul insisted on the superiority of love to knowledge (1 Cor 13). Now it appears he is reversing that order, where knowledge is the more perfect form. In his Letter to the Philippians, however, Paul may be thinking of a form of knowledge different from the one he warned the Corinthians against. The *gnôsis* he spoke of to the Corinthians was a special charism among many others and one that could cause factions in the community. The *epignôsis* he prays for here rather is one that specifically develops out of love.

C. News of Paul's Situation (1:12–26)

Paul refers to his own adversaries in a milder tone than previously (see 2 Cor 11:13–15). He still accuses them of selfish motivation, but in the end states, "What difference does it make as long as...Christ is being proclaimed?" (1:18).

As he reflects on his imprisonment and the very real possibility that he might be put to death, Paul expresses an extraordinary hope in life after death. He starts by expressing his willingness either to continue living or to die: "For to me life is Christ, and death is gain. If I go on living in the flesh, that means fruitful labor for me. And I do not know which to choose. I am caught between the two" (1:21–23). He then explains what he means by "death is gain." "I long to depart this life and be with Christ, for that is far better" (1:23). The implications of this statement are important in Paul's **eschatology trajectory**. Paul seems to be describing a personal blessed existence immediately after death. Life in **union with Christ** is here also seen as the ultimate grace.

D. Exhortations (1:27—2:18)

Paul understands the Philippians as "struggling together for the faith of the gospel, not intimidated in any way by our opponents" (1:27–28). Paul sees this situation as an example of "suffering for Christ" (1:29). Later in this letter, he will speak of "sharing in Christ's sufferings" (Phil 3:10), both references important for Paul's **union with Christ trajectory**.

When Paul describes the opponents who are causing his readers to suffer, his mild attitude (1:18) evaporates. Here he returns to dividing people into those marked or designated for "destruction" (*apôleia*) and those for "salvation" (*sôteria*) (1:28), identifying the opponents with the first group. The vocabulary and the opposition here suggest **eschatological** judgment and consequences. Writing later about the "enemies of the cross," Paul again speaks of their end as "destruction" (3:19).

The exhortation then moves to an encouragement toward humility, leading then to a hymn or poem describing the humility of Christ (2:6–11). One of the most famous christological hymns in the New Testament, perhaps second only to the prologue of John in importance for later theology, this poem forms a veritable climax in Paul's **Christology trajectory**.

The hymn appears to have been composed earlier than the letter, perhaps by Paul, perhaps by another, and then used in this letter as an exhortation to humility. The signs of its autonomous literary existence are its dense theological expressiveness, its poetic rhythm, and its loose connections with its present context. The hymn describes Christ in three successive stages: preexistent (2:6), alive as human (2:7–8), and gloriously exalted after death (2:9–11).

The hymn as a whole reflects a structure seen in two other christological formulas of Paul, both found in 2 Corinthians, where two phases of Christ are described and then connected with a result clause:

Phil 2:6–11	*2 Cor 5:21*	*2 Cor 8:9*
Existing in the form of God [present participle]	Not knowing sin [present participle]	Being rich [present participle]
He did not think… he emptied himself… he humbled himself… God exalted him… and bestowed on him… [all aorist]	God Made him sin for us...[aorist]	He made himself poor for you [aorist]
so that [*hina*] at the name of Jesus every knee shall bend…	so that [*hina*] we might become the justice of God in him.	so that [*hina*] you might be enriched by his poverty

After concluding the hymn, Paul abruptly returns to a string of exhortations. One describes **God**, who "is the one who for his good purpose works in you both to desire and to work" (2:13). This activity of God is given as a motive to Philippians "to work out your salvation with fear and trembling" (2:12).

E. Plans Concerning Timothy and Epaphroditus (2:19–30)

We then learn a bit more about Paul and his companions. He describes his hopes to send Timothy to Philippi and himself to be freed to travel there likewise (2:19–24). The situation of Epaphroditus is a bit more complicated. He was sent by the Philippians to Paul after word got to the Philippians that Paul was in prison (two trips). He became ill; word got to the Philippians that he was ill; and finally word got back to Epaphroditus that they were worried (two more trips). As a result, Paul is about to send Epaphroditus back to Philippi (one more trip coming up).

F. Exhortations (3:1—4:9)

In the various exhortations that follow, Paul emphasizes several diverse aspects of living the life of faith. He shows special insight, perhaps the result of his experience of prison, being stripped of everything, where he could reflect on some thirty years of his life in Christ.

1. Christian Gnôsis *(3:4–11)*

After a brief sketch of his life as an exemplary Jew (3:4–6), Paul refers again to his knowledge of Christ and its surpassing superiority over his former accomplishments under the law:

> Those things I used to consider gain I have now reappraised as loss in the light of Christ. I have come to rate all as loss in the light of the surpassing knowledge [*gnôsis*] of my Lord Jesus Christ. (3:7–8a)

This text is the unique place in Paul where he refers to "my Lord Jesus Christ." We detect here a special intimacy never expressed before.

A few lines later Paul explains what he means by this "knowledge."

> I wish to know Christ and the power of his resurrection, to know a share in his sufferings by being formed into the pattern of his death. Thus do I hope that I may arrive at the resurrection from the dead. (3:10–11)

We see here also a sense of "knowledge" that expresses a full experience of some reality. The Hebrew word for knowledge, *daʿat,* directed to a person, described a full, personal experience of another. Thus Paul can speak here of "knowing" a share in Christ's suffering.

Sandwiched between the two references to this "knowledge of Christ" is Paul's familiar theme of "justice" from faith.

> For his sake I have forfeited everything; I have accounted all else as dung so that Christ may be my wealth and I may be in him, not having any justice of my own based on observance of the law, but rather the justice which comes through the faith of Christ, the justice which comes from God and is based on faith. (3:8b–9)

The two themes belong together in Paul's mind. They may be simply two sides of the same coin. This knowledge of Christ is the normal experience of being "in Christ," the place where God brings about his justice for us. If there is any distinction between the two concepts, "knowledge of Christ" here appears to be the full maturation of this "justice through faith."

2. The Effort of Faith (3:12–16)

As if anticipating a criticism of spiritual laziness, Paul describes the "athleticism" of his faith. He writes about his activity "pursuing," "taking hold," "straining forward," and "pursuing the goal"(3:12–14)—language typical of a competitive runner. He insists that he has not yet achieved or completed the course (3:12), adding a barb intended for those who think they have (3:15).

3. Eschatology (3:20–21)

Paul then adds a note of **eschatological** hope: "Our citizenship is in heaven, and from there we await our savior, the Lord Jesus Christ" (3:20). If we leave aside the letters we consider Deutero-Pauline, this is the only time Paul calls Jesus "savior" (*sôtēr*). As he did earlier (3:11), he speaks of his hope in the resurrection of the dead. Again, in an untypical way, Paul attributes the transformation of the resurrection to Christ. It could be that Paul is incorporating a current formula developed by someone else, one similar to Titus 2:13. The descriptions here are important for Paul's **eschatology** and **Christology trajectories**.

4. Various Instructions (4:1–9)

Paul adds six detached short exhortations: (a) for all to stand firm (4:1), (b) for four individuals in the community, Euodia, Syntyche, Syzyge,[1] and Clement, to help one another (4:2–3), (c) for all to rejoice (4:4), (d) to manifest kindness because the Lord is near (4:5), (e) to avoid worry (4:6–7), and (f) to think good thoughts and keep up the good work (4:8–9). Paul maintains his focus on **God**, with the references to "the peace of God" and "the God of peace" (4:7; 4:9) along with an insistence on confidently making petitions known to God (4:6).

G. Paul's Gratitude and Closing (4:10–23)

As Paul expresses his gratitude for the Philippians' concern and material help, he adds another list of deprivations and abundances that characterized his life (see 2 Cor 6:9–10). The final greetings lead to Paul's typical letter ending: "The grace of the Lord Jesus Christ be with your spirit" (4:23; 1 Thess 5:28; 1 Cor 16:23; Gal 6:18; Rom 16:20).

III. The Thematic Summary of the Letter

A. God

Without the intense concentration on God that he had in writing Romans, Paul sprinkles this letter also with references to God, opening and closing the letter with a reference to "God, the Father" (1:2; 4:20). As he did in his previous letters, Paul insists on giving praise and glory to this God (1:11; 2:11; 4:20).

What stands out in this letter is the insistence on the initiative and effective agency of God in matters of salvation. "I am confident of this; the one who began a good work in you will continue to complete it until the day of Christ Jesus" (1:6). Paul sees this effective agency as occurring within the human being accomplishing both the desire and the work, "for God is working in you [*ho energôn en hymin*] to bring about both the will and the work of his good intentions" (2:13). Paul gives this as the motive for our intense efforts for our own salvation (2:12).

If we are correct in the chronology of this letter, Paul here appears to be building on the thoughts he developed in Romans about predestination. "Those he foreknew, he predestined…called…justified…glorified" (Rom 8:29–30). In Philippians, he is applying this divine work precisely to the human decision. He does not explain how God's work does not diminish human responsibility, which Paul in both letters stresses, except to indicate here that God is acting "in you." Paul rarely describes God the Father as living in or working in human beings. An earlier parallel to Paul's wording is his description of God in the production of the spiritual gifts: "The same God who works all things in all people (*ho energôn ta panta en pasin*") (1 Cor 12:6; see also 15:28).

Another salient aspect of God in this letter is the portrayal of God as "the God of peace" (4:9). God listens to our petitions and needs. Therefore, we should live without anxiety (4:6). By placing our petitions in the hands of God, we should experience "the peace of God which surpasses all understanding" (4:7). These thoughts give special meaning to the formula he has been using to open his letters, "Grace and peace from God our Father" (1:2).

In this letter, the outstanding qualities of God are mercy and kindness. God has mercy on Epaphroditus and Paul (2:27). God listens to prayers (4:6). As a result, Paul has an intense sense of offering thanksgiving to "my God" (1:3).

B. Christ Jesus

Although written as a personal letter, exchanging news, geared toward practical matters, Philippians is distinctive and intense in its Christology. Never before had Paul spoken of "the affection of Christ Jesus" (1:8). Paul cites it here as the dimension in which he felt his own longing for the Philippians. Never before had Paul called Jesus "savior" (3:20). For Paul, Jesus is savior as coming from heaven to transform our bodies by his power. Never before had Paul spoken of "the knowledge of Christ Jesus, my Lord" as "the important thing" in his life (3:8). Paul longs to be with Christ more than life (1:23).

The hymn about Christ inserted into this letter, however, is the place where Paul's Christology is most developed. Composing this hymn or just simply using it, Paul here describes Jesus moving sequentially through three phases—preexistence, life on earth, and exaltation after death.

1. Preexistence (2:6)

Verse 6 describes Christ before the particular action of becoming a human being. While other texts of Paul suggested this preexistence (2 Cor 5:21; 8:9; Gal 4:4; Rom 8:3), this verse and the next clearly describe Jesus having a personal attitude and actively moving on to the next phase, explicitly described as "becoming human." Paul names the preexistent one "Christ Jesus," thus stressing the identity of this preexistent one with the person of the crucified and risen Christ.

Paul describes Jesus at this stage with a positive and then a negative description. He was in the form of God, and he did not consider equality with God to be "loot." In the positive description, the word *form* (*morphê*) in Paul's language is very close to the word *image* (*eikôn*), with perhaps a bit more stress on the interior (see 2 Cor 3:18; Rom 12:2). Paul's description of Christ may be another way of describing him as an image of God. In the negative description we find another ambiguity. To think of something as "loot" (*harpagmos*) could mean to think of this as something already held after some violent seizure or something not held and about to be seized. The expression here is ambiguous; it could have either meaning.[2]

The Jewish picture of divine wisdom provides parallels to this description of the preexistent Christ. Wisdom is described as "an image" of God having multiple divine attributes (Wis 7:24–27). She is consistently described as a person acting and existing from the foundation of the world (Prov 8:1–32; Job 28:12–27). *First Enoch* also describes a journey by Wisdom to earth and a return to heaven (42:1–2).

2. Earthly Life (2:7–8)

Verses 7–8 describe Jesus as an earthly human being. The tone is grim. The descriptions insist on the lowliness, even the degradation, involved in becoming human. The life of Jesus is all subsumed under the image of his cross and death. Two qualities of Jesus are mentioned, humility and obedience, the two qualities characteristic of a good slave.

Earlier Paul described the earthly Jesus as "in the likeness of sinful flesh" (Rom 8:3), "a curse" (Gal 3:13), "under the law" (Gal 4:4), and even "sin" (2 Cor 5:21). Here in Philippians the earthly stage of Jesus is important for Paul only as leading up to Jesus' death. Christmas for Paul was simply the dawn of Good Friday. For Paul, there is nothing glorious or joyful about Jesus becoming human.

3. Postresurrection Glory (2:9–11)

The last part of the hymn describes the recompense given to Christ for his humiliation ("because of this"). This exaltation includes a divine name bestowed on Christ and a universal veneration given to him. "The name above every other name" suggests God's proper name, "Yahweh," often referred to in late Judaism as simply "the Name" (*ha-Shem*). "Yahweh" was a name so sacred that Jews avoided pronouncing it, substituting expressions like *ha-Shem* or *ʾAdonay*, Hebrew for "my Lord(s)." The climactic proclamation of this hymn, "Jesus Christ is Lord" (2:11), could well be another reference to the divine name and its regular substitution.

As possible background for Paul, the great angel Iaoel of Jewish literature, like the "angel of Yahweh" of Exodus 23:20–21, is a superhuman person in whom God's name dwells.[3] The great angel in the story of *Joseph and Aseneth*, on the other hand, has an "ineffable name" (15:12). Whereas these angels appear to have always had these names, Paul describes Jesus as receiving this name at a particular time (aorist tense), namely after his death.

According to the general movement of the hymn, Jesus now is higher than he was at first "in the form of God." The recompenses of stage three appear as something that God gives, not simply restores. The whole exaltation of Jesus, furthermore, is geared "to the glory of God the Father" (2:11). Paul seems to be maintaining the theocentric position he has expressed all through his letters. God the Father remains in the central position and on top. Jesus reigns under the Father (see 1 Cor 15:28).

Nevertheless, the glory of Jesus after the resurrection is clearly a divine glory. It is one that draws universal homage, "in heaven, on earth, and under the earth." It is homage proper to God. Citing Isaiah 45:23, Paul had earlier spoken of this "every knee bending" and "every tongue confessing" as the universal homage God receives (Rom 14:11). The Jewish figure of divine Wisdom, portrayed as a person with divine qualities, combined perhaps with the figure of the great angel, may well be on Paul's mind as he describes Jesus this way (see 1 Cor 1:24; 2 Cor 4:4).

A functional subordination of Christ to the Father also appears in the combined imagery of the hymn. To describe Christ as in the form or image of God is to suggest also another person in scripture known as made in the image of God, namely, Adam (Gen 1:26–27). The snake's temptation to Adam and Eve was "to become like God" (Gen 3:5) by a kind of robbery. Their sin was therefore one of pride as well as a disobedience of a specific prohibition of God (Gen 2:16–17). When Paul describes Jesus "in the form of God," not thinking about robbing equality with God, and becoming both humble and obedient, Paul could be thinking of Jesus also as a "new Adam," undoing the damage of the first Adam (see also 1 Cor 15:45–49; Rom 5:12–19).

4. *Eschatological Agent*

Toward the end of the letter, Paul exhorts his readers to await the Lord Jesus Christ who will transform our bodies to conform to his glorious body (Phil 3:20–21). For the first time, Paul presents the exalted Christ as the agent of our resurrection. This is a shift from Romans where Paul describes the Father as "giving life to your mortal bodies through his Spirit" (Rom 8:11). In Philippians, Paul insists on the power of the risen Jesus to transform the dead as the same power by which Jesus subjects all creation to himself (Phil 3:21). This description of Jesus subjecting all to himself is a clear allusion to Paul's description of "the end" (*to telos*) in 1 Corinthians 15:24–28 when the warrior Christ exercises absolute power over his enemies.

C. The Spirit of God

Paul does not seem to be thinking much about the Spirit in this letter, briefly mentioning the divine Spirit only three times. Paul speaks of "the support of the Spirit of Jesus Christ" (1:19), which along with the prayers of the Philippians becomes Paul's hope of deliverance.

He appeals to the "encouragement in Christ," the "consolation of love," along with the "fellowship [*koinônia*] of the Spirit" (2:1) plus "compassion and mercy" as motives for the Philippians to unite in mind and heart. The first three elements of this appeal echo the concluding prayer of 2 Corinthians: "The grace of our Lord Jesus Christ, the love of God, and the fellowship of the Holy Spirit be with you" (2 Cor 13:13).

In a polemic against circumcisers, Paul evokes the "Spirit/flesh" antithesis he had developed in Galatians and Romans to describe believers as "worshiping in the Spirit of God and...not trusting in the flesh" and thus becoming the community of "circumcision" (3:3). The thought here depends on the discussion of the Spirit in Galatians 5 as giving freedom from the law and circumcision. The connection with "worshiping in the Spirit" may possibly reflect Paul's exhortation and development of "mental (*logikê*) worship" in Romans 12:1–2.

D. Salvation

Salvation and justification appear in this letter in two contexts, (a) in Paul's attempts to come to grips with his own situation and (b) in Paul's reflections on the opponents.

1. *Justice from Faith*

As Paul reflects on his life now in prison, he speaks of the one thing that matters, "to know Christ Jesus my Lord" (3:8), "to gain Christ and be found in him" (3:8–9), "to know him and the power of his resurrection" (3:11). This personal relationship with Christ, twice described as "knowledge" is then described as "not having any justice which comes from the law but that which comes from the faith of Christ, the justice from God, depending on faith" (3:9). Paul also prays that the Philippians be filled with the same "fruit of justice" that he describes as "that which comes through Jesus Christ" (1:11) and is connected also with love growing into "knowledge and every kind of perception" (1:9).

Paul here is building on the thoughts of "justification through faith," which he developed in Galatians 2—3 and Romans 3—8, where he stressed the connection between such faith and the risen life of Christ in the believer. In Philippians, he adds the element of "knowing Christ." By connecting closely "the faith of Christ" with "the knowledge of Christ," Paul adds what looks like an experiential element to faith. At the same time he shows that the nature of faith, like knowledge, is less a matter of deciding the outcome as rather letting the object, Christ, influence us. Faith, like knowledge, is determined by the object. Faith, again like knowledge, is opening one's eyes and hearts to the reality of God's saving power. Thus faith and this knowledge are inseparable from love.

2. The Scope of Salvation

In his reflections on "the opponents" of the Philippians and the "enemies of the cross of Christ," Paul returns to identifying his community by a boundary that divides people into those marked or designated for "destruction" (*apôleia*) and those for "salvation" (*sôteria*) (1:27–28), as he had done in the Corinthian correspondence (1 Cor 1:18–25; 2 Cor 2:15–16; 4:3–4). The evidence or proof of salvation is "struggling together for the faith of the gospel" (Phil 1:27–28). On the other hand, intimidation by "the opponents" or "the enemies" is the evidence of their "destruction" (1:27–28). Their end is "destruction" (3:18–19). All this sounds like a serious limit to the scope of salvation for human beings, a return to the Jewish pessimism that only a few will be saved.[4]

If, however, Paul is writing this letter after Romans, then his general reflections about "vessels of wrath made for destruction" (*apôleia*), reflections connected with his thoughts about the nonbelieving Israel (Rom 9:21–24), help us understand his intentions in Philippians. In Romans, Paul is using Jeremiah's image of the potter who smashes his clay until it pleases him (Jer 18:1–12). As we saw, this image leaves Paul the opening for his conviction, "Thus all Israel will be saved" (Rom 11:25), even though they appear to be in Paul's mind "made for destruction." It would appear in Romans that Paul had in mind some form of intermediate or temporary "destruction," one that shows the wrath of God against sin, but one that leaves open the possibility of the salvation of the sinner, who is loved by God while he or she is still a sinner (Rom 5:8).

3. The Role of Christ

In his typical manner, Paul maintains the agency of God the Father in salvation as he describes, "Your salvation...and this is God's doing" (1:28; see 3:9). What is unlike Paul, however, is the absence of any description of the past activity of Christ as instrumental in justification or salvation. Yet in this letter, for the first time, Jesus is called "savior" (*sôter*), who in the future will come and transform our bodies (Phil 3:20).

The absence of the instrumental activity of Jesus is all the more striking because of the lengthy meditation on the death of Jesus on the cross and subsequent exaltation by God (2:6–11). The result of this death and exaltation is not the benefit of others but Jesus' own exaltation. In this christological hymn, it is Christ who is "saved" and recompensed. Likewise, the sufferings and death of Jesus are mentioned another time (3:10–11), not as the means of salvation but as simply something Paul needs to know and be conformed to, and through that knowledge and conformity Paul hopes to share in the resurrection.

Perhaps, in the light of Paul's earlier description of Christ as "firstfruits" of the resurrection (1 Cor 15:23) and his theology of humanity's inclusion into Christ, these descriptions can be understood here as part of Paul's soteriological trajectory.

E. Union with Christ

1. Life Is Christ

This letter contains significant descriptions of a life in union with Christ mostly in Paul's reflections on himself and his spiritual life. We see this first in Paul's reflections on his imprisonment. He is confident of deliverance. He eagerly hopes and expects that he will not be put to shame, but rather that "now and always Christ will be magnified in my body" (1:20). Paul could be referring simply to the honor that will be given to Christ through the events in Paul's life. However, as he reflects on the uncertainty of his future, Paul goes on to say, "For to me life is Christ" (1:22). He connects this life with necessary work for the Philippians (1:22–24), but the identification of his life with the person of Christ echoes the words he wrote to the Galatians, "Christ lives in me.... I live by the faith of the Son of God" (Gal 2:20).

As we will see, this union of life with Christ is reflected also in the eschatology of this letter. Paul longs "to depart from this life and be with Christ" (*syn Christô; 1:23*). Paul presents this as the ultimate goal of his life. In 1 Thessalonians, he had described the goal as being "with the Lord for ever" (1 Thess 4:17). In the earlier text, Paul saw this union as occurring after the resurrection from the dead. In Philippians, Paul speaks of this union as happening at death.

2. *The Knowledge of Christ*

The distinctive aspect of this union of life with Christ as described in Philippians is Paul's connection with "knowledge." He speaks of "the supreme good of knowing Christ Jesus my Lord" (3:8) and then goes on to explain this as "to know him and the power of his resurrection and the sharing of his sufferings being conformed to his death, if somehow I may attain the resurrection from the dead" (3:10–11). Paul is not referring to an arms-length view of Jesus, but to a personal experience and a union with the dying and rising Christ.

This description of union specifically in the death and resurrection of Christ is a variation of a familiar theme of Paul generally associated with faith. He first expressed it in 2 Corinthians. "Just as the sufferings of Christ have abounded in us, thus through Christ has also abounded our encouragement" (2 Cor 1:5). "We are always carrying about the dying of Jesus in the body, so that the life of Jesus may be manifested in our body. For we who live are constantly being given up to death because of Jesus so that the life of Jesus may be manifested in our mortal flesh…since then we have the same Spirit of faith" (4:10–13; see also 12:9). In Galatians, Paul wrote, "I have been co-crucified with Christ.… I live by faith" (Gal 2:19). In Romans, he wrote, "If we have grown into union with him through a death like his, we shall also be united with him in the resurrection.… If, then, we have died with Christ, we believe that we shall also live with him" (Rom 6:5–8).

The religious knowledge that Paul speaks of appears to be a developed form of faith by which one is united to Christ, dying and rising. He had prayed that the love of the Philippians develop into this knowledge so that they be "filled with the fruit of justice that comes through Jesus Christ" (1:9–10).

3. *Suffering for Christ*

Paul also speaks of the suffering of the Philippians as a suffering "for the sake of Christ." This suffering for Christ is a development out of faith. The Philippians have been granted "for the sake of Christ [*hyper Christou*] not only to believe in him but also to suffer for him [*hyper autou*]" (1:29). Paul sees this as the same as his own "struggle [*agôn*]" (1:30). In 2 Corinthians, Paul had seen his own hardships and persecutions as sufferings "for the sake of Christ [*hyper Christou*]" (2 Cor 12:10).

Perhaps the best way of understanding this theology of suffering is to read it in the context of Paul's sense of "sharing in" the suffering, death, and resurrection of Christ (Phil 3:10). Paul and the community's suffering thus becomes a part of Christ's sufferings, given meaning by the purpose of Christ's sufferings. In that sense it can be "for Christ."

F. Eschatology

Philippians combines two somewhat conflicting aspects of Pauline eschatology, first, a sense of life immediately after death and, second, an expectation of "the day of Christ."

1. Life Immediately after Death

The most distinctive eschatological idea in Philippians is the clear implication that eschatological salvation can begin at death. He expresses this faith in his reflections about his own execution as a real possibility, where "death is gain" (1:21). Referring to life and death, he writes, "I do not know which to choose. I am caught between the two. I long to depart this life and be with Christ, for that is far better" (1:22–23). Here we see hope in a life immediately after death, not simply one that must wait until the resurrection of the dead. Paul longs for this development, as it were, the sooner the better! He clearly contrasts this gain with remaining on earth to serve his friends. One excludes the other.

The term Paul uses to describe this condition after death, "with Christ" (*syn Christô*), expresses personal closeness. The Greek preposition *syn* is far more intense, entails a far deeper closeness, than the alternative *meta*. Paul implies a personal existence in relationship with his Lord, an existence "far better" than his present one on earth.

Paul appears to be adopting an anthropology rooted in Platonic thought, an anthropology that saw the human person as composed of two parts: a perishable body and an immortal mind or spirit. About a century before Paul, this anthropology had made its way into the faith of some Jews and continued to develop as a vehicle of hope in some circles contemporary with Paul.[5] This is the view that forms the backdrop of Paul's desire to die and be with Christ. Only in this view could he maintain the superior existence of the person after death in the face of the apparent corruption of the body.

In Paul's own trajectory of faith, we saw somewhat similar thoughts in 2 Corinthians 5:1–10. Paul here, however, does not mention any new body or "tent" or "clothing" provided by God at death—although perhaps he is still imagining life after death that way. However, he is clear that the "I" who faces death is the same "I" who will be with Christ after death.

2. *Expectation of a Future Day of Christ*

Three times in this letter Paul refers to "the day of [Jesus] Christ" (1:6, 11; 2:16). Paul ends the letter with the reminder, "The Lord is near" (4:5). Despite his move toward a more Greek anthropology of an immortal soul that enjoys salvation immediately after death, Paul vigorously maintains his Jewish apocalyptic sense of future material salvation in the "world to come."

Following the scenario he consistently maintains, Paul writes about this future climax of salvation as the coming of Christ and a transformation of the body (3:20–21). Paul mentioned the possibility of his own "resurrection of the dead" earlier (3:11). The portrayal of believers awaiting Jesus from heaven evokes the scene in 1 Thessalonians 4:16–18. The transformation of earthly bodies as well as the subjection of all things to Christ recalls Paul's instructions about the resurrection in 1 Corinthians 15:27–28, 42–44.

Paul also expresses this hope as involving a present reality that now distinguishes the believer: "Our citizenship [*politeuma*] is in heaven" (3:20). The Greek term, *politeuma,* did not exactly mean "citizenship" in the Roman sense of the word, but it often indicated an officially recognized status of a colony of people from another land, just as Philippi was a colony of Rome. In 1 Thessalonians, Paul attempted to establish this same idea of a realized eschatology by describing the believers as "children of the light and children of the day" (1 Thess 5:5), an imagery that suggests a kind of anticipation of the day of the Lord. In Philippians, the realized eschatology is built on a kind of parallel universe view, where believers are already official members of the "heaven" that now exists and whence the Lord Jesus Christ will come.

IV. The Message of the Letter

Paul in Philippians presents a simple view of Christian living. It focuses on "knowing Christ Jesus my Lord." Nothing else really matters. It is a bit surprising to see this contemplative spirit in Paul, the man of action, the planner and founder of communities, the world traveler preparing his next trip before he has finished the one he is on. Perhaps it is prison that has led Paul to this view. Perhaps it is a perspective derived from a life of frustrating activity. In any case, this theme of knowledge will characterize the last letters of Paul.

Here Paul is in prison. He faces possible death. The tranquility expressed in this letter, however, is striking. Paul has been emptied of all things, like the Christ who emptied himself (2:7). Like the humble Christ on earth, Paul places all his hopes for glory in God. Stripped of everything on earth, Paul looks to a heavenly realm for his fulfillment. The Christians' center of gravity is outside this world: "We have our citizenship in heaven" (3:20).

No other letter stresses humility as does Philippians (see 2:3–4). No other letter stresses with such striking language the need to place one's efforts entirely in the Father's hands. "He who has begun the good work in you will carry it through to completion" (1:6).

Repeatedly, Paul stresses the role of suffering in life. Suffering has meaning in God's eyes, not just in terms of Christ suffering for us, but also in terms of us "suffering for him" (1:29). Such is the special privilege of the Philippians. Paul sees his life "poured out," like the libations of the Temple, "in sacrificial worship" for the faith of the Philippians (2:17). All this suffering like the suffering of Christ, however, is geared toward the resurrection. "Thus do I hope to arrive at the resurrection of the dead" (3:11).

11

Colossians and Philemon

The city of Colossae lay about one hundred miles due east of Ephesus in the Lycus River valley. In this part of the valley, Colossae was part of a cluster of cities, along with Laodicea, a much larger city, and Hierapolis, a type of resort town known for its hot springs and religious shrines. This area of Phrygia was a veritable hotbed of cults.

I. Background for the Letters

Now an old man,[1] Paul is in prison (Col 4:3; Phlm 9–10), probably not too far from Colossae. The letters are both occasioned by other individuals coming to Paul. Epaphras, who apparently founded the community at Colossae (Col 1:7), has come to Paul asking him to address specific problems in the church. Onesimus, a slave who has run away from his master, Philemon, has also made contact with Paul, probably asking for help to get away. Philemon is a member of the church probably at Colossae. With Epaphras, he is well known by Paul.

Although Paul had traveled the road running by Colossae on his way to Ephesus, he did not stop to found a church there (Col 2:1). Epaphras was very probably an associate of Paul in Ephesus operating under Paul's direction when he laid the seeds of Christianity in Colossae (see Col 1:5–7).

A. The Difficulties at Colossae

As we read Paul's warnings against "any empty, seductive philosophy" (2:8), we detect a mishmash of unchristian positions. He speaks of submission to "the elements of the world" (2:8), of the "the worship of angels" (2:18), as well as pride-filled forms of bodily asceticism (2:23). These positions all suggest a type of Gnosticism.

Paul also warns against those who insist on rules that prohibit eating certain things or touching certain things (2:21) and on the observance of religious feast days and Sabbaths (2:16). These positions clearly suggest Judaizers in Colossae.

The descriptions of these positions resemble those in Paul's warnings to the Galatians, where he also mentioned "the elements" as enslaving powers along with the observance of "days and months, seasons and years" (Gal 4:9). We identified the prevalent difficulty in Galatia, not far from Colossae, as that of a Gentile form of Judaizing. We are probably seeing much the same in Colossae.

B. The Authenticity of Colossians

For several reasons, a good number of modern scholars have come to see this letter as "Deutero-Pauline," that is, written by another person in the name of Paul. This is the issue of "authenticity," a literary question, asking about the "authorship" of a document. It is not a questioning of the value of the document, and, in the case of biblical texts, it is not a questioning of the inspiration of the document. We will return to a fuller study of this question in our treatment of Ephesians.

1. Arguments against Authenticity

Strong arguments can be adduced against authenticity. For one thing, the style is very unlike the earlier letters of Paul. In this letter we see long strings of genitives, "the richness of the fullness of the knowledge...of the mystery of God" (2:2). We see long strings of synonyms, "holy and blameless and irreproachable" (1:22). At times, sentences go on ten or more verses (see 1:9–20). This way of writing reflects a hieratic or liturgical style, the style of hymns and prayers.

The vocabulary is likewise very different from Paul's usual vocabulary. We find here thirty-three words unique (or *hapax*) in the New Testament. Another fifteen words are not found again in any of the Pauline epistles; eighty-six are not found again in the "sure" Pauline epistles. On the other hand, we miss such typically Pauline words as *to believe, just, justice, salvation,* or *law*.

Several theological shifts also distinguish this letter, which we will look at in more detail below. Here we note simply (a) the image of Christ as "the head" of the body, (b) the person of Christ as the content of "the mystery" that Paul preaches, (c) the emphasis on the cosmic role of Christ, as well as (d) the insistence on "realized" eschatology. These characteristics all suggest a hand other than Paul's in the writing of this letter.

2. *The Arguments for Authenticity*

Since the letter presents itself as from Paul (1:1), the prima facie case rests with authenticity. In addition, we can note a number of typically Pauline expressions such as "in Christ," "his holy ones," "every good work," and others. The "new theology" of Colossians, moreover, has roots in earlier Pauline ideas. These shifts appear more as enlargements of Paul's thought rather than as radically new positions.

Perhaps the strongest argument for authenticity, however, lies in the connection between this letter and Philemon, a letter indisputably authentic. Both letters appear to be written from the same captivity and relatively at the same time. This connection can be seen especially by a comparison of the persons either supposedly with Paul at the writing or among the intended readers of these letters. We can make the following comparison:

	Philemon	*Colossians*
Companions:	Timothy, "our brother" (1)	Timothy, "our brother" (1:1)
	Epaphras, "fellow prisoner" (23)	Epaphras, "fellow slave," "faithful servant" (1:7)
	Mark (24)	Mark (4:10)
	Aristarchus, "fellow worker" (24)	Aristarchus, "prisoner with me" (4:10)
	Demas (24)	Demas (4:14)
	Luke (24)	Luke (4:14)

	Onesimus (11), sent to Philemon	Onesimus (4:9), sent to Colossae Tychicus (4:7) Jesus Justus (4:7)
Recipients:	Philemon (1), Apphia (2) Archippus, "fellow soldier" (2)	Nympha (4:15), in Laodicea? Archippus (4:17), recipient of a ministry

The identical names in both groups strongly suggests one of two things: Either the two letters are written by Paul very close to each other or another writer copied the names from Philemon to construct a more realistic picture of Paul as the writer. The second alternative, however, cannot easily account for the differences of the two lists. An exact correspondence of both the names and the descriptions associated with these names would look very much like copying. The differences suggest that the writer did not have a copy of Philemon. The names therefore argue that Colossians and Philemon were written during the same imprisonment, with just enough of a time difference to permit the change of Epaphras's and Aristarchus's circumstances.

3. *The Work of a Secretary*

Colossians ends with Paul adding a greeting in his own hand. Such an ending comment is common in Paul (l Cor 16:21; Gal 6:11; Phlm 19) and presupposes the work of a secretary writing the rest of the letter. We do not know exactly how the secretary functioned. His or her work could have been anything from taking dictation to composing under the direction of Paul.

In Colossians, the free work of a secretary—perhaps Epaphras—would explain the unusual vocabulary and style of this letter. Responding to Epaphras's request for help, Paul in prison may have coached Epaphras or another secretary to compose the letter expressing the major ideas of Paul. The final form would have been approved by Paul and then sent to Colossae. Pauline authorship of this letter would then have to be taken in a larger sense—written under his authority but composed by another.

The actual writer knew the thought of Paul well and was able to express Paul's basic ideas yet take them a step beyond Paul's own position. If we imagine Paul still alive and authorizing the contents of the letter, then we must see Paul recognizing the thought of this letter as basically his or as an organic development of his thought.

The jury is still out for the question of authenticity. It is difficult to envisage what now could advance the discussion. The argument against authenticity is by no means overwhelming, especially if we accept the scenario of another writer under Paul's direction. For the sake of simplicity, we will continue to refer to the author as "Paul," always keeping in mind, however, the complexity of this issue.

II. The Sequential Study of Colossians

A. The Outline of Colossians

After a lengthy introduction that includes an early Christian hymn, this letter breaks easily into two parts. The first is instructional (chapters 1–2); the second is exhortatory (chapters 3–4):

I. Opening (1:1–20)
   A. Address (1:1–2)
   B. Thanksgiving and prayer (1:3–14)
   C. Christological hymn (1:15–20)
II. Instructions (1:21—2:23)
   A. Review of the Colossians' faith and Paul's work (1:21—2:3)
   B. Warning against errors; description of life in Christ (2:4–23)
III. Exhortation (3:1—4:6)
   A. Basis of moral life: life with the risen Christ (3:1–4)
   B. Vices and virtues (3:5–17)
   C. Duties of the Christian home (3:18—4:1)
   D. Various advice (4:4–6)
IV. Conclusion: plans, final greetings, blessing (4:7–18)

B. The Address and Thanksgiving Prayer (1:1–14)

Paul returns to the practice of identifying himself as "an apostle." He associates Timothy with him in this letter writing (1:1). As in Philippians, he identifies his readers not as "church" but as "the holy ones," to whom he wishes "grace and peace from God our Father" (1:2), without the mention of "the Lord Jesus Christ," which appears in every other opening greeting written by Paul.

Paul thanks God for the Colossians' faith, love, and hope (1:3–5), the triad of "theological virtues" Paul mentioned in the opening prayer of 1 Thessalonians (1 Thess 1:3). His prayer, like his prayer in Philippians, is for his readers to grow in "the knowledge of God." In this letter, however, this knowledge is more concerned with the will of God and thus echoes the Jewish theme linking knowledge of God with observance of God's law (see especially Jer 31:34; also Jer 22:16; Isa 1:2–4; Deut 4:32–39).

The prayer ends with a thanksgiving for two forms of **salvation**, one yet to come, the inheritance of the holy ones for which we are now made fit (1:12), and one already achieved, God delivering us from the power of darkness into the kingdom of his Son (1:13).

C. The Christological Hymn (1:15–20)

Like the christological hymn in Philippians (Phil 2:6–11), the hymn that Paul inserts here is dense with thoughts important for his **Christ trajectory**, at the same time reflecting Paul's **God trajectory**. Also like the hymn in Philippians, this hymn stands out from the surrounding letter by its rhythmic verse form, by the intensity of its content, and by its loose connection with its immediate context. It thus appears to have been composed prior to the letter and inserted, perhaps by Paul, perhaps by someone else in the tradition of Paul.

Written out in verse form, the hymn falls into three parts or strophes: The first and the last describe two major roles of Christ under God, that in creation and that in redemption; the middle strophe forms the hinge from one role to the other. The structure appears by the repeated words, here italicized:

A. *Who is* the image of the invisible God,
the firstborn of all creation
because in him were created
all things in the heavens and on the earth
the visible and the invisible
whether thrones or lordships, principalities, or powers
all things *through him* and for him were created,
B. *And he is* before all things and all things in him hold together
And he is the head of the body, the church,
A'. *Who is* the beginning
the firstborn of the dead
in order that he become in all things the first
because in him all the fullness[*to plêrôma*] was pleased to dwell
and *through him* to reconcile all things for himself
making peace through the blood of his cross
whether those on the earth or those in the heaven.

Like that in Philippians, this hymn seems to presuppose a personal existence of Christ before his human life. The first strophe (A) gives Christ a profound significance in God's act of creation (1:15–17). The third strophe (A') then continues with the role of Christ in **salvation** (1:18–20).

D. Instructions (1:21—2:23)

The instructional section that follows takes the **christological** focus of the hymn and develops it further, adding more descriptions of **salvation**. This saving grace is described as an act of reconciliation accomplished through Christ and his death (1:22).

As he said in 2 Corinthians and Philippians (2 Cor 12:10; Phil 1:29), Paul sees his own suffering as part of Christ's redemptive sufferings, suggesting an intense **union with Christ** (Col 1:24).

This **union**, described then as "Christ in you" (1:27), is the content of the great "mystery hidden from ages…now manifested to his holy ones," for which Paul is a minister (1:25–27). Paul had introduced the theme of "the mystery" in 1 Corinthians (1 Cor

2:6–10) and referred to it again in the concluding doxology of Romans (Rom 16:25–27). In Colossians, the mystery is given a distinctly **christological** focus. Later in this letter, he describes this mystery of God as "Christ, in whom are hidden all the treasures of wisdom and knowledge" (2:2–3).

After warning about errors dealing with "the elements of the world" (*ta stoicheia tou kosmou*)[2], Paul continues his instructions on **Christ** with the declaration, "In him dwells the whole fullness of the deity bodily" (2:9). The "fullness" (*plêrôma*) mentioned here seems to pick up the cryptic line of the christological hymn, "In him all the fullness was pleased to dwell" (1:19). Likewise picking up from the christological hymn, Paul describes Christ again as "the head" (*hê kephalê*). Here, however, Christ is head of "every principality and power" (2:10), later depicted as vanquished hostile enemies (2:15).

The instructions on Christ then flow into instructions on our **union with Christ**. We are "filled in him"; we are "circumcised in him" (2:10–11). Developing a theme from Romans, Paul describes baptism as being buried with Christ (2:12; Rom 6:3–5). Here, however, Paul shifts his **eschatology** to describe baptism as also a realized resurrection.

The instructional section ends with warning about errors dealing with a slew of cultic practices, including several apparently Jewish and Gnostic elements (2:16–23). In the midst of the warnings is the reminder, "You died with Christ to the elemental powers of the world" (2:20), referring again to cosmic powers opposed to Christ (2:8).

E. Exhortations (3:1—4:6)

Like Romans and Galatians, the second part of this letter is mostly an extended exhortation to specific behavior. The link between the exhortation and the previous instruction, however, is clear. "If then you were raised with Christ, seek what is above… think of what is above" (3:1–2). The link involves Paul's **eschatology**, at first presented as realized. "You have died and your life is hidden with Christ in God" (3:3). However, Paul then moves immediately to a future view: "When Christ your life appears, then you too will appear with him in glory" (3:4).

New behavior must follow "the new self," which is a renewal of the image of God in us. Morality is the continuation of "putting to death the earthly parts" described with a list of vices (3:5–10). All this is part of our **union with** Christ. As Paul said in Galatians, the great social distinctions are gone because "Christ is all and in all" (3:11; Gal 3:28; see also Rom 10:12).

The list of good attitudes and actions (Col 3:12–15) echoes the fruit of the Spirit and the law of Christ in Galatians (Gal 5:22; 6:1–2). The list of liturgical actions (Col 3:16–17) then flows into the "household code" (3:18—4:1), where Paul seems to acquiesce in the dominating role of the husband and father. He simply exhorts love, perhaps as the way of preventing this dominating role from becoming brutally oppressive, as it often was. Paul did not try to reform society, but he did try to infuse love into it.

Similar household instructions appear also in Ephesians 5:21—6:1; 1 Timothy 2:8–15; 6:1:1–10; Titus 2:1–10; and 1 Peter 2:17—3:9; 3:1–7. These later instructions follow different orders and address different groups. The diversity yet frequency of this type of instruction tells us that the authors of these letters were probably following a general literary form of instruction popular among the Christians at that time, the "household code," a form that permitted a great deal of freedom in its application.

F. Conclusion: Plans, Final Greetings, Blessing (4:7–18)

The concluding lines with the descriptions of Paul's co-workers and other prominent people in the local churches give us an insight into early church life (4:7–17). Paul signs off wishing "grace" to his readers, but omitting the reference to "the Lord Jesus [Christ]" found in every other letter Paul writes (4:18).

III. The Sequential Study of Philemon

A. The Outline of Philemon

The outline of Philemon is simple:

I. Opening greeting and prayer (1–6)
II. Request regarding Onesimus (7–22)
III. Conclusion (23–25)

B. Opening Greeting and Prayer (1–6)

In the opening lines of the Letter to Philemon, Paul associates Timothy with the writing. At the same time he addresses not only Philemon but the whole church that meets in Philemon's house. In this very personal letter, Paul is anything but private.

Writing to Philemon about the delicate question of receiving back his runaway slave, Paul describes himself as "a prisoner of Christ."[3] By pointing to his own condition parallel to that of the slave, Paul has a clever preparation for the message of the letter in which he will ask Philemon to accept back his runaway slave and will hint that Philemon should free him.

Paul singles out the "faith and love" of Philemon as the object of his thanksgiving. This love and faith is toward other people but it is exercised "in the Lord Jesus." Paul reminds Philemon of the love he has for all "the holy ones," including his runaway slave.

Paul adds the petition that Philemon's "partnership" (*koinônia*) in the faith develop into a knowledge (*epignôsis*) of all that is good in Christ (6). This theme of knowledge as a form of developed faith is another link of this letter to Philippians and Colossians. The reference to the "partnership" of Paul and Philemon may show how Paul wanted to work with rich people, on whom he depended for support. He did not want them as his "patrons." A "partnership" put both on an equal footing.

C. Request Regarding Onesimus (7–22)

In the body of the letter, Paul basically asks Philemon to free Onesimus, to treat him "no longer as a slave but...a beloved brother, especially to me, but all the more so to you, in the flesh and in the Lord" (16). Paul does not condemn slavery or even challenge Philemon about his slaves—as we would probably want Paul to do. Perhaps his sense of the nearness of the end prevented him from thinking about reforming the structures of society. However, he does insist on the role of love, as he had done for the oppressive form of marriage with which he was familiar (Col 4:19).

D. Conclusion (23–25)

Paul ends the letter with his usual conclusion, "The grace of the Lord Jesus Christ be with you" (Phlm 25).

IV. The Thematic Study of Colossians

There is very little material in Philemon to add to the trajectories we have been tracing. On the other hand, Colossians is rich in theology. Our thematic study will concentrate on that letter.

A. God

For the most part, we see in Colossians the usual Pauline ideas and images of God, especially those of Paul's early letters. Paul is an apostle by the will of God (1:1; 1 Cor 1:1), according to the plan (*oikonomia*) of God given to Paul (1:25; see 1 Cor 9:17). God is to be given thanksgiving always (1:3; 1 Cor 1:4). The work of Paul and his co-workers is geared toward "the kingdom of God" (4:11; 1 Thess 2:11–12). God raises Jesus from the dead and raises us by the same power (2:12; 1 Cor l6:14). God's anger is coming against sin (3:6; 1 Thess 1:10). God "opens doors" for Paul in his preaching (4:3; 1 Cor 16:9). God reveals the mystery of his salvation (1:27; 1 Cor 2:10). God is the agent in our movement into "the kingdom" (1:13; 1 Thess 2:12). Growth in

Christ comes from God (2:19; 1 Cor 3:6–7). By use of the theological passive voice, God appears as the agent of creation (1:16).

Paul seems to be referring to God as "the fullness" (*ta plêrôma*), a term that had a special cosmic meaning in Gnosticism.[4] Perhaps Paul is borrowing this term from the errors he is trying to refute. In the hymn, this "fullness" is described as a person, who "was pleased to dwell" in Christ, and is described as the subject of the verb infinitive "to reconcile all things," an action previously ascribed to God (2 Cor 5:19).

B. Christ Jesus

The Christology of Colossians is quite innovative in comparison with other letters of Paul. Christology dominates this letter. In fact, Paul approaches the problems at Colossae precisely by recalling the role of Christ in the lives of the Colossians and in the cosmos. We will look at the most distinctive aspects of the Christology of Colossians especially as they appear in the hymn of 1:15–20. It forms one of the most important statements about Christ in the Pauline letters.

1. The Cosmic Christ (1:15–16)

Once again, the first role strophe (A) of the opening hymn celebrates a cosmic role for Christ: Paul had briefly alluded to a role of Christ in creation (2 Cor 8:6; Rom 8:20–23), but never had he articulated so explicitly the way Jesus gives meaning to creation.

Describing Jesus as "the image" of God is an example of Paul applying wisdom categories to the person of Jesus (see also 2 Cor 4:4). Wisdom is "the spotless mirror of the power of God, the image of his goodness" (Wis 7:26). In the next strophe, Christ is also called "the beginning" (1:18), as is wisdom (Prov 8:22). Christ is the one "in whom all things hold together" (Col 1:17). Similarly, wisdom "reaches from end to end" (Wis 8:1) and "fills the world" (Wis 1:7).

In this Colossians text, Christ is placed in the order of creation as "firstborn" (*prôtotokos*), an indication of honor and preeminence in a family, with special birthrights and liens from God (Gen 43:33;

Exod 13:2; Ps 89:28). Paul described Jesus with this term in Romans to indicate his priority among human beings, with some connection to justification and glorification (Rom 8:29).

By use of the "theological passive," the hymn ascribes the act of creation to God, but an action that operates through and for Christ. "In him [*en autô*] were created all things...all things through him [*di' autou*] and for him [*eis auton*] were created" (1:16). The first two prepositions, "in" and "through," suggest something of an instrumental role, God operating in and through Christ to bring about creation. Such an instrumental role in creation recalls the role of personified wisdom in Jewish theology (Prov 8:27–31; Wis 7:22). The third preposition, "for," denotes a relationship toward a goal or purpose. People do something *for* some purpose. The purpose gives meaning to the activity. To say all things were created *for* Christ is to say that Christ is the very purpose of creation. This is to say that the meaning and value of all things derive from Christ.

In 1 Corinthians, Paul described all things as *through* Christ but all things *for* God. "There is one God, the Father, from whom all things come and for whom we live; and one Lord Jesus Christ, through whom everything was made and through whom we live" (1 Cor 8:6). In this earlier text, Paul as a good Jew sees all of creation stemming from God as creator and aiming at God as judge. Paul sees God and his glory as giving meaning to all things. In Colossians, Paul has placed Christ in this spot proper to God.

This hymn brings out the cosmic role of Christ in an unprecedented way. Yet the descriptions of the "cosmic Christ" here can easily be seen as developments of Paul's earlier descriptions of the preexistence of Christ (2 Cor 8:9; Phil 2:6) as well as Paul's view of the cosmic nature of redemption (2 Cor 5:19; Rom 8:20–23). There is a theological shift here, but one connected with earlier positions.

2. Christ, the Mystery

Several times in Colossians, Paul speaks of "the mystery" (*to mysterion*), a term dear to the pagan cultists of the Hellenistic world. In Colossians, Paul speaks of this "mystery, hidden from ages and generations past but now revealed to his holy ones" (1:26). He identifies the content of the mystery as "Christ in you, your hope of glory" (1:27). It is "the mystery of God—namely Christ—in whom every treasure of wisdom and knowledge is hidden" (2:2–3).

Paul used the term, "the mystery," in two contexts before in his earlier epistles to refer basically to the gospel or its basic content, hidden in ages past and now revealed.[5] In 1 Corinthians Paul speaks of preaching the "mystery of God" (2:1) and the "wisdom in mystery" revealed by the Spirit to enable us to recognized the wisdom and power of God in the crucifixion (2:7; see also 4:1). Romans ends by praising God for "the mystery" hidden in past ages, now revealed, which consists in the gospel Paul preaches (Rom 16:25–27).[6]

In Colossians, the identification of "the mystery" with the person of Christ again illustrates the general focus of this letter on Christology. Paul is drawing the Colossians' attention to the very person of Christ. It is this person who guarantees the Colossians a freedom from fear of the cosmic powers now haunting them. It is this person who shows the ritual practices of the law to be merely a shadow of the real body of Christ (2:16). If the Colossians can focus on the person of Christ, now seated at the right hand of God (3:1), their syncretistic tendencies will disappear.

3. The Exalted Divine Christ

In the context of warning against "empty, seductive philosophy," Paul again draws attention to Christ: "For in him dwells all the fullness of the deity bodily" (2:9). The description picks up the line in the christological hymn, "For in him all the fullness was pleased to dwell" (1:19), adding the reference to "deity" (*thotês*), an abstract noun for "God" (*theos*), which in Paul's vocabulary is the proper name of the Father. The expression "all the fullness" (*pan to plêroma*) stresses the intensity of this indwelling, "the total completeness of the deity." Like the "name" that God gives Jesus (Phil 2:9), this indwelling of God or deity in Christ brings a divine character to Jesus. The expression comes very close to the

Johannine view of Jesus as divine Word who "became flesh," through whom all things are created (John 1:1–14).

The difference in Paul seems to be the association of this "divinization" with the resurrection rather than the birth of Jesus. In the christological hymn, the indwelling of "all the fullness" is associated with Jesus "the firstborn of the dead" and the preeminence that stems from this status. The indwelling of "all the fullness" in that text is part of God's reconciliation of all things, on earth or in the heavens. Paul maintains a sense of the "advancement" of the humanity of Jesus through the resurrection (see Rom 1:3–4), which is not really found in John. Paul also maintains a sense of the agency of God ("it pleased…to dwell") in this progress.

It is also in connection with the resurrection that Paul will refer to "Christ seated at the right hand of God" (3:1). Again this is an image of the risen Jesus sharing in the authority and power of God, a favorite of Luke,[7] but one that also Paul used earlier in Romans, "Christ Jesus…who also is at the right hand of God" (Rom 8:34).

C. The Spirit of God

"The Spirit" retreats into the background somewhat in Colossians, showing up by name only in the brief descriptions of two things qualified by "the Spirit." Paul thanks God for the readers' "love in the Spirit" (1:8). He also writes about being present to the Colossians "in the Spirit," as he had written to the Corinthians (2:5; 1 Cor 5:3).[8]

Paul may also be thinking of the Spirit when he uses the adjective "spiritual" (*pneumatikos*). He prays that the Colossians be filled with "wisdom and spiritual knowledge" (Col 1:9) and exhorts them to sing "spiritual hymns" (3:16). The "wisdom and spiritual knowledge" may be an echo of 1 Corinthians where Paul wrote of the "wisdom…revealed by the Spirit" that enables believers "to know" the gifts of God (1 Cor 2:10–12). However, in comparison with Paul's earlier letters, nothing appears in Colossians about the theological significance of the Spirit, especially as regards the resurrection, a major theme in Colossians.

D. Salvation

1. The Transfer into the Kingdom of His Beloved Son

At the conclusion of the letter prayer, Paul describes the saving act of God: "He rescued [*errysato*] us from the power of darkness and transferred [*metestêsen*] us into the kingdom of his beloved Son, in whom we have redemption, the forgiveness of sins" (Col 1:13). This apocalyptic language for evil is not foreign to Paul. He described salvation as being delivered "from this present evil age" (Gal 1:4). He had referred to "darkness" (*skotos*) as an image of evil in general (1 Thess 5:4–5; Rom 13:12). He spoke of sin as a demonic power (2 Cor 4:4), an enslaving force (Rom 7:7–24), an enemy to be destroyed (1 Cor 15:26).

In any case, the salvation of God in Colossians involves the movement from this realm of darkness into the "kingdom of the Son" as a past accomplishment of God. Up to now, Paul spoke of "the kingdom of God" as a future inheritance (1 Cor 6:9–10; 15:50; Gal 5:21). Paul had also spoken of God "calling us into his kingdom of glory" (1 Thess 2:12), where the future perspective is somewhat muted. In Colossians, however, Paul insists on a present reality. As the aorist tense of the verbs indicates, the "rescue" and "transfer" took place already at some specific point. Perhaps the unusual reference to "the kingdom of *his Son*" is an attempt to distinguish the present kingdom from the future. In 1 Corinthians, Paul had envisioned a triumphant Christ at "the end, when he will hand over the kingdom to his God and Father" (1 Cor 15:24).

Connected with this transfer is "redemption" (*apolytrosis*) and "the forgiveness of sins" (*aphesis tôn hamartiôn*). While "redemption" is a common Pauline term (1 Cor 1:30; Rom 3:24; 8:23), "the forgiveness of sins" is not. Paul earlier wrote of God "not counting" trespasses (2 Cor 5:19), of God's "overlooking" (*paresis*) of sins (Rom 3:8), of "sins being covered" (Rom 4:7, citing Ps 32:1), and God "taking away" sins (Rom 11:27, citing Isa 27:9). In Colossians, the secretary is apparently adopting a more Lucan view of redemption, where sins like debts are subject to "forgiveness" or "cancellation."[9]

2. The Reconciliation of All Things

Again in the opening christological hymn of Colossians, the third strophe describes Christ through whom God reconciles all things, "And through him to reconcile [*apokatallaxai*] all things for [*eis*] himself" (1:20).

The description of God reconciling all things for or unto himself links back to Paul's description in 2 Corinthians of God reconciling (*katallassôn*) the world to himself in Christ (2 Cor 5:19). In 2 Corinthians, Paul associated this reconciliation with "the new creation" by which all things have become new (5:17). This saving act is not just a matter of getting human beings to change their conduct and attitudes, but is a redoing of creation. In Colossians, this description of reconciliation comes after a strophe on Christ's role in creation.

The expression in the Colossians hymn, "Making peace through the blood of his cross" (1:20), echoes Paul's description of justification in Romans, where he declares, "We have peace with God through our Lord Jesus Christ.... [W]e are now justified by his blood" (Rom 5:1, 9). The description of Colossians stresses even more the universal scope of this saving act of God. God reconciles "all things...whether those on the earth or those in the heaven" (Col 1:20). In Romans, all of creation is presently groaning for a liberation from corruption (Rom 8:20–22). In Colossians, the involvement of all of creation in heaven and on earth in God's saving act is now present.

Paul speaks of the reconciliation of all things "in the heavens and on earth," without mentioning "under the earth," as he had regarding the universal veneration of the exalted Christ (Phil 2:10). The early description of salvation as "rescue from the power of darkness" (1:13) could presuppose this power as such remains for the present—under the earth. Paul's point is an assurance that we are no longer subject to that power.

The connection of this strophe with the first one in the christological hymn demonstrates Paul's concern to maintain the redemptive picture of Christ, even in his most lofty speculations about his being. Christ's role in creation is not to be separated from his role in redemption, and conversely, his role in the redemptive "new creation" stems from his place as the cornerstone of creation itself.

E. Union of Life with Christ

Throughout the letter, Paul maintains the vision of an intense union of the believer with Christ. At one point he describes the great mystery precisely as "Christ in you" (1:27). If the fullness of the deity dwells in Christ, "you share in this fullness" (2:9). His readers should "walk in" Christ, "rooted in him and built upon him" (2:6–7). As he said before (Gal 3:28; Rom 10:12), the great social distinctions between "Greek and Jew," "slave and free" are now removed. In Colossians, however, the removal is based on the fact that "Christ is all in all" (Col 3:11).

1. Christ, the Head of His Body

Perhaps the most vivid portrayal of union of life between the believer and Christ in Colossians is the description of Christ as "head of his body, the church" (Col 1:18; see 2:19). The image of the church as "the body of Christ" is typically Pauline. He stressed it in both Romans 12:4–8 and 1 Corinthians 12:12–27. In the earlier epistles, however, Christ was pictured as the whole. Christians with their diverse gifts made up the organic unity of the body of Christ.

In Colossians, the image shifts to place Christ as the head, a member along with the other members. The stress here is less on the union of the members with each other than on their union with Christ from whom life and growth flow. Christ is "the head, from whom the whole body, supported and held together by its ligaments and bonds, achieves the growth that comes from God" (2:19). Paul makes no efforts here to relate the body image to the diversity of gifts and functions in the church.

2. The Union of Death and Suffering

Colossians picks up the theme of sharing in Christ's death, a theme now steady since 2 Corinthians (Col 2:12, 20; 3:3; see 2 Cor 4:10; Gal 2:19; Rom 6:3; 7:4; Phil 3:10). In Colossians more than in any previous letter, this theme becomes the undergirding for moral life. "If you have died with Christ...why do you submit to regulations as if you were still living in the world?" (2:20). "You have died.... Put to death, then, the parts of you that are earthly: immorality, impurity, passion, evil desire, and the greed that is idolatry" (3:3–5).

In Colossians, Paul is even more vivid about his sufferings as part of the suffering of Christ, even to the extent of talking about how his sufferings complete the sufferings of Christ! "I rejoice in my sufferings for your sake, and in my flesh I am filling up what is lacking in the afflictions of Christ on behalf of his body, which is the church" (1:24). As Christ suffered for "his body," so does Paul. Paul's sufferings are "for your sake" (*hyper hymôn*).

Earlier, Paul spoke of his own hardships as "for Christ" (2 Cor 12:10) and he described the Philippians as suffering "for Christ" (Phil 1:29). What is new here is the way he moves the issue through Christ back to the people for whom Christ suffered, "I rejoice in my sufferings for your sake" (Col 1:24), because this suffering is part of the larger picture of Christ suffering and dying for humanity, a picture that will never be complete until "the end." In this sense, Paul could easily see himself and other suffering people of faith as "co-redeemers" with Christ. If people of faith share in the divine fullness of Christ, they share in his redemptive function.

F. Eschatology

Colossians boldly goes where earlier Paul had hesitated. This boldness appears in its view of the resurrection as in some way accomplished. According to the specific eschatology of Colossians, not only have we died with Christ but we are also already raised with him:

> You were co-buried with him in baptism, in which you were also co-raised with him through faith in the power of God who raised him from the dead. (2:12)

The statement parallels an earlier one he wrote to the Romans:

> Through baptism into his death we were buried with him, so that, just as Christ was raised from the dead by the glory of the Father, we too might live a new life. If we have been united with him through likeness to his death, so shall we be through a like resurrection. (Rom 6:4–5)

Both texts speak about an anticipation of our death. Romans, however, specifically reserved the resurrection for the future. In Colossians, the resurrection has already happened, and it becomes the motive for moral life. "If then you were raised with Christ...seek what is above" (Col 3:1).

The shift is very significant. As theologians today say, Paul has shifted into a perspective of "realized eschatology," in which the future physical end of the world is considerably de-emphasized in favor of the present spiritual or internal realization of the eschatological promises.

This shift, however, is not without some basis in Paul's earlier thought. Writing to the Romans, as we have seen, Paul spoke of a past death of the Christian with Christ and a future resurrection, but he also mentioned a present "new life" (Rom 6:4). Thus, Paul also had in mind a present transformation defined in terms of "life." He apparently was thinking of a present transformation of a person's inner life when he wrote to the Corinthians, "We do not lose heart, because our inner self [inner man] is being made new day by day" (2 Cor 4:16). In 1 Corinthians Paul spoke of the final resurrection as the change from a "natural" (*psychikos*) body to a "spiritual" (*pneumatikos*) body (15:42–44) but also describes the present distinction between the "natural" (*psychikos*) person and the "spiritual" (*pneumatikos*) person (2:14–16). The transformation has already begun by the Spirit that the Christian receives (2:12). This transformation is a progressive intensification of "life" ("from life to life," 2 Cor 2:16) and a progressive intensification of "glory" ("from glory to glory," 2 Cor 3:18).

The continuity with earlier Pauline thought appears also in the way Paul ascribes this realized resurrection to faith as directed to "the power of God who raised [Christ] from the dead." From his earliest letters, Paul associated faith with the resurrection of Christ (1 Thess 4:14; 1 Cor 15:13–14; Phil 3:9–10). More specifically for Paul, faith is aimed at the action or power of God raising Jesus. Just as Abraham believed in God "who gives life to the dead," so we "believe in the one who raised Jesus our Lord from the dead" (Rom 7:17, 24). "If you believe in your heart that God raised him from the dead, you will be saved" (10:9; see also 2 Cor 4:13–14; Rom 4:17, 24). The shift in Colossians consists in its insistence on this power of the resurrection as already active and producing its effect in the life of the believer.

Future eschatology, however, is not totally absent in this letter. In a brief statement, Paul expresses his usual view toward the future: "After all, you have died! Your life is hidden now with Christ in God. When Christ our life appears, then you shall appear with him in glory" (3:3–4). We still live in hope, but this is a "hope reserved for you in heaven" (1:5). The future glory already exists, but "in heaven."

Faith in Colossians now seems to be a way in which the reality of heaven can be started and lived now on earth. In effect, Paul says this as he identifies the mystery, "It is Christ in you, the hope for glory" (1:27).

The eschatological shift in Colossians thus appears as a remarkable development of Paul's thought rather than as some sort of reversal. Colossians thus becomes an important link between the earlier letters of Paul and the later, even more intensely "realized eschatology" of Ephesians and the Gospel of John.

V. The Message of Colossians

In Colossians, Paul develops an intense focus on the person of Christ. It is this focus that Paul sees as the remedy for the problems of Colossae. For those who are so fearful about the "elements of the cosmos," Paul reminds how the universe fits into the love God has for his Son. They must remember the christological meaning that the universe has by its very creation. Furthermore, they must remember the intense union that they have with Christ, like the bond that unites a body to its head.

With this understanding of the role of Christ in their lives, the people of faith should be less inclined to a slavish submission to old ritual practices and should even laugh at their old superstitions. The practices, as Paul explains, were only a shadow of Christ. The hostile powers of the universe have been despoiled by Christ.

PART III

Letters Written in Paul's Name

In the late nineteenth century, scholars began seriously doubting the authenticity of 1 and 2 Timothy and Titus, generally known as the Pastoral Letters. The vocabulary of these letters differed greatly from the generally accepted Pauline letters. The setting of these letters suggested a time after the death of Paul. Later, letters like Colossians and Ephesians, along with 2 Thessalonians, became suspect.

Of course this hypothesis of inauthenticity raised serious theological or faith issues for many. These letters begin by saying it is Paul the apostle writing them. Would this be a lie if Paul in fact did not write them? If so, how could they be inspired by the Holy Spirit?

The tension here between a scientific observation and a faith position led church leaders and theologians to consider the issue of literary form. With letters of questionable authenticity, we could be dealing with a form of writing that flourished in the period roughly from the second century BC to the second century AD. The literary form is called "pseudoepigraphy." Examples of pseudoepigraphy abound in both Jewish and Christian circles.

As we saw in chapter 3 of this book, Jewish examples begin to appear around the second century BC, about the time that Jewish authorities were telling the people that prophecy was in hiatus (See 1 Macc 4:46) and when the idea of closing the canon of scripture was gaining ground. Writers convinced that they had a Spirit-filled message for the people tended then to ascribe their writing to someone living during the "accepted" times. Thus the author of Daniel, an Aramaic-speaking Jew writing around 169 BC, ascribes his writing to a man supposedly living in the sixth century BC.

Christian examples of pseudoepigraphy abound in the second century AD. From that period we have *The Gospel of Peter, The Acts of Paul, The Protevangelium of James,* and many others. Behind these attributions of works to past heroes was a sense of property and appropriation very different from ours. Also behind these Christian writings was apparently the idea of making the now-dead heroes of the preceding generation come alive and speak again to new situations. Invoking a person's name as the author of a document was for people of this time a way of making that person present as author.

Today with our intense sense of individuality and "intellectual property," we call such use of another's name "fraud" or "identity theft," concepts that for some seem incompatible with divine revelation. The question of whether God can be conceived of using fraud to mediate his message remains intriguing. However, to categorize all pseudoepigraphy by these modern concepts is really to oversimplify the phenomenon with which we are dealing. Ancient cultural presuppositions warn us against a hasty application of modern categories.

With this understanding, the issue of other authors writing in the name of Paul becomes less an issue of faith than one of literary analysis. We are not denying the inspiration of these writings. We are not even relegating them to some second-class status in scripture. However, if enough literary indications of inauthenticity argue that Paul did not write a particular letter, then we should understand this letter in a different literary context than that used for the authentic letters of Paul. Such a letter becomes an important indication of how Paul was interpreted by the generation following him. Such a letter becomes an important testimony to the stature of other anonymous ancestors of the faith. However, it should not be used to interpret Paul's expressions and theology.

We refer to such letters as Deutero-Pauline. The classification of individual letters remains hypothetical, as does all science. We deal here with probability. We will never fully understand this mentality for which the past was never really past and persons whose names were known were never really absent. Hence, we will never fully understand the phenomenon of pseudoepigraphy that stems from this mentality. For us the most appropriate attitude toward this manner of writing is a respectful observation of the phenomenon as such, a certain detachment that lets it be what it is, and a refusal to impose blanket condemnations. My inclination here is pragmatic. Barring any conflict with faith, I will follow a literary hypothesis to the degree it makes the document more understandable.

12
Ephesians

Ancient Ephesus lay on the west coast of what is now Turkey. A city of about 200,000 inhabitants, Ephesus was at once the capital of the Roman province of Asia and the province's principal commercial and financial center. A serious earthquake destroyed the city in AD 17. The emperors Tiberius and Hadrian restored the city, which then remained an important commercial center of the empire until the eighth century AD, when it was largely abandoned because of wars and the silting up of its harbor.

Ephesus was Paul's base of operations in the mid-50s. It was from there that he wrote 1 Corinthians and a part of 2 Corinthians. Ephesus may also have been the place of Paul's imprisonment sometime in the 60s for the writing of Philippians, Colossians, and Philemon.

I. Background for the Letter

Introducing his course entitled, "Paul's Letter to the Ephesians" Max Zerwick, SJ, started by saying that this writing probably is not written by Paul, not a letter, and not to the Ephesians. The expression "in Ephesus" appears to be added to the manuscripts in the fourth century. Before that, the address in 1:1 read something like "to the holy ones and faithful ones in Christ Jesus." In this form the writing addresses a very general audience, more or less as does James, 2 Peter, or Jude. For the sake of convenience, however, we will continue to refer to this writing as "Ephesians."

In its literary form, Ephesians appears to be a letter only in its opening (1:1–2) and closing lines (6:21–24). In between, this writing is pretty much a theological essay. According to the distinction made earlier in our study, we can with good reason call this writing an "epistle," an essay in letter form.

A. Arguments Against Authenticity

Several aspects of this epistle argue convincingly against Pauline authorship. Perhaps most important is the way this writing depends on Colossians. At times, the author of Ephesians simply copied sentences and expressions from Colossians. At other times, the author copied and deliberately modified the text of Colossians. A total of sixteen verses in Ephesians have strings of words that are exactly the same as lines in Colossians and often follow the order of Colossians. A number of these verses contain long sentences and clauses with this verbatim similarity. Appendix four contains a table of the verbatim similarities.

Some of the similarities could be explained by letter formulas or common Pauline phrases. Most of the verbatim similarities, however, require a literary dependence of one writing on the other. Even the differences in the parallels do not seem possible without a direct modeling on the corresponding Colossian text. The differences in the wording seem to be the attempt in Ephesians to improve the text, to drop some strange language ("the foreskin of your flesh," Col 2:13) or to add something to make the text ring more Pauline ("and the Lord Jesus Christ," Eph 1:2).

Such copying is unlike Paul. Even letters as close as Romans and Galatians do not show evidence of copying. Paul was too much a master of his own thought and diction to need to copy in this way.

Furthermore, attempts to see Colossians as copied from Ephesians raise more problems than they solve. In effect, Ephesians expands considerably on Colossians at several points, usually adding a more specifically Christian perspective. (See the advice to husbands and wives, Ephesians 5:22–33, compared with Colossians 3:18–19.) It is difficult to imagine why the supposed author of Colossians would have dropped these ideas. Likewise, Ephesians, as we will see, includes several shifts in theology further from the typical Pauline perspectives as found in Colossians. Such a development suggests again that Ephesians developed as a spin-off of Colossians rather than vice versa.

We can only speculate on why the author of Ephesians would have written the way he did. One theory suggests that the author is one who gathered and "published" the letters of Paul. A reference to Paul's letters as a whole occurs in 2 Peter 3:16, suggesting the existence of collections at the time of that writing. The author of Ephesians may have written it as a type of cover letter, representing what he thought to be the synthesis and final stage of Paul's thought. He would not have addressed such a letter to any one church, but would have left the salutation general enough to refer to any church.

II. The Sequential Study of the Letter

A. The Outline of the Epistle

As mentioned above, Ephesians looks more like an essay than a letter. The essaylike character of this writing appears in its simple and coherent structure. Apart from the opening greeting (1:1–2) and the conclusion (6:21–24), the writing falls into two main parts, a chiastic-structured doctrinal section (chapters 1–3) and an exhortatory section (chapters 4–6):

I. Opening address (1:1–2)
II. First part: the mystery of the call of the Gentiles (chapters 1–3)
  A. Blessing and praise (1:3–14)
  B. Prayer for knowledge (1:15–23)
  C. The unity of the church (2:1—3:13)
    1. Realized salvation—eschatology (2:1–10)
    2. The reconciliation of Jew and Gentile through Christ (2:11–22)
    3. Paul's office, servant of the mystery (3:1–13)
  B'. Prayer for knowledge (3:14–19)
  A'. Praise (3:20–21)
III. Second part: exhortations (chapters 4—6)
  A. The call to unity: faith, love, the gifts (4:1–16)
  B. The new life in Christ (4:17—5:20)

C. Duties of the Christian home (5:21—6:9)
D. The spiritual battle (6:10–20)
IV. Conclusion: recommendations and blessing (6:21–24)

B. First Part: The Mystery of the Call of the Gentiles (1—3)

After the letter address, which is a close copy of the opening of Colossians, the author begins a letter prayer, which is also the first part of a chiastic structure extending through chapter 3.

In one long sentence (1:3–14) the author starts by praising **God** for the blessings of holiness and blamelessness bestowed on us "in Christ" and "in the heavens" (1:3–5). Paul never made a claim to moral perfection for himself and his congregations, although he did address the Philippians and Colossians as "the holy ones" (Phil 1:1; Col 1:2) and the Romans as "called to holiness" (Rom 1:7). The perspective here as "in the heavens" alerts us to what we might call a "transcendent idealism" whereby the author is speaking of realities as willed by God, as existing apart from earthly and sinful imperfections, of which the author seems quite aware (4:25–32; 5:4–5).

In the prayer for knowledge, Ephesians maintains the cosmic **Christology** we saw in Colossians but immediately connects this view with the church. God put "all things under his feet" (1:22), but as "head of all things" Christ is given to "the church" (1:22–23).

Back at the end of the prayer of praise, the author distinguished between "we" and "you," apparently distinguishing between Jew and Gentile Christians (1:11–14). "We" are the ones "chosen" who "first hoped in Christ" (1:11–12). "You" are the ones who "have also heard the word of truth" and "are sealed with the promised Holy Spirit" (1:13). Later the author will be more explicit. He is writing to Gentiles from the perspective of a Jewish Christian, welcoming them into the covenant and community of Israel:

> At one time, you Gentiles in the flesh, called the foreskins by the people of the circumcision,...were at that time without Christ, alienated from the community of

> Israel and strangers to the covenants of promise....But now in Christ you who were once far off have become near by the blood of Christ....You are no longer strangers and sojourners, but you are fellow citizens with the holy ones and members of the household of God. (2:11–19)

In Ephesians the great mystery, hidden from ages past and now revealed, is the unheard-of unity of Jews and Gentiles:

> When you read this you can understand my insight into the mystery of Christ, which was not made known to other generations of sons of men as now revealed to his holy apostles and prophets by the Spirit, that the Gentiles are co-heirs, members of the same body, and co-partners in the promise in Christ Jesus through our gospel. (3:4–5)

Here we have a clear parallel with Colossians:

> I became a minister of this church according to the dispensation of God given to me for you, to fulfill the word of God, the mystery hidden from ages and from generations, now however manifested to his holy ones, to whom God willed to make known the richness of the glory of this mystery among the Gentiles, which is Christ in you, the hope of glory. (Col 1:25–27)

The mystery of Christ in Colossians has become in Ephesians the mystery of the church, the central focus of this epistle. The distinctive **soteriology** of Ephesians revolves around this mystery of the church, which also describes the author's distinctive **Christology** and **union with Christ trajectory**. The revelation of the mystery includes a quick allusion to **the Spirit**.

In general, the emphasis in Ephesians is ecclesiological. For instance, instead of being revealed to "the holy ones," an expression Paul uses for Christians as such (see Col 1:1; Phil 1:1), the mystery in Ephesians is revealed to a special group of church

authorities, "the holy apostles and prophets." Eventually the mystery is "made known" to "other generations of the sons of men." However, as an illumination by the Spirit, Ephesians limits the revelation to "the holy apostles and prophets." This group becomes, as it were, the channel by which God's grace of revelation passes on to the rest of the church and humanity. The consequences of this new perspective on later ecclesiology will be enormous and will stand in a real contrast to the more democratic picture drawn by Paul.

The role of "apostles and prophets" in Ephesians is important. They are the foundation of the church:

> You are built up on the foundation of the apostles and prophets, with Christ Jesus as its cornerstone. (2:20)

Colossians spoke of the Christians "rooted and built up on Christ" (2:7), a thought similar to that in 1 Corinthians 3:11: "No one can lay a foundation other than the one that has been laid, namely Jesus Christ."

The shift in imagery here in Ephesians is best seen as a shift to the perspective of the next generation after Paul. Looking back from this later perspective, the apostles and prophets are now seen as a group of people on whom the rest of the church depends for its existence. Christ has not really been displaced. He still holds the preeminent position in the building. However, the perspective differs from that of Paul, who walked among the apostles and prophets of the church and looked back to Christ.

Another theme in this first part of Ephesians is heavenly eschatology. The author adopts the realized **eschatology** of Colossians, taking it another step. Earlier Paul wrote, "You were co-buried with him in baptism, in which you were also co-raised with him through faith in the power of God who raised him from the dead" (Col 2:12). Reflecting on this text, the author of Ephesians writes, "Even when we were dead in our transgressions, God brought us to life with Christ—by faith you are saved—and co-raised us and co-seated us in the heavens in Christ Jesus" (Eph 2:5–6).

Ephesians repeats the Colossian imagery of having already died and being raised with Christ. The author then adds that we have also ascended into heaven. The reference to baptism is dropped, and the death implied in the "co-burial" is explained as a spiritual death, "dead in our transgressions." Ephesians maintains the role of faith in this process, but omits Paul's specific view of faith as being directed to the power of God raising Jesus.

This description of realized eschatology flows into Ephesians' **soteriology trajectory** in a line that looks like a commentary on Romans 3:24–28: "By grace you have been saved through faith, and this is not from you; it is the gift of God; it is not from works, so no one may boast" (2:8–9).

C. Second Part: Exhortations (4—6)

Following a typical division within Paul's letters, the author of Ephesians moves more or less from instructions to exhortations. He calls the readers to unity: "One body and one Spirit...one hope of your call; one Lord, one faith, one baptism, one God and Father of all" (4:4–6).

Perhaps reflecting Romans 12:3–7, the author of Ephesians relates the diversity of authoritative ministries in the church to "the body of Christ" (Eph 4:12), again touching on Paul's **union with Christ trajectory**. Seen as "gifts of Christ" (4:7), the offices include the apostles, the prophets, the evangelists, and the pastors and teachers (4:11). Compared to Paul's earlier lists of diverse functions within the body of Christ (1 Cor 12:8–10, 28–30; Rom 12:6–8), the list in Ephesians is shorter and geared more toward governance.

After a lengthy exhortation regarding specific behavior (4:17—5:20), the author incorporates the household code of Colossians 3:18—4:1, developing each of the relationships with more intense connections to Christian themes (Eph 5:21—6:9). The list in Ephesians contains far more theological motives for accepting the instructions, far more allusions to Christ and other gospel themes.

The expansion of the code dealing with husbands becomes an important development for an understanding both of Christian marriage and of **Christology**:

Husbands, love your wives, as Christ loved the church
and gave himself up for her
in order to make her holy,
purifying [her] in the bath of water in [the] word,
in order to present to himself a glorious church,
without stain or wrinkle or anything of that sort,
in order that she be holy and immaculate,
Thus husbands should love their wives as they do their own bodies...
as Christ cares for the church, for we are members of his body.
"For this reason a man shall leave his father and mother,
and shall cling to his wife,
and the two shall be one flesh."
This is a great mystery.
I mean that it refers to Christ and the church. (5:25–32)

This conjugal imagery given a religious spin is one that the Old Testament prophets had developed to describe the relationship between Israel and Yahweh (Hos 1—3; Jer 3; Ezek 16; 23).[1]

The letter ends with a reference to the spiritual battle (6:10–20), final recommendations (6:21–22), and an unusual blessing, "Grace be with all who love our Lord Jesus Christ in immortality" (6:24).

III. The Thematic Summary of the Letter

A. God

The image of God in Ephesians as principal agent in salvation fits well with the Pauline trajectory. It is God who has blessed us, and chose us, and destined us for adoption (1:3–5; Rom 8:29–30). It is God who reveals the mystery (1:9; 1 Cor 2:10; Col 1:27). It is God who raises Christ from the dead (1:20; 1 Cor 6:14; Rom 4:24). It is God who raises us up (2:6; Rom 8:11).

He is the "one God and Father of all" (4:6; Rom 4:11; 1 Cor 8:6). Ephesians insists that God is also "the God and Father of our

Lord Jesus Christ" (1:3) or simply "the God of our Lord Jesus Christ" (1:17), tying back to a vocabulary in Romans and 2 Corinthians (Rom 15:6; 2 Cor 1:3; 11:31).

B. Christ Jesus

1. Christ under God

In a striking parallel with Lucan Christology, Ephesians provides a glimpse at an "ascension" of Jesus to heavenly power (Eph 4:8–10). Yet this letter appears to pull back from the high Christology of Philippians and Colossians, where Paul seemed willing to dabble with a kind of divinity that can be attributed to the human Jesus, at least from the resurrection. In Ephesians, there is no divine name and universal veneration received by Jesus (Phil 2:9–11). There is no "fullness of deity" (Col 2:9) residing in Christ from the resurrection. In this epistle, the "fullness (*plêroma*)" is the body of Christ, the church (Eph 1:23), and "the fullness of God, of which we may be filled" (3:19). Ephesians apparently knows of the text in Colossians that describes Christ as virtually divine, but changes the meaning of "the fullness" to something of which all believers can have a part.

The cosmic role of Christ does appear clearly in Ephesians. Christ is "head over all things," with "all things beneath his feet" (1:22). Having been raised to the right hand of God in the heavens, Christ is now "above every principality, authority, power, and domination, and everything that is named" (1:21) and is now the one "who fills all things in every way" (1:23). Yet the author is clear that it is God who actively establishes this universal subjection to Christ (1:22; see also 1:10). Colossians, on the other hand, describes Christ far more actively as "despoiling the principalities and powers…leading them away in triumph" (Col 2:15; see also 1 Cor 15:24–25). Ephesians seems uneasy with the picture of Christ as military *pantocrator*. In this letter, we "are created in Christ Jesus" (Eph 2:10) and "chosen in him before the foundation of the world" (1:3). However, this association with God's creating and electing action does not presuppose Christ's personal preexistence.

Far less taken with late Jewish wisdom traditions than was Paul, the author of Ephesians might be concerned about any picture of Jesus as a second or rival God. Reviving an expression from Paul, Ephesians insists that the Father is "the God of Jesus Christ" (1:17; contrast Col 1:3).

2. Our Peace as One New Person, One New Temple

On the other hand, Ephesians sees the role of Christ in the church as central. In its interest on the unity of Jews and Gentiles, this epistle sees Christ Jesus as the place where "those who were far off" have "become near" (2:13). He is "our peace" breaking down "the dividing wall of enmity...abolishing the law with its commandments and legal claims" (2:14). Christ does this "by his blood" (2:13), "through his flesh" (1:14), "through the cross" (1:16), reconciling both parties to God "in one body" (2:16), creating "in himself one new person in place of the two" (2:15).

The author describes the unifying work of Christ this time also with the imagery of a building. Christ is here the "capstone" (2:20), and through him "a sacred temple in the Lord" is held together and grows (2:21–22), thus grafting a bit of plant imagery to that of building. In his early Corinthian correspondence, Paul had insisted on the community as the "temple of God" (1 Cor 3:16–17; 2 Cor 6:16), without referring to Christ. Paul had also combined the planting and the building metaphor to refer to his own work in general, in which he saw the role of Christ as the foundation (1 Cor 3:6–11).

3. Christ as Husband of the Church

Ephesians ties into the prophetic imagery of Yahweh and Israel as husband and wife. Using the household code as regards husbands, the author shifts Jesus into the role of Yahweh as he shifts the church into the role of Israel (5:25–32). Paul had alluded briefly once to this image of Christ the husband (2 Cor 11:2), an image Paul probably received from the developing traditions about Jesus and his preaching (see Mark 2:19; John 3:29).

As describing the church, this image of the wife of Christ expresses the intense love Christ has for his church. It also expresses a certain autonomy of the church in regard to Christ. The image of the church as "the body" of Christ (5:23; see 1:23–24; 2:15; 4:4,12,16) does not leave much room for the church's independent personality. Depicted as wife, the church appears in Ephesians to be in need of purification as well as the object of an incredible love affair.

C. The Spirit of God

1. Sealed by the Spirit

The Spirit of God returns in Ephesians from relative retirement in Colossians. Twice we are told about "being sealed" with the Holy Spirit or the Spirit of God. In one text this "being sealed" is connected with having believed in Christ. The Spirit here is also called the "down payment of our inheritance" (1:13–14). This portrayal is as close as Ephesians gets to the central Pauline vision of the Spirit's role in the resurrection (Rom 8:11). In a second text the author warns his readers, "Do not sadden the Spirit of God with which you were sealed for the day of redemption" (Eph 4:30). In general, the wording is Pauline: the Spirit as the "down payment" (2 Cor 5:5; see 1:22), being sealed by God (2 Cor 1:22), not quenching the Spirit (1 Thess 5:19).

2. The Spirit and Knowledge

Ephesians also repeatedly ascribes a role to the Spirit in revelation and religious knowledge. The great mystery is revealed to apostles and prophets "in the Spirit" (Eph 3:5). God has given us a Spirit of wisdom and revelation (1:17), an expression that parallels the Colossian text referring simply to "wisdom and spiritual knowledge" (Col 1:9). The author prays that the readers "be strengthened with power through God's Spirit in the inner self" so that they may comprehend the depths of God and know the love of Christ (3:16–19). All this echoes 1 Corinthians, where Paul wrote of the "wisdom…revealed by the Spirit" that enables believers "to know" the gifts of God (1 Cor 2:10–12). All this also echoes the Jewish sense of the "the spirit of prophecy."[2]

3. *The Spirit and Community*

Community life and prayer is also for Ephesians a function of the Spirit. Where the author rather obviously copies from Colossians (Col 3:16–17), he adds an exhortation to "be filled with the Spirit" rather than with wine[3] in connection with singing "psalms, hymns, and spiritual songs" (Eph 5:18–19). The readers should pray "at every opportunity in the Spirit" (6:18). As a community where Jews and Gentiles are brought together, the readers are to become a temple, "being built into a dwelling place of God in the Spirit" (2:22). This unity of Jews and Gentiles, which is so important for the author, is attributable to the Spirit. He urges the readers to "preserve the unity of the Spirit...one body, one Spirit" (4:3–4). In his own letters, Paul wrote about the *koinônia* of the Spirit (2 Cor 13:13; Phil 2:1).

Although the author prays that the readers be strengthened through the Spirit "in the inner self," Ephesians does not describe the Spirit dwelling in the individual believer or functioning from within the heart of the believer, a favorite image of Paul (1 Cor 3:16; Rom 8:9, 11; see 1 Thess 4:8; 1 Cor 6:19; 2 Cor 1:22; 3:3; Gal 4:6; Rom 5:5; 8:26–27).

D. Salvation

1. *Pauline Images*

Ephesians contains several references to typically Pauline images of salvation, usually in isolated mention without development. In one breath the author describes salvation "by grace...through faith" (2:8), pointing out the equivalence of the two aspects in good Pauline fashion (see Rom 3:22–24).

Copying a line in Colossians that expresses redemption as the forgiveness of sins, Ephesians writes of Christ, "in whom we have redemption through his blood, the forgiveness of transgressions (1:7; see Col 1:14). While "the forgiveness of sins" is not typically Pauline,[4] Ephesians moves it in the direction of Paul by adding the reference to Christ's blood, a key image in the soteriology of Romans (Rom 3:8; 5:9; see Col 1:20).

Ephesians also picks up the Pauline image of Christ's death as a cultic sacrifice: "Christ handed himself over for us as an offering and sacrifice [*prosphora kai thysia*] to God" (Eph 5:2; see 1 Cor 5:7; Rom 3:25). Whereas Paul earlier wrote in the passive voice of Christ as being "put forth" or "being sacrificed," Ephesians stresses the image of Christ actively involved in the sacrifice.

As Paul writes in Romans 8:23, Ephesians describes redemption (*apolytrosis*) as a future reality, with the Spirit as the down payment or the seal for this future redemption (Eph 1:14; 4:30; see 2 Cor 1:22; 5:5). This "redemption" is for a future "inheritance" (Eph 1:14; Gal 3:18; Rom 8:17; Col 3:24). Ephesians also speaks of "justice" (*dikaiosynê*) but shifts from the typically Pauline meaning. In Ephesians it is always paired with "truth" and described as a personal virtue or good moral quality (4:24; 5:9; 6;14).

2. Distinctive Images

What occupies the distinctive center stage in the soteriology of Ephesians is the unity of Jew and Gentile in the church. The great cosmic reconciliation now is the reconciliation of the two hostile groups of human beings (2:16), rather than the reconciliation of sinners or the universe to God (2 Cor 5:18–19; Col 1:20). The great mystery of salvation, held secret in ages past, is the unity of Jew and Gentile in the church, "Gentiles are co-heirs, members of the same body, and co-partners in the promise in Christ Jesus through the gospel" (Eph 3:6).

The blood of Christ is the means by which "those who were far off have become near." Christ is "our peace" by breaking "the dividing wall of enmity" between the two groups (2:13–14). The death of Christ on the cross reconciled the two groups into one body, "putting that enmity to death" (2:16). What Paul had said earlier about the role of Christ uniting humanity to God, Ephesians now uses to describe the uniting of Jews and Gentiles in the church.

E. Union of Life with Christ

The principal image in Ephesians for a life in union with Christ is the Pauline image of the "body of Christ." Like Paul in 1 Corinthians and Romans, the author of Ephesians uses this image to describe the coordinated functions of diverse offices in the church (Eph 4:11–12; see 1 Cor 12:12–26; Rom 12:4–8). Ephesians, however, speaks about the "gifts/offices" in the church as given or distributed by Christ (4:7–11), shifting from the image of the Spirit distributing these gifts (1 Cor 12:11).

Ephesians sees this body as a progressive reality. The ministry of these offices is specifically for "building up the body of Christ" especially in regard to "unity" (4:12–13). As in Colossians, Christ is pictured as "the head" from whom the body brings about its own growth and builds itself up in love (4:15–16; see Col 2:19). Specific to Ephesians, however, is the way this body functions in the central concern of the letter, the unity of Jews and Gentiles. Christ reconciles Jews and Gentles "in one new person" (2:15), "in one body" (2:16), as "members of the same body" (3:6). It is "in him [Christ]" that both "we" Jews and "you" Gentiles are united (1:11–14; 2:13; 3:6).

Again building off the words of Colossians, the author of Ephesians describes the realized eschatology of this letter as a union with Christ. God "brought us to life with Christ...raised us up with him, seated us with him in the heavens in Christ Jesus" (2:5–6; see Col 2:12).

The author of Ephesians also prays for the indwelling of Christ in the hearts of the believer. "May Christ dwell [*katoikêsai*] in your hearts through faith" (3:17). While Paul did insist on Christ "living in me" and of Christ simply "in" the believer (Gal 2:20; see 2 Cor 13:5), Paul never wrote of Christ "dwelling" in the believer. For Paul, the function of dwelling in the believer was rather that of the Spirit. In Ephesians, the indwelling of Christ is meant to lead us ultimately to "being filled with all the fullness of God" (Eph 3:19).

The image of Christ as the husband of the church is suited to give the church a certain distinct and separate existence from Christ, setting up Christ's role as sanctifying and cleansing the church (5:26). However, with this image, Ephesians insists also on intense unity: "For no one hates his own flesh but rather nourishes and cherishes it, even as Christ does the church" (5:29). Then citing the description of the union of man and woman in Genesis, "And the two shall become one flesh" (5:31; Gen 2:24), Ephesians emphatically applies the description to Christ and the church (5:32). Thus the church becomes "the flesh" of Christ—obviously not in the Pauline sense of the word.

F. ESCHATOLOGY

Of all the writings in the New Testament, Ephesians is the most consistent in its realized eschatology. Some allusions to a future eschatology do occur in the letter. The author makes a brief mention of "the day of redemption" for which we are sealed by the Spirit of God (4:30). To this he adds the Spirit as called "the down payment of our inheritance" (1:14), an implication of a future blessing. The author also sprinkles apocalyptic "two-age" theology in the earlier part of his letter (1:21; 2:2, 7).

On the other hand, the author drops Colossians' allusion to Christ coming in glory (Col 3:1). Furthermore, Ephesians repeats the realized eschatology of Colossians in which we not only have died and have been raised from the dead with Christ, adding that we have also ascended to heaven with him (Eph 2:5–6; Col 2:12).

The author speaks of "the plan for the fullness of time, to sum up all things (*ta panta*) in heaven and earth in Christ" (Eph 1:10). The expression could ring like an allusion to the future end time. However, the author then describes how God has already "put all things [*ta panta*] under Christ's feet" and how Christ is the one who now "fills all things in every way" (1:22). "The fullness of time" seems to be a present time as it was in Galatians 4:4.

The general transcendent idealism of this letter becomes clearer in the light of this view of realized resurrection and ascension into heaven. The author began with a praise of God "who has blessed us with every spiritual blessing in the heavens" (Eph 1:3). He sees his readers as chosen "to be holy and blameless" (1:4). "The church" here appears far less as a congregation of people in some city and more the "fullness" of God's actions, the body of Christ in heaven (1:22–23). The church as the assembly of those already seated in heaven must be seen as "holy and without blemish" (5:27).

This realized eschatology paradoxically also sheds light on the author's exhortations to moral growth. Ephesians is no longer waiting for the immanent climax of history accomplished by God's power alone. Although we are seated in heaven, there is work to be done, the "work of ministry" (*ergon diakonias*). This is the work of "building up the body of Christ" (4:12). In an extended section of his exhortatory part of the letter, the author heaps up body metaphors to explain this task. It means moving to "the unity of faith and knowledge of the Son of God, to mature manhood [*andra teleion*], to the extent of the full stature of Christ" (4:12–13). "Being truthful in love, we grow in every way into him who is the head" (4:15). From this head "the whole body ...with the proper functioning of each part brings about the body's growth and builds itself up in love" (4:16).

IV. The Message of the Letter

The transcendent idealism of Ephesians carries with it the danger of triumphalism in the church. For a discouraged church, however, this perspective comes to the rescue. Our hope lies not in the achievements of Christians on earth, but in the powerful plan of God. We stumble along, but in God's heaven, secure in God's hands, lies a beautiful and glorious form of the church and of our lives. This touch of Christian Platonism might be important in a culture where absurdity and frustration are trumpeted as the norm.

By incorporating his ecclesiology into this household instruction, the author of Ephesians has likewise given us a theology of marriage, saying in effect that Christian husbands and wives manifest in a visible way the love that Christ has for his church. The love of Christian spouses becomes more than just a personal or civil affair. For better or for worse, the world can look upon their love and see the love of Christ.

13

The Pastoral Epistles: 1 and 2 Timothy, Titus

Three letters form a special group of Pauline writings. First and Second Timothy and Titus are addressed not to churches but to heads of churches. They are less concerned with doctrine than with church order. They exhibit a vocabulary and literary style very different from the earlier letters of Paul. Since the eighteenth century, these writings have been known as the Pastoral Epistles.[1]

Two letters address Timothy as presiding over the church at Ephesus. He is supposedly the companion of Paul recruited at Lystra, the son of a Jewish mother and a Greek father (Acts 16:1–3).

One letter addresses Titus as presiding over the church of Crete. Although not mentioned in Acts, Paul refers to him frequently, especially in 2 Corinthians, where he played a key role in restoring order to the church at Corinth.

I. Background for the Pastorals

A. Paul's Circumstances as Described in the Letters

Writing 1 Timothy, Paul appears to be working in Macedonia. He reportedly traveled there after leaving Timothy in Ephesus to resist the false teachers in that church (1:3).

Writing to Titus, Paul is supposedly headed toward Nicopolis (3:12), which has been identified with modern Prevesa, on the west coast of Greece. He had recently been to the island of

Crete, where he left Titus to complete the organization of the congregations (1:5). Paul expects to see Titus soon (3:12).

Writing 2 Timothy, Paul is described as in prison in Rome (1:8, 16–17). The situation of Paul is desperate. He is preparing to be put to death (4:6–8). Except for Luke and Onesiphorus, Paul's friends have left him (4:6–22). Paul was recently in Troas (4:13) and Miletus (4:20). Timothy, probably in Asia, is to hasten to Paul before winter (4:9, 21).

B. The Authenticity of the Letters

In the nineteenth century, when critical Pauline scholarship began asking seriously the question of authorship, the Pastoral Epistles were the first to fall under deep suspicion. Since then, the controversy about Pauline authorship has not ceased. The issue, however, is not one of faith or inspiration, but one of literary analysis.

Several scholars of the nineteenth century pointed especially to the vocabulary of the Pastorals as arguing against authenticity. Of the vocabulary, 36 percent is not found in other Pauline writings. That is about two-and-a-half times the normal frequency of new words in Paul. Words that are used in other Pauline letters have shifted their meanings. For example *faith* has shifted from an attitude of trust to a rule of doctrine.

The most persuasive argument against authenticity, however, lies in the background presupposed in these letters. We glimpse a church being torn by internal forces. The issue of "false teaching" is of first importance, particularly that of "falsely called knowledge" (1 Tim 6:20). Apostolic authority, particularly that of Paul, appears not as a link in the chain of tradition (see 1 Cor 11:23; 15:3) but as an ultimate source and guarantee of truth. Teaching and discipline within the church are falling more and more under the authority of local church leaders. These clues suggest the situation of the church at the end of the first century.

It was at that time that Christian doctrine became critically important. Once all of the apostles had died, continuity with that first generation could no longer be based on personal association or acquaintance. The unity of a community could no longer be built up around the person of an apostle like Paul present by letter or spoken word. The church seemed to go through a shift typical of any movement lasting beyond the first generation of leaders. Once the first generation of church leaders died, conformity of ideas and teachings became the source of apostolic identity and church unity. A Christian could identify another Christian by a common profession of positions, by a common understanding of the traditions. Membership turned more to the ideas and positions of the old leaders, expressed in teaching.

Of course, doctrinal conformity demands doctrinal authority. Thus this period of the church was also the period of the development of ecclesiastical offices, particularly that of the teacher, the one who could expound orthodoxy and refute heresy.

Such a situation lurks behind the descriptions and admonitions of the Pastoral Epistles. As documents of the 50s or 60s, these writings look out of place. In fact it is not clear why Paul would be writing lengthy and detailed instructions to Timothy and Titus at all. In 1 Timothy, Paul has just left Timothy in Crete. In 2 Timothy and in Titus, Paul expresses his hopes to see them both soon. The extensive regulations do not appear as emergency instructions, but as orders for a considerable length of time. On the other hand, as documents of the 90s, they make a great deal of sense.

The personal elements in 2 Timothy (see 1:15–18; 4:9–21) along with the loose train of thought, typical of some of Paul's exhortations, could be arguments in favor of authenticity. Pseudoepigraphers generally do not write about such things in another's name. As in the case of Colossians, the jury might still be out for 2 Timothy, but the vocabulary and the setting lead me to place it hesitantly among the Deutero-Pauline writings.

A pseudoepigrapher(s) may have incorporated fragments of Paul's own notes in 2 Timothy, adding the personal details and greetings typical of Paul. In this way, the writer shows greater skill than other Deutero-Pauls. Apart from these short patches of personal material, however, even 2 Timothy bears the earmarks of a work calling Paul back from his grave to speak to a new situation, recording the memories of Paul's destiny in Rome, giving tribute to the apostle who wrote with such authority.

C. Chronological Order of the Writing

If we consider these writings as Deutero-Pauline, the chronological order of their being written down is difficult to establish. As such, the actual writing of these "letters" is separated from the internal story line of the three writings. The present order in the New Testament of these three writings is of no help since it is determined for the most part by size.

First Timothy and Titus are supposed to have been written before the imprisonment that forms the setting for 2 Timothy; however, other progressions suggest 2 Timothy was written first and the other two letters written later as "prequels." In a way typical of Paul, 2 Timothy incorporates newsy sections with many names of early co-workers. It also expresses deep affection. Titus has a few names and a brief glimpse at travel plans, but not much emotion. First Timothy has no newsy section and mentions no one except Timothy. Second Timothy does not mention any special offices in the church, although it has a great concern for teaching the correct doctrine. Titus mentions the presbyter-bishop as the one responsible for the teaching. First Timothy lists several church offices and seems to separate that of bishop from presbyter, a separation that will become normative in the second century. Second Timothy mentions a worry about "women weighed down by sins" into whose homes false teachers infiltrate (2 Tim 3:6–7). Titus is also worried about whole households being ruined (Titus 1:11) and insists on all women being "subject" to their husbands (2:5). First Timothy is virulent in its anger against women (1 Tim 2:11–15; 5:13).

II. The Sequential Study of 2 Timothy

As a working hypothesis for the sequential study of the letters, therefore, we will place 2 Timothy as the earliest written, followed by Titus and 1 Timothy.

A. Outline of the Letter

I. Opening (1:1–5)
  A. Greeting (1–2)
  B. Thanksgiving (3–5)
II. The hardships and responsibilities of Timothy and Paul (1:6—2:13)
  —concluding hymn (2:11–13)
III. Refuting heresy (2:14—4:5)
  A. Handling pointless quarrels (2:14–26)
  B. The difficulties and heresies of the last days (3:1–9)
  C. The example of Paul's suffering and exhortations to Timothy (3:10—4:5)
IV. Conclusion
  A. News of Paul's situation (4:6–18)
  B. Final greetings and farewell (4:19–22)

B. Opening (1:15)

Of the three Pastoral Letters, 2 Timothy opens with a style that sounds the closest to the way Paul opened his letters. "Mercy" from God and the Lord, however, is added to the greeting (1:2). Paul expresses his own emotions as he greets Timothy ("my dear child") and as he prays, "I am grateful.... I yearn to see you again" (1:3–4). References to "Lois" and "Eunice" also make this letter more personal than the other two (1:5).

C. The Hardships and Responsibilities of Timothy and Paul (1:6—2:13)

The author refers to the Paul's own "laying on of hands" that produced a "gift" for Timothy (1:6) and then mentions **God** giving a "Spirit of love and self-control" (1:6–7). Paul had never before mentioned this gesture. Similar to the Acts (6:6; 8:17–19; 9:12, 17; 13:3; 19:6; 28:8), on the other hand, the Pastorals speak frequently of the "laying on of hands." This was a gesture used in Judaism to designate an authorized rabbi. In the Pastorals we read of Paul laying hands on Timothy (2 Tim 1:6), then of the presbyters laying hands on Timothy (1 Tim 4:14) and of Timothy laying hands on others (1 Tim 5:22). As in Acts, the gesture is associated with the gift of the Spirit (Act 9:17, 19; 19:6).

The author refers to "the epiphany [*epiphania*] of our Savior Christ Jesus" as an event in the past referring to the ministry of Jesus (2 Tim 1:10). Paul never used this term, "epiphany," in any **christological** sense before. In the Pastorals it is a common term (see also 1 Tim 6:14; 2 Tim 4:1, 8; Titus 2:13) and suggests a new approach to understanding **God's** work in Christ. Although here referring to the historical mission of Jesus, this "epiphany" theme is part of the author's **eschatology trajectory** (see 2 Tim 4:1, 8).

The author urges Timothy, "Guard the rich deposit [*parathêkê*] with the help of the **Holy Spirit** that dwells within us" (2 Tim 1:14). Here we have one of the few references to the **Holy Spirit**. The "rich trust" appears to be the "sound words" that Timothy received "in faith" from Paul (1:14). "What you heard from me" is what Timothy is to entrust to other faithful people (2:2). Later, the author returns to the theme that the true doctrine is evident from its source in the apostle Paul (3:14). False teachers "upset others' faith" and are themselves "disqualified in the faith" (2:17–18; 3:8).

This sense of "faith" as words or doctrine to be guarded as a deposit is characteristic of the Pastorals (see 1:12; 1 Tim 6:20). The author is referring to the faith now considered as *something* to be conserved, something to be held on to (1 Tim 1:19; 3:9). The opposite of "the faith" are "things taught by demons" (1 Tim 4:1). The "words of faith" are in effect the same as "sound doctrine" (1 Tim 4:6). This is a shift in the meaning of the term "faith" from the earlier Pauline sense of an openness to God's power and a trust in his grace.

The author ends the section on a **christological** note: "Remember Jesus Christ, raised from the dead, a descendant of David" (2:8). The text echoes Romans where Jesus is described for the first time by Paul as a "descendant of David" and "son of God in power...by the resurrection" (Rom 1:34). The "saying" that follows is probably a creedal formula:

> If we have co-died [with him], we will also co-live
> [with him];

> If we persevere, we will also co-reign.
> If we deny [him], he will deny us.
> If we are unfaithful, he remains faithful, for he cannot deny himself. (2 Tim 2:11–13)

In the light of this formula, Paul is willing to bear suffering for the sake of the chosen ones, "so that they too may obtain the **salvation** that is in Christ Jesus, together with eternal glory" (2:10).

D. Refuting Heresy (2:14—4:5)

Timothy is urged again to impart "the word of truth" (2:15), avoiding the false talk of those who say "the resurrection has already taken place" (2:18). Timothy should be able "to teach, correcting opponents with kindness," hoping that opponents will escape the devil's snare and engage in the "repentance that leads to a knowledge of the truth" (2:24–26). The "sacred scriptures" in particular should equip Timothy for this task as "a man of God" (3:14–17), echoing an Old Testament term for a prophet (see also 1 Tim 6:11).

Here the author sees the problem of false teachings as a sign of the end times. In this **eschatology**, the author interprets the rise of immorality and opposition to the truth (3:1–8). As a battle between sound doctrine and false doctrine, the great eschatological conflict between good and evil is seen to be beginning now:

> For the time will come when people will not tolerate sound doctrine but, following their own desires and itching ears, will multiply teachers and will stop listening to the truth and will be diverted to myths. But you, be self-possessed in all things; put up with hardship; perform the work of an evangelist; fulfill your ministry. (4:3–5)

The author focuses on the way homes and households are used as the basis of these false teachings, with women perceived to be the key problem:

> For some of these infiltrate homes and make captives of women burdened with sins, led by various desires, always trying to learn but never able to reach a knowledge of the truth. (3:6–7)

Homes, of course, were the base of operations for Paul when he would move into a new city. They were probably the base of operations for other religious innovators. Wealthy women were often the managers of the households. Thus the author's anger against false teachers slides to an anger against women who open their homes to such teachers. We have here the beginning of an antifeminism that will become virulent in 1 Timothy (see 1 Tim 2:11–14; 6:13).

E. News of Paul's Situation and Farewell (4:6–22)

Paul's situation is dire. He is envisioning his death (4:6). His trial has gone badly (4:16). In effect, this letter becomes Paul's last will and testament. This letter thus testifies to the ancient tradition of Paul being executed in Rome (1:17), which tradition places around the year AD 67.[2]

III. The Sequential Study of Titus

A. Outline of the Letter

Titus is far less personal in tone than 2 Timothy, alternating between issues of church order and combating heresies, with theological reflections on the manifestations or epiphanies of God.

I. Opening greeting (1:1–4)
II. Church order: appointing *presbyteroi-episkopoi* (1:5–9)
III. Fighting heresies (1:10–16)
IV. Church order (2:1—3:8)
  A. Household advice (2:1–10)
  B. Epiphany theology (2:11–14)

C. Obedience to outside authority (2:15—3:3)
D. Epiphany theology (3:4–7)
V. Fighting heresies (3:8–11)
VI. Conclusion (3:12–15)

B. The Opening Greeting (1:1–4)

In the opening greeting, the author includes a nutshell description of the "faith" as "knowledge of the truth in the hope of eternal life," according to which Paul is an apostle (1:2). The mention of "eternal life" touches Paul's **salvation trajectory**. In this greeting, both **God** and **Christ** Jesus are given the name "savior" (1:3–4).

C. Church Order: Appointing *Presbyteroi-Episkopoi* (1:5–9)

At this point in the letter, the author introduces an important office in the church, that of "presbyter," one which we have not seen in any of the Pauline writings thus far. The office will become extremely important in the future development of the church.[3]

If "faith" is now seen as "true doctrine," something to be preserved and taught, then the church will need strong authoritative teachers as leaders. This will be the role of the presbyter. This leader will have to decide what is the "correct teaching." This leader will have to determine with authority which particular doctrines reflected the teaching of Paul and the apostles and which did not. These decisions were of vital importance. According to them, membership in the community was determined.

The letter to Titus describes the presbyter as such an authoritative teacher. In this first description, the presbyter is also given the name "bishop" (*episkopos*).[4]

> My purpose in leaving you in Crete was that you might accomplish what had been left undone, especially the appointment of presbyters [*presbyteroi*] in every town. As I instructed you, a presbyter must be irreproachable,

> married only once, the father of children who are believers and are known not to be wild and insubordinate. For the bishop [*episkopos*] as God's steward must be blameless.... He should be hospitable and a lover of goodness; steady, just, holy, and self-controlled. In his teaching he must hold fast to the authentic message, so that he will be able both to encourage men to follow sound doctrine and to refute those who contradict it.
> (Titus 1:5–9)

Although two names are used for this official, it is clear from their connection ("for") that the author is speaking about only one office. In this instance, the term *episkopos* is probably used in the generic sense of "overseer," according to the very etymology of the Greek word, *epi* and *skopos*. We saw this term in the greeting of Paul's Letter to the Philippians, probably with the same generic meaning (Phil 1:1).

High moral demands are placed on this person, but his principal responsibility is that of teaching. He is the authoritative teacher who determines and defends orthodoxy. The author speaks, however, about several presbyter-bishops in every town. Hence they rule, not yet as a monarch, but as a type of college. Once again, dating these letters around the 90s allows us to make sense of their content.

D. Refuting Heresies (1:10–16)

The author now takes aim at false teachers. He singles out "rebels" especially "among the circumcised" (Tit 1:10). The concern for the "whole households" that are ruined by this teaching (1:11) reflects again the social condition where early Christian teachers needed a wealthy person's home as a base of operations. The Letter to Titus again warns against "Jewish myths and rules invented by men" (1:14). In response, the author gives the slogan, "To the clean all things are clean, but to those who are defiled and unbelieving nothing is clean" (1:15), suggesting that the false teachings had to do with ritual purity and defilement (see Mark 7:1–23).

E. Church Order and Household Advice (2:1—3:8)

The letter includes a "household code," referencing several groups:

a. Old men are to be dignified and sound in faith (2:2).
b. Old women are to teach younger women to be self-controlled and good homemakers and to remain subject to their husbands (2:3–5).
c. Young men are to be self-controlled and models of good deeds (2:6–8).
d. Slaves are to remain subject to their masters (2:9–10).

The author then develops a theme introduced by 2 Timothy, the "epiphany" (*epiphania*) of **Christ** (2 Tim 1:10; 4:8). The theme is mentioned twice here (Titus 2:11–14; 3:4–8), bracketing an instruction about obedience to outside authorities (2:15—3:3).

In this letter, the author speaks of two epiphanies, one of "God's grace" or "beneficence," which has already happened (2:11; 3:4–8), presumably in the ministry of Jesus, and the second, which we await, "the epiphany of the glory of our great God and savior, Jesus Christ" (2:13). From the Greek grammar, it is clear that the author is talking about one person, whom he names both "God" and "savior." This is the first time in the Pauline writings that Jesus is named "God." Thus in its statement about **eschatology,** the text forms a climax in the **Christ trajectory** in the Pauline writings.

After the instruction on obedience to outside authorities (2:15—3:3), the author speaks about the first epiphany, in what may be another early Christian hymn or creedal statement:

> When the kindness and beneficence of our God and savior appeared [*epephanê*],
> Not from works which we did in justice, but according to his mercy,
> He saved us through the bath of the regeneration and renewal of the Holy Spirit,

Whom he poured out on us in rich measure through Jesus
 Christ our savior,
So that justified by the grace of him, we may become heirs,
According to the hope of eternal life. (3:4–8)

The creedal formula thus weaves threads from the **Christology**, the **Spirit,** and the **salvation trajectories**.

F. Fighting Heresies and Conclusion of Letter (3:8–15)

In a final instruction to Titus about controversies in the church, the author basically advises avoiding dialogue. "After a first and second warning, break off contact with the heretical person" (*hairetikos anthropos*) (3:10).

Paul had spoken earlier about *haireseis* in the context of factions or divisions in the church (1 Cor 11:19; Gal 5:20). The verb form, *haireomai,* simply means to "prefer" or "discriminate." Later the term *haireseis* is associated with "false teachings" and takes on the sense of "heresy" (2 Pet 2:1). The text here in Titus clearly has developed the later meaning—another piece of evidence about the late writing of the letter.

The author concludes on a personal note, with instructions about specifically named Christian travelers and about "Paul's" plans along with an exchange of greetings. (3:12–15).

IV. The Sequential Study of 1 Timothy

A. Outline of the Letter

The least personal writing with no mention of names and no news about Paul's situation, 1 Timothy appears to alternate between two topics, fighting heresy and church order:

I. Opening greeting (1:1–2)
II. Exhortation to fight heresy (1:3–20)
III. Church order (2–3)

A. Prayer for authorities (2:1–8)
B. Instructions about women (2:9–15)
C. Instructions about *episkopoi* (3:1–7)
D. Instructions about *diakono*i (3:8–13)
E. Conclusion (3:14–16)
—hymn (3:16)
IV. Refuting heresy (4:1–16)
A. The heresies (1–3)
B. Correct teaching (4–11)
D. Personal example (12–16)
V. Church order and the care of members (5:1—6:2)
A. Men and women in general (5:1–2)
B. Widows (3–16)
C. *Presbytero*i (17–22)
D. Miscellaneous advice (23–25)
E. Slaves (6:1–2)
VI. Refuting heresy (6:3–16)
A. The heresies and venality (3–10)
B. Personal example (6:11–16)
—hymn (6:15–16)
C. Instructions about the rich (6:17–19)
D. Final exhortation (6:20–21)

B. Exhortations to Fight Heresy (1:3–20)

Issuing a stern warning, 1 Timothy introduces us quickly to the problems facing the community:

> Stay on in Ephesus in order to warn certain people there against teaching false doctrines, concerned with interminable myths and genealogies, which promote only questions.... The aim of this instruction is love from a pure heart, a good conscience, and sincere faith. Some people have neglected these and instead have turned to meaningless talk, wanting to be teachers of the law but actually not understanding the words they are using, much less the matters they discuss with such assurance. (1:3–4)

We have not seen reference to "myths and genealogies" before this in Paul. On the other hand, the Judaizing element is familiar, particularly in its dilettante form (see Gal 5:3). The issues in this epistle clearly center on teachings. The appeal to faith over idle questions indicates an intensely defensive posture against an intellectual attack on orthodoxy.

The adversaries here seem to represent a combination of several positions, including Judaizing elements, "wanting to be teachers of the law" (1:6). The stress in these letters clearly lies on what these adversaries are teaching. The situation provoked by these false teachers is apparently serious and dangerous. The author advises only trying to silence these teachers. There is little effort to show where the error lies in this teaching or, as in earlier letters of Paul, to argue against the positions.

As he describes God's mercy and Paul's role as a former persecutor, the author refers to a "trustworthy saying" or creedal formula important for **Christology** and **soteriology**: "Christ Jesus came into the world to save sinners" (1:15).

C. Church Order (2—3)

The section on church order begins with a request for prayers, especially for those in authority, so that peace and tranquility might reign (2:1–2). The thought then quickly moves to a second creedal statement as an example of "the truth" to which all are called, a statement that weaves together the themes of **God, Christ,** and **salvation:**

> God is one. One also is the mediator between God and men, the man Christ Jesus, who gave himself as a ransom for all. (1 Tim 2:5–6)

The author then begins the instruction on gender roles in the church. Men are told to pray lifting up hands without anger or argument (2:8). No further details or explanation are given. It is not at all clear what exactly the author is driving at, if anything.

Women are then scolded. After insisting on simple and modest attire for women, the author moves into the most antifeminine text in the New Testament. In a reference to Eve, she is described as secondary in creation and primary in sin. Therefore, women are to remain quiet, receiving instructions silently and "under complete subjection." Women may not teach or have any authority over a man (2:9–15).

This antifeminism is best understood in the historical context of this letter. The church is in crisis. False teachers, who would probably operate like Paul from within wealthy homes, are the source of this situation. Several times, we have seen concern about the disruption of households (2 Tim 3:6; Titus 1:11). Since often the wife was the manager of the household, these women in charge of these households are assumed to be irresponsible religious innovators and became the focus of the author's anger.

The instructions then shift to "offices" in the church. Bishops, no longer related to the office of presbyter, are described as having a "noble" office. They are required to exhibit a long series of virtues and need to prove themselves as capable managers in their own households, keeping their children under control before they can take care of the church (3:1–7).

Deacons (*diakonoi)* are also required to show virtues in their personal lives and prove their ability to manage their own children and household (3:8–13). Paul had frequently described himself and his co-workers as deacons (1 Cor 3:15, along with Apollos; 2 Cor 3:6; 4:6; 11:23, Col 1:23, 25). Outside of Philippians, the only other mention by Paul of a deacon as possibly an office in the church are the references to Phoebe (Rom 16:1), Epaphras (Col 1:7), and Tychicus (Col 4:7).

The author concludes this section by incorporating what appears to be an early christological hymn or formula that gives a comprehensive description of **Christ** from his earthly manifestation to his being taken up. Apart from the "flesh/Spirit" antithesis, the description has little in common with Paul's view of Christ:

> Who was manifested in the flesh, was justified in the Spirit,
> was seen by angels, was preached among the Gentiles,
> was believed throughout the world, was taken up in glory.
> (3:16)

D. Refuting Heresy 4:1–16

The author then warns against "those who are turning from the faith…to things taught by demons in hypocritical lies" (4:1–2). In a rare reference to **eschatology**, the author sees this development as a sign of the "last times." Among the heresies, he mentions "forbidding marriage and abstaining from foods which God created" (4:3). Such antimaterial asceticism reminds us of Gnosticism, as does the final warning against "falsely called knowledge [*gnosis*]" (6:20).

Timothy, called here "a good deacon," is charged with dealing with these heresies, having been nourished by "the words of faith and of the sound teaching," where clearly faith appears as doctrine (4:6). Timothy is to remain courageous in this difficult task by remembering "the gift" he received "through the prophetic words with the laying on of hands by the presbyterate" (4:14).

The office of teaching and refuting heresy is serious, even a matter of **salvation**. As the author states, "Attend to yourself and to your teaching; persevere in both tasks, for by doing so you will save both yourself and those who listen to you" (4:15).

E. Church Order and the Care of Members (5:1—6:2)

The author then switches back to groups in the church. The sequence is confusing in its shift from household categories to church categories, perhaps indicating the close relationship between the two. He begins with brief descriptions of the "older man" (*presbyter*), "younger men," "older women," and "younger women," instructing the readers on how to treat these people (5:1–2).

The topic then shifts to "widows." The group seems to have special status in the church, since the author is worried about the church being "burdened" with them (5:16). Likewise, they are supposed to engage in several works of service, especially menial tasks (5:10). Very specific qualifications are listed for widows to be "enrolled" (5:9–12).

At this point, the author's anger against women flares up again. He warns against women "idlers, going about from house to house, and not only idlers but gossips and busybodies as well, talking about the things that ought not to be mentioned" (5:3–16). The description would apply to wealthier, more educated women, whom apparently the author did not like.

The author then describes "presbyters" again. They appear now as a paid professional office. The "laying on of hands" is mentioned in connection with this role and may have been the "ordination" ceremony for the office (5:17–22).

"Slaves" close the list, with some attention to the special duties incumbent on the slave of a Christian master (6:1–2).

F. Refuting Heresy (6:3–16)

The author returns one more time to the importance of refuting heresy. Timothy is to do this by sound teaching (6:3) and by "guarding the deposit" (6:20; see 2 Tim 1:13–14). Characteristic of these letters and of earlier Paul, the heretical teaching is attacked by assailing the moral quality of the teachers. They are described as evil people (6:4–10).

In contrast, Timothy is to exemplify a good character, which he is to maintain "until the epiphany [*epiphania*] of our Lord Jesus Christ, that the blessed and only ruler will make manifest at the proper time, the King of kings and Lord of lords, who alone has immortality, dwelling in unapproachable light, whom no human being has seen or can see. To him be honor and eternal power. Amen" (6:14–16; see also 1:17). This concluding doxology weaves important descriptions of **Christ, God** and **eschatology**.

V. The Thematic Summary of the Letters

A. God

This concluding doxology to 1 Timothy with its extended description of the majesty of a rather distant God (6:14–16) is unlike any other description in the Pauline letters. Titus and

1 Timothy are also distinctive by their persistence in calling God "savior" (*sôter*; Titus 1:2; 2:10; 3:4; 1 Tim 2:3; 1:2). Paul does not use this term for God, although he insisted throughout his writings on the principal agency of God in salvation. On the other hand, the Pastorals are silent about God initiating salvation with any specifics, such as sending Christ or the Spirit (Gal 4:4–6), shining his light into our hearts (2 Cor 4:6), or reconciling the world (2 Cor 5:19).

When describing the role of God in the life and work of the apostle, his co-workers, and other officials in the church, the Pastoral Letters speak in loud Pauline tones. Paul is an apostle by the will of God (2 Tim 1:1; see 1 Cor 1:1; 2 Cor 1:1) or by the command of God (1 Tim 1:1; see Rom 16:26). The most common relationship to God seen in Paul's and Timothy's life is "before God" (2 Tim 2:14; 4:1; 1 Tim 5:21; 6:13); see 2 Cor 4:2; 7:12; Gal 1:20; see also 1 Thess 3:9), a relationship that should be found in other believers (1 Tim 5:4). The bishop is "God's steward" (Titus 1:7; see 1 Cor 4:1). The church is the "house" (*oikos*) of God (1 Tim 3:15), perhaps an echo of Paul's image of the church as the "temple (*naos*) of God" (1 Cor 3:16–17).

B. Christ Jesus

Second Timothy mentions the resurrection of Christ once: "Remember Jesus Christ, raised from the dead, a descendant of David" (2 Tim 2:8; see Rom 1:3–4). This resurrection, which forms the key of Paul's theology, is not mentioned at all in Titus or 1 Timothy.

Second Timothy and Titus apply the term "savior" to Christ (2 Tim 1:10; Titus 1:4; 2:13; 3:6), a title that Titus also applies to God and that 1 Timothy uses only for God. Paul used the title only once for Christ in what looked like a formula (Phil 3:20).

One description of Christ as savior in Titus is remarkable because of the way it applies the term "God" also to Jesus. The author describes "us…awaiting the blessed hope and the epiphany of the glory of our great God and savior, Jesus Christ" (*tou megalou theou kai sôtêros hêmôn Iêsou Christou*) (2:13). The Greek unites "great God and savior" with one article (*tou*) at the beginning of the expression and the possessive pronoun, "our" (*hêmôn*), at the end, an indication that the whole description in between applies to one person.

Paul never called Jesus "God." For him the title was the proper name of the Father. However, we have seen a trajectory in Paul that makes this affirmation possible by a follower of Paul. From the beginning of his writings Jesus was "Lord" (*kyrios*) in a sense that suggested the divine title of the Old Testament (see 1 Thess 1:1; 4:16). In later writings, Paul suggested preexistence (1 Cor 1:24; 2 Cor 8:9; see esp. Phil 2:6–7). Then in his late writings he implied divinity through the images of God conferring "the name above all names" on Christ (Phil 2:11) and by the indwelling of "the fullness of deity" in Christ (Col 2:9), a divinity that begins with the resurrection.

The theme of preexistence is proclaimed briefly in 1 Timothy with the line, "Christ Jesus came into the world" (1 Tim 1:15). The expression echoes Johannine Christology (John 1:9; 3:19; 6:14; 9:39; 11:27; 12:46–47; 18:37).

On the other hand, one title for Jesus in 1 Timothy seems out of place in Paul. This is the title "mediator" (*mesitês)* (1 Tim 2:5). Paul typically portrays God saving humanity through Christ (see 2 Cor 5:18; Rom 3:21–26). However, Paul is so insistent on the direct action of God that he seems to rule out the role of any "mediator" (Gal 3:19–20).

The christological hymn celebrating the comprehensive career of Jesus from "manifested in the flesh" to "taken up [*anelêmphthê*] in glory" (1 Tim 3:16) introduces the Lucan portrayal of an "ascension" (see Act 1:1; 1:22, *anelêmphthê*). The exaltation of Jesus described in the Philippians hymn (Phil 2:9) is closely related but portrays God with an action, *hyperypsoun*, that directs attention to a transformation at the resurrection rather than a change of place from one world to another.

C. The Spirit of God

In this same christological hymn (1 Tim 3:16), the Spirit is mentioned: "In the Spirit" Christ "is justified." This part of the hymn may be a development of the formula in the opening of

Romans, which described the resurrection as the time when Christ was "established Son of God in power according to the Spirit of holiness." There too Paul applied the Spirit/flesh antithesis to Jesus (Rom 1:3–4).

Apart from this christological hymn, the Pastorals make three brief references to the Holy Spirit. In 2 Timothy, the author urges Timothy, "Guard this rich trust [namely, the sound words that you heard from me] with the help of the Holy Spirit that dwells within us" (2 Tim 1:14). The image of the Holy Spirit dwelling within us is typically Pauline (see Rom 8:11; 1 Cor 3:16). The author does not explain how the Spirit assists in this work of guarding and preserving.

The second reference is in Titus, in one of the "epiphany" hymns where the author explains, "When the kindness and generous love of God appeared,...he saved us through the bath of rebirth and renewal by the Holy Spirit whom he richly poured out on us through Jesus Christ our savior" (Titus 3:5–6). Paul spoke of "the renewal of our minds" but does not directly connect it with the Spirit (Rom 12:2). He did connect baptism and the Spirit (1 Cor 6:11; 12:13). The portrayal of the Spirit as a liquid "poured out" is used by Luke to describe the gift of the Spirit at Pentecost (Acts 2:17–18). In turn, Luke is citing the words of Joel 3:1. Paul speaks of God "sending" his Spirit, not "pouring" it (Gal 4:6).

In 1 Timothy, the third reference is apparently supposed to be a description of a Christian prophecy: "Now the Spirit expressly says [*rhêtôs legei*] that in the latter times some will turn away from the faith" (1 Tim 4:1). The image of the Spirit speaking is very Lucan. In Acts, Agabus, the Christian prophet, introduces his prophecy, "Thus says [*legei*] the Holy Spirit" (Acts 21:11; see also 20:23). With other verbs of speaking, the Holy Spirit directs the church (Acts 10:19; 11:12; 13:2; see also 28:25). Although Paul sees a role of the Spirit in Christian knowledge and prophecy, he never portrays the Spirit as speaking a message or "saying" anything.

D. Salvation

Titus and 1 Timothy repeatedly refer to "eternal life" as the great hope promised by God (Titus 1:2; 3:7; 1 Tim 1:16; 6:12).

Second Timothy speaks of "eternal glory" (2 Tim 2:10). Several times in Romans Paul had referred to "eternal life" and "glory" as the fundamental gift of God offered to humanity (Rom 2:7, 10; 3:21; 5:2, 21; 6:22–23).

Nowhere in the Pastorals, however, is there any mention of a general resurrection of the dead or the eschatological transformation of creation. The divine will for "everyone to be saved and come to a knowledge of the truth" (1 Tim 2:4) appears to be more of a spiritual salvation in a realm of eternity, as it links salvation and knowledge.

Although 1 Timothy uses the title "savior" only for God, this letter describes an essential role of Jesus in salvation. Christ Jesus "gave himself as ransom [*antilytron*] for all" (1 Tim 2:6), a concept that Paul may have had in mind with his image of Jesus "purchasing" sinners (Gal 3:13; 4:5; see also Mark 10:45; 4 Macc 17:21). The author of this letter also quotes the formula, "Christ Jesus came into the world to save sinners" (1 Tim 1:15). Second Timothy and Titus explicitly name Jesus as "savior" (2 Tim 1:10; Titus 1:4; 2:13; 3:6). Titus describes Jesus as the one "who gave himself for us in order to redeem us from all lawlessness and to cleanse for himself a people as his own" (2:14).

The hymn or creedal formula toward the end of Titus weaves together Pauline and non-Pauline themes concerning salvation. We are saved "because of God's mercy" not by our deeds. We are saved "through the bath of regeneration and the renewal of the Holy Spirit," who in turn is "poured out on us through Jesus Christ our savior." Thus we are "justified by grace" and "heirs of eternal life" (Titus 3:4–8). The theme of divine mercy in contrast to human deeds is Pauline. For Paul, baptism is incorporation into Christ (Rom 6:3; 1 Cor 12:13; Gal 3:27). The expression "regeneration" (*palingenesia*) is found again only in Matthew to describe the eschatological age (Matt 19:28). The general idea of salvation as regeneration is Johannine (John 3:3). "Renewal" of the mind or inner person is a Pauline image (Rom 12:2; 2 Cor 4:16; Col 3:10) but Paul does not directly connect it with the Holy Spirit.

What perhaps is the most distinctive aspect of salvation for the Pastorals, at least for 1 Timothy, is the role of doctrine in salvation. The author of this letter commands, "Attend to yourself and to your teaching; persevere in both tasks, for by doing so you will save both yourself and those who listen to you" (1 Tim 4:15). "Being saved" and "coming to a knowledge of the truth" are mentioned in one breath to describe the will of God for everyone (2:4). Second Timothy sees "knowledge of the truth" as a way of escape from "the devil's snare" (2 Tim 2:25). Thus the office of teaching and refuting heresy is serious—even a matter of salvation. "Sound doctrine" or authoritative teaching becomes the key element in Christian life. Adherence to orthodoxy becomes the clear and emphasized key to membership in the Christian community and by implication a key to salvation.

In his own letters, Paul earlier had shown by his anger that false teaching was a serious matter. He warns against being seduced by the preaching of "another Jesus than the one we preached...another Spirit than the one you received, or another gospel from the one you accepted" (2 Cor 11:4). He described the teachers of such positions as "deceitful workers," comparing them to ministers of Satan (2 Cor 11:13–14).

The early Pauline anger at false teachers and their teachings, however, is not exactly the same as the Pastorals' insistence on sound doctrine. The shift is subtle. Paul was insisting on himself in the act of preaching and on the gospel he was preaching. The Pastorals are stepping back and insisting on the body of doctrine that Paul passed on. Paul's focus is on the realities of God's salvation in Christ. The Pastorals' focus is on the words now used in the church to explain and communicate those divine saving realities. When Paul insisted that we are justified by the faith of Christ and not by works of the law (Rom 3:21–31), he was moving human activity back to the role of grateful response to divine salvation. When the Pastorals place correct teaching and adherence to correct teaching as a means of salvation, they are focusing on one human action, albeit mental, by which we bring about our salvation.

E. Union of Life with Christ

The great Pauline theme of sharing in the death and resurrection of Christ almost disappears in the Pastorals. Second Timothy does use the expression "in Christ" several times. The author refers to several things that are in Christ: "the promise of life" (2 Tim 1:1), "faith and love" and "faith (1:13; 3:15), "grace bestowed on us" (2:1), and "salvation" (2:10). Once a reference is made to the act of "living religiously in Christ Jesus" (3:12). The expression "in Christ" is not found in Titus. First Timothy refers to "faith and love" and to "faith" in Christ Jesus (1 Tim 1:14; 3:13).

F. Eschatology

Besides the warning against any doctrine of realized eschatology (2 Tim 2:18) and the isolated deprecations of "this age" (1 Tim 6:17; 2 Tim 4:10; Titus 2:12), eschatology in the Pastorals appears in two ways. The first connects with the theme of the great "epiphany" of Christ. Second Timothy uses the term to describe both the historical ministry of "our savior Jesus Christ" (2 Tim 1:10) as well as the eschatological coming of Christ. The author describes Christ Jesus as the one "who will judge the living and the dead at his epiphany and his kingdom" (4:1). "The Lord" is also described as the one who "on that day will repay...all those who lovingly await his epiphany" (4:8). Titus uses the term "epiphany" only for the eschatological coming of Jesus Christ, "the epiphany of the glory of our great God and savior Jesus Christ," for which we await with blessed hope (Titus 2:13). First Timothy likewise speaks of the "epiphany" only as eschatological (1 Tim 6:14).[5] While Paul in his early letters encourages hope and expectation in the "parousia" of Jesus (1 Thess 2:19; 3:13; 4:15; 5:23; 1 Cor 15:23), neither the noun, *epiphania*, nor the verb, *epiphainô*, appear in Paul's vocabulary.

The second context for the eschatology of the Pastorals is the deep concern for the presence of false teaching and general immorality. Second Timothy laments, "Know this, in the last days [*eschatai hêmerai*] stressful times will arise. There will be people...who are self-centered, greedy, proud...who slip into homes and make captives of women weighed down by sins...always trying to learn, but never able to reach a knowledge of the truth... disqualified in regard the faith" (2 Tim 3:1–8; see also 4:3). Similarly, 1 Timothy refers to "the latter times [*hysteroi kairoi*]" when "some will turn away from the faith by paying attention to deceitful spirits and demonic instructions" (1 Tim 4:1).

These warnings use the future tense for their predictions. However, the purpose of the warnings is to explain the contemporary situation of the author and his readers. This purpose is clear from the context of the letters with their concern for heresy now in the church. The implication, of course, is that the author and the readers are now living in the "last times." The author is following the Jewish apocalyptic schema that movement toward the end of the world will involve a progression of both good and evil.[6] When the "sound doctrine" that Paul taught (1 Tim 1:10–11) is attacked within the church, things are really bad. The end must be near.

Portrayed as expecting to die shortly, Paul expresses his hope in God in terms of a "crown of justice" that "the Lord, the just judge" will give him "on that day" (2 Tim 4:8). Here the author appears to be retreating from the immediate spiritual eschatology of Philippians 1:23. On the other hand, this same dying Paul voices his hope that "the Lord will rescue me from every evil threat and will bring me safe to his heavenly kingdom" (4:18), a hope that suggests something more immediate.

VI. The Message of the Pastorals

Our thoughts and judgments about God and salvation are very important. We can get it wrong, and that can be very bad for us and for others. In a nutshell, that is the message of the Pastorals. It is not enough just to be sincere. Just being sincere is much easier than trying to sort out the truth, but the job of "sound doctrine" is very important.

The Pastorals instruct the readers to look to Paul for help in sorting out the truth of doctrine. The teaching of the apostles is becoming an authority. As time separates us from the historical Jesus, this teaching, which in some ways does not slowly walk the earth and is not bound by time, becomes the link over distance and time.

The importance of the Pastorals is also in their ecclesiology. They give us a picture of a structured, hierarchical church, one that developed to combat the crisis then facing the church. Perhaps it was a development that allowed the church to survive the crisis. But this new form of the church was a development. It was a change from the church we saw in Corinth, probably some forty years earlier. The diversity of church form portrayed in the New Testament by the ecclesiology of the Pastorals in comparison with the ecclesiology seen in the earlier letters of Paul should allow us to envision new possibilities of church form today and at any time.

14
Second Thessalonians

Second Thessalonians is the second-shortest letter in the Pauline writings. Yet no other letter of Paul has provoked such interest and such an abundance of commentaries and explanations. History is filled with attempts to decipher the obscure references in this letter to events connected with the end of the world. Today scholarly studies abound on the authenticity of this letter.

In some ways it is a fascinating letter. It presents a whole program of events to allow Christians to prepare for the end of the world (2:1–12). Yet in other ways it is a disappointing letter. Its eschatological program is confusing and gives us little substantive instruction. Paul appears as an authoritarian grouch, advising starvation for the lazy (3:10) and ostracism to any who would not obey his orders (3:14).

I. Background for the Letter

Unlike 1 Thessalonians and all his other recognized authentic letters, 2 Thessalonians gives little information about Paul's situation and the circumstances leading up to the writing of the letter. If Paul indeed is the author of this letter, he would have had to write it very soon after writing 1 Thessalonians. As in 1 Thessalonians, Paul is with Silvanus and Timothy. Much of the wording in this letter is the same—perhaps too much the same—as that of 1 Thessalonians. The dominant topic is the same for both letters: the end of the world. However, the instructions about the end are almost diametrically opposite from those in 1 Thessalonians. Whereas 1 Thessalonians insists on the end coming unannounced, "like a thief in the night" (1 Thess 5:2), 2 Thessalonians stresses a visible program preliminary to the end allowing people to prepare for its coming (2 Thess 2:1–12). As an authentic letter, 2 Thessalonians would have to be a quick retraction and explanation of things said in 1 Thessalonians.

Some have suggested that Paul may have written this letter before 1 Thessalonians. Our present order of the letters reflects more the size of the letters than their historical order. A major difficulty with this view, however, lies in the reference in this letter to instructions already received "either by our word or by our letter" (2:15). It is unlikely that "our letter" is a self-reference by 2 Thessalonians, since "our letter" is related to past instructions, "traditions which you were taught [*edidachthête*]...by our letter."

If Paul wrote the letter, he most likely would have written it around AD 52 probably from Corinth, a situation that can be correlated with the end of his second journey as described in Acts.

A. The Question of Authenticity

While not as clear as for Ephesians and the Pastorals, a number of arguments taken together lead to a strong case against the authenticity of 2 Thessalonians.

1. Copying from 1 Thessalonians?

The first argument arises from the verbatim similarities of parts of 2 Thessalonians with 1 Thessalonians. A total of nineteen verses in 2 Thessalonians contain strings of words that are identical to expressions in 1 Thessalonians. Unlike the verbatim similarities between Ephesians and Colossians, those in 2 Thessalonians are shorter expressions from different parts of 1 Thessalonians, rather than whole sentences and clauses. These similarities appear most in opening, transition, and ending sections (1:1–2; 2:13–17; 3:1–12), suggesting that the writer of 2 Thessalonians used bits and pieces of 1 Thessalonians as the mortar for his specific message. Appendix 5 contains a table of the verbatim similarities between 1 and 2 Thessalonians.

Do these similarities demonstrate copying by a later author knowing and using 1 Thessalonians? These common expressions could be explained perhaps also by Paul writing this letter almost immediately after writing the first letter.

Yet what is curious is the way the common expressions are used with shifts of meaning. For instance, the expressions in 1 Thessalonians about the Lord directing Paul's travels (3:11) become expressions about God directing the hearts of the readers (2 Thess 3:5; see 2:16–17). In fact, no travel plans appear in 2 Thessalonians. In 1 Thessalonians, Paul refers to his "labor and hard work night and day" to prove his love for the readers (1 Thess 2:9). In 2 Thessalonians, the reference is part of a command to make the lazy get to work (2 Thess 3:8)! First Thessalonians describes Jesus coming with "his holy ones" (1 Thess 3:13), whereas 2 Thessalonians shifts the common expression to Jesus coming with "his angels" (2 Thess 1:7; see Matt 24:31). Paul's references to "angels" are usually to dangerous or hostile forces (Rom 8:38; 1 Cor 4:9; 6:3; Gal 1:8), and he never otherwise associates Jesus with them except as subjugating them (1 Cor 15:24–25). This use of words with a shift of meaning suggests another foot trying to wear Paul's shoes.

2. Absence of a Developed Reference to 1 Thessalonians

Another detail argues against authenticity. This is the absence of any clear reference specifically to 1 Thessalonians as a letter that he had *just written* to the same church, containing instructions that conflict with those in 2 Thessalonians. When Paul does have to modify an earlier instruction, he does so in a very explicit way by referring to the earlier letter and explaining it (see 1 Cor 5:9).

Second Thessalonians does have two references to other letters. One, as we have seen, commands the readers to a blanket acceptance of the instructions received "either by our word or by our letter" (2:15). The other reference is a warning against instructions about the end of the world "by a letter *as if* [*hos*] from us" (2:2; emphasis mine). If Paul's purpose in 2 Thessalonians is to correct an impression given by his very recent writing of 1 Thessalonians, both references—the blanket acceptance and the blanket rejection—seem strange. The warning against gullibly accepting a letter about the end of the world is particularly perplexing coming after he has just written the Thessalonians a letter precisely on that topic.

3. An Impersonal Tone

A third detail that argues against authenticity is the complete absence of any personal news about Paul, any remembrances about his experiences with the community, any personal greetings. There are no names of friends mentioned, other than in the first line, which repeats 1 Thessalonians 1:1 verbatim. Compared to 1 Thessalonians, this letter looks very impersonal.

Putting these arguments together, we begin to see the plausibility of this letter not being written by Paul, but rather written by a later person using 1 Thessalonians—perhaps explaining a misunderstanding of 1 Thessalonians—writing probably to another church and therefore not wanting to provide any concrete data about the situation of the author to the church receiving this letter so as not to blow his cover.

4. Clarification of Meaning

Finally, an argument that might settle the question for many is simply that the letter makes much more sense if written by someone as the first century draws to a close. As we will see in the examination of the letter's eschatology, the issue seems to be the delay of the parousia. The author's intention here seems to be to explain this delay. Paul was not faced with this problem. The church of the last decades of the first century was.

The strongest argument against the hypothesis of pseudoepigraphy is the insistence at the end of this letter that it is from Paul (3:17). We have found this reference to an autograph common to many of the recognized authentic letters of Paul. This way of signing a letter in another's name, however, may have been a characteristic of the pseudoepigraphy at the time.[1]

II. The Sequential Study of the Letter

A. The Outline of the Epistle

After an extended prayer (chapter 1), the letter basically falls into two sections: instruction about the end of the world (chapter 2) and various exhortations (chapter 3):

I. Opening (1)
  A. Greeting (1:1–2)
  B. Thanksgiving and encouragement (1:3–10)
  C. Prayer (1:11–12)
II. Instructions about the parousia (2)
  A. The day of the parousia (2:1–12)
  B. Exhortation to persevere (2:13–16)
  C. Prayer (2:17)
III. Exhortations (3:1–15)
  A. Request for prayers (3:1–5)
  B. Instructions regarding the disorderly (3:6–15)
IV. Concluding prayer and final greeting (3:16–18)

B. Thanksgiving and Encouragement (1:3–10)

After the opening greeting, the author expresses a duty to give thanks to God: "We ought to thank God" (1:3). The object of the thanksgiving is the faith and love of the readers and their endurance in persecution [*diôgmos*] and affliction (1:3–4). In 1 Thessalonians, the only description of something like a persecution appears in the section that looks like a later addition (1 Thess 2:14).

This "thanksgiving" prayer then abruptly shifts to a description of **eschatology** and final judgment, where Jesus appears "in blazing fire, inflicting vengeance [*ekdikêsis*] on those who do not acknowledge God," a punishment that consists in "eternal ruin [*olethros aiônios*] separated from the presence of the Lord" (2 Thess 1:8–9). The **Christology** here is that of a mighty eschatological avenger. This text is also the first description of hell in the Pauline writings, where people are definitively excluded from **salvation**.

C. Instructions about the Parousia (2:1–12)

In the central part of this letter, the major development of the letter's **eschatology**, the author describes the events leading up to "the parousia of our Lord Jesus Christ and our assembling with him" (2:1). Unlike 1 Thessalonians, which insisted on the suddenness of the end, coming "like a thief in the night" (see 1 Thess 5:1–4), 2 Thessalonians provides an observable program of events leading up to the end, by which the faithful will be warned of its coming. The expressed purpose of the author here is to cool the readers' expectation of the end, particularly to debunk the assumption that the end has already come and to calm fears that the readers somehow missed it (2 Thess 2:2).

As presented in this letter, **God's** program consists of three interrelated events. First, the real tell-tale sign of the end will be the mass apostasy or falling away from the faith (2:3). Second, this mass apostasy will be provoked by the actions of "the man of lawlessness" who will appear on the scene as a false god (2:3–4) and as a false prophet (2:8–11). Third, for this "man of lawlessness" to go into action, there needs to be removed whatever is presently restraining him (2:6–7). Only when these events occur will the end come.

The section ends with a description of the condemnation of "all who do not believe in the truth and approve of wrongdoing" (2:11). All this is part of God's plan against those who "have not accepted the love of truth so that they may be saved" (2:10). **God** is in control even here since he is "sending a deceiving power" so that these wicked people "may believe the lie" (2 Thess 2:11), an echo of the story in 1 Kings 22:1–38.

D. Exhortation to Persevere (2:13–16)

The author concludes the eschatological section with another expression of duty: "[W]e ought to give thanks to God" (2:13). The readers are described as chosen "to acquire the glory of our Lord Jesus Christ" (2:14), where the word *glory* (*doxa*) is substituted for *salvation* (*soteria*) in a line taken from 1 Thessalonians (1 Thess 5:9).

The author includes here an admonition to "stand firm and hold fast to the traditions" taught by Paul (2 Thess 2:15). Previously, when Paul spoke of handing on traditions, he would refer to himself as link rather than as a source (1 Cor 11:23; 15:3). Seeing Paul as the source of the authoritative teaching would be the understandable perspective of the next generation of teachers. As in the Pastoral Epistles, apostolic teaching was becoming the key to authentic Christian life.

E. Instructions regarding the Disorderly (3:6–15)

This perspective would explain the great insistence in the last section of the letter on obeying Paul's teachings:

> We command you, brothers, in the name of the Lord Jesus Christ, to avoid any brother who wanders from the straight path and does not follow the tradition you received from us.... If anyone will not obey our injunction, delivered through this letter, single him out to be ostracized that he may be ashamed of his conduct. (3:6,14)

When we read this letter as though written by Paul, we can easily be bothered by his authoritarianism. Paul simply does not speak that way in his earlier letters. He did once advise an excommunication, but that was a person publicly engaging in incest (1 Cor 5:1–5). Paul's concern there was far more about the harm done to the community than about the recognition of his authority.

If, however, we see this letter as written by a person long after Paul, then the descriptions insisting on Paul's authority become expressions of homage. When the church was beset by heresies, it leaned heavily on "apostolic authority" as a way out of the morass. Hence we detect in this letter a great respect for Paul's writing (2:15), a respect that this letter intends to exploit (3:14).

III. The Thematic Summary of the Letter

A. God

For the author of 2 Thessalonians, God is the one who encourages the hearts of good people and strengthens them so that good deeds and words issue forth (1:11; 2:16–17). This stress on the effective agency of God in the hearts of the believers reminds us of the similar theme in Philippians (Phil 1:6; 2:13). This is the God who "loved us and gives us an eternal encouragement" (2 Thess 2:16).

For evil people, however, this God is also an avenging judge. He "repays with affliction those who are afflicting you" (1:6). The goal of God's action is the condemnation of all "who have not believed the truth but have approved of wrongdoing" (2:12). To this end, God leads evildoers into deeper trouble by sending them "a deceiving power so that they may believe the lie" (2:11). Like the Yahweh who sent a "lying spirit" to deceive King Ahab in the story of his ill-advised and disastrous military campaign against Raboth-gilead (1 Kgs 22:19–23), God here is still in control even when things are going poorly.

Paul had talked about the wrath of God at length in Romans. He had also described human blindness as God's punishment for sin, a punishment that leads to even more sin (Rom 1:18–32). However, in Romans, Paul balanced this picture of the angry God with the God who loves us while we are still sinners (Rom 5:8) and thus shows his justice so that he might justify sinners (Rom 3:21–28).

God does not appear in this letter as reconciling a sinful world to himself or freeing human beings from sin. People are already divided by their behavior, believing the lie or believing the truth, and God reacts accordingly.

B. Christ Jesus

Jesus appears in a pattern similar to that of God. The author promises the good people, "The Lord is faithful. He will strengthen you and guard you from the evil one" (3:3). He will "direct your hearts to the love of God and the endurance of Christ" (3:5). With God, therefore, Jesus is effectively in control.

For evildoers, however, Jesus is an avenging warrior. The author promises "revelation of the Lord Jesus from heaven with his mighty angels in blazing fire, inflicting vengeance [*ekdikêsis*] on those who do not acknowledge God and on those who do not obey the gospel of our Lord Jesus" (1:7–8). It is Jesus who without effort destroys the man of lawlessness. "With the breath [*pneuma*] of his mouth, the Lord Jesus will kill the lawless one" (2:8), like the sprout of Jesse promised by Isaiah (Isa 11:4).

Paul had suggested the eschatological warrior image in 1 Corinthians, when he described Jesus subjecting all enemies under his power "when the end comes" (1 Cor 15:24–27). There Paul was focused on cosmic powers. Apocalyptic imagery tended to focus on the effortless destruction of superhuman forces of evil (see Rev 20:7–10). Second Thessalonians describes Jesus destroying evil human beings in "eternal ruin" (2 Thess 1:9).

This image of Jesus here shows significant and noteworthy contacts with the Gospel of Matthew. It is Matthew who also portrays Jesus coming with "his angels" to "assemble [*episynagein*] the elect" (Matt 24:31). Second Thessalonians also describes "the assembly" [*episynagogês*] of the faithful with Jesus at his coming (2 Thess 2:1). In Matthew's Gospel, it is Jesus who comes as eschatological judge, precisely to separate the good from the bad and to cast the bad "in the eternal fire prepared for the devil and his angels" (Matt 25:41).

Like Matthew, the author of 2 Thessalonians is following a Jewish strand of theology. In this apocalyptic Judaism, the heavenly mediator is at times portrayed as an avenging warrior on earth destroying the oppressive people at the end times. *First Enoch* briefly describes "the Son of man," who "shall loosen the reins of the strong and crush the teeth of the sinners" (46:4; see 62:2–6). *Second Baruch* speaks similarly of "the Anointed One" who will destroy the armies of the fourth and last kingdom of the world (40:1–3). All the surviving inhabitants of the nations "will be delivered into the hands of my Servant, the Anointed One" (70:9). *Second Baruch* also speaks of this work of the Anointed

One judging the nations as occurring "after the signs have come of which I have spoken to you before" (72:2).

The author of 2 Thessalonians puts great stress on the "glory" (*doxa*) of Jesus as eschatological judge. Eternal condemnation consists in being separated from "the glory" of Jesus' power (2 Thess 1:9). Jesus comes at the end "to be glorified among his holy ones" (1:10). The author prays that "the name of our Lord Jesus may be glorified in you and you in him" (1:12) and states that good people are called "to possess the glory of our Lord Jesus Christ" (2:14). Perhaps this stress also points to a contact with Matthew's Gospel where the final judgment consists in "the Son of man coming in his glory" and "sitting on his throne of glory" (Matt 25:31; see also 19:28; 24:30).

C. The Spirit of God

The Spirit of God is not prominent in this letter, mentioned clearly only once in a reference to "salvation through sanctification by the Spirit and belief in truth" (2:13). Nothing is said about the power or joy of the Spirit, themes in 1 Thessalonians, or about the later themes of indwelling of the Spirit or the connection between the Spirit and the resurrection.[2]

D. Salvation

Second Thessalonians speaks briefly of a basic gift of God for human beings coming prior to any human action: "God chose you as the firstfruits for salvation through sanctification by the Spirit and belief in truth. To this end he has also called you through the gospel to possess the glory of our Lord Jesus Christ" (2:13–14). This choice and this calling come close to the Pauline view of grace anticipating human action. These lines occur in a transition section where the author appears to imitate a Pauline thanksgiving prayer by borrowing phrases from 1 Thessalonians (see 1 Thess 4:7 and 5:9).

Most of what this letter says about salvation deals with eschatological salvation. The present time is an evil time, and will only get worse. In the future, however, God will wreak vengeance on evildoers but "grant rest to you who are undergoing afflictions" (1:7). Salvation here is rescue from bad people, not liberation from sin, death, and the law. The author prays that "we may be delivered from perverse and wicked people...strengthened and guarded from the evil one" (3:2–3).

This rescue presupposes a grouping of people already into the good and the bad. Suffering persecution will show the good "to be worthy of the kingdom of God" (1:5). God "will grant rest to you who are undergoing affliction" (1:7), while those who cause the affliction will suffer the punishment of "eternal ruin" (1:9). The saving action of God is thus determined by prior human performance.

Thus in 2 Thessalonians, there is no salvation for those who "have not accepted the love of truth...all who do not believe in the truth and approve of wrongdoing" (2:10–11). The author here is echoing the late Jewish view of hell, a punishment that continues for eternity in a realm of suffering beyond earth. *Fourth Ezra* describes the fate of the wicked as "the pit of torment" and the "furnace of hell" (7:36). *First Enoch* describes the "chains of Satan" being prepared for the kings and potentates of this earth" (53:4–5). Again, similarities with Matthew appear in this portrayal of eternal damnation (see Matt 13:40–42; 25:41).

While Paul spoke of the destruction and the divine wrath facing sinners (1 Cor 1:8; 2 Cor 2:15; 4:3; Rom 2:5–11), he never spoke of "eternal ruin." In 1 Thessalonians Paul clearly distinguished the good person from the sinner (1 Thess 4:5; 5:5). However, he did not carry over that distinction into his view of the parousia of Christ, where no one among the living or the dead is excluded from being "with Christ forever" (4:17; 5:10).

E. Union of Life with Christ

Twice the author uses the Pauline expression "in the Lord," both in a section with other phrases apparently copied from 1 Thessalonians. "We are confident of you in the Lord" (3:4), and "We order and urge in the Lord Jesus Christ..." (3:12; see 1 Thess 4:1). Apart from those two instances, there is no indication in 2 Thessalonians of any sense of life in union with the dying and rising Christ.

F. Eschatology

As we have seen above, the distinctive eschatology of 2 Thessalonians lies in the unusual description of God's program for the end, which consists of "a restrainer" eventually removed, holding back "the man of lawlessness," who provokes a "mass apostasy" (2 Thess 2:3–11). This description is hyped by assertion that the readers are supposed to know what this is all about (2:5–6). It is in the interpretation of these details that the issue of authorship becomes critical. We can consider the two possibilities:

1. *As written by Paul.* As instruction of Paul, this eschatological program poses great difficulties for the interpreter, even apart from the difficulty of seeing how Paul could have changed his mind so quickly regarding the suddenness of the end. In this description, Paul refers to the way "I spoke to you about these things when I was with you" (2:5), indicating that the three elements that form God's program for the end had some precise meaning. In particular concerning "the restrainer," Paul expects his readers to know what he is talking about (2:6). The interpreter of Paul today then is faced with the question of what Paul meant by the mass apostasy and the man of lawlessness. What future events could Paul have intended to describe that would be meaningful for his original readers?

Attempts to identify "the man of lawlessness" have ranged from the pope to Attila the Hun, as every generation looks to the person they love to hate. Attempts to identify "the restrainer," mentioned first with a neuter noun (2:6) and then with a masculine noun (2:7), have ranged from Paul and his preaching of the gospel, on the one hand, to the emperor and the Roman Empire, on the other. We have no clue in the rest of Paul's writings as to which interpretation comes closest to his.

Any attempt to identify this figure with persons close to Paul leads to the theological difficulty of the end not coming. Attempts to identify these realities with events still in our future, known to Paul by a miraculous revelation, lead to the problem of how they could have been meaningful for Paul's audience. Moreover, the general issue of predictions in apocalyptic literature lies in the way most of these often conflicting "predictions" are based on literary stereotypes circulating during these early centuries, suggesting that the writers of the predictions did not have specific information about the end.

2. *As written by someone after Paul.* A very different perspective appears if we consider these texts as not written by Paul, but composed by someone perhaps years after Paul. In this perspective, the author may not have had any specific reality in mind when he wrote of "the mass apostasy," "the man of iniquity," or "the restrainer." In this perspective, the expressions, "Do you not remember how I used to tell you about these things," or "You know what restrains him," are part of the general fiction involved in pseudoepigraphy. The author is imagining Paul and his readers.

In this perspective, our investigation is directed, not to specific realities that correspond to these eschatological descriptions, but rather to motifs or general stereotypes that would have led the author to think of these realities and impute knowledge of them to Paul.

We find such a motif behind the image of "the mass apostasy" in general apocalyptic literature. The Book of Revelation, for example, speaks of the great masses led astray by the beasts of evil (Rev 13:14–16). The actual expression "apostasy" (*apostasia*), as referring to a mass defection from the worship of God, appears in 1 Maccabees 2:12, where the systematic religious persecution of Antiochus IV is described.

The general figure of the "man of lawlessness" suggests the anti-God character also common in apocalyptic writings. The description in 2 Thessalonians 2:4 in particular, however, suggests a text in Daniel where again Antiochus IV was described:

> The king will do as he pleases, and he will exalt himself and make himself greater than any god. He will utter blasphemies against the God of Gods. He will prosper until divine wrath is fulfilled, for what is determined will take place. He will have no regard for the gods of his ancestors or for the desire of women. For no god

will he have regard, because he will extol himself over all. (Dan 11:36–37)

Antiochus's desecration of the Jerusalem Temple in 168 BC left a lasting imprint on Jewish consciousness. In many ways, he became a figure of evil personified. Like Hitler in the twentieth century, Antiochus IV terrorized the Jews and would remain in the Jewish memory as a symbol of evil.

"The restrainer" is unique to 2 Thessalonians as an apocalyptic motif. We do not find clear parallels in other apocalyptic literature or in the religious history of the Jews. When speaking of this restrainer, the author may not have had any particular thing in mind, although he writes as if Paul and the Thessalonians had something specific in mind. As described in this text, "the restrainer" is the reality that is holding up the whole show, the reality, as it were, responsible for the delay of the end.

In fact, the principal difficulty provoking this writing could be precisely the delay itself. The end of the world was so late in coming that some in the community are worried now that they missed it, that the day of the Lord has already come and the community slept through it (see 2:2). Second Peter witnesses to the great concern that the delay of the end was causing the Christians at the end of the first century (see 2 Pet 3:3–4).

In this perspective, then, "the restrainer" may simply be the author's dramatic way of referring to the delay itself as planned by God. Something or someone is holding back the events immediately preliminary to the end. And this situation should not be cause for alarm. Events are going as expected. After all, did not Paul and the Thessalonians know all about this?

In this way, the eschatological teaching of 2 Thessalonians begins to make sense. We begin to see that the author, like other apocalyptic authors, is not really predicting specific events. He is not giving us information about the end. Rather, he is giving us an attitude with which to consider the end.

IV. The Message of the Letter

Like most apocalyptic writings of its time, 2 Thessalonians directs us to the end and goal of history. This is the point from which the flow and development of history is supposed to make sense and demonstrate its meaning. History is supposed to progress toward that point.

The progress of history toward that end point, however, is not a simple linear movement. In fact, as is typical of apocalyptic writing, it appears as a double progression of both good and evil. In the line of goodness, we progress in hope. We move closer to the coming of the Lord and our assembling with him (2:1). In the line of evil, we are subject to growing persecution. The "mystery of lawlessness" is already at work (2:1) and has only begun to wreak havoc. The triumph of the Lord comes at a time of mass apostasy.

Thus real historical progress is God's progress and not human progress. It is a mysterious, paradoxical progress, to which we can commit our efforts only through hope, only through acknowledging God (1:8), which means acknowledging God as future in some absolute and unmanageable form. This progress, which is God's, is essentially out of our control.

Yet hope is also for the present. We place our trust in God now. Even in bad times, God is in control. Even raging evil fits into God's plan, as it did at the crucifixion of Jesus.

Conclusion

I. Paradox and Vector Theology in Paul

It all started with a paradox. Why Paul? After Jesus spent years training his twelve apostles, he throws the ball into Paul's lap—a legalist and persecutor of the church. Paul's gospel continues with more paradoxes. Jesus the Jewish Messiah becomes the hero and savior of the Gentiles. And Paul's life ends with the paradox. He is beheaded as a criminal to become perhaps the single most influential figure in Christianity after Jesus.

Paul would chuckle, "See I told you. It all looks like foolishness and weakness, but it is really God's wisdom and strength." He would insist on embracing the paradox, even in our unavoidable attempts to make sense of it, our inevitable attempts at theology.

He gives us an example of embracing the paradoxes. In one extended breath, he describes the destructive anger of God and proclaims God's love for all sinners. The message of salvation is the message of death on the cross. Paul speaks of judgment after death but insists that the dead person is absolved from sin. He insists on belonging to the community of Christians for salvation and declares that all the Jewish people will be saved.

To use a different image, Paul is thinking with theological vectors. Vectors are lines of force on some object, lines of force often distinguished by their conflicting directions. Vector resolution is a way of determining where the object will ultimately move, given the force and direction of the vectors. In the end, the object moves in a direction that is *other than that of any of the applied vectors*. Simple mechanics allow us to see that final direction by simply completing the box or parallelogram started by the first two vectors, whose length represents the magnitude of their force:

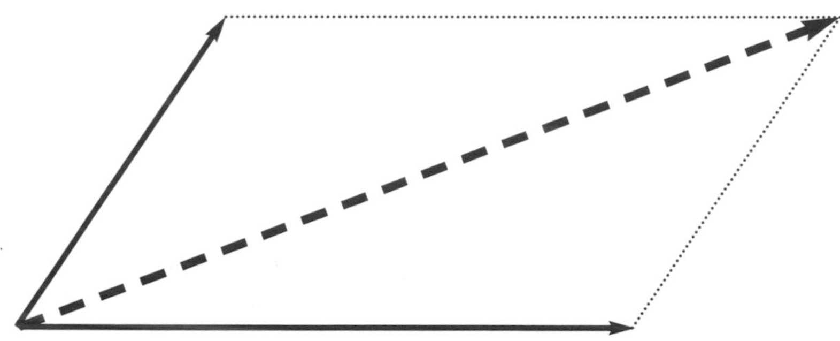

Paul, for instance, insists on human responsibility for a good life and declares it is all God's work. He has given us two theological vectors. If we hang on to both, we will move in a direction that Paul did not explicitly describe. We will be moved toward the mysterious reality that perhaps only God knows. However, if we disregard one of these vectors, we lose the accurate direction toward the mystery.

Along come the "Deutero-Pauls" and the Lucan accounts of Paul that add more vectors to this theology, and our movement toward the mystery shifts. Along come Matthew and James and other writings that seem almost antagonistic to Paul, and the movement shifts again. Paul, however, would not mind. "Oh, the depths of the riches and wisdom and knowledge of God! How inscrutable are his judgments and how unsearchable his ways" (Rom 11:33).

Our faith in inspiration and the biblical canon assures us of a mysterious continuity among the biblical authors. They all aimed at the same divine reality. The task thus arises to search for the continuity—despite the bumps and jolts—between Paul and the author of the Pastorals, between Paul and Luke or Matthew, between Paul and the rest of scripture. The final goal is not the biblical text (or any other text) but the mysterious reality of God.

Later Christian theology will pick up the Pauline themes of God, Christ, and Spirit as well as his views on grace and redemption and develop them into different forms. Sometimes these developments were wrong. Almost always they were diverse and conflicting.

However, diversity and conflict in faith positions are not a problem in good Christian theology, aimed at the reality of God. Diversity is the only way the limited human mind can aim at the infinite. What is crucial is an experience of continuity from one position to the other and with the themes of Paul. Like a crowd of observers very slowly walking around a great cube in our midst, talking to others on the other sides of the cube, we try to see what the cube really is in itself. Now, however, with all the different facets of scripture and theology, the cube is beginning to look like a mirrored disco ball. No angle will allow us to see all the facets, but we know our limits and we sense the continuity as one side slides out of view and another appears, and our heart senses a joy at letting the reality in itself make its claim on us.

Thus, we constantly come back to Paul and the rest of scripture. If we could just comprehend God and his ways, we could forget the vectors in their distinctiveness and diversity. But, of course, we do not have this divinelike theology. On the other hand, descriptive historical theology allows the various voices their diversity and distinctiveness. This descriptive historical approach was the method intended through most of this study.

II. Principles and Expository Theology in Paul

Paradoxically, this intention was not shared by Paul. He was not very tolerant of divergent voices. He insisted on his message as a coherent whole. For all his adaptation to his readers, Paul had something specific and important to say. He intended to talk about God and God's saving love in Christ. In this intention Paul connected with an eternal and universal mystery, as he attempted to communicate with all the diverse people and situations he addressed. This was why he traveled from one place to another. This is why he wrote. This is why he worked with passion.

To give voice to this intention, Paul chose expository writing incorporated into his letters. Like a good Hellenist, Paul provides abstract expositions of the reality that he encountered and that summoned him to take a position. "The mentality of the Spirit is life and peace" (Rom 8:7). "All things were created through him and for him" (Col 1:16). These are statements that seem valid for all times and places. These are statements of principles, whose stability and universality help us understand the sandstorms of life.

Paul chose this form of speaking rather than that of telling a story. Stories and narratives tend to have great power in particular places. That is why we speak of a story as the story of this or that people. In their abstraction, however, principles are intended to have power for all and in some way for all times. In effect, Paul chose abstract theology, not historical descriptive theology.

Paul would be the first to say that he did not do an adequate job of expressing that mystery. Like all of us, he fumbled and stammered, trying to talk about what he did not really understand. Like all of us, Paul ran into the problem of expressing these principles. He needed words and images that have meaning for a particular time and place. Paul had to build his theological castles from the sand of this world. He changed his tone and his thought as he journeyed and his perspective shifted. At one point, he comes close to retracting something he wrote earlier (1 Cor 5:9–11). He drew from whatever concepts he had at his disposal, however material and earthly, however limited and sterile.

However, his intentions were aimed at something beyond the shifting sands of our world with its concepts and images. In this intentionality, Paul breathed new vigor and power into these concepts and images. In this intentionality he inserted a subtle dimension of stability and universality into what otherwise could be stopgap measures. He becomes, in effect, the father of Christian theology.

III. Understanding Paul and His Letters

In our windy and sandy world, of course, this attempt to grasp Paul's intentions is no simple matter. It never was (see 2 Pet 3:15–16). Two extremes can destroy our theological efforts. One extreme is intent on transposing the universal principles of Paul to our day in such an inflexible way that it distorts and destroys the meaning of the images and words Paul used. This extreme neglects the perspective of Paul, refusing to see Paul's statements in their historical contexts. The other extreme is intent on rejoicing in the shifting sands and refusing to seek the principles. Paul's very efforts to express theological principles are often dismissed as Hellenizing distortions in favor of the narrative of the gospels. The eternal and universal reality disappears in the sandstorm that inevitably blows.

Can we work between the two extremes? Can we recognize our own fragile perspectives as well as those in which Paul worked? Can we move from one perspective to the other—perhaps through a long history of shifting perspectives—constantly evaluating the continuity of one perspective with the next as one flows into the other?

The key to such an understanding, I think, is listening to our hearts. In matters of good theology, we recognize the limits of any one perspective and the need to communicate with others. In good theology, we also recognize the experience of continuity as one description seems to flow into another. We also recognize the excitement or passion that comes when contact seems to be made with the intended reality. These recognitions of limits, continuity, and summons are not things we observe. These spontaneous recognitions arise more from the heart with its sense of the real and whole rather than from the analytical intellect.

Through this heartfelt experience of limit, continuity, and summons, we can understand Paul and continue his theological effort. We can rejoice in the fragile character of our words and concepts—we never leave them. Instead of trying to leave these fragile words and concepts, we study how words and concepts of one culture can be translated into another culture and historical context.

Like that of all great thinkers, Paul's thought carried with it the seeds of its own development. The Deutero-Pauls were quick to spot this. Luke, in his interpretation of Paul, jumped on this bandwagon. Paul may have the first word. He does not have the last word. If Paul and the other biblical authors form the "canon" or criterion of later theology, it is not because they have said everything there is to say about God and salvation. It is because they have a privileged perspective and an inspired say. Thus all subsequent theology needs to be in continuity with the biblical authors. The subsequent statements cannot contradict the biblical intentions and must remain in continuity with the intentions of the biblical authors, who intended the same mystery. New perspectives provide new and changing insights, but the mystery of God is universal and eternal.

Appendices

Appendix 1
Stoic and Hellenistic Texts on the Social "Body"

Chrysippus, 280–207 BC, one of the founders of Stoicism

Fragment 367: "Here then we have a single body [*soma*] composed of diverse bodies, like an assembly [*ekklesia*] or an army or a chorus" (cited by Plutarch, *De defectu oraculorum*, 29).

Cicero, 106–40 BC

De finibus bonorum et malorum, 3.19 [62–64]: "[The Stoics hold that] nature brings about that children be loved by their parents. From this beginning we trace the common association of the human race. This is understood by the figure of the body and its members [*figura membrisque corporum*].... It follows that we are made for gatherings, assemblies, and societies [*coetus, concilia, civitates*].

Dionysius of Halicarnassus, 60–6 BC

Roman Antiquities, 6.86.1–5: [Menenius Agrippa:] "A society [*polis*] resembles in some measure a human body [*soma*]. For each of them is composite and is of many parts; and no one of their parts among them either has the same function or performs the same services.

"If, now, these parts of the human body should assume each for itself perception and a voice of its own, and a sedition should then arise among them, all of them uniting against the stomach alone, and should the feet say that the whole body rests on them; the hands, that they work the crafts, secure provisions, fight wars and contribute many other useful things toward the common good [*to koinon*]; the shoulders, that they bear all the burdens; the mouth, that it speaks; the head, that it sees and hears and possesses the other sense by which the thing is preserved; and then they say to the stomach, 'And you, fine thing, which of these things do you do? Of what use are you to us?... Why do we not assert our liberty and free ourselves from the many troubles we undergo for the sake of this thing?' If, I say, they are of such opinion and none of the parts should any longer perform its own work, could the body possibly exist for long and not rather be destroyed within a few days by the worst of all deaths, starvation? No one can say otherwise.

"Now consider the same thing for a society. For this also is composed of many peoples not at all resembling one another, every one of which contributes some particular service to the common good [*to koinon chreios*], just as its member do to the body.... If then all of these different peoples should rise against the senate, which is composed of the best men, and say, 'As for you, senate, what good do you do us, and for what reason do you presume to rule over others?'... If, I say, they should take this resolution and quit their usual employments, what will hinder this miserable society from perishing miserably by famine, war, and every other evil?

"Learn, therefore, plebeians, that, just as in our bodies the stomach thus reviled by the multitude nourishes the body even while it itself is nourished, and preserves it while it itself is preserved, and is a kind of feast, as it were, provided by joint contributions, which as a result of the exchange duly distributes that which is beneficial to each and all, so in cities the senate, which administers the public affairs and provides what is expedient for everyone, preserves, guards, and corrects all things...."

Seneca, 4 BC–AD 65

De clementia, 1. 5. 1: "You [Nero] are the soul [*animus*] of society [*res publica*], which is your body [*corpus*]."

De ira, 2, 36.7: "To harm one's country is wrong; consequently, therefore, likewise, to harm a fellow-citizen—since he is a part of the country, and if the whole is venerable, the parts are sacred—consequently to harm any man [is wrong] for he is your fellow-citizen in the greater city [*maior urbs*]. What if the hands should desire to harm the feet, or the eyes the hand? So that all the members [*membra*] agree among themselves—since it is in the interest of the whole for an individual to be protected—thus mankind spares the individual...."

Epistle 95, 51: "All this which you see, which is comprised of the divine and the human, is one. We are members [*membra*] of a great body [*corpus*]."

Plutarch, AD 46–147

Lives. Solon, 18, 5: "The lawgiver in this way rightly accustomed the citizens, as parts of one body [*hosper henos mere somatos]*, to feel and sympathize with one another."

Greek and Latin texts from Loeb Classical Library; translations mine.

Appendix 2
"Hymn of the Pearl" from the Acts of Thomas

When I was a speechless child, I dwelt in my father's kingdom and constantly enjoyed the wealth and delicacies of those who nurtured me. From the East, our homeland, my parents provisioned and sent me forth. From the wealth of the treasury they gathered for me a load.... They took off the golden clothes that in their love they had tailored for me and the yellow robe woven to my stature. They made an agreement with me, writing it in my mind that I might not forget, saying, "If you go down to Egypt and rescue from there the one pearl that is in the midst of the sea serpent, you will put on your splendid clothes and that robe which goes over it. With your brother, next in rank, you will be herald in our kingdom."

I went from the East and went down with two guides, for the way was dangerous and difficult and I was inexperienced in such travels.... I entered Egypt, and my guides who were journeying along with me left. Rushing to the serpent as fast as I could I stayed near his hole watching for him to become drowsy and fall asleep, that I might seize my pearl. Since I was all alone, I washed my face and appeared a stranger to my companions. However, I saw there one of my race, a noble out of the East, a youth handsome and attractive, a son of the nobles. Coming to me he conversed with me and I made him my companion, my friend and associate in my affairs. I urged him to guard against the Egyptians and against consorting with those unclean ones. But I clothed myself in their garments that I might not be thought of as a stranger from without, come to take the pearl, lest the Egyptians waken the serpent against me. I do not know how, but they learned of my pretense, that I was not of their country. They dealt with me treacherously. I was given to eat of their food. I thus became ignorant that I was a king's son and began to serve their king. I forgot about the pearl for which my parents had sent me.

While all this befell me, my parents observed and were grieved for me.... They wrote to me, and the nobles stamped their seal thereto, "From your father, the king of kings, and your mother, the keeper of the East, and from your brother, our other son, to our son in Egypt, peace! Rise up and awaken from your sleep and listen to the words of our letter. Remember that you are a son of kings. See the yoke of slavery that you are subject to! Remember the pearl for which you were sent into Egypt. Remember your splendid clothes. Your name is read in the book of life along with that of your brother who waits in succession."

Because I sensed it, I awoke from my sleep. Picking it up and kissing it, I read it. In my heart was written the words that had been recorded. I suddenly remembered that I was a son of kings, and my noble birth began stirring. I remembered the pearl for which I was sent to Egypt. I came as on a war chariot to the dreadful serpent. I overcame him reciting the name of my father. Then I snatched away the pearl and turned about to my father's house. Taking off the filthy garment, I left it in their land. I directed my way to the light of the East, my homeland. I found my awakener on the way. Just as it had awakened me from sleep with its proclaiming voice, so it led me with its light. For then before my eyes were the royal clothes of silk. Leading me and drawing me forward with its love, it passed by Babyrinthos....

Indeed I had not remembered its glory, for as a child and still quite young I had left it in my father's palace. Suddenly as I saw the garment as in a mirror, it became like me. I saw myself wholly in it, knowing and seeing myself through it. In part we were divided from each other, yet again one in single form....Again I saw that all over it the motions of knowledge were stirring. It was ready to utter a word. Its royal movements rested on me with such a growing force. It strove from his [?] hand, stretched out that I might take it. My desire also spurred me to run to meet it and receive it. I stretched out and was carried off by the colors. I drew completely over myself my excellent royal robe. I clothed myself and mounted up to the place of peace and worship. Bowing my head I worshiped the splendor of the father who had sent the robes to me, for I had accomplished his orders, and he also had done what he promised. At the gate of the royal one, who is from the beginning, I mingled. For he rejoiced over me and received me with him in his kingdom. All his servants praised him with favorable voices. He promised to send me with him to the gate of the king that I could appear with him before the king with my gift and my pearl.

My translation from the Greek text in Acta Apostolorum Apocrypha, *ed. M. Bonnet (Hildesheim, Germany: Georg Olms, 1959), II, 219–24.*

Appendix 3
Jewish Sources

I. Pseudoepigrapha

These books are Jewish writings of the "intertestamental" period, never making it into any of the major Jewish or Christian canons, with the exception of *1 Enoch*, which the Coptic Church considers a canonical part of the Old Testament. Like many of the canonical books, the authors ascribed their works to well-known characters of the Bible, identifying themselves with pseudonyms. Hence, the name "pseudoepigrapha." Perhaps the best collection in English translation is James H. Charlesworth, ed., *The Old Testament Pseudepigrapha*, 2 vols., Anchor Bible Reference Library (London: Doubleday, 1983 and 1985).

- *1 Enoch* is attributed to the seventh descendant of Adam and Eve and father of Methuselah (Gen 5:18–24). The book describes the heavenly journeys and visions of the patriarch in an elaboration of the Genesis description of his death: "He was no longer here for God took him" (5:24). It is also known as *Ethiopic Enoch*, from the language of the principal extent manuscripts. It was written most likely in Hebrew or Aramaic or a combination of both, originating in Judea over a span of about one hundred years, from about 200 to 100 BC. One of the last sections to be added, chapters 37–71, called "the Similitudes," is of particular interest to us with its description of "the Son of man" or "the Elect One."
- *2 Enoch*, also known as *Slavonic Enoch*, appears to be written in the late first century BC by a Hellenized Jew perhaps in Alexandria. It is a midrash on the life and heavenly jour-

neys of Enoch continuing then up to the Flood (Gen 5:21–32). Two principal but often divergent Old Slavonic manuscripts give us the text of this work. Manuscript A is the shorter; manuscript J, the longer. Therefore, references have to indicate which of the two is being cited.

- *2 Baruch* is attributed to the secretary of Jeremiah writing at the time of the Babylonian destruction of Jerusalem in 587 BC. In this book, Baruch addresses the people after the city is destroyed and predicts events as the end of time approaches. It actually appears to have been written around the end of the first century AD in Palestine. Originally written probably in Hebrew, our present Syriac texts are clearly translations from an earlier Greek. It is now called "second" to distinguish it from the biblical Book of Baruch.
- *4 Ezra* is attributed to the fifth-century priest, scribe, and leader of the Jewish people after their return from exile in Babylon, whom we know from the two biblical books of Ezra and Nehemiah. In this book, Ezra describes a series of visions about eschatological times. The book is called "fourth" to correlate it in a complicated relationship with the two biblical books, known in the Latin Bible as 1 Esdras and 2 Esdras, along with a book called *3 Esdras* that included material from the two biblical books, from 2 Chronicles as well as some nonbiblical material. Although written probably in Greek, *4 Ezra* exists today only in Latin manuscripts. It appears to stem from around AD 100.
- *4 Maccabees* is a philosophical discourse with reflections on the events of the Maccabean revolt of the early second century BC as described in the deuterocanonical books of 1 and 2 Maccabees. In some manuscripts of the Greek Bible it is placed after a book called *3 Maccabees*, an imaginative historical sketch of the persecutions under Ptolemy IV. Scholars date this book anywhere from the middle of the first century BC to the middle of the first century AD. The major manuscripts of the Greek Bible (LXX) all include this work, which most likely was written in Greek.

- *Apocalypse of Abraham* is an imaginative retelling by the patriarch of his story up to his leaving his father's house in Mesopotamia as briefly recounted in Genesis 12:1–3. The book then transitions to a series of visions seen by Abraham about the end times. We have this book only in Old Slavonic translation. Some evidence suggests it was originally written in Hebrew around the end of the first century AD.
- *Letter of Aristeas* purports to describe how the Septuagint (LXX) was written under the auspices of the Egyptian king, Ptolemy II. Written probably in Alexandria, Egypt, anywhere from 250 BC to AD 100 in Greek, this document exists today in several Greek manuscripts.
- *Joseph and Aseneth* is a midrash on Genesis 41:45 describing Joseph's marriage to Aseneth, the daughter of Potiphera, the priest of the Egyptian god, On. Most of the story imagines a way in which Aseneth converts from her Egyptian religion and becomes a devout Jew. The book exists today in several Greek manuscripts, probably its original language of composition. It was probably written in Egypt in the early second century AD.
- *Jubilees* is a midrashic retelling of Genesis and Exodus stories. It is presented as an extended revelation of God and God's angel to Moses. Our present text is based mainly on four Ethiopic manuscripts, with some help from a Latin manuscript and some Greek fragments. Scholars agree that the book was originally composed in Hebrew as early as the late second century BC in Palestine.
- *The Martyrdom and Ascension of Isaiah* tells in legendary form the story of the death of Isaiah, roughly chapters 1–5. This is followed by a Christian addition recounting a series of visions experienced by the eighth-century BC prophet, roughly chapters 6–11. The early legendary account appears to be not later than the first century AD. The visions appear to be from a century later. The older Jewish part of the book was composed in Hebrew, which was then translated into Greek, and then Greek into Ethiopic, the only language in which the entire book can be found.

- *Psalms of Solomon* is a collection of eighteen psalms by devout Jews in response to the oppressive annexation of Jerusalem by the Romans in 63 BC. Solomon's name is attached to the collection probably because of the influence of the biblical Psalm 72, a "psalm of Solomon," on this collection. We have these psalms from several Greek and Syriac manuscripts. They appear to have been written originally in Hebrew probably before AD 70.
- *Testament of Abraham* is part of the *Testament of the Three Patriarchs*, written by a Greek-speaking Jew of the first century AD. The *Testament of Abraham* deals with the events just preceding the death of the patriarch. It is mostly in the form of a dialogue between Abraham and Michael the archangel about life after death. Our present reconstruction of the text is based mostly on Greek manuscripts with some help from Romanian, Slavonic, Coptic, Arabic, and Ethiopic manuscripts. Attempts to bring these manuscripts together results in two forms of the story, a longer one (A) and a shorter one (B). Chapter and verse references have to note therefore which form they pertain to.
- *Testament of Moses* is a farewell address by Moses to Joshua in the form of a prediction of what is to come for Israel, from the conquest of the land to the return from the Babylonian Exile. Moses then warns about general apostasy under the Hasmoneans. The book then transitions into a description of the cosmic catastrophes at the end of the world. Our only copy of this story is a Latin manuscript. This Latin is clearly a translation from Greek, probably the original language of the document. The story most likely was written in the first century AD before the fall of Jerusalem in AD 70.
- The *Testament of Levi* and the *Testament of Naphtali* are parts of the *Testament of the Twelve Patriarchs*, which purports to be the final words of the twelve sons of Jacob. Each testament is modeled on the biblical story of Jacob's own final words in Genesis 49. Our text is based mostly on Greek manuscripts, and the work appears to be composed originally in Greek, following the Septuagint style

with its Semitic idioms. In the course of the manuscript transmission, many Christian interpolations, additions made by Christian copyists, have been identified. Apart from these interpolations, however, the book seems to have been written in the early second century BC, probably in Syria.

II. Essene Writings

In 1947, large jars containing ancient scrolls and fragments were discovered in caves overlooking the Dead Sea. The writings were identified as produced by a Jewish monastic separatist group who lived in a community now identified as Khirbet Qumran. They seemed to be affiliated with the Essenes that Josephus described in his writings. The community settlement by the Dead Sea (the Salt Sea) was destroyed by the Romans around the year AD 70. The jars and caves appear to have been the secret repositories of the sectarians desperate to preserve their theological treasures, many of which were already a hundred years old before their burial.

For scientific purposes, the scrolls were identified first by a number to indicate the cave in which they were found, by the letter Q to indicate Qumran, and then by a letter or word to distinguish the scroll from others found in the same cave. One exception to this method of identification is the *Damascus Document* (*CD*), two copies of which had been found in 1897 in a Cairo synagogue. Numbers are then used to indicate the column on the scroll and the line(s) in the column to reference specific statements or words.

For an English translation, see *The Dead Sea Scriptures*, trans. T. H. Gaster (Garden City, NY: Anchor Books, 1964).

- *CD* are the letters for the *Damascus Document*, also known as the *Zadokite Document*. It describes an Essene community that called itself "the New Covenant in the Land of Damascus." Two incomplete copies of this document were found in a storeroom of an old Cairo synagogue. Fragments of the same document were discovered in caves

4 and 6 at Qumran.

- *1 QS* is the scroll discovered in cave 1 of Qumran that describes the rule (*serek*) of life of the community. It is known also by the names *The Rule of the Community* and *The Manual of Discipline*. It may be the oldest of the documents at Qumran, dating perhaps from the later part of the second century BC.
- 1 *QSa* is a fragment that appears to belong to the end of *1 QS*, although it is different in its content.
- *1 QM* is known as *The War Scroll* (*milchama*) and depicts realistic battle plans against the forces of evil, that is, the Roman army, cryptically called the "Kittim." The author seems to have been inspired by the apocalyptic war scenes in Daniel 11. It was probably written around the turn of the era.
- *1 QH* is a booklet of twenty-five hymns of thanksgiving (*hodayoth*).
- *1 Q Genesis Apocryphon* consists of midrashic accounts in Aramaic of patriarch stories based on Genesis. The book starts with the birth of Noah, whose father thinks the angels of Genesis 6 were involved. The story then skips to a midrash about Abraham's journey to Egypt and subsequent return to Canaan as told in Genesis 12—15.
- *11 Q Melchizedek* is a fragment with barely two columns. It describes the role of Melchizedek in the year of Jubilees and its liberation. This document is also listed as 11 Q13.

III. Philo

Philo of Alexandria lived from 20 BC to AD 50. He was a devout Jew who wanted to show the congruence of his faith with Greek philosophy. Historians remember especially his efforts to defend the Jewish people of Alexandria against Roman persecution, even to the point of leading a delegation to Rome to speak to the emperor Gaius Caligula—to no avail. His many writings include commentaries on scripture, philosophical treatises, and works defending Judaism.

The works of Philo are translated into English sometimes with different titles. The earlier Latin titles help with identification. The Greek with an English translation of thirty-seven works of Philo can be found in the Loeb Classical Library series, *Philo*, trans. F. H. Colson and G. H. Whitaker, 12 vols. (Cambridge, MA: Harvard University Press, 1949–79). (An earlier, weaker translation is now online at http://www.earlyjewishwritings.com/philo.html, which publishes the classic study, *The Works of Philo Judaeus, the Contemporary of Josephus*, translated from the Greek by C. D. Yonge [London: H. G. Bohn, 1854–90].) His works include:

- *Questions and Answers on Genesis*, books I–III, in Latin, *Quæstiones et solutiones in Genesin*, consists of a series of questions verse by verse of Genesis.
- *Allegorical Interpretation*, books I–III, known in Latin as *De legum allegoriae*, may be the best source of Philo's ideas. It is a philosophical commentary on the Pentateuch.
- *On the Confusion of Tongues*, in Latin, *De confusione linguarum*, is a philosophical treatise on life, using Genesis 11:1–9 as springboard.
- *On the Special Laws*, books I–IV, in Latin, *De specialibus legibus*, is a philosophical treatise on morality in connection with the various prescriptions of the Pentateuch.
- *On the Creation*, in Latin, *De opificio mundi*, consists of spiritual and theological reflections on Genesis 1—3.

IV. Josephus

Josephus Flavius lived from AD 37 to 101. He was a strong pro-Roman Jewish historian determined to show the loyalty of his people to the emperor, despite the war of AD 67–70 when the Romans put down a rebellion and destroyed the Temple in Jerusalem. His two major works give us precious information about the Jews at this critical time. For an English translation, see *The Works of Flavius Josephus*, trans. by William Whiston (Grand Rapids, MI: Baker Book House, 1974).

- *Jewish War*, books I–VII, describes his memories of the Jewish-Roman war. It spans the time from AD 66 to 73.
- *Jewish Antiquities*, books I–XX, is meant to span the entire history of the Jews from creation to the outbreak of the Jewish–Roman war.

V. Rabbinic Writings

After the destruction of the Temple in AD 70, the lawyers or rabbis formed the nucleus for the reconstruction of the Jewish people, now without king or Temple. Their focus was on the law and moral precepts, eventually to the total exclusion of apocalyptic speculation. Successive rabbinic periods are named as Tannaic (AD 70–200), Amoraic (AD 200–c. 500), Savoraic (c. AD 500–700), Genoic (AD 600–1000), and Reshonic (AD 1000–1400). The importance of the later periods for this study lies in the way the writers conserved much earlier material, some of which could testify to the Judaic culture of Paul.

- *Shemoneh 'esreh*, or "Eighteen [Benedictions],"also known as the *Amidah*, is the central prayer of the synagogue. It is one of the oldest parts of the service, dating back to the first century AD. It consists of actually nineteen prayers in a row. It is said that Rabbi Gamaliel II introduced the twelfth prayer, a curse on the heretics, sometime after AD 80, without changing the name of the collection. For the English and Hebrew, see *Shemoneh Esrei: the Amidah: the Eighteen Blessings: Inspirational Expositions and Interpretations of the Weekday Shemoneh Esrei*, ed. Avrohom Chaim Feuer (Brooklyn, NY: Mesorah Publications, 1990).
- *Sifra on Leviticus* is part of a halakic (or ethical) midrash-type commentary on Leviticus. It incorporates the tradition of Rabbi Aqiba from the late first century, with additions from the school of Rabbi Yishmael from the early second century, one of the compilers of the Mishnah. For an English translation, see *Sifra*, ed. Jacob Neusner (Atlanta, GA: Scholars Press, 1997).

- *Mekilta Beshallach.* The *Mekilta* is an ancient halakic midrash on Exodus, probably written around the second century AD or the Tannaitic period (AD 70–200) of rabbinic tradition. The *Mekilta* is divided into 9 *massektot* or "treatises," the second of which is *Massekta de-Vayehi Beshallach,* or simply *Beshallach.* It covers Exodus 13:17—14:31 and consists of an introduction and six sections. For an English translation, see *Mekilta de-Rabbi Ishmael,* ed. and trans. by Jacob Z. Lauterbach (Philadelphia: Jewish Publication Society of America, 1976).
- *Targum Onkolos* was the official translation of the Pentateuch into Aramaic. No one knows for sure who made this translation, which is named after a first-century Jew. References to it from other sources, however, suggest a major part of it could be from as early as the first or second century AD. The translation often incorporates new interpretative details or digressions in the form of short midrashim on the biblical stories. For the Aramaic, see *Targum Onkelos,* 2 vols., ed. A. Berliner (Berlin: Gorzelanczyk, 1884).
- *The Mishnah* was edited around AD 200 by Yehudah ha-Nasi "Judah the Prince" as the first written recording of the Jewish oral law. It incorporates the teachings of the Pharisees as debated in the period AD 70–200 by the group of rabbinic sages known as the Tannaim. The Mishnah consists of six orders, each containing seven to twelve tractates, each divided into verses. The orders include: *Zeraim* ("Seeds"), dealing with agricultural laws and prayers; *Moed* ("Festival"), dealing with the Sabbath and the Festivals; *Nashim* ("Women"), dealing with marriage and divorce; *Nezikin* ("Damages"), dealing with civil and criminal law; *Kodashim* ("Holy things"), dealing with sacrificial rites and dietary laws; and *Tohorot* ("Purities"), dealing with purity and impurity. *Mishnah Sotah* is a tractate in the order *Nashim. Mishnah Yoma* and *Mishna Pesahim* are tractates in the order *Moed.* For an English translation, see *The Mishnah: a New Translation,* trans. Jacob Neusner (New Haven: Yale University Press, 1988).

- *Babylonian Talmud* was edited around AD 500 and is a discussion of the *Mishnah* and other related topics. It is sometimes referred to as the *Gemara*. However, in the technical sense as the written record of the early rabbinic discussions of the Jewish law, the *Talmud* is the combination of both the *Mishnah* and the *Gemara*. It is often designated as the *Babylonian Talmud* to distinguish it from a much smaller but later *Jerusalem Talmud*. The organization of the Talmud follows that of the *Mishnah* into six orders, then into tractates and verses. *Babylonian Talmud Hagigah* and *Yoma* are tractates in the order Moed. *Babylonian Talmud, Zebachim* is a tractate in the order *Kodashim*. For an English translation see *Hebrew-English Edition of the Babylonian Talmud,* 3 vols., trans. by Maurice Simon (London : Soncino, 1960ff.).
- *Midrash Rabbah* is a large collection of ten commentaries on the Pentateuch and the Megilloth. They include *Midrash Rabbah on Exodus* from the eleventh and twelfth centuries AD, known also from the Hebrew names of the biblical book as *Shemoth Rabba;* the *Midrash Rabbah on Leviticus* from the middle of the seventh century AD, known also as *Wayyiqra Rabba;* and the *Midrash Rabbah on Numbers,* from the twelfth century AD, known also as *Bamidbar Rabba*. For an English translation, see *Midrash Rabbah,* 4 vols., trans. and ed. by H. Freedman and Maurice Simon (London: Soncino, 1977).

Appendix 4

Verbatim Similarities in a Comparison of Ephesians and Colossians

Ephesians	*Colossians*
[1:1] Paul an apostle of Christ Jesus through the will of God to the holy ones who are... and faithful ones in Christ Jesus	[1:1] Paul an apostle of Christ Jesus through the will of God and Timothy the brother [2] to the holy ones in Colossae and to the faithful brothers in Christ.
[2] Grace to you and peace from God our Father and the Lord Jesus Christ	Grace to you and peace from God our Father.
[3] Blessed be the God and Father of our Lord Jesus Christ...	[3] We thank the God, the Father of our Lord Jesus Christ...
[15] Therefore, I also, hearing of your faith in the Lord Jesus and of your love to all the holy ones...	[4]...hearing of your faith in Christ Jesus and of the love which you have to all the holy ones
[2:5] And you being dead to transgressions were brought to life to Christ Jesus...	[2:13] And you being, dead to transgressions and to the foreskin of your flesh, were brought to life with him...
[3:7]...the gospel, of which I became a minister according to the gift of the grace of God given to me...	[1:25]...the church, of which I became a minister according to the dispensation of God given to me for you to fulfill
[4] the mystery of Christ which was not made known to other generations of the sons of men as now revealed to his holy apostles and prophets...	[26] the mystery hidden from ages and from generations, now however manifested to his holy ones.
[4:2]...with all humility and	[3:12]...humility,

meekness, with patience, bearing with one another with love,	meekness, patience, [13] bearing with one another and
[32] forgiving one another, just as God in Christ forgave you.	forgiving one another,… just as the Lord forgave you.
[5:5] No fornicator or unclean or or lustful person, which is an idolater can have inheritance…	[3:5] Put to death…fornication, uncleanness, passion… that lust which is idolatry,
[6] For through such comes the anger of God on the sons of disobedience	[6] Through which comes the anger of God on the sons of disobedience
[15] Walk, not as unwise but as wise	[4:5] In wisdom walk with outsiders,
[16] redeeming the time	redeeming the time
[19] speaking to one another in psalms and hymns and spiritual songs praising and singing psalms in your heart to the Lord,	[3:16] admonishing one another with psalms, hymns, spiritual songs in grace praising in your hearts the Lord.
[20] giving thanks always for all things in the name of our Lord Jesus Christ to the God and Father.	[17] And all that you do in word or work, do all in the name of the Lord Jesus, giving thanks to God the Father through him.
[6:21] In order that you might know news about me, what I am doing, Tychikos, the beloved brother and faithful minister in the Lord, will make all known to you. I sent him to you for this purpose that he might make known to you matters concerning me and comfort your hearts.	[4:7] All the news about me Tychikos, the beloved brother and faithful minister and co-slave in the Lord, will make known to you. I sent him to you for this purpose that he might make known to you matters concerning me and comfort your hearts.

Appendix 5
Verbatim Similarities in a Comparison of 1 and 2 Thessalonians

The opening lines of the two letters are almost exactly the same:

2 Thessalonians	*1 Thessalonians*
[1:1–2] Paul and Silvanus and Timothy to the church of the Thessalonians in God our Father and the Lord Jesus Christ. Grace to you and peace...	[1:1] Paul and Silvanus and Timothy to the church of the Thessalonians in God the Father and the Lord Jesus Christ. Grace to you and peace.

The letter prayer in 2 Thessalonians also contains a number of expressions common to 1 Thessalonians:

2 Thessalonians	*1 Thessalonians*
[1:3] We ought to thank God always for you, brothers...because your faith flourishes...and love multiplies...all for each other.	[1:2] We thank God always for all of you remembering...your faith and...love... [3:12] May the Lord multiply and cause to abound the love you have for each other and for all.
[1:5] for you to be worthy of... the kingdom of God	[2:12] God who calls you into his kingdom
[1:7] the revelation of the Lord Jesus from heaven with the angels of his power	[3:13] at the coming of our Lord Jesus with
[1:10] to be glorified among his holy ones.	all his holy ones.
[1:11] we pray always for you	[1:2–3] We thank God always

that God fulfill…a work of faith	for all of you …calling to mind your work of faith

The next batch of common expressions occurs in the words of encouragement (2:13–17) that follow immediately after the eschatological instructions:

2 Thessalonians	*1 Thessalonians*
[2:13] We ought to thank God always for you…because God chose you…in sanctification of the Spirit	[1:2] We thank God always for you all [4:7] God calls us…in sanctification
[2:14] the firstfruits for salvation…to acquire the glory of our Lord Jesus Christ	[5:9] to acquire salvation through our Lord Jesus Christ
[2:16] May now our Lord himself, Jesus Christ and God our Father…	[3:11] May now God himself, our Father, and our Lord Jesus direct our way…
[2:17] comfort and strengthen your hearts	[3:2] We sent Timothy…to strengthen and comfort you [3:13] May the Lord…strengthen your hearts

The last chapter abounds with these common expressions:

2 Thessalonians	*1 Thessalonians*
[3:1] For the rest, brothers,	[4:1] For the rest, therefore, brothers,…
pray for us	[5:25] brothers, pray for us…
[3:5] May the Lord direct your hearts…	[3:11] May the Lord Jesus direct our way to you…
[3:6] brothers…shun any brother behaving unruly	[5:14] brothers, admonish the unruly…
[3:8] In labor and hard word, night and day, working in order not to be a burden to any of you	[2:9] our labor and hard work, night and day, working in order not to be a burden to any of you
[3:10] and for when we were among you we announced to you	[3:4] and for when we were among you we foretold to you
[3:12] We order and urge such people in the Lord Jesus Christ	[4:1] We ask and urge you in the Lord Jesus

so that working with tranquility…	[4:11] to be tranquil…working with your own hands
[3:16] May, however, the Lord of peace, himself,	[5:23] May, however, the God of peace, himself,…
[3:18] The grace of our lord Jesus Christ be with you all.	[5:28] The grace of our Lord Jesus Christ be with you.

Notes

Introduction

1. See William K. Wimsatt Jr. and Monroe C. Beardsley, "The Intentional Fallacy," in *The Verbal Icon*, ed. W. Wimsatt (Lexington: University of Kentucky, 1954), 3-18; [*The Bible and Culture Collective,*] *The Post Modern Bible* (New Haven, CT: Yale University, 1997).

2. The modern technical word *eschatology* is built on the Greek word *eschaton*, "the last (thing)."

3 Second Vatican Council, *Dei Verbum*, n. 12.

Chapter 1

1. At the turn of the twentieth century, the German scholar G. A. Deissmann made the distinction between a letter and an epistle in his *Light from the Ancient East. The New Testament Illustrated by Recently Discovered Texts of the Graeco-Roman World*, trans. L. R. M. Strachan (Grand Rapids, MI: Baker Book House, 1965; orig. German: 1909), 227–45. Scholars today question any rigid use of this categorization, yet the classification of Deissmann remains useful.

2. *Les Papyrus grecs du Musée du Louvre*, 43, in A. S. Hunt and C. C. Edgar, *Select Papyri*, Loeb Classical Library (Cambridge, MA: Harvard University Press, 1932), 1:286–87.

3. *Greek Papyri in the British Museum*, 42, in Hunt and Edgar, 1:282–85. These two rather funny letters (see note 2) were pointed out by C. K. Barrett, *The New Testament Background* (London: SPCK, 1958).

Chapter 2

1. First Maccabees 15:21 tells of such extradition rights for the Jewish leader in Jerusalem around 140 BC. However, after the Romans deposed Archelaus in Jerusalem in favor of direct rule by Roman prefects, the authority of the Sanhedrin in Jerusalem was restricted to Judea.

2. Compare Acts 9:3–7 with Revelation 1:10–19, Ezekiel 1:26–2:3, or *1 Enoch* 14:8—15:2.

3 A postbiblical tradition identifies the author of the third Gospel and the Acts of the Apostles as "Luke the physician" and companion of Paul mentioned in Colossians 4:14; see 2 Timothy 4:11. The "we" passages in Acts (16:10–16; 20:6–16; 21:1–18; 27:1—28:16) are better explained in terms of incorporation of a travelogue or journal into Acts.

4. For a study of this Roman law, see D. Ernst Haenchen, *Die Apostelgeschichte* (Göttingen: Vandenhoeck & Ruprechte, 1968), p. 647, especially note 2.

5. See *De viris illustribus*, 5.

6. *I Clement* 5:5—6:1.

7. *History*, II, 22.

Chapter 3

1. Perhaps the best examples of Greek expository writing are the studies of Aristotle, who wrote about everything from animal natures to human virtues. Plato's dialogues are in the form of narratives where the characters present abstract expositions. We no longer have the purely expository writings of Plato, referred to by others as his "esoteric" writings because they were for the inside (*eso*) group of his students.

2. See *Republic*, VII, 514–17.

3. See *Phaedo*, 93–94.

4. See Chrysippus in Plutarch, *De Stoicorum Repugnantiis*, 47; Origen, *Contra Celsum*, V, 14; Diogenes Laertius, *Lives of the Philosophers*, VII, 68 and 74.

5. *Epistle 95*, 51.

6. Chrysippus, fragment 310, 414, 440, 479. The texts of Chrysippus are all from von Arnim's collection (Leipzig: B. G. Teubneri, 1903–24), vol. II.

7. Chrysippus, fragment 443.

8. See Epictetus, *Dissertationes*. IV, 1; Dio Chrysostomos, *Orationes*, 14, 1.

9. Fragment 367, cited by Plutarch, *De defectu oraculorum*, 29.

10. *De ira*, 2, 31, 7.

11. *Lives*: *Solon*, 18, 5.

12. *De ira*, 2, 36, 7; see also Cicero, *De finibus*, 3.19 [62–64].

13. *De clementia*, 1. 5. 1

14. *Roman Antiquities*, 6.86.1–5. This text was brought to my attention in the study of Michelle Lee, *Paul, the Stoics, and the Body of Christ* (New York: Cambridge University Press, 2006).

15. *Discourses*, III, 2. English text from *Epictetus: Discourses and Enchiridion*, trans. T W. Higginson (Roslyn, NY: Walter J. Black, 1944).

16. *Discourses*, I, 8.

17. *Discourses*, I, 12.

18. The gist of the Isis and Osiris cult is given to us especially by L. Apuleius in his *Metamorphoses*, XI. See also Plutarch, *Isis and Osiris*, 12–19.

19. Our knowledge of the Eleusis cults is from many fragments. See the study of W. Dittenberger, *Sylloge Inscriptionum Graecarum*, 3rd ed. (Leipzig: S. Hirzelium, 1915).

20. We know about Gnosticism mostly from the Christian writers who wrote against it, for example, Irenaeus, *Adversus haereses*, I and II. The largely pagan Gnostic work, *Corpus Hermeticum*, from probably the second century AD, and the later Christian Gnostic documents of Nag Hammadi, Egypt, are some of the few original sources for our knowledge of this movement.

21. See E. Hennecke and W. Schneemelcher, eds., *The New Testament Apocrypha*, trans. R. McL. Wilson, 2 vols. (Philadelphia: Westminster, 1963), vol. 2, 425–531, especially 498–504.

22. The term "the Writings" (*ha-Katubim)* refers to the third major part of the Hebrew Bible, which together with "the Law" (*ha-Torah*) and "the Prophets" (*ha-Nabi'im*) form the Bible (*ha-Tanak*) for Jews today.

23. See Josephus, *Jewish Antiquities*, XIII, 297–98; *Jewish War*, II, 162–66.

24. A common understanding of the name *Pharisee* is that it derives from the Hebrew *parush*, which means "separated." This understanding is disputed by scholars, but see the later rabbinic commentary on Leviticus 11:44–45 where the original word *qadosh* (holy) is replaced by *parush* (*Sifra on Leviticus [ad locum]*).

25. For an English translation, see *The Dead Sea Scriptures*, trans. T. H. Gaster (Garden City, NY: Anchor Books, 1964).

26. See *Midrash Rabbah on Exodus*, 15, 1–6; Philo, *Allegory of the Law*, III, 162–68; *The Confusion of Tongues*, 253–63. A similar technique is found among the Essenes: see *CD* 4–7, 11, along with the many scripture commentaries found at Qumran.

27. The name and the abbreviation came from the contemporary Jewish story describing seventy-two scholars working for seventy-two days to make this translation. See *The Letter of Aristeas*, 38–40, 301–8.

28. Most of these texts are available in English in the collection edited by James H. Charlesworth, ed., *The Old Testament Pseudepigrapha*, 2 vols., The Anchor Bible Reference Library (London: Doubleday, 1983 and 1985). Charlesworth includes sixty-three "books" in his edition, which does not include the Dead Sea Scrolls. My citations of this literature will be taken from this edition.

Chapter 4

1. I want to use the word *heuristic* to describe the basic structure of all discovery. The term comes from the Greek verb, *heuriskein*, to discover, as in "Eureka!" Every discovery presupposes some knowledge of what will eventually be discovered. We cannot simply go out and find "it." The discoverer has to know what to look for even without having seen it. Hence, our need to study these six Jewish faith themes. For this chapter I am deeply indebted to the classic study of W. D. Davies, *Paul and Rabbinic Judaism* (London: SPCK, 1965).

2. Thus the modern mistake of seeing the name of God as "Yahowah," which then through the complications of German spelling and pronunciation becomes "Jahovah."

3. For example, W. Bousset, *Die Religion des Judentums in späthellenistischen Zeitalter*, 3rd ed. (Tübingen: Mohr, 1926).

4. See E. P. Sanders, *Paul and Palestinian Judaism* (Philadelphia: Fortress Press, 1985), especially pp. 55–56. L. Hurtado, *One God, One Lord: Early Christian Devotion and Ancient Jewish Monotheism, 2nd ed.* (Edinburgh: T & T Clark, 1998), especially pp. 17–39.

5. See *Shemoneh 'esreh*, petitions 5 & 6. See Appendix 3 for a fuller description of the Jewish sources used in this chapter.

6. I prefer to translate *dikaiosynê* as "justice" in order to maintain the linguistic connection with the verb *dikaioô*, which is translated almost always as "to justify."

7. For an interesting study of Old Testament texts and methods used to understand Jesus in these texts, see Eugen Pentiuc, *Jesus the Messiah in the Hebrew Bible* (Mahwah, NJ: Paulist Press, 2006).

8. On this topic see especially Larry Hurtado, *One God, One Lord: Early Christian Devotion and Ancient Jewish Monotheism, 2nd ed.* (Edinburgh: T&T Clark, 1998).

9. Scholarship confirms that the book of Isaiah is a progressive work, the product of at least three major authors: the eighth-century prophet Isaiah, responsible more or less for chapters 1–39; an anonymous prophet in exile during the Babylonian Captivity, responsible for chapters 40–55; and an anonymous postexilic prophet, responsible for chapters 56–66.

10. *Questions and Answers on Genesis*, II, 62; see also *Allegorical Interpretation* II, 86.

11. *Questions and Answers on Genesis*, IV.110–11.

12. *On the Confusion of Tongues*, 146

13. *Testament of Abraham* A.1:4—2:12; see also *2 Enoch* J 22:6; 33:10; 71:28; 72:5.

14. *Apocalypse of Abraham*, 10:1—11:6. The name of the angel, also written "Yahoel," is apparently a combination of Yahweh and 'El, meaning "Yahweh is God."

15. *1 QM* 17:6–8.

16. *11 Q Melchizedek* 2:4–25. For this identification of Michael and Melchizedek see Kobelski, *Melchizedek and Melchisesha'*, (Catholic Biblical Quarterly—Monograph Series, 10; Washington, DC: Catholic Biblical Association, 1981).

17. For this identification, which is not explicit in the text, see C. Burchard, in Charlesworth, *ad loc.*, II, 225.

18. Scholars debate whether the Son of man in these texts is eventually identified with Enoch himself. In *1 Enoch* 71:14, Enoch is declared a righteous "son of man." However, the Ethiopic uses different vocabulary for Enoch than it does for the exalted Son of man. See the notes at this verse in Charlesworth.

19. In both its Greek form, *christos*, and in its Hebrew form, *mashiach*, the title simply means "anointed one." They derive respectively from the Greek verb *chriein* and the Hebrew verb *mashach*, both of which mean to anoint or smear with an oily liquid.

20. The description of the high priest as anointed (Exod 29:7; Lev 21:10) may well be an anachronism based on the post-exilic high priests assuming royal or governing functions.

21. In biblical Hebrew the expression "son of..." (*ben*) was a way of describing someone, an alternative to using an adjective. Thus a "son of Israel" is an Israelite, or a "son of iniquity" is an evil person, much like a "throne of glory" is a glorious throne and the "holy of holies" is the most holy place.

22. Among the Essenes we find a teaching about two messiahs, one priestly and the other apparently royal: 1 *QS* 9:11 "until there shall come the prophet and the messiahs of Aaron and Israel"; *CD* 12:23 "until the coming of the anointed of Aaron and Israel" (also 14:19). We also find a description of "an anointed one" who summons the congregation at some future assembly and dinner. He is "head of the whole congregation," seated before all "the chiefs of the clans of Israel, the heads of families, the wise." He waits for the priest to bless the food, then he blesses the bread (1 *QSa* 2:11ff.).

23. The late Jewish book, the Wisdom of Solomon, connects the images of divine wisdom and spirit. Wisdom is called a "philanthropic spirit" (1:6). The author prays for prudence and is given

a "spirit of wisdom" (7:7), and "in her [wisdom] is an intelligent, holy...spirit" (7:22).

24. Capitalization is strictly a decision of the translator. Hebrew has never had a distinction of upper- and lowercase letter. The ancient Greek script was all in uppercase. The lowercase script in Greek was introduced in the Middle Ages and gradually the capitalization of certain words or names took place.

25. See the *Targum Onkelos* at Genesis 41:38; Exodus 35:31; Numbers 11:25, 29; 24:2, and so on. For a discussion of this topic and for many other rabbinic references, see H. L. Strack and P. Billerbeck, *Kommentar zum NT aus Talmud und Midrash*, 5th ed. (Munich: Beck, 1969), II, 127–29, especially note a.

26. See *Midrash Rabbah on Leviticus* 32:4: "The holy spirit enlightened Moses" in an allusion to Leviticus 24:10–12 and Moses' depending on Yahweh for a judicial decision.

27. See *Midrash Rabbah on Numbers* 15:25.

28. See *Babylonian Talmud, Hagigah* 15a: "And the spirit of God was hovering upon the face of the waters, i.e., as a dove which hovers over her young, but does not touch them."

29. See 1 Maccabees 4:46; 9:27; 14:41; Josephus, *Jewish Antiquities*, 13.1.1.

30. *Mekilta, Beshallach* 7.

31. *Mishnah, Sotah* 9:15.

32. 35:7; see *Midrash Rabba on Song of Songs* 1:8.

33. Careful scholarship shows the original disunity of the Exodus story (Exod 1—18) and the Sinai covenant story (Exod 19—24). The earliest hymnic sketches of the origins of Israel, including the patriarchs, the Exodus, and the conquest of the land, do not include the Sinai story (for example, Deut 26:5–9; Josh 24:2–18). Furthermore, the Exodus story, with its focus on Joseph seems to be more the heritage of the northern tribes. How the Sinai covenant story came to be fused with the Exodus remains obscure.

34. Philo called it "the greatest of the feasts" (*The Special Laws*, II, 32).

35. See *Mishnah, Yoma* 5:2.

36. *Babylonian Talmud, Yoma* 5a; *Zebachim* 6a.

37. After the first destruction of the Temple in the sixth century BC, Pentecost, or the Feast of Weeks, was celebrated to commemorate the gift of the law. However, this did not focus on the bloody ratification of the covenant.

38. By exception: Job 15:7: "The first born of mankind," apparently Adam, is described as brought forth before the hills. Ezekiel 28:12–16 makes a strange allusion apparently to Adam "in Eden" to describe the original state of the king of Tyre, who then sins.

39. *4 Ezra* 3:4–23; 7:11–12; *2 Baruch* 17:3; 23:4.

40. *Allegorical Interpretation,* I, 31; see also *On the Creation,* 134.

41. *2 Baruch* 24:1; 44:14; *Testament of Levi* 13:5; *Testament of Naphtali* 8:5; see also Matt 6:19–20.

42. *Midrash Rabbah on Exodus* 15:3ff.

43. *Midrash Rabbah on Exodus* 21:8; *Mekilta Beshallach* 4.

Chapter 5

1. First Thessalonians 4:4 poses a problem of translation. Paul refers to guarding one's *skeuos* in holiness and honor. The Greek word is often translated "vessel" and used to designate the human body (2 Cor 4:7). Possibly, then, Paul here is referring euphemistically to a man's penis. This meaning would correspond to the preceding instructions of Paul. However, the word was also used in ancient literature to designate one's wife. In this understanding, Paul would be warning against adultery or other forms of conjugal abuse. This meaning would fit well with the following verse.

2. The Greek text is ambiguous; the expression "through Jesus" could modify either the participle "those having fallen asleep" or the verb "will lead." Although "through" (*dia*) often describes divine activity through Christ, the structure of the sentence here suggests the phrase describes the manner of death of human beings.

3. An unnamed "archangel" shows up also in Jude 9, but not in an eschatological context.

4. The eschatological functioning of the Messiah appears clearly in *4 Ezra* 7:28–44; *Psalms of Solomon* 18:5–7; *2 Baruch* 39:7;

40:1–3. *Fourth Ezra* 7:28 describes God speaking of this Messiah as "my son."

5. Once, to the human spirit at 5:23.

6. See also *1 QS* 8:16.

7. See the second-century *Mekilta, Beshallach* 7; the third-century *Mishnah, Sotah* 9:15; the fifth-century *Midrash Rabba on Leviticus* 35:7.

8. See also Luke 16:8, "children of the light" in contrast to "children of this age"; also 1 *QS* 1:9–10; 3:13ff.; 1 *QM* 1:1, 3.

9. *2 Baruch* 50:1–3; see 2 Maccabees 7:9; 12:43–44; 14:46.

10. *Phaedo,* 93–94. The image of an immortal soul remaining in some spiritual state until the general resurrection is found in some apocalyptic literature. A clear picture of conscious happiness for good souls appears in *4 Ezra* 7: 88–99. The "treasury" of departed souls in *2 Baruch* 21:23; 30:2 is more like Sheol.

Chapter 6

1. The much more common translation was *synagogê,* without any apparent difference of meaning. Note the use of the word *synagogê* for the Christian church in James 2:2.

2. The translation of *psychikos* by the English word *natural* is a compromise. Paul has nothing against "nature." And he is not distinguishing "natural" from "supernatural." He is contrasting the *psychikos* from the "spiritual"; hence, the most accurate translation would be "unspiritual." But this word lacks grit. We could use the word *psychic,* basically transliterating the Greek, but that word sounds like the ability to read minds.

3. The eschatological kingdom of God is an image found occasionally in the Judaism at the time of Paul that used the expression "his kingdom." See *Testament of Moses* 10:1; *2 Baruch* 73:1; see also the Kaddish prayer: "May he establish his kingdom during your life and during your days." The phrase "kingdom of God [heaven]" dominates the gospels of Matthew, Mark, and Luke and most likely should be attributed to the preaching of Jesus.

4. The rock in the desert is an allusion to the story in Exodus 17:5–6 about the rock that supplied water to the Israelites. In at least one midrashic rewriting of this story by a later first-century

writer, the rock moves along with the Israelites. See *Pseudo-Philo* 10:3.

5. The Greek word *teleios* can be translated either as "perfect" or "mature." Those two words ring very differently in English. That difference is blurred in the Greek word, which basically means having achieved one's goal (*telos*). Hellenistic mystery cults used the term to denote the full stage of membership in the cult or full moral development through systematic exercises. Matthew's Gospel links the term to God's very being (Matt 5:48) and actually contrasts it with moral perfection, defining it rather by a following of Jesus (19:21).

6. *4 Ezra* 4:30.

7. Philo, *Allegory of the Jewish Law*, 1, 31–32.

8. The recently discovered documents of the Palestinian dialect of Aramaic show an imperative form for the verb "to come" as *atha*. Although ancient manuscripts generally placed no spaces between words, we should separate the two words as *maran atha*.

9. *2 Baruch* 39:7; 40:1–3.

10. *1 QM* 17:6–8.

11. *1 QH* 12:11; 13:18–19.

12. *4 Ezra* 7:50.

13. See for instance the refusal of Jesus in Mark to draw boundaries as he declares, "Whoever is not against you is with you" (Mark 9:40), in contrast to the Jesus in Q, "Whoever is not for you is against you" (Matt 12:30; Luke 11:23).

14. Mark 14:24 makes a closer connection with Exodus 24:8 by the clear citation, "the blood of the covenant."

15. See Exodus 12:21–23; *Mishnah Pesahim*.

16. *Exod Rabba* 15:3ff.; 21:8; *Mekilta Beshallach* 4. See especially the reflections on the martyrs in Maccabean times where the deaths of heroes were seen as "ransom" (*antipsychon*) (4 Macc 6:28–29; 17:21–22).

17. In later letters, Paul will use this word for "sharing" or some form of "fellowship" in regards to "light" and "darkness" (2 Cor 6:14), his ministry (8:4), "the Holy Spirit" (13:13; Phil 2:1), Christ's sufferings (Phil 3:10) and "faith" (Phlm 6), all with the genitive construction to indicate the reality in which one shares.

Four times he uses the term by itself, mostly to refer to a collection of money (Rom 15:26; 2 Cor 9:13; Phil 1:5) as well as to refer to an agreement with the leaders of Jerusalem (Gal 2:9). Luke, on the other hand, uses the word by itself for the church community (Acts 2:42).

18. See especially Dionysius of Halicarnassus, *Roman Antiquities*, 6, 86, 1–5; Plutarch, *Lives, Solon*, 18, 5; Seneca, *De ira*, 2, 36, 7; *De clementia*, 1, 5, 1; Cicero, *De finibus*, 3, 19.

CHAPTER 7

1. See the *Testament of Levi* 3:3; 18:12; *Ascension of Isaiah* 4:2.

2. *1 QS* 3:7–9.

3. The verb Paul uses in 3:18, *katoptridzô*, could indicate the action of reflecting like a mirror or that of gazing into a mirror. Paul's interest here on the glory of Christ shining on his face as an image of God (4:4–6) strongly suggests the second option of gazing into a mirror.

4. It is difficult to translate Paul's statement, *ei tis en Christô, kainê ktisis*. Most translators add words to the line to stress a more restrictive sense, "If anyone is in Christ *that one* is a new creation." However, the Greek reads simply, "If anyone is in Christ, [there is] a new creation." The verb "to be" is often not expressed in Greek.

5. In the Greek, *peri tês hamarias*, or simply *hê hamaria*.

6. See *1 Enoch* 42:1–2.

7. *1 Enoch* 47:3; 90:15–27; *4 Ezra* 7:33–44.

8. Wisdom 3:1–4; *4 Ezra* 7:88–99; *1 Enoch* 39:4.

CHAPTER 8

1. Most likely Leviticus 18:5. Paul refers to this same Torah text in Romans 10:5.

2. Genesis 17 (the P tradition?) also describes a divine covenant between God and Abram but one explicitly and emphatically demanding circumcision (17:10–14), yet Paul's emphasis in the rest of this letter will be to avoid circumcision.

3. In this context, Paul shows the inferiority of the law by the fact that it involved a "mediator" (*mesitês)* between God and

human beings, in effect then rejecting this function of "mediator" for Jesus (Gal 3:19–20). By contrast, the author of Hebrews will develop the image of Jesus the "mediator" (Heb 8:6; 9:15; 12:24).

4. The formula can be found again in 1 John 4:9 and John 3:16–17 as well as in Romans 8:3. Common to all these instances is a confession of faith in God (*ho theos*) sending the Son (*ton hyion*), followed by a purpose clause (*hina*) expressing salvation in one form or another.

5. The expression "born of a woman" can simply mean "a human being." See Luke 7:28.

6. See *Shemoneh 'esreh*, petitions 5 and 6.

7. The prefix *ex-* does not seem to change the meaning of the verb *agorazo* ("to buy") except perhaps to intensify the action, like the English expression "to buy out." Perhaps for this reason, this intensified verb is used more for the religious sense of "to redeem" or "to deliver."

8. *4 Ezra* 4:30.

Chapter 9

1. *Life of Claudius*, 25.

2. *History*, II, 25.

3. See chapter 1 above.

4. As an explicit and documented theological position, Adoptionism appears only in the eighth century AD. However, there is evidence that some early Christians saw Jesus "adopted" by the Father as his Son at the resurrection, implying that Jesus during his human life was not the Son of God. Mark's baptism scene seems to attempt to draw such a status change back to the baptism (Mark 1:10–11), whereas Luke appears to establish the divine Sonship of Jesus at his conception (Luke 1:35).

5. See 1 Thessalonians 1:3; 5:8; 1 Corinthians 13:13; Colossians 1:3–5.

6. The expression *talaipôros ego anthropos* reminds us of almost the exact expression of Epictetus, the master of the Stoic diatribe (*Discourses*, I, 3, 5).

7. A pottery maker once told me, when the clay turns out bad, the potter feels disappointed in herself because she did

something wrong. Jeremiah may be telling us much more about God than about sinful Israel.

8. This doxology concludes the letter in the earliest and best manuscripts. In two eighth-century manuscripts this prayer occurs after 14:23. One second-century papyrus places it after 15:33, and a ninth-century manuscript omits it altogether.

9. Romans 8:35; 2 Corinthians 5:14; see also "the love of the Spirit" (Rom 15:30).

10. The imagery of circumcision of the heart also appears in Deuteronomy 10:16 and 30:6.

11. Paul also speaks of the "witness" of the Spirit in connection with his own conscience and his concern for his Jewish compatriots and relatives (Rom 9:1).

12. Later Luke will write about prophetic praises of God inspired by the Spirit. See Luke 1:67–79; 10:21–22. Luke is far more interested in Spirit-inspired proclamation to a human audience. See Luke 1:41; Acts 2:1–41; and so on.

13. See especially *1 QS* 4:7–8: "eternal joy in life without end."

14. We are leaving aside 1 Thessalonians 2:13–16, which appears as a later insertion.

Chapter 10

1. The Greek word, *syzygos*, means "co-yoked." No one has yet found it used alone as a proper name in the ancient literature and inscriptions, although it appears in connection with other names, perhaps as a description. If Paul is not here naming someone in Philippi, it is difficult to know why he is being so vague about the person's identity, here also described as *gnêsios*, "genuine" or "legitimate."

2. English translators often make a decision to go one way or the other with such translations as "something to cling to" and "something to grasp at."

3. *Apocalypse of Abraham* 10:8.

4. Daniel 12:2; *4 Ezra* 7:36, 47; 9:14–22; 53:4–5; Matthew 7:13–14 [Q].

5. See Wisdom 3:1–4; *4 Ezra* 7:88–99; *1 Enoch* 39:4; see also Luke 16:27–30; 23:43.

Chapter 11

1. In Philemon 9, Paul calls himself a *presbytês*, an old man. Earlier we estimated that his "calling" was around AD 35, when Luke describes him as a powerful person with authority to arrest and extradite. According to that picture, Paul or Saul would have been born around AD 5. That would make Paul around sixty years old at the writing of Colossians and Philemon.

2. See the same expression in Galatians 4:3 and *to asthenê kai ptôcha stoicheia* in Galatians 4, 9. In both places the *stoicheia* seem connected to elements of the Mosaic law.

3. The "of" here probably indicates the subjective rather than the objective genitive, that is, as we find in the expression "a prisoner of conscience" rather than "a prisoner of the state."

4. The Gnostic Valentius, a Christian of the next generation after Paul, apparently used this term frequently in a Platonic sense to mean the upper world of perfection in contrast to the lower world of change and incompletion. See Epiphanius, *Heresies*, 31. 10. 13; Irenaeus, *Against the Heresies*, 1, 1, 1. For the typically Pauline sense of *plêroma* as "total sum" or "completeness," see Romans 11:12, 25; 15:29; Galatians 4:4.

5. He also uses the term twice to refer to eschatological events (1 Cor 15:15; Rom 11:25) and twice in connection with spiritual gifts (1 Cor 13:2; 14:2).

6. In Jewish theology, the closest parallel to the great secret specifically in the Colossian context is the description of the Son of man in *1 Enoch*: "For the Son of man was concealed from the beginning, and the Most High One preserved him in the presence of his power; then he revealed him to the holy and the elect ones" (62:7; see also 48:2–6; *4 Ezra* 12:32). Paul does not use the title "Son of man" for Jesus, but this Enoch text may have been behind a notion of the Messiah as coming out of some heavenly hiding place and appearing suddenly on earth (see also John 7:27).

7. See Luke 20:42; 22:69; Acts 2:33; 5:31; see also Acts 7:55–56.

8. In Colossians, the presence "in the Spirit" is contrasted with absence "in the flesh" (Col 2:5). In 1 Corinthians, it is contrasted with absence "in the body" (1 Cor 5:3). In fact, the secre-

tary of this letter generally fails to pick up the Pauline meaning of "flesh." Because of its contrast with another "part" or aspect of the human being, the "spirit" in both 1 Cor 5:3 and Col 2:5 could be read as an anthropological spirit. But Paul blurs the line between the human spirit and the divine Spirit. And it is difficult to see how he would see an individual human spirit as overcoming spatial distance.

9. The expression *aphesis tôn hamartiôn* ("forgiveness of sins") is a common Lucan term (Luke 1:77; 3:3; 24:47; Acts 2:38; 5:31; 10:43; 13:38; 26:18; see also Luke 5:20–24; 7:47–49; 11:4).

Chapter 12

1. The three prophets, Hosea, Jeremiah, and Ezekiel, use the image of the unfaithful wife to dramatize Israel's sin. Although it does not even mention God in its songs celebrating sexual love, the Canticle of Canticles was included in the Jewish canon because religious authorities could recognize in this writing an allegory about God's love for his people.

2. See *Targum Onkelos* at Genesis 41:38; Exodus 35:31; Numbers 11:25, 29; 24:2; 1 *QS* 8:16.

3. The comparison of being filled with the Spirit and being drunk is found also in Acts 2:4–15.

4. See the discussion of Colossians 1:14 in the preceding chapter.

Chapter 13

1. P. Anton is identified as the first to suggest the title "Pastoral" for these letters in 1726. See W. Lock, *A Critical and Exegetical Commentary on the Pastoral Epistles* (ICC: Edinburgh: T&T Clark, 1973), xiii.

2. See *The Acts of Paul* 11:3–5; Jerome, *De viris illustribus*, 5. See also chapter 2 above, 34–35.

3. The term in Greek, *presbyteros*, is the comparative form of the adjective *presbytês*, which means "an old man." The comparative form was used at the time of Jesus for a member of the Sanhedrin in Jerusalem, whom we know in English either as "elders"

or "presbyters," depending on whether the English translator translates the Greek or simply transliterates it (see Mark 7:1; 8:31; 14:43; 15:1). As Luke describes them, Jewish Christians in Jerusalem very quickly adopted the term for their leaders (see Acts 15:2–6, 22–23; 16:4). We can suspect the influence of James the brother as leader of the church in Jerusalem (see Acts 15:13–21). Writing some thirty years after Paul, Luke also described Paul and Barnabas as appointing "presbyters" in the churches of Antioch in Pisidia, Lystra, Iconium (Acts 14:23) and of meeting with the "presbyters" of Ephesus (Acts 20:17).

4. The title *episcopos* does not appear to be Jewish. It appears in Hellenistic writings describing officers in clubs and voluntary associations. The title designates a middle manager, often in charge of resources other than the property of the club.

A decade or so after Titus, Ignatius, the Christian bishop of Antioch, will speak of an individual or "monarchical" bishop in a city, ruling in the name of God, surrounded by a council of presbyters and deacons. (*Letter to the Magnesians*, 6; see *Letter to the Philadelphians*, preface.) The Letter to Titus functions precisely as the link between the earlier congregational type of church founded by Paul and the later episcopal form connected with Ignatius. In the Letter to Titus, the bishop is not yet a distinct office from the presbyter, and the bishop does not yet rule as a monarch but rather in connection with others in a governing council.

5. Using a related verb, both Titus and 1 Timothy describe the ministry of Jesus as an epiphany or manifestation. Titus describes the grace of God that was manifested (*epiphanê*) to all human beings (2:11; also 3:4), while 1 Timothy uses a similar verb (*phaneroô*) for the historical appearance of Christ (1 Tim 3:16).

6. *The Testament of Moses* 10:1–4; *4 Ezra* 9:2–4.

Chapter 14

1. A pseudoepigraphical letter of Jesus Christ to Abgar of Edessa, a writing of about the fourth century AD, was found in which "Jesus Christ" autographs the letter to insist on himself being the author. This example, however, is a bit late and may be an imitation of the letters of Paul.

2. The term *pneuma* occurs again in 2 Thessalonians 2:8 in reference to the man of lawlessness, "whom the Lord Jesus will slay [*anelei*] with the breath [*pneuma*] of his mouth." The author is alluding to the figure of Immanuel in Isa 11:4 (LXX), who "with the breath [*pneuma*] of his lips will slay [*anelei*] the wicked."